Detail from the
map Orestes Lorenzo used for
his flight back to Cuba

Wings of the Morning

Orestes Lorenzo

Wings

of the

Morning

The Flights
of Orestes Lorenzo

Translated by
E. K. Max

St. Martin's Press / New York

For Vicky, who rescued love within me. For my sons, Reyniel and Alejandro, with the hope that they'll fight to ensure that stories such as this one will never be repeated.

Design by Jaye Zimet

Library of Congress Cataloging-in-Publication Data

Lorenzo, Orestes.
   [Vuelo hacia el amanecer. English]
   Wings of the morning : the flights of Orestes Lorenzo /
Orestes Lorenzo.
      p.   cm.
   ISBN 0-312-10008-6
   1. Lorenzo, Orestes.   2. Cuba—History—1959–
3. Refugees, Political—Cuba—Biography.   4. Refugees,
Political—United States—Biography.   5. Fighter pilots—
Cuba—Biography.   6. Fuerza Aérea Rebelde (Cuba)—
Biography.   I. Title.
F1788.22.L68A313   1993
972.9106'4—dc20   *93-21523*
                                                              CIP

First Edition: January 1994

10   9   8   7   6   5   4   3   2   1

Contents

Chapter 1.   Welcome to the United States   *1*

Chapter 2.   Poverty Lost   *12*

Chapter 3.   The New Man   *25*

Chapter 4.   Vicky   *48*

Chapter 5.   Memories of Development   *67*

Chapter 6.   On the Brink of War   *86*

Chapter 7.   Angola   *110*

Chapter 8.   Patriotic Posturing   *127*

Chapter 9.   Perestroika   *146*

Chapter 10.   Oh, God . . . Forgive Me   *161*

Chapter 11.   History Is the Way It Is   *171*

Chapter 12.   Enemies of the People   *183*

Chapter 13.   A Doorway Out of Hell   *197*

Chapter 14.   I'll Never Give You Up!   *208*

Chapter 15.   The First Day   *221*

Chapter 16.   Waiting   *241*

Chapter 17.   Love Will Triumph   *266*

Chapter 18.   Friendly Hands   *285*

Chapter 19.   Someone to Confide In   *298*

Chapter 20.   Messengers of Love   *311*

Chapter 21.   The Final Day   *326*

Afterword   *345*

Chapter 1

—

Welcome to the United States

Alabama, March 20, 1991, 10:45 A.M.

Colonel Barton halted in front of the door, glancing at the panel of buttons to his left and swiftly pressing in the required code. A green light went on above the door and, simultaneously, the whir of an electric motor could be heard from somewhere behind it. The fifteen-ton mass of the door began to open with a groan, revealing a familiar room lit with a pale glow that appeared to emanate from nowhere in particular.

Their backs to him and their eyes fixed attentively on a twenty-foot screen looming above, the team of operators sat comfortably ensconced in swivel armchairs facing a wide panel cluttered with a variety of switches and myriad colored lights. Moving across the screen in all directions within the contours of a map of the United States were hundreds of luminous dots with a trail of digits and symbols. The eerie hum of high voltage, together with occasional beeping sounds, contributed to an atmosphere of intense silence interrupted only now and then by brief communiqués uttered over the loudspeaker system. Although the overall effect was something out of science fiction, the thick walls of leaded concrete enclosing an operations room several stories below ground level and the miles of communications lines emanating from its core, both marvels of engineering, framed the neurological hub of a very real United States Early Defense Warning System. This was the control room, situated under the Southern Strategic Air Command Headquarters. At their posts for coordinating and directing the system's resources were the men and women who formed the complement of the morning watch.

The colonel waited for the door to close behind him, then with a confident stride made his way over to the central panel. He stood behind one of the operators seated at the controls of the radiolocation system, glanced up at the screen and its accompanying data monitors covering the entire wall, and, setting his hand gently upon the young officer's shoulder, inquired in a barely audible voice, "How are things, Captain?"

"Everything in order, sir," Captain Lee replied.

"Has the reserve line on Point Three been repaired yet?"

"Yes, sir. I confirmed it myself, once they checked it out okay."

"Good. Did you sign off today's entries?"

"Yes, sir."

Colonel Barton assured himself that everything was running smoothly on the morning watch. Despite the evidently normal routine and the outstanding quality of his subordinates, he liked to keep an eye on things personally and always felt better for having sounded out a bit of precise data from his operations crew.

A few years back, upon learning he was to be reassigned Stateside to head one of the teams stationed at the command post in Alabama, the colonel had assumed that at last he would be relieved of the constant stress that pervaded his years of service in Southeast Asia and then in Europe, where the missiles and tanks of the Warsaw Pact sat just a few miles across the iron curtain. His reassignment was the best piece of news he had had in quite a while. Back in Alabama, not only was there no enemy with nuclear striking capability within a radius of several thousand miles, but the climate was also superb. And his daughter, Kathy, who had moved back to the United States once she got married, happened to live less than three hours from his new post. The day he brought home the good news to his wife, Elizabeth, she had thrown her arms around his neck and broken into tears of relief.

More recently, however, his peace of mind had been troubled by a certain preoccupation. A brigadier general of the Cuban air force, Rafael del Pino, defecting to the United States in 1987, had suggested at a debriefing that Fidel Castro was prepared to launch a MiG attack upon the Turkey Point nuclear reactor complex in Florida in order to produce the equivalent of a nuclear strike against the southern *perimeter. And Castro's MiGs were based just a few minutes away from their target.*

Unconsciously, he was now smiling at the thought of his four-year-old granddaughter racing across the front lawn to greet him with "Grandpa, Grandpa!" He would scoop her up in his arms and then wait for that mischievous look in her eyes and the question "What'd you bring me, Grandpa?"

Only a few more hours till the end of his shift. Then he was all set to enjoy five days' leave, and he had already made plans with Elizabeth to visit their daughter. His son-in-law had promised to take him fishing, but what appealed to him most was the thought of just playing with his little granddaughter out in the backyard. He came back to reality once again, letting his eyes wander from the large screen to the digital clock above it. Ten-fifty A.M. . . .

In Cuba, less than 750 miles to the southeast, fourteen MiG-23s sat under a blazing sun awaiting the pilots who might have to board them at any given moment. The squadron of MiG-23 BN fighter-bombers was poised to carry out the day's mission.

"Permission to address the major!"

The request, barked directly from behind me, interrupted my thoughts as I stood examining the meteorological map for details on weather conditions to the north of Cuba.

"Go ahead," I replied, turning around.

"Number seven-twenty-two is ready to go, sir!"

"Have you checked out the inertial guidance system?"

"Checked and ready, Major."

"Thank you, Gutiérrez, now let's try it out," I told the young engineer, patting him on the shoulder and inviting him to precede me onto the field as I realized that I'd probably never see him again.

Gleaming in the sunlight, N°722 stood waiting for me—and for its maiden voyage following the complete overhaul to which it had been subjected, including a fresh coat of dark green and blue paint. It was also to be my first flight in a 23. For the past ten years I had flown only the less sophisticated MiG-21s. Now we had fourteen MiG-23 BNs, all recently arrived at the base, and this was to be my first mission in one—and most certainly my last in any MiG.

I was about to make the most dangerous journey of my life. This time there would be no points of reference on my navigational chart for the voyage I was undertaking, nor any parameters for my heading, airspeed, altitude, or fuel consumption. Nothing about this flight had been programmed into the aircraft's computer. The only data I would be able to make use of was in my own head: two alternate routes to my secret objective, two configurations of numerical data jealously guarded in my brain. My worldly possessions consisted of a pack of cigarettes, a lighter, my wallet, and a pair of photographs painstakingly cropped the previous night in order to fit the size and contours of my pockets, keepsakes of all that was dearest to me in life: my wife, Vicky, and my sons, Alejandro, four, and Reyniel, nine.

As I walked up to the plane, I found the flight technician and his mechanics waiting for me, standing at attention and saluting, preparing to inform me as to its readiness for my flight. Instead of hearing them out I greeted each of them with a quick handshake and approached the boarding ladder to climb into the cockpit.

"How're you feeling for your first flight in a twenty-three, Major?" my technician asked with a smile while helping me to adjust the harness of my parachute.

"Just like a beginner," I answered, hoping to deflect the real reasons for my anxiety. In fact, contrary to what would normally have been the case, the prospect of flying this particular aircraft, new to me, had failed to trigger the slightest emotion.

"Falcon, one-four-six-one, permission to start engine," I asked the control tower after hearing my flight technician tell me over the headphones that I could proceed with ignition.

"Engine start, six-one."

"Roger, Falcon."

As I flipped the engine-start switches I noticed that my hands were trembling. I set the throttle to "Minimum Thrust" and pressed the button that would begin the cycle, all the while attempting to control the nervousness that was welling up in me.

"One-four-six-one, permission to taxi."

"Cleared for taxiing, six-one."

The aircraft overcame its inertia with the release of the brakes, succumbing to a slow, wheeling passage toward the start of the runway.

You sure you want to go through with this? I asked myself, staring through the Plexiglas windshield at that landscape I loved so dearly, wanting my eyes to caress every last palm tree for a final farewell.

In the heat of the narrow cockpit I was already sweating heavily and feeling the discomfort of the oxygen mask glued to my face. I noticed how rapid my breathing had become. I was panting the way one would expect during aerial combat maneuvers under the effect of g-forces; only I was still on the ground, lumbering barely faster than a man might walk. I stopped just short of the runway. Someone was coming in for a landing and I would have to wait for him to taxi off the runway before I could proceed to takeoff. Meanwhile the heat, the sun, the lack of ventilation, the galling oxygen mask . . . everything on earth seemed meant to torture me.

Something happens now and I don't take off. That'd be just my luck!

How long before I see Vicky again, and the kids? Maybe never.

A second plane was about to land. *Did they all decide to come in at once? What'll my parents say when they find out? How will they take it . . . and my brothers? My friends? God, how will Vicky explain to the children?*

Still another plane. *Aren't they ever going to stop! What's going to happen to Vicky once they realize what I've done? Will she be able to hide her feelings and manage to do what she has to?*

Finally the runway was clear.

"One-four-six-one requesting permission to access runway."

"Taxi into position and hold, six-one."

Well, here goes! Manual control of nosewheel disengaged, trim tab neutral, compass synchronized, autopilot engage-switch on, thrust 85 percent, pressure and temperature normal.

"Falcon, one-four-six-one, request takeoff."

"Six-one, cleared for takeoff, zone one."

"Roger, Falcon."

Thrust 100 percent. Revolutions, temperature, hydraulic and oil pressures—all normal. Voltmeter okay . . .

I was sitting on the brakes!

. . . afterburner!

A sudden, overwhelming force mushroomed behind the plane, shuddering its nineteen tons of aluminum and steel straight forward, despite everything the pneumatically braked tires, squealing against the tarmac, did to hold it back.

Afterburner indicator on, nozzle at maximum open . . .

At last I released the brakes, and in a few seconds I was airborne.

Gear up, flaps . . . airspeed 600 kilometers per hour—disengaging afterburner . . .

I racked my mind, attempting to summon the data I had memorized.

Heading 347°, minimum possible altitude, airspeed 900 kilometers per hour.

My breathing was becoming desperate. Finally I tore off the oxygen mask, leaving it dangling from my helmet.

This is like meeting death face-to-face.

———

Not far from the base, Vicky was on her way to the market with Alejandro when they felt the deafening noise produced by an afterburner at takeoff. They glanced up to watch a MiG soaring into the air, impetuous, blue, and gleaming in the sun.

"Mommy," Alejandro asked, "is that Daddy's plane?"

"Yes, Alé, that one is Daddy's."

"Mommy, I don't want Daddy to fly those awful airplanes,"

Alejandro declared with all the authority innocence lent to his four years of age.

Vicky swallowed dryly and felt a knot tightening in her throat. She did her utmost not to cry and asked God to see me safely to my destination. She knew it was going to be my last mission.

Help him, Lord. Help him get there safely. And please, dear God, help us to be reunited with him again, she prayed, hurrying off with Alejandro to pick up their daily ration of milk and bread.

—

Meanwhile, I sat struggling with myself in the terrible confinement of that narrow cockpit, absorbed in fevered speculation.

What in God's name are you doing? Have you lost your mind? What about your parents, your two brothers, your friends, everybody who knows you. . . . How betrayed they'll feel!

What makes you think you know the truth? How can you be sure what you saw on the Russian television, or read in the Soviet papers, isn't all lies as well? Besides, how do you know they won't just turn you back over to the Cuban authorities? Or send you to the electric chair? Or to prison? After all, you've been their enemy practically from the day you were born.

But what about my sons? Am I going to let them have the same kind of life I had? Do I just let them grow into slaves, without a word of protest? Do I watch while their lives are poisoned with the hatred that infected my own?

I'd rather die first! If that world is just as bad as the one I already know, if whatever I've read and seen lately turns out to be just as false, then there's no point in living, then . . . but I've got to find out!

In a cold sweat, panting for breath and struggling with my conscience and my soul, I was taking my 722 out over the blue waters of the Straits of Florida, to a destination known only to Vicky and myself.

"One-four-six-one . . . four-seven here."

The voice exploded, sharp and clear, from the headphones of my helmet, severing my thoughts. I was already halfway gone, keeping just a couple hundred feet above the water; and those few minutes had been enough to lose contact with my flight controller out of Santa Clara.

"Go ahead, four-seven. Six-one here."

"Falcon is calling you."

"Tell Falcon I don't read him."

"Falcon, four-seven here. Six-one reporting he cannot read you."

The pilot repeated to the tower that he had talked to me, and that he himself was flying at an altitude of approximately 15,000 feet, fixed for a landing on an instrument approach.

"Six-one, Falcon is asking your position," he resumed after a pause.

"At the center of zone one," I answered him, "and about to go into my dive."

Four-seven relayed my reply to Falcon, then after a few seconds, he added, "Six-one, Falcon has you cleared to proceed."

"Roger, four-seven," I replied.

Cleared to proceed, all right!

That was my last radio contact with the Falcons of Santa Clara.

Alabama, 11:10 A.M.

Colonel Barton's vacation plans were unexpectedly shattered by the syncopated howling of the control room's computerized alarm system. Disoriented, he searched the screen for some indication, but his reflex was interrupted by the ringing voice of one of his subordinate officers.

"Enemy target approaching at sea level. Quadrant two-five-three-two, heading three-fifty, airspeed four hundred eighty-five knots . . ."

A luminous dot to the southeast of Key West was moving directly north at high speed. The colonel hurriedly read its flight parameters and was struck with a feeling of foreboding. He was more than accustomed to picking up various approaching aircraft proceeding from the south and attempting to evade radar detection, but those were generally small craft flying at low speed, hoping to penetrate U.S. airspace covertly to deliver narcotics from Central and South America. The target he now observed on the screen, heading toward the Florida coast, implied far greater danger. This was a supersonic fighter, very likely armed with bombs and missiles, and in an attack profile. It was already less than twenty-five nautical miles from the coast of Key West. It would take that baby under three minutes to overfly Boca Chica Naval Air Station, and only ten minutes to hit the nuclear complex at Turkey Point!

The magnitude of the implication froze Colonel Barton's blood. Although it seemed highly improbable, no one could afford to ignore the possibility of a surprise attack by Castro against the United States. As a career officer entrusted with the responsibility of safeguarding his country, he knew that no possibility was ever too remote—and the slightest miscalculation, unpardonable.

"Scramble interceptors out of Homestead and put out a yellow alert for ground-to-air for Southern Strategic and for the interceptors at MacDill," he ordered smoothly with no detectable alarm in his voice, though the order certainly seemed to galvanize his complement as they ran to their stations.

One of his officers began demanding something over the inter-com, talking to some distant radar operator from whom he evidently hoped to obtain more precise data on the approaching target, but the operator seemed unable to come up with the answers. Another was snapping out orders over his scrambled line of communication, as if hoping somehow, by his shouting, to gain precious time on his target. The colonel kept checking the screen for incoming data sent up by the computer tied into the aerial scanning systems, only to have con-firmed what he had suspected all along. He felt a chill creep up his spine.

Barton knew that approximately one minute had already elapsed from the instant the target had been picked up by radar. At this point they were tracking it some eight nautical miles farther north. It would take another minute to issue and digest the various commands needed to implement a military response from appropriate units of the armed forces. The ground-to-air missiles would need another four minutes to be operational, an additional minute to locate the target, and a final minute to destroy it. At the same time, the pilots on duty at Homestead Air Force Base would require about three minutes to get to their fighters and settle into the cockpits, then another two minutes to be airborne, lock onto and knock out the target still approaching with God knows what intentions.

The decision to put the squadrons at MacDill also on alert had been taken in view of the distinct possibility that his lone aircraft was actually part of a much larger strike force, a diversionary tactic to launch a more devastating attack from some other direction. Any-thing was possible.

The only thing certain was that, as the seconds ticked away, the enemy aircraft would continue to make for its unknown objective. If its intention was to hit Boca Chica Naval Air Base, the base itself could barely take any preemptive measures now, because you couldn't knock that target out of the air before it reached Key West. But if its mission was actually to strike the Turkey Point reactor complex, then at least there were some opportunities left to intercept and destroy it before it hit the power plant and produced a disaster worse than Chernobyl.

The colonel suddenly thought about his granddaughter and other innocent millions, children and adults, working or just relaxing at the beach, completely unconscious of the impending danger fast ap-proaching the Florida coast. Now he doubly comprehended what his entire military career had taught him—that mistakes were simply not permissible. Instead of filling him with dread, the extraordinary responsibility that had fallen upon his shoulders in just a matter of seconds gave him the courage to act with precision and determina-tion. He picked up the phone, a direct line to the chief of staff of the Southern Strategic Air Command, and briefly explained the situation to his superior. *The orders came back over the wire just as briefly and to the point.*

Secret communiqués went out over the scrambled lines of communication connecting the various military units scattered throughout the south of Florida. Instructions were relayed back and forth with increasing urgency. What had been rehearsed so many times in practice drills until it had become little more than a conditioned reflex now produced the kind of excitement that ultimately only real and present danger can provoke. This time, the adrenaline was of a different order among the men and women under Barton's command, not to mention in Barton himself. This was not one of those unexpected surprises introduced in training exercises. The change that came over the control room was, even to Barton, dramatic.

"We're going to take out the enemy target at the second line."

His voice was firm, sure. It was the voice of a commander who had confidence in the ability of his subordinates and the effectiveness of his arsenal.

The F-16s out of Homestead could only lock on to their target a few miles south of Turkey Point, but the ground-to-air missiles could take him out well before that—in fact, just as soon as he crossed the second line of antiair defenses. Both fighter pilots and missile crews were already rushing to their aircraft and the silos. The military response had been set in motion, and the only thing left for Colonel Barton to do was to wait and see who would come out the winner. The element of surprise, he knew, favored the enemy.

By the time the alert reached Boca Chica, however, it was already too late.

*T*ime to climb and cut back power, I told myself after calculating that I ought to be about fifty nautical miles off Key West. I had no wish to alarm the United States authorities any more than I had to, and I expected to be able to climb to an altitude of approximately 7,000 feet and to reduce my airspeed to about 240 knots while still at a prudent distance. Radio contact was out, since I had only the twenty preset channels with coded military frequencies, impossible to adjust from inside the cockpit. I was not going to have the opportunity for direct communication with North American traffic controllers. With such flight parameters I hoped to facilitate being peaceably intercepted by some of the fighters based at Boca Chica. Once the North American fighters reached me, I could easily make sight contact through internationally recognized visual signals to explain my intentions. So my luck would depend on how they interpreted my presence.

I'd better not cross the line at Key West, not a hair's breadth farther north, I warned myself.

As I climbed, however, the outline of Key West rolled over the horizon and, looking down, I was thrown into a panic. This was much closer than I had expected. I had plotted two alternate routes and was navigating by dead reckoning—I couldn't risk detailing my plans anywhere but in my own head—but my memory had deceived me. I was flying at the correct heading but calculating my time from the wrong route! I was already on top of the Keys, with no alternative but to overfly the naval air base at Boca Chica.

They must have already given the order to take me out at the slightest penetration farther north, I told myself, desperate at my blunder. *Just keep yourself this side of Key West if you want to stay alive,* I swore, scanning the horizon to avoid any small airplanes overflying the vicinity.

I cut back on power and, banking gradually to the left in order not to pass the perimeter I had established for myself, I dropped altitude to make a low pass over Runway N°07 at the base, waggling wings to signify my peaceful intentions. I would have to check my fuel-quantity indicator to see what remained in the tanks.

Too much weight . . . I've got to use up another 250 gallons to be able to make a landing.

I extended the wings sixteen degrees and activated the air brakes, lowering the landing gear and fifteen degrees of flaps.

One more pass over the runway—low, slow, and dirty—to let them know on my next pass I'll be coming in for a landing. . . .

—

At eleven hours, eighteen minutes that morning, a Cuban MiG-23 touched down on the runway before the astonished eyes of flight controllers and other naval personnel on duty at the time. The pilot exited from the unfamiliar runway on the first available taxiway, to the left, and brought his plane to a halt; then he waited.

—

I felt my legs trembling. Where were those Colonel Bartons or Captain Lees from my fevered imaginings as I had flown across the straits? I couldn't figure out the stillness around me, and I sure as hell didn't like it.

Could they be consulting with the Cuban government before coming to a decision? Well, whatever happens now, let it! Nothing can be worse than waiting like this.

Suddenly I noticed someone up in the control tower observing me through binoculars. It was the flight controller, evidently at pains to describe over the telephone exactly what he saw, presumably to his commanding officer, saying something like, *"A MiG-23 BN fighter-bomber with Cuban air force markings is just sitting tight out there on the taxiway off Number Seven, obviously waiting for some sort of instruction. There's a drag chute swinging from the tail, from when the pilot set her down on the runway.''*

The chute rose and sank at intervals, whenever the exhaust from the engine's tail nozzle and an occasional gust of wind conspired to fill its canopy. It just hung there, lifting and falling back onto the concrete in agonized convulsions, like a dying bird, imparting a feeling of captive desolation to the flat, deserted landscape of the base.

Eventually a light truck with a yellow blinking light above the cab pulled up to the front of the aircraft, signaling me to follow. Slowly, with the drag chute clawing me back, I managed to taxi behind him, crossing the length of the airfield under a bright sun: the driver and his truck, me and my MiG-23, as if we were all that was left on earth.

When we reached a small ramp at the far end of the field, the driver got out of his truck long enough to raise his arms above his head and cross them, indicating that I should cut the engine. First I made a slight turn, however, to point the tail of the aircraft into the grass; then I pressed the button to jettison the drag chute, which whirled off in a final gust. Seconds later, after the shrill drone of the turbine had ceased, a red automobile drove up to my plane. At the wheel was an officer who turned out to be the base commander, accompanied by a sergeant who seemed to be Hispanic. Both stepped out of the car as soon as they saw the MiG's canopy slide open, revealing the frightened face of a Cuban pilot unable to conceal his emotion.

There they are, I thought to myself, observing them. *We've been enemies ever since I could walk. Let's see what's going to happen!*

I took off my helmet, dropped it into the cockpit, and sprang onto the pavement, presenting myself at military attention to the senior officer. Then I proceeded to declare in Spanish with a trembling voice, *"Mi nombre es Orestes Lorenzo."*

"His name is Orestes Lorenzo."

"Soy mayor de la Fuerza Aérea Cubana . . ."

"He says he's a major in the Cuban air force."

". . . y pido protección a las autoridades de este país . . ."

"He's asking for protection by the authorities."

". . . por razones políticas."

"Political asylum."

The colonel kept nodding to the sergeant as he listened; then he fixed his eyes on me. Suddenly he broke into a smile, stepped forward, and extended a hand, saying, "Welcome to the United States."

Chapter 2

—

Poverty Lost

My earliest memories go back to my birthplace in Cabaiguán, a small town almost exactly at the center of Cuba. In the language of the Cuban aborigenes, "cabaiguán" means "land of the iguanas." In those days Cabaiguán was famous for its tobacco and its women. "The most beautiful women in Cuba come from Cabaiguán," the grown-ups would say over and over again. "This black soil is the richest on the whole island. We have the best vegetables and the finest tobacco."

But more than once when I left the area with my parents, someone would manage to tease me with: "So you come from the town of the *verracos*, eh?" And I would feel ashamed, because the word *verraco* can mean "idiot" in Cuba. Still, for any native of Cabaiguán, the town's nickname derives from its magnificent breeding hogs, which are referred to by the same term: *verracos*.

Cabaiguán also boasted several *escogidas*, or stripping barns, where tobacco leaves were sorted and graded, their midribs manually removed, and the remainder of the leaves sprayed with water so that they could be easily bundled and sent to the cigar factories, where artisans called *torcedores* hand-rolled them into the distinctive *puros* from Cabaiguán. Generally it was the women who worked in the stripping barns and the men who worked in the cigar factories.

It was in 1950 that my parents met each other at the *Zorrilla* stripping barn, where they had both been driven by more or less the same destiny. My mother was the seventh of nine daughters and a son, from the marriage of María, a young peasant woman from the fields of Pedro Barba, to Casildo, a Spanish emigrant from the Canary Islands, both of whom had found each other in the midst of the direst poverty. My grandmother María was only twelve years old when her mother died in childbirth and her father disappeared, driven insane by the tragedy, leaving María to raise nine brothers and sisters. It was an uncle who came to their rescue, assuming the responsibility of feeding that brood of famished children. He worked from dawn until dusk in the fields of a tenant farm, but didn't have sufficient energies to feed so many mouths, and little by little he was drained by exhaustion, which translated itself into less and less food on the table.

That was when that happy young man with lively blue eyes named Casildo appeared, having fled Spain to avoid military service and looking for some work to survive on that island where he had neither relatives nor friends. María's uncle offered him a job on the farm and the young man accepted readily in exchange for a place to sleep, which he found in the stable, and a plate of food, which they set out for him together with the rest of them at the table. Months of hard work passed under the forceful tutelage of the uncle, while each day Casildo felt more and more drawn to that fourteen-year-old who took care of the hearth like a mother, exchanging timid glances for his insistent ones as she served him his meals.

One afternoon when María was washing clothes on the patio, he went out to the well, pretending to fetch water in order to go up to her and say, "María, I want to marry you."

She shrugged her shoulders, lowered her head without saying a word, and continued scrubbing the dirty shirt she had in her hands even harder. And he knew that she had accepted. He ran back to the field where her uncle was bent over sowing and asked for the hand of my grandmother in marriage. But the uncle, true to his reputation as a hardheaded man, replied furiously with the blood rushing to his face, "Scoundrel! I don't want to ever see you in my house again!"

Then he pointed with one hand to the Royal Road while reaching with the other for his machete.

That night María wept in the solitude of her hammock and Casildo slept in the mountains beneath the stars, since he was determined not to go far, knowing that necessity would finally overrule the uncle's obstinacy. Three days later my grandfather returned once more to ask for the hand of my grandmother, and this time her uncle grumblingly assented to the marriage, which they immediately contracted.

Casildo turned out to be an intelligent, industrious young man who, hearing of a number of men who needed work then at any price, proposed to the uncle to go hire them to work on the farm. And thus there arrived additional journeymen, who were put up in the stable and ate seated in the kitchen next to Casildo and the uncle, while extolling the excellent food prepared by young María, who also looked after the brood of her younger siblings. With time the farm prospered and my grandmother's brothers were already working there as well, while each year she brought into the world one daughter after another until she had her ninth—and only male—child. It didn't seem to bother my grandfather or her uncle to have more and more women in the family. They took them along to the fields every morning, giving them less arduous work, which the girls were only too happy to help with.

They were able to hold on to the farm, which grew more and more productive, by renewing their contract as tenants for additional ten-year periods, slowly attaining a level of prosperity that allowed my grandfather to hire a teacher from town who would come for six months each year to educate his daughters during the evenings after work in the fields. It seemed that their very lives had taken root in that land, like the fruit trees crowding next to the house, when the owner of the farm decided he no longer wished to renew their lease.

"I'm very sorry, Casildo, but you'll have to leave," he had told my grandfather.

Casildo returned to the house that day without his habitual smile, and his daughters joined him in his mournful silence, walking about the house taciturn and disconsolate amid occasional sighs of "What's to become of us?"

"Enough tears," my grandmother suddenly exploded in the midst of the collective drama, "we can't let ourselves die of misery!" And throwing back her head, she turned to Casildo to announce resolutely, "We're going to move to town!"

A few days later, with their bundles on their backs and their life's savings in their pockets, they left in search of a house to rent and some work that the daughters might perform in that town called Cabaiguán, where four years earlier my father's family had also arrived, with bundles on their shoulders.

My paternal grandparents, María and Cristino Lorenzo, hadn't been able to afford to rent any land whatsoever. They had lived with their nine children on a farm where the owner had allowed them to build a shack with a dirt floor, which my grandmother swept down each afternoon with the ashes left from the charcoal she used for cooking. One day the owner sold the farm, and the new owners insisted that my grandparents get off the place. The family then set out on the Royal Road, since they were afraid of life in town and hoped their five young sons might make enough to pay for a home if they worked as journeymen with my grandfather.

My father shared in the chores by tending to the pigs they raised in the back of the house, and he sadly watched his hopes evaporate for a Christmas Eve dinner pig, as they were sold off one by one to pay the bills for the food they'd had to buy on credit that year at the nearby bodega. Once again they'd have to celebrate Christmas with the same old fare.

One afternoon as my father was returning from the tobacco fields mounted on horseback sitting behind my grandfather, he leaned to one side to look for the origin of that strange sound coming down the road, and saw for the first time that mass of iron set upon four wheels heading straight for them as it bumped over the holes in the road. The driver of the automobile honked his horn to announce his approach, and my father jumped off the horse, fleeing in terror from that "monstrous animal" before the astonished gaze and laughter of my grandfather.

My father was then fourteen and had never worn a pair of shoes in his life since they were too expensive, and he boasted to other children that he was able to stamp out lighted cigarettes with his bare, callused feet. He had only been able to study up to the third grade in a small public school along the Royal Road with a teacher hired to instruct the peasants, but he had already begun to discover what would turn out to be one of the passions of his life: reading.

Hounded by debt and despair, my paternal grandparents decided finally to move to the long-feared town, where after a few years my father found work as a "reader" in the *Zorrilla* stripping barn. My mother had also arrived there at fourteen years of age, in search of the six pesos she could earn weekly by stemming and sorting tobacco leaves during the three months of the year that the stripping barn was operative. And here was that young man of twenty, seated in the middle of a room filled with young working girls, looking up at intervals from the newspaper he was reading aloud to them as they worked, to fix his eyes on the wild adolescent girl who remained seated there before him with her head bent over the table full of tobacco leaves.

One day my father paused next to the window adjacent to my mother's work station and remarked to the friend in his company, "That girl is going to be the mother of my children."

Hearing what he said, the young girl blushed, then turned to him with an arrogant stare that made my father burst into laughter.

My mother was now fifteen and allowed to wear lipstick and go with her older sister to the movies shown at noon on Sundays in the only cinema in the town. Filled with curiosity and held tight by her sister, she entered that dark theater, which momentarily frightened her, and together they took seats in one of the nearly empty rows in the back.

"May I sit here?"

She recognized the familiar voice of the reader beside her after only a few minutes had passed.

"Why not, it's a public place," she answered as roughly as if she had just left the fields of Pedro Barba, and she watched him out of the corner of her eye as he sat down two seats away. But he didn't seem interested in what was on the screen. Instead, he kept talking to her about the stripping barn and how he'd like to visit her house, when she turned her head to him and asked with evident annoyance, "Tell me something . . . are you courting me?"

"No, no. How could you think that? I'm incapable of such a thing."

They were soon engaged, and my father visited my mother's house on days appointed by Casildo—he ever anxious to kiss her, and she terrified of his doing so, until the required six months had passed.

It was 1955 when they decided to marry and go to live in a small, fragile wooden house in the neighborhood called "De La Cafetería," because of its having the only coffee-bean roasting plant in the region. There they spent their first years together, watching every centavo of their meager salaries to be able to eat and pay the rent. Around that time the government had passed a law requiring the owners of stripping barns to pay a higher salary to their workers in response to their demands. But the owners decided to move their *escogidas* to other towns with more docile labor forces instead of paying the increased wage. My parents suddenly found themselves in the desperate situation of not having five centavos each morning with which to purchase the liter of milk needed by their first wailing little glutton, born in 1956.

At that time the men from the Twenty-sixth of July Movement were already in the mountains, promising to make a Revolution that would give justice to the country, and my father began to collaborate with the rebels by selling the movement's bonds to finance the movement. In the last days of 1958 the troops commanded by Ché Guevara entered Cabaiguán in triumph after a few skirmishes, to establish their headquarters in the *Manuel Gutiérrez* stripping barn, very close to our house. Three days earlier my father had left to join the combatants of the twenty-sixth of July before the taking of the town, and now my mother was cowering in a corner of the kitchen, already eight months pregnant with their second son, her face extremely pale with the panic she felt at the sporadic gunfire she could still hear nearby. She was worrying about my absent father when she suddenly heard the desperate cries of her neighbor. The woman was ill and had sent her adolescent nephew to the pharmacy for medicine some two hours earlier. Now they brought her the news that an army sniper, stationed on a rooftop, had killed the boy as he crossed the street attempting to reach the pharmacy. My mother felt invaded by the terror of her neighbor's tragedy, and was running with me in her arms back to the house when she heard the familiar sound of an airplane swooping over the house followed by the sound of explosions.

"Everybody into your houses! They're machine-gunning headquarters!" she heard someone yell, running down the street. She hurled herself under the bed with me, convinced that there we'd be sufficiently protected. After the bombardment, my mother went out to the patio to get the mattress left in the sun to dry out her two-year-old son's wetting, and discovered to her horror that several large-caliber shells had perforated it.

The old government fled and the guerrillas entered the capital like heroes enveloped in the triumphal rejoicing of the adulating masses. All the *escogidas* returned to Cabaiguán, and the owners agreed now to pay the established wage, increased to some twenty pesos a week. The rent for houses had been lowered significantly, and each day more and more laws were passed in favor of the poor. The rejoicing was great; the Revolution had triumphed!

My father was now employed as "reader" in the *Bouzac* tobacco factory. He had a small room in the factory loft that he reached by narrow stairs. In the room was a huge cast-iron amplifier, with an old microphone facing a small chair. Here, my father spent the workday hours reading aloud from works by the great authors, from Cervantes to Victor Hugo and Hemingway, as the *torcedores* carefully rolled the cigars. Thus the cigar workers of Cabaiguán acquired a remarkable literary education.

—

In those days we lived with my grandparents in a small wooden house, which was later rebuilt in brick, thanks to the money my father's younger brother, who was living in the United States, brought back on one of his vacations to Cuba. The house was situated at the end of a narrow stone lane that ambled over a gentle hillside. This lane was trafficked almost exclusively by our neighbors, and our house was separated from it by a flagstone terrace and a shallow ditch through which water would drain copiously whenever it rained. I used to love to run out to the terrace and wet my bare feet in that warm, muddy water. "You're going to get sick, boy!" my grandmother would yell from the doorway, ordering me back into the house.

Shading the patio at the back of the house were two mango trees that my cousins and I would gorge on during the month of June. One day I noticed a discarded pit at one corner of the patio which had sprouted a green shoot. I asked my grandfather what it was, and he explained a little about sowing to me as he pushed the pit deeper into the ground. I then began to look for the centavos my uncles always gave me, and ran to plant them, too. But despite my longing to make a gift to my grandparents, no money tree ever bloomed on our patio.

I spent a lot of time with my grandparents, watching them roll their own cigars, the leaves of which they'd guard jealously in a wooden box on the dining room table at the back of the house. My grandmother smoked her rough-hewn *puros* mostly in the kitchen, while my grandfather chose an old easy chair next to the living room window, where he'd spit out a caramel mixture which formed dark stains on the flagstones. Tobacco permeated every facet of our lives back then. When I was only fourteen months old, my father brought me to a photographer's studio, where they took my picture with a lighted *puro* between my lips.

My grandfather had the habit of starting up a conversation with whomever happened to be passing by. I would often hear him call my grandmother to tell her jokingly, "Come, María, have a look at this girl going by. Now, there's one heck of a woman!" My grandmother would start out of the kitchen, but then, hearing his pronouncement, turn right around with a "Bah!" Grandfather always responded with a roguish laugh while my grandmother went on with her chores, muttering to herself.

Those who knew him well said that my grandfather remained faithful, although he never gave up teasing my grandmother to work up her jealousy. And she would chastise him with: "But Cristino, when are you going to grow up?"

Years later, when he died unexpectedly, my grandmother fell to waiting silently for her own death, which took less than a year to occur. She said over and over that she preferred being with him, wherever he might be. And she continued wasting away in his absence, awaiting the death that would unite them once again.

In the evenings, when my father arrived home from work I'd be waiting for him by the doorway. I remember how I'd try to catch sight of him as he came up the lane, always with something in hand. Then I would take off for him like a bullet, and he'd crouch down for me to throw myself into his arms, kissing him on both cheeks. He would carry me back into the house and sit me up on the table, to show me what he had brought. Sometimes a sweet; other times, some fruit juice. The first time he brought me tomato juice I remember I didn't like it, but my father told me that the juice of the tomato made men's balls grow strong. Then I drank eagerly, in hopes of being a man as soon as possible. From then on I loved tomato juice, and now I use the same technique with my sons whenever they refuse some food rich in vitamins.

—

Late one night someone woke me with a kiss. It was my Uncle Orlando, the youngest and the only bachelor among my father's brothers. He had just arrived from the United States, and was holding up a large airplane that he'd brought for me. We all sat up in the living room that night, excited at his arrival, and no one could persuade me to go back to bed. There I was with my new toy, taxiing between the legs of my parents and grandparents, taking such pleasure in that winged apparatus that transported me on a fantastic voyage around the world, a voyage I was not about to have interrupted by bedtime. From that night on, whenever anybody asked me what I was going to be when I grew up, I would answer: "A pilot!" That airplane, the first I ever flew, on the imaginative wings of my four or five years of age, would be my last toy.

It was December 1960 or 1961, and Orlando was only the first of many relatives who arrived for the Christmas holidays. My father had three other brothers and four sisters, all with children of their own, who filled our home that season with an intimate and happy ambience I was not to experience again in the remaining years of my childhood. Miladis, the youngest of my father's sisters, came from the United States as well, along with her husband and children. One afternoon they brought over a projector with slides from "up North," which they projected that night onto the white wall of the house across the street, causing a sensation among the kids and adults of the neighborhood.

On Christmas Eve, all the men sat out on the back patio with my grandfather. The women stayed in the kitchen, while the boys ran through the house in an all-out war with their cap guns blazing away. In the midst of the fray the older boys managed to instigate our storming the dollhouse that the girls had set up on the patio, disturbing their peaceful playing and thereby prompting a rain of complaints on my aunts, who passed them along to the men outside, saying, "Will you get those kids under control before they drive us all crazy!"

My uncles and grandfather were already gathered around the rectangular fireplace, swigging occasionally from their beer bottles and laughing boisterously as the dinner pig roasted.

They had begun to prepare the pig two days earlier. He was brought to the patio still alive and we children all stayed there to watch the spectacle. "They're about to kill the pig!" one of the younger boys yelled, sounding the alarm, and the rest of us ran out there to see what it was like to die.

There he was—a rope tied around his neck and also to a stake driven in the ground, to prevent his escape—busy rummaging the earth with his snout and at the same time letting out muffled squeals. Meanwhile, Grandfather was sharpening a long knife. First he poured out some water from an old metal pitcher, letting it run over the blade and onto the circular stone beneath, against which he repeatedly scraped the edge of the knife back and forth. From time to time he would wipe the blade and run the tip of his thumb carefully along its edge, murmuring, "Still not sharp enough." When the knife was finally ready, we children watched, breathless, as Grandfather walked over to the pig, took it by one of its legs, and flipped it onto its back with a yank. Next he swung around to position himself on top of the outstretched pig, leaning the full weight of his knee on its ribs and, amid deafening squeals, lifting back one of the fore-hocks to locate the heart. Holding his right hand behind him, he asked one of my uncles for the knife. This he brandished firmly by the handle, and with a final motion he drove it into the chest of the animal, piercing its heart. Then blood gurgled out of the wound, while the pig's screams were drowned in intermittent convulsions that became slower and slower, all beneath our frightened stares.

Next, an uncle poured some boiling water, which had been prepared just beforehand for cleaning the animal, onto the ribs of the pig, who reacted with a final shudder. Then someone bellowed, "Don't skin it yet, it's still alive!" Once it was finally dead my uncles began scurrying about, between swigs of beer, emptying pitchers of boiling water over the carcass, which they rubbed with some porous stones to remove the black hide. The pig was soon left milky white, and the men proceeded to open the belly in order to take out the guts. Next they poured buckets of fresh water into the cavity to wash out the blood, and they hung the animal from the kitchen rafters with a basin set underneath, where the last of its blood would drain overnight.

The following day they made slits into the flesh and rubbed in some marinade, which had been made with sour oranges from the countryside, cumin, garlic, and salt. Then they set the pig on the table, covered it with plantain leaves, and left it for another night to allow the marinade to permeate the meat. It would be ready for roasting the following morning, on Christmas Eve.

Chrismas Eve day, while the pork was roasting out on the patio, my father sat down in front of a crate of empty beer bottles. He took out one of the bottles, wrapped a rayon cord around it halfway from the bottom, made it taut at both ends, and drew first one end and then the other, back and forth a number of times, rubbing the cord against the glass. Then he quickly submerged the bottle in a basin of cold water, which caused it to crack around the middle, leaving on one side the discarded neck, and on the other, a rustic glass for the feast.

Christmas dinner was held in the living room, around a table lengthened by crates and boards and covered with an assortment of white tablecloths. There we all sat, children and grown-ups together, to partake of the suckling pig and to hear Grandfather give thanks to God and offer a toast for the preservation and happiness of our family. Those were the last and the only Christmas memories I have.

One day the leaders of the Revolution decided that Christmas traditions were imported and harmful to the economy since they coincided with the most important period of the sugar harvest, the best moment to cut the cane for its highest yield in sugar. Nor was there any reason for the children to be celebrating the "Day of the Magi" on the sixth of January. That children's celebration could be shifted to the end of July, to celebrate the attack on the Moncada Barracks by a group of young men led by the Highest Leader. Those charming figures on camels who answered our letters by leaving toys under our beds before dawn were to disappear henceforth from our dreams.

Never again would the entire family be seated around the table, never again would thanks be given to God. Soon I would not even receive a blessing before going to sleep.

Our life returned to its accustomed routine when the new leaders of the town offered to send my father to the School for Revolutionary Instruction, since they needed new cadres to direct the creative tasks of the Revolution. And we watched him go off, content to seek wider horizons than those of a tobacco reader.

My father spent what seemed to me to be a long time away at school, and was then working in the Ministry of Education, when one afternoon I saw him emerge from my room furious, holding a picture of the Virgin Mary that had hung over my bed. "I told you I don't want any more of this garbage in the boy's room!" he cried, and with a curse flung it onto the patio. My mother broke into sobs, while my grandfather sat in his old chair by the window, seemingly unmoved. And I, confused and frightened, ran for my grandmother's skirts. In the kitchen among her pots and pans, she put her arm around my shoulder and pressed me to her.

Before going to bed at night I would often find my grandparents by the radio, listening to a faraway station with the volume turned very low. From my bedroom I would call out to them for their blessing and they'd respond, almost in unison, "May God bless you, my boy."

In the morning, after my parents had gone off to work, my grandmother's brother Modesto, a dry pedant who never said a word to me, usually stopped by. While he and my grandparents awaited Grandma's delicious coffee, he invariably brought up the previous night's broadcast. At the time I couldn't figure out what they were talking about, or why they had to listen to the radio so cautiously.

"What we need is for the Americans to come here and straighten things out," Modesto insisted.

"This guy is worse than Batista," my grandmother would add in a sad, low voice while Grandfather nodded his head.

One day my father was brought home barely conscious. My mother, grandmother, and aunt managed to prop him up in bed while he vomited profusely, leaning over a bucket they'd placed beside the bed. I watched from the doorway, horrified. "He's drunk out of his mind," I heard my aunt say. The friends who had brought him home explained that they'd all been out celebrating the reported rescue of Camilo Cienfuegos, a hero of the Sierra Maestra, who had just disappeared mysteriously with his plane during a storm. That was the only time I've ever seen my father really drunk.

—

The following year my father went off to another province, eventually returning for us in a Russian truck, with a tough young driver at the wheel named Mario. My father eagerly described his new job as "director of education" to his brothers and friends. Then, piling the few things we owned onto the back of the truck, we all took off together—my father, my mother, my little brother, myself, and the driver—all crammed into the front under an endless downpour, headed for the town of Matanzas. That day I discovered that the world went much father than Cabaiguán.

My brother and I spent the better part of the trip fascinated by the burly driver, who told stories of boxing matches in which he'd always come out the winner. Weeks later, my father came home from work to tell us that Mario had killed himself accidentally with a gun, while working as a school guard. To us it seemed impossible that something as small as a bullet could kill a big man like Mario, and the fact troubled us for the longest time.

Our home in Matanzas was on the fourth floor of a modern apartment building where we were the first tenants, and where my parents and my brother Orlando still live. From up on the balcony we caught our first glimpse of the sea—the sea, which was going to be the focal point of all our adventures and our mother's greatest worry. Soon the other apartments had tenants as well: blond, blue-eyed foreigners who did not speak our language. "They're German technicians," people said, and from then on the building was called the Technicians' Quarters. These Germans were rather reserved and spoke very little, except when they had a party. Then they would throw glasses and beer bottles down the stairs, leaving a trail of broken glass, but they'd always clean up everything the next morning. On one occasion they were celebrating a wedding and instead of glasses and bottles they threw down coins; and all the neightborhood kids, myself included, scrambled after them.

Each afternoon I'd grab an inner tube and head out into the bay with a group of boys to dive for sea snails. The Germans would trade us chocolates and other sweets for them, and the more snails we brought them, the more they wanted. Soon other boys from other neighborhoods would also tag along, tubes over their shoulders, lured by the promise of sweets.

At night I would hang out with a bunch of friends at a small park near our building. We'd play hide-and-seek or gangsters. Sometimes we made up more original games, like who could catch the most fireflies from the bushes on the other side of the street. Once Pedrito came out of the bushes cursing and holding up his hands. Someone had smeared excrement all over the branch of a small tree and stuck a firefly in it. When Pedrito grabbed for that firefly gleaming in the darkness, his fingers sank into the foul mess of excrement. "Damn— it's shit! Which one of you mothers did it?" We never found out but we never played that game again.

Behind our group of buildings rose a rocky hill, covered with agave plants and traversed by the railroad. The bigger boys used to go there to wait for the freight trains laden with sugarcane which rode past very slowly. As soon as they heard the sound of a locomotive they'd rush to the tracks and yank off any cane stalks hanging over the side of the heavily loaded cars. Then, once the train had passed, we'd all sit on the rails to enjoy sucking the cane juice out of the stalks.

Grazing among the agave were the local peasants' horses, which we would mount to ride bareback. More than once we ran away, utterly terrified when an angry peasant threatened us with a machete because we were tiring his workhorses. Once as we tried to catch one of those horses the animal lashed out and kicked Luis Alberto in the mouth, splitting his lower lip, an accident that was to mark him for the rest of his life.

Luis Alberto was quite a dreamer, with ideas even crazier than mine or my brother's. One day he came to tell us he was building a space laboratory to establish contact with extraterrestrial civilizations. He took us to the ruins of a building abandoned in the middle of construction. In one of its filthy rooms Luis Alberto had installed a few cables, some tubes, and other odds and ends with which he meant to talk to the Martians. Little by little Luis Alberto's laboratory got turned into a kind of minizoo, where we raised all sorts of animals our mothers didn't allow us to bring into the house. Among our favored mascots was, I remember, a snake whose home was a small cardboard box. We would move the box around to different parts of the room to watch the poor animal crawl about, searching for its home. One day my brother and I took the snake home with us to demonstrate its skills to our mother. When we set it on the floor in front of her, she jumped onto a chair, shrieking with terror: "One of these days you're going to kill me with your pranks."

Thus she threatened us with the swift loss of her infinite patience in dealing with our continual adventures, but she always ended up overlooking even our most outrageous antics when they were based on charity.

One afternoon when our mother had sent us to the neighborhood pharmacy with a prescription for some medicine she needed, Faure and I on our way back came across a stray cat with its skin pocketed with sores filled with a repugnant swarm of twisting worms. We scrutinized the poor animal with pity and didn't hesitate to pour the medicine over its wounds, convinced it would thereby be cured.

"Mommy'll understand," we told ourselves.

Meanwhile our mother had already lost patience waiting, when she saw us arrive with the empty flask and a repulsive cat in our arms. A few minutes later she was painstakingly administering the proper medication to cure the poor animal.

During this period my father worked tirelessly throughout the province, often returning home dirty and exhausted. Then he would explain how he had been to Ciénaga de Zapata, inaugurating some little school for the illiterate charcoal burners who lived there. Our family, however, seldom traveled anywhere, not even for a day, let alone for a weekend. My father's work was his obsession. The word *revolution* was forever on his lips, and he would speak of it—to my brother and to me—as his reason for living.

The few times we went to see a movie or to eat out, he and my mother would argue because he didn't want to dress up properly. He preferred to wear his ordinary gray khakis on such occasions, or the simple blue militia shirt he wore each day to work.

"Orestes, please do me a favor and don't dress so shabbily. We're going out," my mother would scold him.

"A man's worth is on the inside, not on the outside," he insisted. "Dressing fancy is a bourgeois habit, not mine."

Chapter 3

—

The New Man

When I was seven my father told me I was to be sent away to a new school, on a government scholarship. Suddenly I realized he meant I wouldn't be living at home. It was my first baptism by fire.

"I never had schooling," he explained, "but today the Revolution gives everything to children. At boarding school you'll have an education, clothing, meals—all free. Not just you, but every child. It makes no difference if you're the son of a government minister or a shoemaker. That's the justice of the Revolution."

The boarding school was located off in the hills, with a distant view of the city of Matanzas. Our week began Sunday evenings at eight, when parents would drop their children off at the front gate. Thus began the long school week, which ended only on the following Saturday, at noon, when we were let out to go home for the weekend. About sixty of us, all boys, slept in a large dormitory with two rows of bunks. We would make our beds at six in the morning, as soon as our teacher entered shouting, "On your feet!"

After brushing our teeth, we formed two lines outside in the schoolyard, then marched to the dining hall in step with the teacher's commands: "Attention! Forward, march! One-two, one-two-three-four . . ." And as we marched we would sing the revolutionary songs they taught us: "Marching we go, armed with the truth, knowing we'll find the solution. . . . United we stand, the Cuban youth, our faith in the Revolution. . . ." Or sometimes they were the songs of the Young Pioneers: "Eehh, *Malembe*, students don't surrender. . . . Eehh, *Malembe*, students don't sell out. . . . Eehh, *Malembeee*! . . ."

In the afternoon, after classes, we would wash up in a room near the dormitory. We were supervised by a big black woman whom we called the concierge. Her job was to make sure we were clean, and she scared the heck out of us. Each day she would have several five-gallon cans of water ready to douse us with as soon as we were naked and properly soaped up. Then we'd have to wait there like sitting ducks for the moment when the cold water would hit and take our breath away. A country boy by the name of Osvaldo was put in the second grade with us, even though he was already fourteen. Osvaldo was the only one to be spared the concierge's bucket of cold water because it was considered too embarrassing for a young man in his puberty to have to stand naked in front of her.

At night there was always a teacher with an old rifle posted on guard duty. He told us that there was the possibility of a North American invasion; that there were counterrevolutionaries trying to turn us into slaves again; that it was necessary to maintain constant vigilance, which was why he stood guard with his big gun while we slept: to defend us against imperialist aggression.

One quiet afternoon as we were getting ready to take our bath we heard a deafening explosion in the dormitory. One of the boys had sneaked into the teacher's room at the dormitory entrance to play with the "big gun" lying on the bed there, and the gun had fired, putting a gaping hole in the mattress. When we got there we found Esteban dumbfounded and white as a corpse. When I saw that smoking hole in the mattress I remembered Mario, and I finally understood how a small bullet could kill such a huge man.

Whoever behaved badly would be punished at night. At the end of the day each teacher handed the night guard a list of the guilty ones, and they'd be called in by him and made to stand at military attention for several hours. On one of those nights, already half-asleep after such a punishment, hardly had my head hit the pillow when I felt the earth tremble from two distant explosions. The next morning, while getting ready for breakfast, we were told that a plane coming from the United States had dropped two bombs on one of the port factories. That morning was the first time I began to think how bad the Americans were, not even letting us sleep in peace.

———

Being separated from my parents made me very homesick, and often in class I would find myself dreaming about the coming Saturday, when I could go home again. Those weekends were the happiest moments of my life, when, together with my brother Faure, I would go hiking in the "mountains," as my mother called the fields of agave, or off to catch sea snails in the bay.

One afternoon my father came with Faure to pick me up, telling me with a rather preoccupied look on his face, "You have a new brother! He was born yesterday and his name is Orlando." And so

26

the three of us went off in the jeep to the hospital. But we were only allowed to greet Mother from out in the street. She was leaning out the hospital window, waving to us from the fourth floor. Later, we found out that our new brother had been critically ill, hovering between life and death for over a week. "His blood had to be changed," my father told his friends. Later, my mother explained, "It was a problem with the Rh factor."

Every two or three months we'd go off to spend a few days with our grandparents in Cabaiguán. Faure and I awaited those visits anxiously since we missed the place where we were born and the grandparents who indulged us so. On one particular visit we encountered a funereal atmosphere in the house. My grandmother remained seated on a stool in the kitchen, downcast and silent, her eyes all red from crying. My grandfather was in his customary chair, talking with the neighbors who came to express their sympathy, speaking in hushed voices, sharing his grief over the tragedy that had occurred.

Although no one had died, the news that had arrived the day before caused the same reaction: my grandparents' fourth son, Edelso, who lived in the capital, had been arrested for complicity in a theft. He had been sentenced to twenty years in prison.

The eldest son, a lawyer by profession, explained that the felony in and of itself did not merit such severe punishment, but unfortunately The Leader of the Revolution had recently made a pronouncement that had become law: "Your foot gets caught, we'll pry it out; your hand gets caught, we'll cut it off." Years later I understood that the phrase, expressed in "perfect Cuban," established the difference between the punishment received by revolutionary leaders for corruption, in their case called an "error of judgment," and punishing a deliberate theft committed by ordinary citizens. My grandparents' shame at having a son in jail accompanied them to their grave.

My father had changed a lot since we'd moved to Matanzas. I didn't see him often, and when he talked to me it was mainly to scold, contrasting his harsh childhood to my own. "At your age I was a man already," he would tell me. I felt ashamed of my infantile pranks; yet at the same time I felt too shy to ask him what it was I was supposed to know at my age. And of course I never told him about any of my problems for fear of his reproach.

One Sunday evening as my parents were taking me back to the boarding school, I wanted so much to stay at home that I actually told my father.

"Don't be a softy," he replied. "At school you have everything."

"Please, Orestes—why don't we let him stay home this week?" my mother interceded.

"Onelia, you cut out this nonsense, too. He's a big boy now and has to stop his whining. When I was his age I was breaking my back in the fields with my father, working from sunrise to sunset. I couldn't even dream about school. And do you know how many children there are in the world without any school, living in ignorance and misery? Millions!''

My father was getting more and more worked up as he spoke, and his voice grew louder. "What wouldn't those children give for the chance the Revolution offers Orestico today!" He turned toward the backseat where I sat, crushed by his words. "We mustn't forget that it cost a lot of lives to get where we are now and that it still takes a lot of effort to hold on to what we've won, so we're not going to coddle Orestico.''

"But Orestes, try to understand. You hardly ever spend time with the boys. All you do is work day and night, without ever stopping.'' My mother was trying to make him see that we hadn't talked like father and son in a long time. Whenever we did talk, it was as revolutionary to revolutionary, which at my seven years of age made me rather bitter.

"Get it into your head, Onelia, that my sons aren't the only kids in the world, not even the best. I work hard because I owe it to the Revolution, which made it possible to have schools for everybody, schools that I never had.''

"But Orestes, the family—''

My mother couldn't finish her sentence. She was interrupted by my father, who, livid with anger at her insistence, repeated in a choked voice, "They'd better get it into their heads: first the Revolution, and then the family.''

I shrank in the backseat of the jeep, feeling insignificant and ashamed. I wanted the earth to swallow me up, because I was less than dirt. Yet, when they left me at the gate of the school that evening, I ran along the fence in tears, crying out to the jeep, which was already heading down the road: "Daddy, Mommy . . . don't leave me!'' After my father's outburst I never again had the courage to ask directly for his affection, though I often pleaded for it whenever he was out of hearing. I went into the dormitory, where a cold bed awaited me, and cried myself to sleep, buried under the covers.

After the third grade I was transferred to a recently opened school at Varadero Beach, a popular resort. This time Faure would come with me, and for several years we got to share our adventures on the many trips between Varadero and Matanzas. The new school, which specialized in swimming, comprised a large row of mansions at the east end of Varadero Beach, famous for its fine, white sand. These were houses of the "old well-to-do," who had left the country for the United States because the Revolution, we were told, had not permitted them to continue exploiting the poor. A street lined with palm trees and cocoa-plums fronted the row of houses, which differed in style but not in luxury. The houses, with the beautiful beach behind them, were on the north side of the street, while the canal, which crossed the small peninsula, providing rapid access to the bay of Cardenas, was on the south side. We were to live in Residence 3, which, our instructors told us, had been the country house of an ex-President by the name of Grau San Martín. The houses were filled with fine furniture and mirrors, but the pupils, who were mostly peasants from Ciénaga de Zapata or children from modest families, didn't take long to destroy everything. At night, as soon as the lights were turned off, one of us would throw the first shoe, which was always followed by a heavy crossfire of footwear from all directions, smashing some crystal or mirror. The next morning when our swimming instructors and our teachers tried to ascertain who the guilty parties were, they inevitably encountered a group of sheepish boys with heads bowed, unable to recall anything about the previous night.

Since the school was newly opened, additional pupils arrived every week. One day a boy by the name of Nelson showed up. He would eventually become a first-rate swimmer, competing in the Scholastic Games held every summer in the capital. But then he was just a thin, inscrutable nine-year-old who was a native of Ciénaga de Zapata and the son of charcoal burners. After introducing himself and taking possession of his bunk, he went into the bathroom. Soon we heard him struggling with something and, our curiosity aroused, we went in to investigate. There he was, a towel around his neck and his foot in the bidet, trying to stop the water that was gushing in all directions. Upon seeing us, he lifted his dripping face and grumbled, "Boy, the rich sure were gross. Imagine flushing the water back up to wash their feet!"

—

Every afternoon we were taken by bus to the finest hotels in Varadero for swimming lessons. But soon an Olympic-sized pool was built on the grounds of the school, and we would train there three times a day. Our lives became a constant shuffle between swimming pool, classrooms, and dining hall, always marching to the instructors' orders, always intoning revolutionary songs. After dinner at twilight we would go to the canal, where fishermen spent hours with their nets and lanterns, catching the shrimp that would come in with the tide. We'd sit among those skinny men with their weather-beaten faces, listening to their fantastic stories about the famous *Cornuda Mocha*, who lived in the deepest waters of the canal and who already had snatched away several victims. Open-mouthed, we would listen to how the legendary shark would devour anyone foolish enough to try to capture her, how she once had sprung out of the water to catch an unwary fisherman sitting by the canal, pulling him forever down with her, and they never heard of him again.

Early in the morning a silver plane would fly over the school to land at the nearby airport. It was the period when those emigrating to the United States would leave from Varadero. One day somebody asked our trainer about the silver plane, which seemed to monopolize our attention at the swimming pool. "It's the shit truck coming to pick up its cargo," he answered, then blew his whistle for us to resume practice. Twenty-six years later I would learn that the Cubans who left the country on those flights had dubbed them "Freedom Flights." Later there would be mass departures of emigrants to the United States from the port of Camarioca, a small fishing village between Matanzas and the sea resort of Varadero—a place we crossed every Saturday and Sunday on our trips between school and home.

My mother's sister Felicia lived in Cabaiguán. She and her husband, Raúl, owned a small store, which provided them with a modest living. Once it was confiscated by the government, they decided to leave with their two little children for the United States. My father would often bring up the emigrant question, saying such people preferred to exchange their love of family and country for the various articles they could obtain in the United States. Those who wanted to leave were referred to as *gusanos*, or worms, meaning those who crawled, unable to hold up their heads. "Those who stay here live modestly but with dignity, and dignity is the most valuable possession one can have," my father would say.

One day I heard him arguing with my mother but I didn't understand why. "Even if it is your sister, they're not going to spend the night in this house." It was my Aunt Felicia's turn to leave the country via Camarioca, and as they lived quite a distance away, in Cabaiguán, someone in the family had called to see if they could spend the night with us before their departure. "I will have nothing to do with anybody who is against the Revolution," my father declared. My mother ran off to her room in tears, thinking of the sister whom she might never see again, unable to comprehend why they shouldn't spend their last night in Cuba at our home.

During this period my mother did custom dressmaking, using an old German sewing machine. A beautiful young woman began visiting the house who loved to talk with my mother while she worked on the dresses. One Sunday morning this woman told my mother that she would love to invite her over, but that state security had to check her file first, as her husband didn't want any enemies of the Revolution coming to his house. Her husband was Joaquín Quinta Solás, commander in chief of the Central Army. My mother listened without saying a word and I went off to sulk, with a feeling of humiliation tightening in my chest.

Aren't we all revolutionaries? I asked myself.

—

Sometimes on Sundays my father's friends, *dirigentes* or "officials" like himself, would meet at our house, where they would spend hours

discussing various political and historical subjects while I listened attentively. It was my father's opinions that gave meaning to the doctrines we learned at school. The conversations always centered around the powerful but fraudulent enemy, our country's honor, and Fidel's greatness. The enemy was a big, powerful country called the United States, which despised us and wanted to humiliate us by imposing its every whim upon us. History, as we learned it in school, provided the basis for my father's discussions with his friends.

For more than a century the giant to the north had coveted our island, giving little credit to the intelligence and honor of its citizens. To prove this, our teachers would cite New York newspaper articles of a hundred years ago, in which journalists lobbied for the annexation of Cuba, referring to Cubans disdainfully as intellectually, spiritually, and morally inferior. Nowadays the Revolution was giving our lives a new dimension; we had dignity and would not allow ourselves to be treated as lesser beings. Death was preferable to accepting that kind of humiliation. Nevermore would we submit to such offenses. The spectacle of a drunken, disrespectful U.S. Marine sitting on top of José Martí's statue in Havana, immortalized by an infamous photograph from the forties, would never be repeated. Whoever came to Cuba today would have to leave his arrogance back home.

My father and his friends also dreamed about the bright future opening up to all Cubans.

"Look at the Soviet Union," my father would remark, "a country that has made the leap from feudalism to socialism, and turned out to be the first to send a man into space. . . . And to think they had to build their own first tractor, while we receive them today by the thousands. What won't we accomplish in just a few years?"

In school we were taught to worship the Revolution, and there wasn't a day we weren't reminded that the sons of peasants like my father were never able to attend school before. "But today," the teachers would all tell us, "you have the benefit of an education, and in the very houses of those who formerly made themselves rich through the suffering of the poor." I went to school with the sons of scientists, military officers, peasants, and poor laborers. Some were already winning medals in the National Scholastic Games, and I felt lucky to be living under a revolution, in a place where the same rights were given to everybody and where our parents' income didn't matter.

Sometimes when his friends were around, my father would call me in to quiz me on some political issue. My knowledge of politics, acquired so early, made him feel proud of me. Once when they were talking about the *gusanos* who were leaving via Camarioca and about the importance of educating one's children to love their country, he asked me, "What would you say if tomorrow your mother and I decided to leave for the United States?"

"I'd rather see you dead than traitors to your country," I

answered quickly in a grave and solemn tone. My father's eyes sparkled with pride as he smiled his approval.

—

The strenuous physical activity of the swimming school made us all insatiably hungry, and late at night, in small groups, we'd sneak down to the dining room, via the beach, to steal the following morning's breakfast rolls. Incredibly enough, at those late hours we still found the energy to hide in the sand and surprise a *kawama* or two coming out of the sea to lay its eggs.

As Young Pioneers, we also had a military unit for a sponsor. From time to time they'd visit the school and teach us how to assemble and load an M-52 rifle. Later, during our Pioneer Festival, they would always organize a student competition that involved assembling and dismantling the rifles against the clock.

Saturdays everybody went home and my brother Faure, six at the time, and I nearly always managed to get a taxi driver to take us to Matanzas for nothing. Faure was a sly one, and whenever we couldn't persuade anybody he would pretend he actually had the pesos for the trip, and then once in Matanzas he'd act astonished and ashamed, turning his pockets inside out while complaining, "I don't understand, I must have lost my money."

When we arrived at home one Saturday we were told that Father had been taken to the hospital. His sisters had come from Cabaiguán to help my mother, who could not care for him and for our baby brother at the same time. Father had been vomiting and passing blood. The doctors diagnosed an ulcer and recommended that he change his job, for his passion in performing his duties—often not eating or sleeping while he traveled about the province inaugurating schools and teaching peasants—was the cause of his illness.

Faure and I also began suffering from heartburn around this time, which was treated with milk and an antacid. It was a type of gastritis caused by the kind of food given us at school and the way it was prepared. Years later this kind of sickness was dubbed the "scholarship syndrome."

With my father's illness, the so-called party officials and others from the Ministry of Education began to visit us, concerned about his health. They were all surprised to see that in our house there was no television or refrigerator, since they took it for granted that, given my father's position, we had been allotted them. They didn't understand that my father was proud of his austerity. "The more humble a man, the greater he is," we had often heard him say. And he truly was an austere man. Nevertheless, while he was still in the hospital, a refrigerator and television were delivered to the house one day. "So he can observe his diet properly," the deliveryman explained to my

mother, pointing to the refrigerator, which was not available in stores, being only assigned by the State.

—

It was during holidays that we undertook our biggest adventures. Among the agave fields of *La Loma*, as we called the hill across which the railroad ran, there were a number of caves filled with mystery for us. We all had visited the famous Bellamar Caves, open to the public and not very far away. But we were fascinated with the idea of becoming the "discoverers" of a new cave, which we expected to be full of crystalline stalactites and perhaps even a secret treasure hidden there centuries ago by pirates.

One morning we organized our own expedition: Faure, Alfredo Formero, his brother Rolando, and myself. With a flashlight and a flimsy rope borrowed secretly from my mother's clothesline, we set out to explore the most intriguing of the caves. Near the entrance was a well called the Blind Well, because of the length of time it took a stone to reach the water below. It was said that down in the cave was an underground river that flowed beneath the well, so we decided to go see it with our own eyes.

Behind a few bushes in an outcropping of rock called Dog's Tooth was an opening that led to a small grotto with a pit at the center. Although we couldn't see to the ground with our flashlight, we figured it was solid enough and—calculating the time it took for stones we had dropped in there to hit the bottom—not too deep for the length of our rope. We tied one end of our rope to a rock and began our descent into what turned out to be the most extraordinary cave of that whole region. One by one we climbed down the rope along the rocky wall. Instead of compact even ground down there, however, we found a slope of soft earth ending much farther below, on the bank of a lovely river of clear water, which flowed from among the limestones. There we played Robinson Crusoe, investigating and discovering new chambers and grottoes along the river. We bathed in the river and drank from its water, naive, carefree, not even thinking about how long the flashlight batteries would last.

All of a sudden Alfredo accidentally turned off the flashlight and such total darkness, like we'd never seen before, frightened us— reminding us we'd better be heading back. It wasn't until we tried to get out of there that we realized the danger we were in. Suddenly we longed to see our parents again, who had so often warned us about the danger of going into those caves. We had to get back up the slope, but our wet clothes caused us to slip on the mud, and each time we tried we ended up sliding back down to the riverbank. The flashlight's glow was growing dimmer and dimmer, but finally we figured out that the best way to get up the slope was to kick repeatedly with our shoes into the clay until we had formed a crude step along which to make

developed a taste for those raw sweet potatoes we dug out of the earth. We would clean them with our hands, bite off the peel, and chew the inside to ward off hunger. Around noon the tractor arrived with lunch, which we ate greedily despite the constant menu of dried hake, chickpeas, and rice. Then back to pulling raw potatoes out of the ground. For dinner, it was more of the same. By the time you went to bed you had only one thing on your mind besides food: home.

One night we discovered that the padlock to the door of the pantry was gone. Curious and hungry, we opened the door and with a lighted match rummaged around in the darkness. We found hundreds of small cartons containing powdered milk, but when we opened one of them we saw a bunch of maggots crawling around inside. We found it nearly impossible to remove so many maggots from the powder with our fingers, so we sent someone off to get a mosquito net and then used it to strain out the maggots. That was one night we went to bed with our stomachs full. But I could never figure out why they would let all that milk simply rot, instead of giving it to us in place of sugar water for breakfast.

The students brought wooden lockers with them to School in the Fields in those days. These contrivances were the divine work of neighborhood carpenters who designed them at the behest of the parents. Since the nourishment was so bad at School in the Fields, parents would bring their children enough food on the weekend visits to supplement their diet for the rest of the week. And as hunger is the strongest reason for becoming dishonest, many stole and ate secretly what didn't belong to them. That was why the lockers tended to be solidly built and airtight with a large padlock to prevent easy access to their contents: condensed milk, homemade sweets, biscuits, the ever popular *gofio* (sweet roasted cornmeal), and other treats that the students would parsimoniously mete out to themselves until their parents' next visit.

I spent my time pining for those weekend visits, when I would get to have my own picnic lunch with my parents off in the trees beyond the fence. When Sunday finally came and the parents began arriving, one by one the students would go off with them into the grass and spread their blankets. There they would sit, talking and eating the meals that their families had so carefully prepared for them. Those hours were the most precious and long-awaited moments of the week. And soon I became the only one still left in the dormitory, pretending to read while awaiting my parents, expecting them to surprise me at any moment, but they never came. One of my friends would occasionally notice that I was still alone and invite me to join his family, but I always thanked him and excused myself, preferring not to go with them. Deep down I was ashamed the other parents would notice that mine hadn't come.

Four lonely and sad Sundays went by like that, and I couldn't figure out why my parents hadn't come to see me. Finally, in despair, I wrote a short note to my mother: . . . *Mommy, please, we're all so hungry. Have someone from Matanzas bring me something, if only some brown sugar.* It's true we were all very hungry, but that wasn't my real reason for writing to my mother. I just wanted to know they loved me and to have them show it like the other parents did. But I didn't have the courage to say that in my letter, being afraid to be branded a weakling by my father. I asked another boy's parents to mail it.

Three days later on a rainy afternoon my mother arrived, despondent and exhausted, with mud up to her knees after having walked the two miles from the highway. She hugged me with tears in her eyes, saying, "My poor boy, you look like a ghost!" I was twelve years old at the time, already a man by my father's standards, and so I refused to let myself cry. I held her and kissed her, breathing hard to choke down the pain inside me. I was deeply grateful for this sign of affection. "Your father's as stubborn as ever," she told me. "I begged him to come but he refused, insisting you were grown up by now and should be acting like a man. This time he got really angry with me and refused to even take me in the jeep. So I made my way as best I could, hitchhiking bit by bit along the highway."

I felt a terrible pressure well up in my chest as I listened to what she told me, and felt terribly ashamed to have made her go through all this for me. *How selfish!* I kept telling myself, doubly grieved at the thought of what she must have suffered, embroiled in a conflict with my father because of her own maternal love and my stupidity.

My mother left at dusk, walking the two miles back to the highway along the winding dirt road. She seemed so sad and bewildered. And I stood there just as sad, wondering why study and work had to separate us so far from each other. Confused, I turned back to the dormitory, remembering those faraway days with my grandparents in Cabaiguán and those lively Christmas holidays with all my relatives, wondering whether I'd really lived them or if they were simply a dream.

The last Sunday I finally did have a surprise. My parents and my brothers came to visit in my father's shiny jeep from the Ministry of Education. I never felt so proud. I wanted all my campmates to meet them and I took my family for a walk all around the grounds. My mother was pleased to have persuaded my father to come, and she kept asking me about conditions there, obviously to have my father hear the answers. In the meantime my brothers ran about playing games, turning into an adventure what would later become a reality for them as well: the School in the Fields.

My father tried not to give much importance to my mother's complaints about the place. "Nonsense," he remarked with a laugh, "they're having a better time than you imagine. I'd love to have these country vacations Orestico is having." But you could see in his eyes he didn't believe what he was saying. It was his way of protecting himself from remorse. When they were ready to leave he turned to me from behind his steering wheel and said, "Don't give in, you can take it. You're a man." Watching the jeep drive away, splashing through the muddy potholes, I suddenly felt able to deal with almost anything. I no longer felt alone.

When I returned home two weeks later, my father was so proud I had passed the test. "You're thinner, but you're more of a man," he said, patting me on the shoulder. "You're becoming a revolutionary." And then he continued, "When I say 'First the Revolution, and then the family,' that doesn't mean I'm against you. On the contrary, you are part of a world I call the Revolution. It's you, the suffering people of the earth. Human dignity, the children everywhere . . . that's the Revolution. I'm tough with you because I don't want you to become selfish, callous about other people's suffering. Millions of human beings die in misery every day around the world because of the self-seeking interests of those who exploit them. These people need us, they need you and they need me, they need all free and honorable men. . . . When the food isn't good, think of those who have none. . . . When life becomes difficult, remember Ché Guevara. A revolutionary doesn't live to provide privileges for his own children. What makes us different is a constant readiness to sacrifice ourselves for others." And my father continued to explain the meaning behind his words, while I began thinking, *Those who have nothing . . . first them, then us—yes, that's what it means! First the Revolution, and then the family!*

—

Having stood the test of the School of the Fields, at twelve years old I was ready to face anything. I was no longer a weakling in my father's eyes, and although I still didn't feel close to him, I looked up to him as the wisest, most important man in the world. I considered myself a model revolutionary—the "New Man" that the highest leader had proposed to be molded in the likeness of Ché Guevara. I wanted to be like the legendary commander, strong and just, ever ready for sacrifice. So I asked my parents to let me continue my studies in the most highly acclaimed military academy in the country. This school, only recently inaugurated, bore the name of the most charismatic commander of the Revolution—Camilo Cienfuegos, the same one whose rumored rescue had caused my father's only drunken episode a few years back. If everything went well, I might eventually be chosen to become a fighter pilot. Of course, that would be many years off, but I was already in the antechamber—military school. The new academy with its impressive five-story buildings occupied a large tract outside of Matanzas. Its elegant uniform—olive green like that of the armed forces and bearing a gold coat of arms on its buttons and cap—was the envy of every boy. And its program was unique among the rest of the schools in Cuba at the time. While I had been spending my two months at School in the Fields, classes at the academy had continued without interruption. However, through the kind intervention of the head physician, a friend of my parents, I was permitted to enter at this later date. Thus I began my first great fiasco.

I arrived full of energy, out to conquer the world, and while the other students were enjoying a short vacation, I spent the time diligently studying to catch up on what I'd missed. One day the school director, Captain Palacios, seeing me studying all by myself, asked, "How old are you, son?"

"Twelve, sir," I replied timidly.

"When you're thirteen I think we'll make you a member of the Union of Young Communists."

My father would be beside himself with pride. To be a Young Communist one had to be at least fourteen years old, but they were going to accept me one year earlier. I'd already be among the academy's elite and my parents would receive congratulations from everybody. Yet nothing could have been further from the truth. Once the other students returned from their vacation I was to discover a different world.

The school itself was composed of two main blocks of buildings centered around an asphalt polygon on which we practiced our infantry drill. We were so well trained that not even officers of the armed forces displayed such elegance and discipline in drill. As a result we were often invited to take part in commemorative parades for which we would practice hours at a time, shouting revolutionary slogans in a chorus as we marched. It was quite an experience to hear more than a thousand young voices rend the air in unison with: "Commander in chief! Whatever the job, wherever the job, come what may . . . we obey!"

Every morning at six we were awakened with, "On your feet!" We had five minutes to be lined up by companies on the polygon. Roll call was immediate and anybody who was late, even a second, paid for it by losing his weekend pass for home. We would run and drill for about thirty minutes and then be given another twenty to wash and line up again downstairs for the march to the dining room, hitting the asphalt with military vigor under the command of Sergeant García.

We were already familiar with the anecdotes circulated by older students about the sergeant. An extremely stubborn and stupid man, García devoted his talents to the art of leading a troop in drill. He imposed an iron discipline in training his cadets, to such an extent that during the long waits outside to enter the dining hall he liked to keep us at absolute attention, with our eyes fixed exactly on that imaginary point directly ahead. The slightest movement was severely reprimanded. But we cadets were forever contriving some way or another to leave formation, impatient to have even a moment's rest from that torture out in the sun. So after calling us to attention he would repeat his customary warning: "I advise you in advance . . . there'll be no permission to get water or take a leak. Bear it or burst, there's no permission." But one day a student asked, "Permission to leave, Sergeant, to take H_2O." "For medicine, okay. Permission granted, cadet," he replied.

—

Each evening most of the professors and instructors would go home, with a small group remaining to keep order. That was when the "officers" in command of our battalions—cadets from the upper grades—took charge. They generally behaved tyrannically, sometimes showing up in the barracks of the lower grades to beat up on a rebellious student and humiliate him publicly. One day they went after Gustavo, a thirteen-year-old boy who had answered one of them back. They simply showed up and invited him outside to settle the matter. Gustavo listened but didn't answer and didn't go outside either, because there was a bunch of husky "officers" out there just waiting to even the score. So they really began to taunt him, calling him the worst names and shouting abuse about his mother. Gustavo still wouldn't leave, so they branded him a coward for his refusal to fight them. From that day forward life became a nightmare for Gustavo. Wherever he went they would call him names. There wasn't a place in the school where he could feel at ease. In class they threw things at him from behind and at drill they pushed him out of line. At night while he slept they'd light strips of newspaper between his toes and he'd wake up screaming and run to the bathroom. Almost everyone got involved in abusing him; everyone enjoyed being tough on Gustavo. We all laughed at him . . . such is the cruelty of adolescents.

Finally Gustavo couldn't take it anymore. Early one Monday morning he showed up with his mother to pick up his belongings. And in seconds the word went out: "Gustavo's cutting out!" A group of students gathered in front of the director's office, where Gustavo and his mother were filling out the papers for his discharge. We had a fifteen-minute recess between classes, and from a window on the third floor I watched the scene unfolding below. When the two of them came out, Gustavo in civilian clothes with his head bowed, obviously afraid to face the crowd of boys, somebody shouted: "Gustavooh, youuu quitter!" And dozens of voices joined in repeating, "Coward! . . . Quitter!" Gustavo and his mother kept walking toward the gate, attempting to ignore the taunting crowd gathering behind them. Suddenly from within that mob of his tormentors a stone was hurled. It described a slow parabolic arc and struck Gustavo on the head with a dull sound I could hear clearly from the window where I stood.

Gustavo put a hand to his head, bending over slightly, but his mother grabbed him by the arm to steady him. Gustavo looked down at his bloodstained hand and I could see more blood running down his neck. And the two of them kept walking slowly past the gate, without once looking back at that gang of boys who were still jeering.

That day was the first time I witnessed the exuberant cruelty of a mob. I couldn't believe who it was that actually threw the stone because he was a boy wholly incapable of doing such a thing on his own. Yet the same scene would be repeated more than once, with other boys who made up their minds to leave. They were looked upon as traitors and ostracized. They were branded weaklings and quitters. And the teachers never did anything to halt the collective insanity. They didn't seem to mind; they even silently approved such behavior.

—

Activities at school all took place under strong military discipline, to inculcate in us an exacting rigor. The teachers always carried with them a little notebook for "reports," as they called them. Most anything would provide occasion for a report: if you didn't respond with enough speed or alacrity when called upon by a superior, you'd be marked "slothful"; if your boots weren't gleaming, "untidy"; if you attempted to explain yourself, "answers back." We always preferred to keep our distance when we saw a teacher coming our way. Every two weeks we had the right to a weekend pass, but first we had to appear before the terrible "court." The court sessions took place in the dormitories every other Friday, after lunch. We all had to line up, at attention, before the commanding officer–instructor of our battalion. He would call us up, one by one, those with "reports." And one by one, the accused would present themselves, stating, "Cadet so-and-so, ready to respond, sir!"

"At ease!" the officer-instructor would reply, observing just how we complied with the order.

Often one received an extra report during the court hearing, losing two or more passes at a time. As a result we always tried to be well pressed and polished, accepting guilt beforehand, even if the report was unjust or simply erroneous. Any attempt to defend oneself or to give an explanation ended in more reports—for answering back.

"You were reported for speaking during drill formation on such-and-such a day at such-and-such a time. Guilty or not guilty?" the sergeant would ask, looking the accused straight in the eye.

"Guilty, sir!" the student invariably replied.

I don't remember ever enjoying the use of a pass. Barely had all the other students returned from vacation and settled down to the normal routine when I started topping the list of those most frequently disciplined by the court. "Dirty boots," "speaking during drill," and especially "answering back" were the reasons I was denied a pass.

And each court appearance only added to the list of my reports for "answering back" because keeping silent in the face of what I considered an injustice was something I never managed, even knowing it would have been the smarter thing to do. Thus I spent weekend after weekend at school, on "perennial watch," waiting for night, when I might escape home secretly by creeping along the dry stream-bed winding past the school grounds. At home, however, it would be the same old problem. My father would accuse me of being unruly and lacking discipline. "You're no good for anything," he railed and made me go back to school, which I began to hate with all my might.

"I've got to get out of this place," I told myself, no longer even caring about my dream to be a fighter pilot. But I wasn't ready to bear the humiliation of a gang of students calling me a quitter, perhaps with my father as the director of the chorus. Little by little my list of reports grew, and my reputation for "always objecting" spread among the teachers, who focused their attention on correcting my rebellious-ness. For me, the school became more and more stifling—but where could I go?

One afternoon while passing some time alone beyond the bushes lining the bed of the stream, I broke off a branch from a *guao* shrub and let the resin drip on my forearm. *I'm getting out of this place, even if I have to go to the hospital to do it,* I had decided, and the result was grim.

I was admitted to the school infirmary, where I spent hours with one poultice after another applied to my swollen arm. When the doctors interrogated me about the incident I tried to make them think it had been accidental. In any case my arm was soon cured and with my sickness went any hope of getting discharged from school on account of poisoning. I was thrust back into the normal routine of the academy, to receive a new string of reports and have even more teachers out to correct me for "always objecting." But I was deter-mined to get out now no matter what the cost. I no longer cared what ranting mob jeered at me or branded me a quitter; it didn't matter. Only what about my father? How was he going to take his son's asking to be discharged? No, he could never accept that. I'd only have his reproaches for ever putting in such a request. Which would be the greater humiliation? What I'd get from the mob of students, or from my father? *But I'm getting out no matter how,* I told myself, *no matter how.*

So one day I locked myself in one of the bathrooms, took a razor blade out of my pocket, and made two cuts in my forearm without reaching the vein. Someone seeing blood seep out from under the door sounded the alarm, and I was taken to the military hospital on a stretcher. I had gotten my way and was never to return. My mother nearly went crazy when she found out. She spent the whole time of my hospitalization by my side, showering me with attention. My father preferred not to speak of the matter with me, but his eyes were filled with anguish a long time thereafter. Then came the consultations with psychiatrists and psychologists, who provided me with a medical discharge from the academy, thereby terminating the treatment as well as the illness.

—

The remaining two months of the school year I spent traveling with my father on his journeys throughout the province, helping with volunteer work cutting sugarcane and visiting peasants. One day I noticed he looked unusually happy, but preoccupied at the same time. He'd been nominated for possible induction into the Communist party. Nothing could have pleased him more than this, his dream for so many years. He had always felt somehow ashamed that he'd never been asked to be a party member, feeling excluded from the great family of revolutionaries to whom he had devoted his life. To him it was as though they didn't have enough confidence in him. He was finally being given his due. But something was still bothering him: A year before the triumph of the Revolution he was forced by the police to vote in elections that the rebels in the Sierra Maestra had asked the people to boycott. If he failed to justify that decision, he might be rejected by the party. Each day he looked more and more preoccupied, lost in his doubts. Until at last the good news came: He had been accepted into the ranks of the Communist party. He turned exuberant as a child and went off to tell his closest friends. The Revolution finally had confidence in him.

For my part I would no longer have to lie when applying to schools, where the first blank to fill in would always be, REVOLUTIONARY ENROLLMENT OF PARENTS. Until then I'd faked it by listing my father as "Party militant."

During those two months that I observed my father meeting with the people and discussing various issues, we shared everything and I was truly happy. My father had changed greatly and I felt him to be close, trusting, a friend. Years later, when I became an adult, I thought that perhaps the psychologists treating me had spoken to him. But whatever lesson he'd had back then had brought a change, and he gave our youngest brother the attention Faure and I had never received when it came time for Orlando to go off to school on scholarship.

I don't think I really wanted to leave the world of the living when I slashed my arm, but obviously I wasn't altogether well at the time. For years I felt haunted by the deed, which I took to be a result of my own cowardice. I never mentioned it to anyone and tried to blot it out of my life, until a certain toughness acquired by bitter experience made me see it differently. At twelve years of age I was still far from being a man.

I understood things a little better when I myself became a father.

After the adventure of traveling around with my father was over, I entered our local secondary school to begin my next year of studies. Leaving for school in the morning and coming home each afternoon was paradise. And so I began my adolescence, thinking about girls and flashy clothes. The latter, however, was something of a problem. The rationing coupons to control clothing purchases had, in my case, nothing to do with reality. I had grown tremendously in the past year and the clothing allotted for my age group was too small for me. My mother pleaded with the saleswomen and even spoke to the managers, but the answer was always the same: "Sorry, but with a minor's coupon you cannot purchase adult clothes." Thus I was often forced to wear shoes that didn't fit and which, under the pressure of my large foot, would stretch out in the back until the heel looked as if it had been moved forward. With shoes ready to burst and my pants always ending above my ankles I looked plain ridiculous and of course felt mortified. My mother, it must be said, performed miracles on her sewing machine to enlarge my clothing by adding patches, which, unfortunately, were never the same color.

—

One day a task force from the Ministry of Education came by the school to tell us that the Revolution needed teachers. "The first calling of a revolutionary is to *be* revolutionary," they told us, reminding us of our ethic of the "New Man," for whom sacrifice is the very meaning of life. Without thinking twice I signed up for one, which involved a year of training at Varadero Teachers' College. Once again I had a scholarship, but this time I was not deprived of my weekend passes. The school was housed in the famous Granma Apartments complex, which originally had been built for tourism but which with the Revolution had become fairly run-down in appearance due to the students.

The apartment buildings, which housed about forty students apiece, contained only one bathroom each. On Saturdays we had to clean up the excrement from the top floor, where those who couldn't wait went for their necessities. We had to do this before going home each weekend, and it was one of the more unpleasant chores I remember. I began to think that all my life I was going to be condemned to perform repellent tasks in order to have the right to visit home.

Upon finishing the program at the age of sixteen, I was sent to teach with a classmate named Victor to the Communist party's regional school, where half-illiterate workers and peasants—members of the party—were being educated. All of our students were over forty years old and most had had only one or two years of schooling in their lives. Yet, though they were unschooled in the arts and sciences, their worldly wisdom taught me a great deal. These simple and honest people had spent their lives working hard to feed their families, never caring much about politics, but the Revolution had embraced them, making them members of the party and sending them to school to raise their "level of culture." We would get up together at five A.M. to cut sugarcane, and there in the fields those students would become our teachers, often joking about our lack of skill in cutting. Classes took place in the afternoon, with Victor and I teaching basic subjects like math and Spanish. The older teachers, who were part of the ideological arm of the party, gave classes in political science. It was amazing to see such students straining to read Marx, Engels, and Lenin at night, struggling to make sense out of their abstract theories.

Located about two miles from the village of Limonar, the school was surrounded by fields growing cane for the regional mills. The students would often take a walk to the village after dinner, using the narrow path that led there from the school. One night Victor and I decided to play a trick on a group of them on their way back from the village. We covered ourselves with white sheets and went down along the path until we heard them coming. We quickly hid among the cane stalks and when they passed we jumped out, grunting like apparitions. One of them yelled, "I'll turn you into real ghosts, you little—" and pulling out his machete, he lunged for us in the darkness, followed by the others shouting, "Get the little bastards!" But all they got were the two empty sheets left behind as we ran like hell to the village. We were the ones who looked like we'd seen a ghost.

—

During that period my parents moved to an apartment in Havana, to be closer to work, and once again I was hounded by those two eternal problems: lack of transportation and scarcity of food. On weekends I would go to the bus station and try to find a space on one of the rare, always overcrowded buses, but most of the time I would have to give up and stay at my parents' empty home in Matanzas, where I would go after having spent most of Saturday at the station. Then the most difficult task would be to find enough food to get through the weekend. The long lines of hungry customers in front of the pizzerias generally discouraged me from the prospect of eventually sitting at a counter to sip a glass of water with a dish of bland pasta and a slice of pizza. There wasn't a single restaurant without those long lines, so it was finally the "Frozens" that saved me. That type of ice cream, then fashionable in Matanzas and dispensed by newly installed Italian machines, was produced by mixing vanilla-, chocolate-, or strawberry-flavored powder with water to create a paste resembling real ice cream. If the Frozen merely satisfied my hunger, the same was not true of the cone, which was delicate and crunchy, a delightful little confection made by a machine imported from Italy. I'd go to one of those Coppelitas stands with a pitcher under my arm to buy a dozen of those ice creams, which I'd then stick in the freezer to serve as my food for the remainder of the weekend.

When the school year ended, I was more than ready to give up my long waits at the bus station and all those Frozens to join my parents in the capital. Once in Havana I went to the Ministry of Education with my provisional work permit stamped and sealed, tucked under my arm, searching for a job; and they sent me to the party school in central Havana. No sooner had I introduced myself to the young principal there than she asked, "Are you a militant of the Young Communists Union?" I told her I wasn't, to which she replied, "Why not?"

"I don't know," I told her, "they never screened me." I was referring to the routine investigation that precedes approval for membership, a sort of inquiry involving the places where one lived, studied, and worked, as well as a report from the Ministry of the Interior verifying that one had no criminal record.

"Leave your papers and come back tomorrow morning at eight o'clock sharp," she told me peremptorily.

When I returned the next morning I was greeted by the principal, along with the school's secretary general of Communist youth. As soon as I walked into the office they eyed me with open distrust; then the secretary general asked, "How do you explain that at seventeen you're still not a member of the Young Communists?"

"I explained yesterday, they never screened me for membership." I could feel my ears flush.

"And why didn't they ever screen you?" she insisted skeptically.

I didn't know what to answer and stood there defenseless and humiliated.

"In that case we can't have you in our collective," the principal concluded abruptly, as if addressing an enemy.

I left, feeling utterly despised.

When I told my father about what had happened his only comment was: "A pair of imbeciles. A Communist's identity card is something you carry in you, not on you. There are those who have one that shouldn't; and those who don't that should." He was referring to both the party and the Communist Youth. And then he added, while writing a quick note, "Go to the National Board of Adult Education and ask for Isabel. Give her this note and she'll place you in one of the schools."

Following my interview with Isabel the next day, I set off for another school, this time the Provincial School for Party Officials. My boyhood pranks and adolescent rebelliousness were definitely behind me. I was a man now, and my parents were proud to see me working and at the same time studying biology at the University of Havana.

—

In the evening I started receiving a lot of telephone calls and my mother would ask, "When are you going to introduce us to the girl you're going with?"

"And who told you I had a girlfriend?"

"Do you think that when you're not here the telephone doesn't ring?"

"It's too early, Mom," I said, kissing her on the cheek. "I'm only going to introduce you to the one I marry." But it wasn't too long before my mother got to meet that very girl. It happened when the neighbors on our block were all celebrating with beer and music the anniversary of the founding of the Committees for the Defense of the Revolution. I spotted a girl in an adjacent patio playing hide-and-seek with some little children there, running about and having fun with them, unaware that she was being observed and totally engrossed in the game. She had the biggest eyes, full of kindness and candor.

"Who's that girl?" I asked a boy sitting next to me.

"Who—that one? Are you crazy, man? Keep your distance from her or her father will kill you. . . . They treat her like she's made of porcelain."

"All right, but what's her name?"

"Vicky."

"Vicky," I repeated softly as I watched her playing.

I didn't see her again that night, but when I went to bed I was still thinking about her.

"Vicky," I whispered before falling asleep.

Chapter 4

—

Vicky

We lived in the capital now, and each day that passed brought new discoveries of Havana's charm: the latest films, the theater, classical music concerts—a life wholly different from anything I had known. In the early morning hours on the streets of Vedado, people coming home from nightclubs would meet up with those going off to work. And at night the Rampa would be filled with young people strolling for hours around the Coppelia, gathering in small groups to chat, sporting the latest bit of clothing or jewelry someone had brought them from abroad. It was not unusual to see some of them carrying huge portable tape systems to regale the air with the booming rhythms of Led Zeppelin, Chicago, Credence Clearwater Revival, and Blood, Sweat and Tears. Older people, feeling that there was something immoral about such behavior and swearing the young were "lost," rejected the complete cultural contrast of a different generation, which went "recklessly parading" in the streets to the beat of North American hard rock or to songs of protest by Silvio Rodríguez and Pablito Milanés, troubadours of the Revolution.

Music to us, as opposed to our parents, was something we didn't judge by its politics. Let whoever sings it sing it. Every young man's dream was to own a portable tape deck with which to show off and prove his worth. Only those who had somebody in the family traveling abroad could indulge in such a luxury. And as a result the sons of diplomats and civil servants, together with those who had relatives abroad, were the natural elite among those taking walks along the Rampa. To have any status among the young, an outfit, a watch, anything at all had to come "from abroad." Thus, the youth of Havana was visibly divided into two categories: those who were with it, and the *guachos*—the latter, slang for "hick," and a term of ridicule applied by those who were "with it" to anyone unfortunate enough to have to wear what the Revolution made available in the shops of Cuba.

"Their parents are so many parasites who live at the expense of the Revolution," my father railed critically when I asked him to use his influence to help me get more stylish clothes. "They raise their children to be idiots, but tomorrow history will settle accounts with them," he predicted, concluding, "There are more important things in life than dressing up, and you ought to know what they are by now."

Once in a while the police carried out a cleanup operation, sweeping through the Coppelia District, arresting crowds of youths and hauling them off in patrol wagons. At the time there was a law in force known as Against Vagrancy, which made it obligatory for every citizen to have a job. And since many of the young were neither employed nor students, they were sent to special prisons where they were to be "reformed." It was one of the Revolution's many attempts to rid society of its undesirables. After tens of thousands of young people had been imprisoned and marked for life, the law was ultimately repealed, reality slowly triumphing as always over the romanticism of our leaders.

—

The Provincial School of the Party where I gave classes in biology was at the west end of town, so I had to get up very early in the morning to catch the bus. Among those waiting at the stop, almost furtively, was an imposing, reserved-looking man whom I greeted each day with a "good morning" and a smile; and he would return the "good morning" but not the smile. His name was Gerardo, and he was Vicky's father. And as much as I tried to strike up a conversation, his abrupt, evasive replies would keep me at a distance.

One evening there was a meeting of the neighborhood Committee for the Defense of the Revolution to approve the slate for the various nominations to the Block Committee: president, secretary, ideologist, secretaries of culture, sports, health, vigilance—in short, a title for nearly everyone in the neighborhood. When I arrived I spotted Vicky, who was accompanied by her parents. She seemed rather naive and extremely timid, hardly opening her mouth during the course of the meeting. And her parents appeared to be guarding her more than accompanying her. The meeting alternated between voting for the candidates and covering the committee agenda, while I gazed obliquely at this girl whose meek aspect I found so charming. Once our eyes met, causing her to blush terribly, which didn't pass unnoticed by her father. From that night on, the morning encounters at the bus stop turned into a forum for Gerardo's thinly veiled interrogation, as he proceeded to learn about my background and my prospects for the future.

Although we were neighbors I never ran into Vicky. Our work and study schedules didn't coincide, so I never managed to catch a glimpse of her even on her way to and from school. Sometimes I would spend the afternoon hours sitting in front of my house with the hope of seeing her, but in vain. She never seemed to go out.

I finally got to meet her at one of those boring Block Committee meetings.

"What's your name?" I asked her during a break.

"Vicky. And yours?"

Her voice trembled as if she were scared. I found that amusing. At the end of the meeting, after I'd finished leading the study group, she approached me.

"They're screening me to be a member of the Communist Youth. Soon I'll be having my interview, and I don't know anything about politics. I'm sure they'll ask me about things like the oil crisis and . . . do you think you could help me with some materials to study?"

"Whatever you need. . . . I'm nearly an expert on oil issues," I replied with a slyness she didn't perceive. "Look, if you want, I could come to your house and go over it with you," I insisted, looking for some way to get to see her before the next block meeting.

"I'll ask my mother. I think it should be all right. No reason I can't have a friend come to the house."

So I began to visit Vicky's house and we'd have long talks, she and I, but always with her mother, María, present. We hardly ever mentioned the international oil crisis.

In the afternoons, when I'd often be out in front of my house busy washing the new government car my father used for work, somebody would always let Vicky know. As water was scarce in Havana, she took over her brother's task of fetching water to refill the two cisterns her father had installed on the roof, each of which held fifty-five gallons. I'd see her coming out holding two small buckets, which she'd fill at a nearby faucet. And during her trips to and from the faucet we would have short conversations that gradually drew us closer. Our meetings at her house grew more and more frequent, and we would pass the time talking of classical music and the theater. Vicky was studying piano and she played beautifully. I loved to sit beside her, listening while she played Mozart and Tchaikovsky.

One evening when we were sitting on the curb together, posted for guard duty by the Defense Committee in the company of a neighbor, I began talking about my feelings for her while running a fingertip over the back of her hand.

"Vicky, I've always been searching for you without knowing you existed."

She moved her hand away nervously, timidly withdrawing as if afraid of what I was about to say, but never taking her eyes off me.

"I've always been looking for you. . . . I already knew you without knowing you."

She opened her eyes wider, as if suddenly surprised at the way things were happening.

"All my life I would have searched for you, because you're the only one I could ever spend a lifetime with."

She lowered her eyes and fixed her gaze on some vague spot in the pavement.

"Can I talk to your parents? I love you and don't want to hide it any longer."

"I, I don't know. . . . It's . . ." she stammered.

Feeling more confident, I took her hand and pleaded, "Don't say anything just now, let's talk more later. Think about it."

"Yes, it . . . I have to think about it," she said with a look of relief, as if glad to find the words to escape from that trance.

Guard duty was over and I escorted her home, still under the vigilant watch of our kind neighbor. When we said our good-byes I saw a joyful light in her eyes. I marched off happily with a dream in my heart.

—

Vicky thought it over for the next two weeks.

"Shall we be joined together forever? And have lots of kids?" I asked with shameless pleasure, enjoying her blushing and nervousness at any mention of our future.

"I have to think about it," she told me.

One day we went to the movies chaperoned by an aunt. There in the half-light of the theater I began to press her for her answer again while running my finger softly over her forearm. "Well . . . ?" She hesitated an instant, drawing her arm away as if pleading for me to stop caressing her, then stammered, "All right."

I felt so happy.

I quickly withdrew my right arm, which was resting against hers, and put it around her shoulders, drawing her to me. She shrank with embarrassment. "I love you," I whispered in her ear, making no further move so as not to scare her.

—

Whenever I visited Vicky her father would remain upstairs, as if he didn't want to see me. At the bus stop he didn't seem to mind talking to me but in his own home, where I was courting his daughter, it was another story.

"Does your mother know?" I asked Vicky in a whisper one day, as she was playing the piano.

"Know what?"

"That we're engaged."

"Yes," she replied, without looking up from the keyboard.

"And your father?"

"No. My mother doesn't dare tell him."

"Then I'll talk to him myself, right now."

"No, please don't, I'm scared to death!"

"Scared of what?"

"I'm not scared, just embarrassed," she chided my lack of understanding.

"But we're not going to keep it a secret forever. After all, you're seventeen and he should trust you by now. And I really love you, so I'm not afraid. I'd face a thousand dragons to win your hand."

"My father's not a dragon!"

"I know that, but I'm not a monster either. So I want to tell him."

"Okay, but please do it when I'm not here."

"When, then?"

"Tomorrow afternoon, while I'm at my piano lesson."

The next day I went to Vicky's house and asked her mother whether I could have a word with Señor Gerardo. As I sat downstairs waiting I could hear their voices above.

"I'm not going down to talk to anybody!"

"But Gerardo, the boy is downstairs waiting—you can't just leave him like that!"

"I have nothing to say to him!" Then after a while I heard his voice again: "All right, María, I'll see him." And with rapid steps he came down.

The staircase was hidden behind a wall, so that I didn't see him until he stood right in front of me.

"Good afternoon!" he said in a not-so-friendly tone, looking me straight in the eye. I got up and stared right back at him. I felt offended by his attitude. I was proud of being a young, serious worker and was not about to be treated contemptuously. A few seconds passed in silence, as Vicky's father tried to see whether I had anything to hide about myself. Finally he smiled, extended his hand, and asked me to sit down.

"Señor Gerardo, I love your daughter and I want to marry her one day. I know it's important to you both that she finish her studies. It's important to me as well. Please let me come see her whatever days and times you decide, here in your home, for which I have the greatest respect."

Gerardo listened carefully as I went on talking; with a certain sadness in his eyes, as if time had surprised him, as if suddenly he comprehended that his daughter was no longer a child. Perhaps he

---

was already anticipating her departure from the home in which she was born and grew up.

When I finished speaking he straightened up in his chair as if awakening from a faraway dream, and called, "María, please bring out some food for us." Then he began asking me a thousand questions about my parents and grandparents, about our places of birth and our Spanish ancestors, about my interests and plans for the future. Afterwards, he philosophized a bit about life and the importance of the family. He ended by saying, "All right . . . you can come see Vicky on Wednesday and Saturday evenings from seven to nine o'clock."

I went home delirious with happiness and called Vicky at the music school. "Your father looked at me and shouted, 'Who put it into Vicky's head I'd ever allow her to be engaged!' and with that he showed me the door."

"But—really? What will we do? How can I face my father now? How do we see each other from now on?"

I began to laugh and told her the truth: "I'm going to pick you up with your brother. . . . Don't worry, I convinced Gerardo. He's letting me come see you on Wednesdays and Saturdays."

From that day on we were "officially engaged" and I began my visits as Vicky's fiancé. The brief hours spent at her house on those evenings were like precious relics of a traditional past that had begun to disappear in Cuba, once young girls started leaving the seclusion of the home to become involved with the Revolution. We were like living fossils in an age when the promiscuity of the young at every turn made us look pleasantly ridiculous.

On the days when I visited, Vicky's mother took special care with every aspect of the household. Everyone dressed more formally, and Vicky would wear one of her nicest dresses, alternating the few she owned for each of my visits.

—

Thus the first month of our engagement passed. We always spoke in the presence of her mother or brothers, with hardly a possibility for the amorous interchanges normally enjoyed by fiancés. I'd write little passionate notes that would make her blush, which she tore up immediately while I looked on with delight. A month had passed, and still we hadn't had our first kiss, while Vicky's lips continued to torment me like a seductive obsession every minute of the day. Finally we were allowed to go to the movies again with one of Vicky's aunts, who was glad to be our chaperone. It was a first-run American film, *Wait Until Dark*, the story of a young blind woman alone in her apartment with a murderer. Vicky was terrified by the plot, not to mention embarrassed and evasive about my insistence on kissing her. At the moment when the entire audience let out a scream, as the criminal jumped out of the darkness at his helpless victim, I turned

Vicky's face toward mine and kissed her lips for the first time. Now we had a real secret, and were already conspiring for the next kiss. Now we were truly engaged.

—

One Sunday afternoon I came home to find my parents extremely upset. My father was sitting in the living room, looking very pale and lost in thought. I asked my mother what was going on and she explained worriedly, "Your father has gotten himself into a terrible fix."

"What happened?"

"He lent the car to someone at work, and the fellow got hit on the passenger side, denting the door."

"Why's that so awful?"

"That's not the problem. It's that your father went to a mechanic this morning to have it fixed because the door wouldn't close properly. And, well, the mechanic does this work on the side, so your father had to wait in line because there were other cars there waiting to have something fixed."

"And?"

"All of a sudden a car from State security appears and they begin photographing all the cars and people there."

"Did they say anything to Dad?"

"No, but he's scared to death. Can you imagine if he gets mixed up in some illegal activity? Nobody's allowed to work on the side like that. And where do you think that mechanic gets the oxygen and acetylene for his repairs? He must steal it from some public company, because the State doesn't supply those products to just anybody, so whatever work he does is illegal."

"But Dad has nothing to do with that."

"What do you mean, 'nothing'! Your father is a militant of the party and one of its *leaders*! Since that car he took to fix belongs to the State, that makes him an accomplice, for using such services instead of denouncing them."

"What?"

"Your poor father didn't even want his lunch."

I turned to my father and it pained me to see him slouched in his chair, absorbed in his thoughts, ignoring us as if he were in some other world. His face reflected one emotion: fear. I'd never seen him in such a state before and it cast a pall over the entire family. The house was filled with an atmosphere of suspense. We all felt like we'd committed some crime and were about to be discovered. My mother kept repeating nervously, "Your father's behavior has always been irreproachable. He's never given them a single cause for complaint. And now this whole thing is destroying him. . . . He's disgraced."

We resigned ourselves with bitterness to something that defied negative assessment for "lack of revolutionary conscience." I felt ashamed and depressed, stunned to watch my whole year of work and study be derailed by friends and colleagues singling out my lack of revolutionary conscience, but still benevolent enough to remark that it was probably due to my youth and inexperience, not to lack of enthusiasm for the Revolution, for which I obviously had a passion.

—

At last the sixteenth of July 1976, our longed-for wedding day, arrived. Vicky had successfully completed her studies and I was enjoying a vacation. Soon we would have those first moments of intimacy we'd dreamed of for so long. We were to be married at the Matrimonial Palace at six P.M., but by three o'clock I was already at Vicky's front door coordinating some last-minute details with her when Gerardo arrived. He took one look at us and said disapprovingly, "If you need to talk, at least do it in the house." Up to the last minute Gerardo was determined to protect his daughter against wagging tongues. "My daughter is a decent girl and no one is going to question her reputation," I had often heard him say. The dignity of his home was his most valued treasure and he was not about to take chances with what people might say.

The ceremony took place among friends and family, along with a photographer sent by someone as a wedding present, who pursued us at every moment. Afterwards we all went home to celebrate in the common courtyard, everybody drinking beer and doing their best to tease the newlyweds. At least I had taken the precaution of leaving our suitcases at a neighbor's house, as it was common for friends to hide the wedding couple's luggage and thereby force them to stay at the reception dancing until dawn.

We had reserved ten days at the Hotel Internacional in Varadero, where we headed at last, after spending enough time with everybody, feeling anxious to be alone and leaving the guests in the company of my in-laws, with whom they could carry on until dawn. When the car was ready to leave, Gerardo came over and kissed his daughter, and looking at me with tears in his eyes, he said, "Take care of her, my son." Then the car began moving away slowly, with the string of cans somebody'd tied to the back bouncing against the asphalt, proclaiming to the whole world that we'd just been married.

That first night, almost the next morning, I heard Vicky's voice from afar in our air-conditioned room, as from the depths of a cave, sobbing and reproaching me for something. I opened my eyes to see her with the face of a two-year-old, complaining, "You left me alone!"

"What do you mean? How did I leave you alone?" I asked drowsily.

"Over there, in the corner," she replied, pointing to the edge of the bed.

human understanding. Our father, who had been the model of a devoted revolutionary, saw himself ruined overnight by a transgression not found in any law book, but nevertheless considered a crime according to the ethics of the Revolution—a law a thousand times more fearful and exacting than anything written in the constitution or the penal code. Every day we waited for my father to arrive home with the news of our undoing. But time passed and nothing happened. Little by little my father put it out of his mind, regaining his confidence and becoming his old self again. But not the rest of us, who had learned through this whole experience to feel guilty even though we weren't. Anything not sponsored by the State could be considered a crime and not to oppose it could also be considered a crime. Such was the philosophy of justice they inculcated in us: Whoever fails to denounce or condemn is guilty.

No one ever bothered my father about the incident, but some of my mother's ominous expressions would come back to haunt us from time to time: "It's destroying him. . . . He's disgraced." How often I would hear that term—disgraced—applied to countless people in politics, science, and the arts, who inexplicably vanished from public life: This one or that one "has been disgraced."

—

Little by little my visits to Vicky's house lengthened and multiplied until there was no longer a fixed schedule to them. As her father and I got to know each other better, we shed our initial misgivings and gradually forged ties of genuine respect and affection.

Gerardo worked as a plumber for a construction firm that generally had contracts for projects outside of Havana. It took him hours to go back and forth to work each day; he devoted some fourteen hours a day thus to a poorly paying job, waiting to accumulate the time needed to retire. As his salary was insufficient to provide food for a family of five in Havana, Gerardo waited impatiently for the weekend to go out to Fontanar, where one of his brothers lived. In the nearby foothills he had found a stony, abandoned plot to grow the only vegetables that would come up there: corn and squash. Those Sundays spent with Gerardo under the hot sun, on that rocky slope full of weeds with patches of corn and squash, cultivated in me a deep affection for this remarkable man, humble and generous, for whom the most important thing in life was the family. His days constituted a never-ending struggle for the well-being of his loved ones, whom he tried to protect, with an almost excessive zeal, from whatever new influences might interfere with their obligations to the family. Gerardo's was a life of constant labor: on the job, on that rocky hill where he'd reap a few ears of corn and a handful of squash, and in the houses and apartments of the Vedado District, where he'd wander with his old toolbox in search of occasional plumbing jobs to add to his income. When he had accumulated a little savings he would travel to the countryside to get some peasant to sell him vegetables and, if he was lucky, even pork. The meat would often be confiscated by the police on his return trip. But nothing could discourage Gerardo in his struggle to feed his family.

Occasionally Vicky's family and mine would get together, but Gerardo and my father didn't have much in common and usually just exchanged the usual formalities. This made me feel embarrassed and hurt because I loved them both.

One day when I asked my father about his behavior toward Gerardo, he replied, "I have nothing against him, but there's little for us to say to each other. His world is totally different from mine."

And that was true. Each had his own different world inside him. For Gerardo, a humble and semiliterate plumber, life consisted of loyalty to family and friend; for my father, party leader and professor of history, it was the Revolution, the party, Fidel. For Gerardo, his daily concern was to feed his family; for my father, it was the tasks of the Revolution, international politics, history, and Marxist philosophy. With time the simple world of Gerardo would win out over that of my father; revealing to his eldest, most indoctrinated son that whatever is opposed to the primary importance of the family ends up weakening the whole society.

—

My parents didn't like the capital very much and at the end of the year they decided to return to their apartment in Matanzas. But I, in love with Vicky, insisted on staying as long as I could in the apartment the government had assigned for their stay in Havana. So I wrote the following letter to the authorities:

I am eighteen years old and teach in the Provincial School of the Party. My parents have moved back to Matanzas while I have preferred to remain here in the apartment lent to them by the Revolution. I would like to get married, and request permission to go on living here for the time being. Should the Revolution have need of the premises, it has only to notify me and I will surrender them immediately.

I never received a reply and I interpreted their silence as acceptance. It was September, and Vicky and I had plans to get married the following summer. I was making 140 pesos a month at the time, and we estimated that we could put aside about a hundred of that a month, so that by July we would have saved about 1,000 pesos. At that time a peso was the equivalent of about fifteen cents in U.S. currency on the black market, but, in our eagerness to be married, we considered that enough savings. Gerardo was surprised and somewhat reluctant to

approve our marriage plans. "M
able to continue her studies afte
reassured him when I told him th
with Vicky's studies was me.

The news of our impending m
the neighborhood, with rumors a
the marriage. "They're just kids,'
few months' time they're sure to
other and are serious," others ins
those two." The months passed wi
to high school, while I taught biolo
the university every afternoon. It v
which our dreams and our eagernes
to overlook the sacrifices we had to

At Vicky's house I had gradual
once my parents had left Havana.
apartment, the rest of my free tim
member of the family. Each morning
door, and have a cup of coffee, wl
before I went off to work. The image
each morning, looking fresh and lov
and prepare the coffee, was somethin
the rest of the day. Then at about se
back with Vicky, while her mother v
delicious meals waiting. In spite of th
plies, María proved her artistry as a c
into a delectable feast. She even got me
they used to feed us by the ton back at

My new family's house was situat
and was reached by a lateral passage
cement courtyard surrounded by eight h
by a family of five or more. It was typ
with its tenements. But unlike places on
was one where the neighbors enjoyed
great consideration for each other. Gera
it's difficult to say which—was located at
a two-story dwelling. The ground floor c
dining room with a staircase leading to the
side were three rooms stretched out ove
which was occupied by Gerardo's brother
side of the stairway was a wooden ladde
against the wall in that limited space. It
through which one could get to the roof.
ladder regularly and it was marvelous to
keeping their balance with one hand while
bucketful of newly washed clothes to hang

Victor, Vic t. The crime
manner tha ing indepen-
pailful of l to beginning
around the ld find out I
Gerardo ra own how to
It alwa y have been
chickens o ably isn't a
maintain a exclude him
similarly in able revolu-
in their bat s it.
by the au r evaluation
removing t, however.
One that had to
their famil r could be
stood rig e masses—
arthritis, y in judging
was a pe ay of open
pension system for
market th e aspects
sacks un k attitude,
and Pina l aptitude,
and othe elf-critical
sion of ndamental
foodstuff ometimes
were fro ost trivial
man, wh eventually
wife of a but they
and the fessional
however- meetings
reunion, a reason
Son so was to
and ho erly criti-
accomp turn be
proved she took
highwa ecies of
planted me each
source e left for
usual ried into
usual stepped
left sc it hara-
others iticism,
later.
every ff with
our tw rocks,
on jut e days
It was ed in a

human understanding. Our father, who had been the model of a devoted revolutionary, saw himself ruined overnight by a transgression not found in any law book, but nevertheless considered a crime according to the ethics of the Revolution—a law a thousand times more fearful and exacting than anything written in the constitution or the penal code. Every day we waited for my father to arrive home with the news of our undoing. But time passed and nothing happened. Little by little my father put it out of his mind, regaining his confidence and becoming his old self again. But not the rest of us, who had learned through this whole experience to feel guilty even though we weren't. Anything not sponsored by the State could be considered a crime and not to oppose it could also be considered a crime. Such was the philosophy of justice they inculcated in us: Whoever fails to denounce or condemn is guilty.

No one ever bothered my father about the incident, but some of my mother's ominous expressions would come back to haunt us from time to time: "It's destroying him. . . . He's disgraced." How often I would hear that term—*disgraced*—applied to countless people in politics, science, and the arts, who inexplicably vanished from public life: This one or that one "has been disgraced."

—

Little by little my visits to Vicky's house lengthened and multiplied until there was no longer a fixed schedule to them. As her father and I got to know each other better, we shed our initial misgivings and gradually forged ties of genuine respect and affection.

Gerardo worked as a plumber for a construction firm that generally had contracts for projects outside of Havana. It took him hours to go back and forth to work each day; he devoted some fourteen hours a day thus to a poorly paying job, waiting to accumulate the time needed to retire. As his salary was insufficient to provide food for a family of five in Havana, Gerardo waited impatiently for the weekend to go out to Fontanar, where one of his brothers lived. In the nearby foothills he had found a stony, abandoned plot to grow the only vegetables that would come up there: corn and squash. Those Sundays spent with Gerardo under the hot sun, on that rocky slope full of weeds with patches of corn and squash, cultivated in me a deep affection for this remarkable man, humble and generous, for whom the most important thing in life was the family. His days constituted a never-ending struggle for the well-being of his loved ones, whom he tried to protect, with an almost excessive zeal, from whatever new influences might interfere with their obligations to the family. Gerardo's was a life of constant labor: on the job, on that rocky hill where he'd reap a few ears of corn and a handful of squash, and in the houses and apartments of the Vedado District, where he'd wander with his old toolbox in search of occasional plumbing jobs to add to his income. When he had accumulated a little savings he would travel to the countryside to get some peasant to sell him vegetables and, if he was lucky, even pork. The meat would often be confiscated by the police on his return trip. But nothing could discourage Gerardo in his struggle to feed his family.

Occasionally Vicky's family and mine would get together, but Gerardo and my father didn't have much in common and usually just exchanged the usual formalities. This made me feel embarrassed and hurt because I loved them both.

One day when I asked my father about his behavior toward Gerardo, he replied, "I have nothing against him, but there's little for us to say to each other. His world is totally different from mine."

And that was true. Each had his own different world inside him. For Gerardo, a humble and semiliterate plumber, life consisted of loyalty to family and friend; for my father, party leader and professor of history, it was the Revolution, the party, Fidel. For Gerardo, his daily concern was to feed his family; for my father, it was the tasks of the Revolution, international politics, history, and Marxist philosophy. With time the simple world of Gerardo would win out over that of my father; revealing to his eldest, most indoctrinated son that whatever is opposed to the primary importance of the family ends up weakening the whole society.

———

My parents didn't like the capital very much and at the end of the year they decided to return to their apartment in Matanzas. But I, in love with Vicky, insisted on staying as long as I could in the apartment the government had assigned for their stay in Havana. So I wrote the following letter to the authorities:

> *I am eighteen years old and teach in the Provincial School of the Party. My parents have moved back to Matanzas while I have preferred to remain here in the apartment lent to them by the Revolution. I would like to get married, and request permission to go on living here for the time being. Should the Revolution have need of the premises, it has only to notify me and I will surrender them immediately.*

I never received a reply and I interpreted their silence as acceptance. It was September, and Vicky and I had plans to get married the following summer. I was making 140 pesos a month at the time, and we estimated that we could put aside about a hundred of that a month, so that by July we would have saved about 1,000 pesos. At that time a peso was the equivalent of about fifteen cents in U.S. currency on the black market, but, in our eagerness to be married, we considered that enough savings. Gerardo was surprised and somewhat reluctant to approve our marriage plans. "My only fear is that Vicky won't be able to continue her studies after the marriage," he told me. But I reassured him when I told him that the one who was most concerned with Vicky's studies was me.

The news of our impending marriage spread like wildfire through the neighborhood, with rumors and predictions both for and against the marriage. "They're just kids," some of them warned, "and in a few months' time they're sure to get divorced." "If they love each other and are serious," others insisted, "then nothing can separate those two." The months passed with Vicky running off each morning to high school, while I taught biology in the mornings and studied at the university every afternoon. It was a difficult but thrilling time in which our dreams and our eagerness to carve out a future helped us to overlook the sacrifices we had to make.

At Vicky's house I had gradually become a kind of adopted son once my parents had left Havana. While I still slept in my own apartment, the rest of my free time I spent at their house like a member of the family. Each morning I'd get up early, knock at their door, and have a cup of coffee, which Vicky would make for me before I went off to work. The image of Vicky coming down the stairs each morning, looking fresh and lovely, to greet me with her smile and prepare the coffee, was something I carried with me throughout the rest of the day. Then at about seven in the evening I would be back with Vicky, while her mother would already have one of her delicious meals waiting. In spite of the scarcity of decent food supplies, María proved her artistry as a cook, turning the humblest fare into a delectable feast. She even got me to enjoy those hated chickpeas they used to feed us by the ton back at boarding school.

My new family's house was situated behind another larger one, and was reached by a lateral passageway. There was a common cement courtyard surrounded by eight little dwellings, each inhabited by a family of five or more. It was typically Cuban, this courtyard with its tenements. But unlike places one often found, this courtyard was one where the neighbors enjoyed excellent relations, showing great consideration for each other. Gerardo's house—or apartment, it's difficult to say which—was located at the far end of the courtyard, a two-story dwelling. The ground floor consisted of a small kitchen/dining room with a staircase leading to the second floor. There on one side were three rooms stretched out over a small apartment below, which was occupied by Gerardo's brother and his family. On the other side of the stairway was a wooden ladder leaning almost vertically against the wall in that limited space. It led to a kind of skylight through which one could get to the roof. Vicky and María used this ladder regularly and it was marvelous to watch them climb up it, keeping their balance with one hand while carrying with the other a bucketful of newly washed clothes to hang out to dry. Gerardo and

Victor, Vicky's younger brother, also went up there frequently in a manner that seemed to me worthy of a circus act. They took up a pailful of leftovers, which Victor collected every afternoon from around the neighborhood, to feed the ten hens and two roosters Gerardo raised for eggs and meat to supplement the family's diet.

It always struck me as amazing how that family managed to raise chickens on such a tiny rooftop in the middle of the capital and to still maintain a standard of hygiene. In time, however, I would discover similarly incredible things in Havana. Other families have raised pigs in their bathrooms. And to silence their pigs so as not to be discovered by the authorities, they invented a popular veterinary surgery for removing the animal's vocal cords.

One of the boldest, most inventive of those struggling to feed their families was Cando, Gerardo's eldest brother, whose apartment stood right next door. Cando was over sixty and suffered from arthritis, which forced him to walk painfully with a cane. Since he was a peasant who had never enjoyed continuous employment, his pension was under seventy pesos. He had created a kind of black market that allowed him to get by. He'd set out with his two empty sacks under his arm, heading for the countryside bordering Havana and Pinar del Río, returning in the evening loaded down with bananas and other produce he bought from the peasants. Then began a procession of neighbors, who would purchase at reasonable prices the foodstuffs Cando brought back from the interior. Those silent buyers were from every social class and profession. They included a policeman, who supposedly should have arrested Cando for contraband, the wife of a party leader, a doctor, an intermediary who bought to resell, and the wife of a common laborer. They all had something in common, however—going in and out of Cando's house as if to a clandestine reunion, with fear and guilt written on their faces.

Sometimes on Sundays, wishing to improve the family's situation and hoping to accumulate enough savings for our wedding, I would accompany Cando just outside of the city to perform a task that proved to be as lucrative as it was ingenious. Near the western highway was a stretch of flat land belonging to the government and planted with coffee. This property would turn out to become the major source of our income. The harvesting was done on weekends by the usual volunteers brought in from the city, who did their work the usual way, without interest or effort. Thus many coffee beans were left scattered on the ground, which Cando and I (along with many others who had the same idea) would furtively collect a week or two later. Bent beneath the coffee trees, we painstakingly gathered up every bean we could find until, after a half-day's labor, we had filled our two sacks. Back home, we cleaned off the beans and placed them on jute bags to dry in the sun up on the roof. Eventually we sold them. It was obvious that the coffee beans we collected would otherwise go

to waste, but still I lived in constant fear of being caught. The crime was not in taking what wasn't ours, but in doing something independent of the State. Later, when I was investigated prior to beginning my training as a fighter pilot, I kept worrying they would find out I had sold coffee on the black market. I wouldn't have known how to explain myself to Counterintelligence and would certainly have been disqualified. Today, of course, I realize that there probably isn't a single person in Cuba without some blemish that could exclude him or her from the right to a position slated for "irreproachable revolutionaries." The fact that they have survived so long proves it.

As the school year was coming to an end, teacher evaluation began. It was not the principal's opinion that carried weight, however. The Revolution was just, so therefore it was the collective that had to do the evaluation, not the official in charge. The latter could be influenced by his or her own likes and dislikes, but not the masses—they never erred. Thus the union was the ultimate authority in judging a worker's performance, and for this purpose they held a day of open meetings in which to review each case. They used a point system for assessing each teacher's level of performance. Among the aspects considered were personal behavior and appearance, work attitude, discipline, political and ideological preparation, professional aptitude, as well as revolutionary outlook, and competency in being self-critical and critical of others. And this last competency was a fundamental criterion for their judgments, leading to discussions that sometimes went on for ten or more hours at a stretch over the most trivial matters. Such evaluations served as the basis for what eventually would be written up on a teacher's permanent record, but they amounted to little more than an opinion based not on professional standards but on purely subjective issues. During those open meetings everybody would wear himself out attepting to find or invent a reason to criticize oneself, placing oneself in the dock. Not to do so was to demonstrate "poor self-critical spirit." Whoever didn't properly criticize the next teacher to be evaluated in public would in turn be accused of showing "poor critical spirit" as soon as he or she took the stand. Thus, these union meetings were turned into a species of public trial, where friends and colleagues suddenly became each other's prosecutors for a few hours. By the end of it everyone left for home with a bitter taste, provoked by the sense of having pried into the most intimate aspects of another person's life, of having stepped where one shouldn't have. The popular expression "to commit hara-kiri," meaning to submit to the inevitable ordeal of self-criticism, dates from this period.

In my evaluation I paid indirectly for having gone off with Gerardo those few Sundays to sow corn and squash among the rocks, and for having gathered coffee beans with Cando, as on those days I'd failed to take part in various voluntary tasks, which resulted in a negative assessment for "lack of revolutionary conscience." I felt ashamed and depressed, stunned to watch my whole year of work and study be derailed by friends and colleagues singling out my lack of revolutionary conscience, but still benevolent enough to remark that it was probably due to my youth and inexperience, not to lack of enthusiasm for the Revolution, for which I obviously had a passion.

—

At last the sixteenth of July 1976, our longed-for wedding day, arrived. Vicky had successfully completed her studies and I was enjoying a vacation. Soon we would have those first moments of intimacy we'd dreamed of for so long. We were to be married at the Matrimonial Palace at six P.M., but by three o'clock I was already at Vicky's front door coordinating some last-minute details with her when Gerardo arrived. He took one look at us and said disapprovingly, "If you need to talk, at least do it in the house." Up to the last minute Gerardo was determined to protect his daughter against wagging tongues. "My daughter is a decent girl and no one is going to question her reputation," I had often heard him say. The dignity of his home was his most valued treasure and he was not about to take chances with what people might say.

The ceremony took place among friends and family, along with a photographer sent by someone as a wedding present, who pursued us at every moment. Afterwards we all went home to celebrate in the common courtyard, everybody drinking beer and doing their best to tease the newlyweds. At least I had taken the precaution of leaving our suitcases at a neighbor's house, as it was common for friends to hide the wedding couple's luggage and thereby force them to stay at the reception dancing until dawn.

We had reserved ten days at the Hotel Internacional in Varadero, where we headed at last, after spending enough time with everybody, feeling anxious to be alone and leaving the guests in the company of my in-laws, with whom they could carry on until dawn. When the car was ready to leave, Gerardo came over and kissed his daughter, and looking at me with tears in his eyes, he said, "Take care of her, my son." Then the car began moving away slowly, with the string of cans somebody'd tied to the back bouncing against the asphalt, proclaiming to the whole world that we'd just been married.

That first night, almost the next morning, I heard Vicky's voice from afar in our air-conditioned room, as from the depths of a cave, sobbing and reproaching me for something. I opened my eyes to see her with the face of a two-year-old, complaining, "You left me alone!"

"What do you mean? How did I leave you alone?" I asked drowsily.

"Over there, in the corner," she replied, pointing to the edge of the bed.

———

Only then did I realize that it was the cold that had awakened her, so I lulled her back to sleep in my arms and felt her curl up like a newborn puppy looking for warmth.

—

Our marriage unfolded like our courtship, only more romantically. Each evening we'd go for walks along the Malecón, an avenue that meandered around the northern part of Havana through an area that had once belonged to the sea. We'd sit on the seawall and dream about the future: the home we would have and the children to come after Vicky finished her studies. Vicky pushed herself to the utmost to achieve her dream of becoming a dentist. Each day we'd go over her homework together after she came back from classes.

Sometimes I'd confess to her that teaching wasn't my real vocation but merely a revolutionary duty. My real passion was to be a pilot in one of those supersonic planes pictured in magazines, but as I told her, "It's something I could never hope to do. The vocation of a revolutionary is, after all, to be revolutionary." I had resigned myself, convinced that I was doing what I was supposed to do. Vicky would listen to me silently, with a certain sadness in her eyes; then, leaning her head on my shoulder, she would say reassuringly, "I like that you're a teacher."

One evening a frail, emaciated man resembling my father showed up at our house. It was my Uncle Edelso, who had been sentenced to twenty years in prison for a petty crime and had now been released for good behavior after having served half his term. Everyone in the house was overjoyed to see him again and, as he came to see us regularly, I gradually became reacquainted with this man whom I'd last seen as a child. He had many incredible stories to tell of life in prison. To my surprise, Edelso turned out to be one of the most gullible people I had ever known. A very weak man, he didn't know how to say no and thus fell prey to any swindle devised by the sharks that inhabit the ocean of society.

Once released, my uncle found himself in the street, without a home, without a ration card, without work. He had to get along as best he could without committing any further offense. As the days passed I began to understand that he would never be reintegrated into a society that had erased from its cultural conscience the meaning of the word *forgiveness*. Edelso would spend hours at our house talking to everybody. You could see how grateful he was for the moments spent with the family, which made him feel like a human being again. Watching him walk off into the night after those long talks, I'd feel as though he were taking part of me along with him to ward off his hopelessness and solitude. And I was crushed by a reality I could not accept: my powerlessness to change something dictated by an inflexible, unrelenting world. Often in talking to my uncle I'd try to

convince him to go live with my parents in Matanzas, where nobody knew him, or back to Cabaiguán to live with his eldest brother. But he refused, and I sensed the feeling of everlasting shame that he carried inside himself wherever he went. My in-laws' honorable home seemed to be the only place in the world where Edelso could lift up his head when he spoke.

—

One day in October 1976, the media were angrily denouncing a shocking crime: Terrorists from Miami had placed a bomb aboard a Cubana de Aviación flight from Barbados, which exploded shortly after takeoff, killing all seventy-three passengers, among them members of the national fencing team. The results of the preliminary investigation were aired on TV, along with recordings of the last contact the pilots had with the control tower. The entire country listened in horror as the pilots reported two explosions onboard, then heard their frantic exclamations as they fell into the sea, disappearing without a trace. The whole island shared those minutes of fear and terror along with the victims.

Accusations concerning the guilty parties quickly followed. Our Leader insisted that the CIA had committed the crime with the help of Cuban exiles in Miami, whom they'd trained and supplied with C-4 explosives for the bombs. The days passed, and we all followed, with growing indignation, events related to what eventually would be called the "Barbados atrocity." Suspects were apprehended in Venezuela and the first mutilated bodies were recovered from the sea, to be sent back to Cuba. The Leader called upon the people to deliver a last farewell to our martyrs, who were lying in state beneath the national flag in Revolution Square. And the people answered his call with a massive demonstration. Vicky and I, along with my father, who'd come from Matanzas for the event, walked the three miles from our house to the square. The spectacle that lay before us would have touched the most unfeeling heart. Hundreds of thousands of people—human rivers—were pouring through the streets of the Vedado heading toward the square. We joined the flow, our heads lowered, our eyes filled with the same pain and indignation felt by all. It was impossible to reach the actual square; the congestion was already such that we had to halt at the corner of Paseo and Zapata to listen to the words of farewell addressed by The Leader, in the name of the Cuban people, to those martyrs.

Fidel's voice, which echoed from the hundreds of loudspeakers placed on the neighboring buildings surrounding the square, was torn by grief and went straight to the hearts of the million or more people assembled there. It was as if time itself stood still when the Commander in Chief paused; only the gentle sound of the sea breeze could be heard above the silent, outraged multitude. Our Leader recounted

the history of CIA terrorist plottings against Cuba. He recalled the ship *La Coubre* exploding in the port of Havana, which caused the death of hundreds of innocent Cubans. He reminded us of all the Cuban fishing boats attacked by pirates on the high seas; of the little girl in the fishing village of Boca de Samá who'd been shot in her sleep; of the diplomats murdered by hired assassins. He reminded us of the aerial bombardment of the Santiago de Cuba and Ciudad Libertad airports prior to the Bay of Pigs invasion; of the brutal killings of the young volunteers from the literacy drive in El Escambray. With this litany of the innocent dead, he reminded us all that we had a cowardly enemy conspiring to bring us to our knees through terrorism.

". . . our athletes could not get to the Olympics," his voice echoed above the cavern of buildings surrounding Revolution Square, "but have been enshrined forever in that greater Olympus—of martyrs for the fatherland." Men, women, and children alike listened with clenched fist and a lump in the throat; and we all felt closer to each other, more unified as a group, sharing our grief like a great family in the midst of tragedy.

"Let it be known to North American imperialists that they will never bring us to our knees," Fidel continued as we clamored with clenched teeth to vent our fury and hatred upon the enemy, "because when a strong and vital people like ours sheds its tears, injustice trembles!" An exclamation of fury broke from our throats, rumbling like a war cry, drowning out the sea breeze in a triumphant ovation. We were invincible! We were unbending—because we were in the right.

We returned home from the funeral feeling as if we had been pushed around for years without reacting to the insult. "Enough is enough!" we told each other with an irresistible urge to go out and battle our enemy, wondering at the same time why Fidel hadn't already declared war on the United States. I wanted to die fighting to avenge our dead rather than silently accept the impunity of their assassins. But Fidel, wise and peaceful, preferred to endure it rather than lead his people into war. "If it were up to me, we'd declare war right now," I proclaimed indignantly in my boundless grief and hatred.

—

Soon thereafter Vicky passed her final examinations and we waited anxiously to find out whether she'd be accepted in the course of study she had chosen. Almost every day we went to the university to check the rosters and every day we would return disappointed because the Stomatology lists hadn't yet been posted. Finally they appeared, but we couldn't find Vicky's name anywhere. I kept scanning the names desperately until at last I heard Vicky exclaim, "Oré, look, here I am!" Sure enough, in our haste we'd passed her name without seeing

it. We hugged each other jubilantly, as if it were a triumph for both of us.

—

One day Vicky's cousin Adolfo, who was undergoing training to become a fighter pilot, came to see us. Fascinated, I asked him about the selection process even though I'd given up any notion of trying such a thing. "It's not completely out of the question. You're only twenty and although you have a profession, you're still technically a student at the university. Tomorrow I'll ask our group leader about what you might do to apply." The next day he returned with a name and telephone number written on a piece of paper. "It's Lieutenant Colonel de la Paz, Chief of the Pilots' Recruitment Commission. Call him and he'll tell you what you need to do."

I went straight to the telephone.

"Why do you want to become a pilot if you're already a teacher?" the lieutenant colonel asked me.

"I'm above all a revolutionary, and that's why I became a teacher. But I love flying and I think I'd be more useful as a fighter pilot. The country needs men to defend it and I want to be one of them."

He asked a few more questions about me, then said, "Report tomorrow morning at eight A.M. to the Marianao Military Hospital. I'll be there with a group of candidates taking their physicals. Bring your papers."

I couldn't believe it. What I'd always considered impossible was turning out to be easier than I could have imagined. I went in to tell Vicky my incredible news.

"But I don't want you to go away to study in the Soviet Union," she said gravely, tears brimming in her eyes.

"I know it's a sacrifice, my love, but it'll make for our happiness in the end. You know I don't like my job, and this has been a lifelong dream. The time will pass quickly. Anyway, let's not get ahead of ourselves. I probably won't even pass the tests and they'll end up rejecting me."

The medical exams were long and intensive, not to mention the interviews with military Counterintelligence, who laid great stress on the fact that I had family in the United States.

"Have you corresponded or in any way kept in touch with them?" the officer queried. Like all such officers, he wore a checked shirt that hung outside his pants.

"No, never."

"And your parents? Have they ever written to any of them?"

"Never."

"What do you think of American jeans?"

"I don't wear them; I never had a pair."

"And what do you think of people who do? With that piece of leather on the back showing the brand name?"

"It's like wearing the enemy flag on your pants."

The man smiled with satisfaction, while telling me, "Write the names and addresses of your closest friends on this form." As I was doing so, he asked suddenly, "Why did you attempt suicide while in Camilitos?"

The question stunned me, taking my breath away. I could feel my ears reddening. *How had they found out?* I glanced up from the form and answered, looking him straight in the eye challengingly, "I was twelve years old then and not in very good shape. I've been ashamed of it ever since. I believe suicide is for cowards."

But I finally passed the tests, including the investigations by military Counterintelligence, and in a few days I was numbered among the thirty young men selected to undergo training in the Soviet Union to become fighter pilots. We were instructed to appear that evening at an address in the Miramar District. "Come dressed as well as you can," we were instructed by staff at air force headquarters, "and come alone." As men chosen to travel outside the country we were given an allowance to buy clothing at a special store set up for that purpose. There for the first time I was able to buy shoes and pants that fit me. They even had us buy a suit, for the trip over, something I'd certainly never planned for. Later, when all thirty of us got together at the airport, we discovered that our suits and suitcases were all alike. Evidently we were not to go unnoticed.

In Miramar they gave us a farewell party in the presence of the commander in chief of the air force, who was surrounded by several colonels. A young man close to Fidel, very popular and very powerful in those days, was there, too—Luis Orlando Domínguez, first secretary of the Union of Young Communists, who brought us a personal message from Castro congratulating us and calling us an example to Cuban youth. "You have won the privilege of defending the Revolution on the front line of battle, as pilots and future officers of the armed forces," he said in his message. And for our part we could only admire Fidel, an extraordinary man down to the smallest details, capable of being at the airport to receive a sports team that had won medals abroad or sending congratulations to a group of young men going off to study in the Soviet Union. (Ten years later that dynamic young man, so close to Fidel, would be condemned to twenty years in prison "for corruption," during a trial conducted in secret. It would be Castro himself who would then go on national television to tell the people the only version of the story they were ever to hear.)

I was proud and happy. The Revolution had given sure proof of its confidence in me, which it had done to few others. And I was also excited at the prospect of becoming acquainted with the Soviet Union, the most advanced country in the world. At last I was to travel abroad and get to know other languages and cultures. Yes, it was clear the Revolution had placed great confidence in me. Yet before we were to leave, there was to be one more meeting, this one with the officers of military Counterintelligence, who made suggestions and also warned us about the dangers we would encounter on our travels.

"There's going to be a stopover in Morocco, a capitalist country in North Africa. Remember to stay together and no talking to foreigners. You're not to go near the newsstands or read any capitalist literature. Remember that reading foreign material is a direct violation of orders from the Supreme Commander of our nation, and you will be liable for expulsion."

They went on: "Something important to bear in mind: If any emergency landing occurs, watch out, because the CIA certainly knows that you're onboard the flight and may attempt to kidnap some of you in order to orchestrate a propaganda show, claiming you deserted."

And more advice: "In the Soviet Union you're going to meet students from other countries, some of whom you are prohibited from having any contact with, especially the Iraqis, the Libyans, the Yemenis, and all those not belonging to the Socialist camp. You are authorized to pursue friendly relations only with students from Vietnam and the socialist European countries, and only after requesting permission from the counterintelligence officer at the Cuban embassy in Moscow."

Vicky, her family, and my parents all came with me to the airport to see me off. Vicky had spent the night in my arms, quietly in tears, while I stroked her hair, thinking about the time we were to be separated. At the airport we all embraced, one by one; Vicky and I last of all. I left her standing there, to watch me disappear into the waiting area for international flights. And I read in her eyes the solitude she would be facing for the next two years. I felt as though I were stealing something from her and at the same time leaving a part of myself behind with her. It was only when the plane was in the air that the full reality of what I was doing finally struck me with all its cruelty—that I would have to endure two whole years without seeing her, while longing for her every moment. A deep sorrow welled up in me, and I realized how much I loved her.

Before me, the vanguard of universal justice and social well-being was opening its doors to me: the Soviet Union. There could be no greater proof of the party's confidence in me.

Chapter 5

—

Memories

of

Development

"I'm First Lieutenant Popov of the Soviet Armed Forces Tenth Command," declared a tired-looking man in perfect Spanish who was waiting at the foot of the ramp as we disembarked from the Aeroflot jet. It hadn't been difficult for him to spot us among the other passengers on that cold fall day, as we were the only ones to emerge dressed in thin suits. "There's a bus waiting for you out front. We'll be spending the night in the artillery school and tomorrow we fly on to Krasnodar, your final destination. Now, if you'll give me your passports so we can get through Customs. . . ."

As we left the airport at dusk, I sat huddled in the cold bus, staring out the window at the landscape unfolding before me. *The earth and grass here aren't any different from in Cuba*, I thought, looking out at the unfolding landscape, site of the bloodiest battles of World War II.

This time it was real—the setting that I had imagined countless times while reading Zhukov and Boris Polevoy. In these skies the Russian pilot Alexey Meriesev had downed more than twenty German planes, even though he'd already lost both legs in aerial combat and flew outfitted with artificial limbs. Polevoy's gripping *The Story of a*

Man had made this fighter pilot, with his courage and iron will, the hero of my adolescence.

To our right suddenly appeared a monument, which somebody said was dedicated to General Panfilov and his small group of soldiers, who had courageously defended Moscow at its gates against the onslaught of German tanks. Soon we saw some rustic fences surrounding a group of scattered cabins whose small-paned windows emanated a dull light. They looked lonely and still, as if frozen in time. I recognized them from films I'd seen about the defense of Moscow, and realized I was no longer imagining all this. The scenes had remained unchanged: History was so close you could touch it with your hands, everything just as it was during the "Great Patriotic War." And without knowing why, I felt depressed and sad.

The next day, after two hours in an old four-engine IL-18 that shook violently throughout the flight, we arrived at Krasnodar. The officer in charge of our training was Major Argatov, a short, stout man with nearly transparent skin that disclosed the capillaries in his face. After we were shown to our dormitories he came by to give us instructions, with our group leader, Gallardo, serving as his translator.

"From now on," Argatov began, "according to agreements signed by the governments of Cuba and the Soviet Union, you will submit to the rules and regulations of the armed forces of our country."

This hardly surprised or bothered us, as we had the same kind of regulations at home.

"You may not leave the school's perimeter for any reason for the first forty-five days, the time required to learn a minimum of the language as well as the laws governing daily life in this country. Later you'll be allowed to go on Saturdays and Sundays, but you must be back always by eleven P.M.—no sleeping out. Anybody absent will be reported immediately to general headquarters in Moscow and subject to expulsion. Tomorrow you'll receive your uniforms and then you'll have your physicals; after that, classes begin. You will take an intensive course in Russian—eight hundred and fifty hours—alternating with classes in Marxist philosophy and the history of the Soviet Communist party, and after this you'll begin your technical training."

Thus began our three years as aviation cadets in a country that for me would only become more and more of an enigma.

Situated some 720 miles south of Moscow on the Kuban River, Krasnodar was a city of Cossack traditions with over half a million inhabitants. Its main avenue was bisected by a spacious walkway covered with gardens, and had a huge circular fountain at each end of it. The walkway began at the steps of the October Theater, which, built on an artificial elevation, seemed poised to observe the entire city. The thoroughfare was lined with government buildings, which alternated with small peaceful parks full of benches shaded almost invariably by some ancient-looking tree. At the far end of the walk-way, facing the theater from a distance of three miles, stood a statue of Lenin with one hand in his pocket and the other hand raised in a gesture that seemd to say, "Forward!" This principal boulevard and the few secondary streets on which trolleys and buses ran were the only paved roads in the city. Beyond them was the old quarter containing mostly wooden huts like those seen on the way into Moscow, and the modern neighborhoods with identical-looking pre-fabricated apartment houses. In the spring and fall one's shoes were always caked with mud.

The School of Aviation was situated at the extreme western end of the city, and occupied an area of several square miles. There was one official entrance for students, with a sentry box for an officer and a guard at the gate. The Checkpoint, as the entrance was called, stood at the beginning of the main street traversing the school grounds and ending behind some hangars on the airfield about a mile off. To the left was the school theater fronted by a small park with a monument to pilots fallen in World War II. In its halls we practiced "brotherhood among peoples" by commemorating from time to time the different national holidays of the various foreign contingents studying there. To the right, opposite the theater, was a monument to Lenin and, behind that, at the top of some steps stood an old, well-preserved, four-story edifice that housed the school's administrative headquarters.

On Monday mornings we would assemble out front between the theater and the administration building to pass muster before the school commander. When he appeared we'd be called to attention by the officer on duty, who marched smartly toward the general with resounding steps amid the otherwise silent ranks. After the order of the day, Major General Paulika would stand before the troops with Lenin's statue behind him and with his right hand just grazing the peak of his cap in a military salute to greet his cadets, whereupon we thundered back: "Morning, comrade Major General!"

Those Monday-morning formations were our only contact with the major general, yet they provided time enough to discover his personality. Rather short and stout, he had a peevish and contradic-tory nature which intimidated everyone to such an extent that who-ever spotted him anywhere in the compound would scurry off to avoid meeting up with him. He enjoyed coming up behind a man, whether an officer or a cadet, then insulting him for negligence of duty or lack of military courtesy. On those Monday mornings, for instance, he always found a reason to rebuke the officer on duty, normally one of the numerous colonels and lieutenant colonels comprising the faculty of professors and squadron chiefs. If he didn't find fault with the duty officer, then it would be with one of the students who'd moved while in formation, or with some stray paper he'd found on the pavement—anything—but whatever it was, the duty officer knew he was in for it.

The first time we witnessed one of Major General Paulika's outbursts we were petrified by the despotism with which he treated his subordinates. As Cubans we'd been accustomed to being treated with politeness and respect, so we refused to accept the major general's behavior for what it was and attributed it instead to some quirk of Russian military behavior.

On both sides of the administration building stretched two gigantic wings curving toward the back to form an enormous U. These housed the classrooms, all excellently equipped with materials ranging from small aerodynamic tunnels to engines and planes, whole or in parts. At the end of the east wing was the school hospital, a series of filthy rooms outfitted with medical tools and instruments as crude as they were antiquated, and run by coarse-looking, male military nurses. That was where we had our medicals, prior to beginning classes, and those dreary rooms became the stage for our first jokes—this group of thirty young men full of Caribbean humor found cause for laughter in almost anything.

There was a fellow in our group, thin, of medium height, who spoke very little and very quietly at that, the few times he participated in any conversation. For that reason we nicknamed him "Tranquillity," and everyone joked around with him without ever managing to draw him out. During our physicals we went in small groups from specialist to specialist, undressing for each exam. When we got to Ophthalmology, somebody noticed that Tranquillity had lagged behind, so we waited for him to catch up and pretended to be redressing after our exam when he walked in. Without saying a word, holding back our laughter, we left the room just as Tranquillity began undressing for his next exam. Out in the hall we stood waiting and listening until we heard the eye nurse let out a shriek and a second later come bolting out of the room, hurling insults at him in Russian.

The dormitories were composed of two four-story buildings situated on opposite sides of the main street, a little beyond the theater and administration building. These were dubbed "hotels," given the comfortable facilities they provided for their foreign "guests." At the entrance to each building was a booth in which sat an old woman we affectionately called "Grandma." The grandmas alternated from shift to shift but proved unvaryingly meticulous about recording the entrance and exit times of the students for the authorities. As a result, on Saturdays after eleven P.M., one or more ropes of knotted sheets would be hung out the back windows of our "hotel" for the convenience of tardy classmates.

Our dormitory housed students from Vietnam, Afghanistan, Yemen, Iraq, Libya, Uganda, the Congo, Zambia, Mozambique, Ghana, and Algeria. We Cuban students enjoyed particularly cordial relations with the Vietnamese, as they were sanctioned by Cuban counterintelligence. The Vietnamese students were generally small-bodied and unpretentious, but with iron wills and a sense of discipline that expressed itself clearly in their eagerness to learn. They would spend countless hours studying Russian—a language that was especially difficult for them. The sincere sympathy and respect we felt toward them we expressed by referring to them affectionately as our "cousins." On the other hand, culture shock was inevitable in the case of the Libyan and Iraqi students, with whom we were absolutely prohibited to have any kind of relationship. They tended to criticize everything and spoke contemptuously of the Soviets, which offended us terribly, as we considered it vile to speak ill of those who were helping us. And to top it off, the officers of those countries were used to meting out corporal punishment to their cadets, something incomprehensible to us. The first time we saw a Libyan officer with a stick administer a beating to one of his cadets who was kneeling in the snow, stripped to the waist in the −4°F weather, we nearly came to blows. We soon grew accustomed to the spectacle, however, swallowing our indignation, aware that we hadn't the right to impose our own views upon a different culture.

Our day as cadets began at six A.M. with twenty minutes of running and exercises outdoors. With the onset of winter, we were wakened nearly every morning by the sound of shovels, as Russian soldiers cleared snow from the street for our daily workout. Before very long we began disputing with our supervisor about the cold, and we finally convinced him that we couldn't do our exercises in weather under −14°F. To prove this we resorted to whatever genetic explanations we could—our tropical origins and so forth—and thus stole another twenty minutes of sleep each morning.

We breakfasted in the dining hall, and the meals they served us were pleasantly varied and tasty. Our classes filled out the rest of the day until seven P.M., with an hour's recess for lunch. All classes were conducted in Russian, a language so different from our own that I found it difficult to follow the lectures much of the time. My longing for Vicky grew deeper each night.

Vicky was writing me every day and sometimes I'd receive ten letters all at once, which I would devour when I was all alone, letting my imagination transport me back to her and my yearned-for Cuba. She explained how she was putting aside my whole salary of 141 pesos, which the government continued to send her each month because I was in the armed forces. Our dream was that she could eventually pay for a ticket to the Soviet Union, so that we might spend the summer together since I would not be permitted to return to Cuba during my first two years away. Yet, no matter how many times we tried to make plans, we continued to run into the same bureaucratic obstacles. The only passage Vicky could manage with Cuban money was as a tourist on one of those vacations the unions awarded to their vanguard workers, but Vicky was a student. Nevertheless, luck came our way when someone who'd been granted such a trip offered her the ticket. Then, full of illusions, we began making plans for the summer in earnest, but new difficulties arose, this time from the Soviet Union. As a tourist Vicky would be required to remain with her group throughout her stay, and thus be prevented from coming to Krasnodar to visit me. On the other hand, I couldn't be admitted to her travel group, as it was not the custom to allow separate visitors to join each other once abroad. After several months of such efforts, worn out and disappointed, we finally gave up our dream of seeing each other that following summer and resigned ourselves instead to the two years of separation, subtracting each day from the time remaining before I would be allowed my first visit back home.

Every month we attempted to talk by telephone and, since my salary wasn't sufficient to pay for the call at my end, I'd spend the early morning hours in the booth with "Grandma," waiting for Vicky's call, which was always difficult to put through. We'd talk for six minutes, meticulously timed by the operator, amid static and echoes that made it nearly impossible for us to hear each other. I'd hear Vicky faintly in the distance, with constant interference, sobbing while she spoke; and I felt my chest tightening, which made it more and more difficult for me to speak clearly, until our conversation was reduced to repeating the same words: "I love you. . . ." Once the operator had pitilessly interrupted our call at the end of the prescribed six minutes, I went off to bed—not to sleep but to stare up at the ceiling, breathing deeply to arm myself with the strength to overcome my homesickness. *You have to bear with it*, I told myself. *The sacrifice will make for our future happiness.* And I endured, funnelling all my energies into my studies and sports, counting the days that still separated me from her.

—

When classes ended Saturdays at two P.M., we'd hurry to change from uniforms to civilian clothes and take off, eager to explore the world that was the Soviet Union. We'd walk the city from end to end, visiting the most unlikely places in order to satisfy our curiosity about this enormous country, so impenetrable to a visitor's first glance. It was in the streets of Krasnodar that I first tried one of those popular soda machines, a kind of gigantic metal cabinet that mixed syrup with compressed gas from a tank behind it and water from the public fountain to which it was attached. In summertime the demand for these soft drinks would soar and it was common to see pedestrians lining to buy a glassful, which was dispensed automatically into one of the two public tumblers placed beneath the tap. Before depositing the money each customer rotated the tumbler on a horizontal wheel, which as it turned sprayed fine jets of water against the inside of the glass, thereby "freeing" it of all possible germs. Thirsty and confident in my own antibodies, I drank liberally from those tumblers used by thousands before me, always first rinsing them out with that miracle water.

As cadets we received a stipend of twenty rubles a month, paid by the school, and a so-called additional supplement of thirteen rubles from the Cuban embassy. With this allowance in hand, a veritable fortune by our standards, we rushed out to the stores looking for the most elementary articles that were scarcely obtainable in Cuba and which here for the first time we were able to purchase without having to present our odious rationing cards. Other students such as the Libyans received a stipend of over three hundred dollars a month from their embassies, which they could exchange on the black market for eight rubles per dollar. They had it good. . . . Some of them bought beer and soda, afterwards leaving their empty bottles outside the door to be picked up by the cleaning help. But we Cubans, neither diligent nor lazy, would collect the bottles and store them carefully in bags to return them eventually to the school's small store for twenty-five kopecks each. The woman who worked for the state collecting bottles there was sixty years old, a veteran of the war who during holidays would bedeck herself with a host of medals. Whenever we would return bottles discreetly, in order not to call attention to our poverty, she'd take them with open hostility. She knew we felt ashamed and always brazenly counted ten bottles less, which allowed her to pocket two and a half rubles. That impudent way of cheating caused more than one Cuban to try to correct her mathematics, but he would immediately be subjected to a stream of cries and insults calculated to attract the attention of passersby, and thus be forced to retreat in embarrassment as swiftly and silently as he'd entered. With no other place nearby to turn in the bottles, and given the disagreeable experience of her tirades, we learned to make our calculation by always subtracting the ten bottles that our picaresque bottle collector invariably pocketed for herself. Eventually, however, when I saw for the first time the elderly women veterans with their World War Two medals pinned to their tattered clothes, shoveling snow from the streets in the harshest winter weather in order to earn a few rubles with which to survive, I understood a lot better our picaresque purchaser and from then on I gladly shared with her my cache of bottles.

I seem to have had a tremendous ability to save my money during that time. With those thirty-three rubles a month, plus what I made on the occasional sale of bottles, I was able to buy soap, toothpaste, and other small articles not provided by the school, as well as clothes and shoes for Vicky and the rest of our families. I even managed a few gifts to give friends on my return. The Russian goods available in the stores were invariably inferior in quality to products of capitalist origin so ostentatiously displayed by the Libyan and Iraqi cadets, but we Cubans were fascinated by the fact that they were available at all.

We all wrote home to our families about the tremendous abundance that existed in the Soviet Union, where it was possible to buy things without the need of a rationing card.

As our Russian improved we gradually enjoyed closer relationships with the school personnel and the townspeople. Little by little we came to know that world which—initially vanguard and subsequently more enigmatic—became by turns unbelievable and intolerable. Our disillusionment with this country we had been taught to admire as the pinnacle of civilization actually began once the first students were hospitalized. A Yemeni cadet had to undergo an appendectomy without anesthesia; dental extractions, too, were performed in medieval fashion. Hygiene conditions in the hospitals were dismal and medical personnel often reeked of alcohol. The corruption present at all levels of society, as we came to know it, left us with an impression of overwhelming ethical deterioration in the Soviet Union. Each time we saw more evidence of such realities, we would resort to making light of it somehow: "Evidently Soviet power hasn't quite made it this far yet," as though the old government of the czar, overthrown sixty years earlier, were to blame.

One Monday there was a crisis at school. The political commissar informed us during morning drill that a gang of young delinquents known as "hooligans" had beaten up two students from Uganda as they waited in town for a bus.

"All students are prohibited from leaving the school grounds until further notice," the commissar informed us after explaining what had happened.

With a mixture of solidarity and curiosity, a few of us went during recess to visit the Ugandans at the hospital and what we saw left us horrified. They had been beaten terribly about the head and face, suffering multiple jaw fractures and loss of some teeth. They looked awful. The police patrol, which had come on the scene by chance, had saved their lives; the hooligans had fled, leaving them kicked and beaten to unconsciousness there on the sidewalk. To our amazement, we later discovered that dozens of passersby had witnessed the event without intervening to stop it.

Eventually we realized the strong antipathy the young Russian peasants felt for foreign students, whom they considered to be intruders and usurpers of their women—reserving special contempt for the African students, whom they disparagingly called "Negroes." The street gangs were filled with these tall, strapping youths, who also made a habit of accosting cadets near the school's entrance to buy dollars, clothing, or foreign electronic equipment. They were capable of offering a fortune for any gadget with a North American brand name. "We make better ones," they would boast, but then offer two hundred rubles for a pair of Western jeans or a thousand rubles for a tape recorder, when they could have gotten Russian versions of the same items for fifteen or two hundred rubles. Such conduct was often carried to ridiculous extremes, and it was not uncommon to see some of them offer forty rubles to a student for a pair of sunglasses that the student had bought for three rubles in town just a few hours earlier. If a foreigner wore them, they couldn't be Russian; that was their logic.

Such gang attacks on foreigners were rather routine in the towns of southern Russia and, as experience revealed to us that complaining about it only led to our being barred once again from going into Krasnodar, we Cubans decided to deal directly with the gangs on our own. We attempted to smooth things over with them in a way they could understand: We went off with their leaders to one of the many filthy, depressing joints where they sold beer, and drank a few mugs with them while nibbling on some of the small, reddish, foul-smelling fish served in those places. And in this way we managed to avoid any problems with them, by making the kind of peace pact generally observed by the "hooligans." To attack a Cuban meant war between our group and theirs, so we rarely had any trouble on the streets.

—

With our first year of studies behind us we were all set to go for a week's vacation to Sochi, a bathing resort on the Black Sea. The holiday was part of the study package agreed upon by the governments of Cuba and the Soviet Union, but it so happened that an additional group of students from Libya had just arrived and requested to go to Sochi. Since additional accommodations were not available at the resort, the school administration decided to grant the Libyans the lodgings reserved for the Cubans and the Vietnamese. We were to stay on at school in Krasnodar for the month of vacation. This was the one occasion when the "indestructible fraternity" between Cubans and Vietnamese and the Soviets had not worked. From then on we noticed that it was the official policy of the Soviet command to show preference toward military personnel arriving from capitalist countries.

After the holidays we were suddenly told to pack. An unexpected number of students would be arriving from the Arab nations, so a change had to be made in our program. The Arabs were to be installed in the more comfortable accommodations at Krasnodar, while we were to be sent to Primoskastarskaia, a village some ninety miles away. There we would continue our technical studies of the jet we were to fly first: the L-29.

Primoskastarskaia was situated on the shores of the Sea of Azof, and the rustic cabins dotting its empty streets were nestled among apple and apricot trees and surrounded by wooden fences. We arrived in autumn and the mud we saw at every turn gave us the impression we'd come to the filthiest place on earth. The villagers were rough, simple peasants who did nothing to hide their mistrust of foreigners, whom they viewed as just so many intruders ready to disrupt their peaceful country ways with a load of newfangled articles and fashions that would make the local youngsters start acting crazy. The school itself was located about three miles outside the village, sealed off like the typical military unit and made up of two blocks of buildings, with dining room and gymnasium, and a small airfield.

We got there in the afternoon and before unpacking had to listen to the instructions of our new training supervisor, who advised, "For the moment you may not visit the village. There have been several cases of aggression against students by local delinquents." The school physician then added, "We also advise you not to have relations with women from the region. Our statistics indicate that more than eighty percent are infected with venereal diseases such as gonorrhea."

How is it possible? I wondered. We realized that good hygiene was rarely practiced in the southern territories, but what I now heard straight from a military doctor left me dumbfounded. These were actual statistics confirming the terrible backwardness of a nation we were accustomed to regarding as the beacon of civilization.

Later, when Major General Paulika visited the school in the jet fighter he treated as his private property, using it to travel from one school to another, we began to understand that corruption was the norm. From the young waitresses who served in the dining hall we soon learned that Paulika had an apartment reserved exclusively for himself at each school air base. And whenever the general came for a visit, the waitresses would get very nervous and some would actually call in sick. Eventually we found out why: Paulika had the habit of requesting by telephone that his meal be brought directly to his apartment by one of the girls, whom he would specify to the dining-room manager; once the waitress arrived with the food she had to accept the general's "kindness," or suffer the consequences.

It was 1978 and the leader of the USSR celebrated his birthday by adorning himself with his fourth Medal of Hero of the Soviet Union. In our classes in Marxism and the history of the Communist party our professors told us that socialism had already been "constructed" in the USSR and that they were now at the threshold of the communist society dreamed of by Marx, Engels, and Lenin. Yet in Cuba the kind of restrictions taken for granted in the Soviet Union simply did not exist. Our state of medicine was incomparably superior and we didn't live isolated from the rest of the world. Our citizens could move about freely on the island without having to obtain internal visas, which the Soviets required of their inhabitants traveling to the larger cities. In Cuba we could see American films on television or listen to capitalist rock stars on the radio. We knew about Barbra Streisand and Charles Bronson. In Cuba we were sure of our ideas and were unafraid of capitalist culture. There we couldn't imagine that a store clerk could cheat you impudently the way the one who redeemed our bottles had done, or that a doctor would demand additional money to give a patient better treatment. Still less, that a general would force a young girl to have sex with him or behave as if a jet fighter were his personal property, or that a colonel would sell special privileges to a Libyan cadet for a tape recorder. "What a fraud against humanity," I said to myself, "and if the Eastern European countries are socialist in the Soviet fashion, then the only country where true socialism exists is Cuba!"

We completed our five interminable months of theoretical studies in that place, which seemed to us like hell. Then we were sent to Morozovsk, which was somewhat larger than Primoskastarskaia and a major rail link between Rostov and Volgograd. Morozovsk was a picturesque village whose courteous inhabitants eyed us with curiosity and a certain pleasure, which made us feel wholly welcome there. We were received by Colonel Jriskovsky, head of the Kachenskoe School base, where we had been sent in the continual shifting of students to make room for more and more Arab and African cadets. We were the first and only foreign students there, which was to our advantage; although we'd lost the comfortable lodgings of Krasnodar, we got to mingle with the Russian cadets billeted in the adjacent barracks and were treated with special hospitality.

Our group had been reduced to twenty-six cadets after four hadn't passed the final theoretical exams and were sent back to Cuba. We were all excited about our upcoming flights and, filled with enthusiasm, we worked out in the gym and spent long hours in the flight simulator, dreaming of our first real solo flight and the vacation to follow back in Cuba when our first two years were up.

Our instructors turned out to be young but professional, solidly grounded in both theory and practice. They spent each afternoon with us going over various details of aerodynamics and flight dynamics, using model planes to demonstrate the maneuvers we were to perform the following day, and quizzing us thoroughly to see how much we'd learned. At the end of each day they signed our notebooks, giving us the go-ahead for the next day's flight. Every day after our flights we reported to each other excitedly on our new experiences. Finally we were able to do what we'd all been dreaming about for nearly two years of grueling preparation.

Each instructor was responsible for three or four cadets, to whom he taught the techniques of navigation and the different maneuvers and stages of a flight. After the cadets had passed the minimum number of exercises necessary for the solo, the instructor presented a designated pilot from base command with a list of those he deemed ready. This pilot would first take a test flight with each cadet before giving him final authorization to fly solo.

I'd completed the course of flying with my instructor in an L-29; so now I presented myself before the base commander to have my flight test—only he could decide whether or not I was ready for my first solo. Once we'd landed and I stood at attention to hear his evaluation, he put a hand on my shoulder, saying:

"But why are you still on the ground? Get up there!"

I ran off, jubilant, to the nearest plane ready for takeoff. For the first time I would fly entirely on my own. Each instrument in the cockpit of that obedient charger would respond to my will alone.

"I'm airborne! Solo!" I shouted to myself as the aircraft lifted off the runway.

Some dark clouds had begun to move in toward the airfield, and I knew I might be ordered back should it start to rain.

"Zero-eight, Rizhnoy." It was the control tower.

"Go ahead to zero-eight."

"How do weather conditions look up there?"

"Excellent!"

They allowed me plenty of time to enjoy my first solo flight, and ever since, the more I've flown, the more I want to fly. I was soon prisoner of that romantic infirmity common to all pilots, for which no one has ever found a cure: the obsession to fly.

It was at this point that our group saw itself dramatically reduced, when eight of our members were unable to handle the plane properly within a given number of qualifying flights. Of those disqualified, it was Rafael who upset us the most. He had a wife and daughter back in Cuba whom he'd sorely missed; yet his passion for aviation had seen him brilliantly through his studies. His medical exams, stress tests, and flight simulations had all gone satisfactorily; but the moment he took off wearing an oxygen mask he was unable to avoid vomiting. He could fly without a mask, but for a fighter pilot that was an impossibility, so he was finally disqualified. And to make things worse, the return ticket to Cuba, which the embassy was supposed to provide, inexplicably took several months to arrive, leaving Rafael to wander disconsolately about the base.

In the meantime I'd receive the letters Vicky wrote me every day and each day I'd write back, giving her details of my new experiences as a pilot. And dreaming, always dreaming about the future, when we would never need to separate again. She had been with me every moment of my two years in the Soviet Union and there was nothing I wanted more in the world than to hold her once again, and to tell her how much I loved her. Every minute now I was thinking about the time left until we'd be reunited, happy that I'd already gotten presents for our family and friends.

In October 1979, we went to Moscow for several days before returning to Cuba. During that time I hardly slept at all, overwhelmed by thoughts of my loved ones, and spending all my time traveling about that immense metropolis on the most' beautiful and efficient subway system I'd ever seen. The city itself gave one the impression it was inhabited by millions of people in transit, human waves streaming everywhere, about to suffocate or crush you. During one of our walks my friend Enrique had to go to the bathroom, so we ran around for blocks and blocks looking for a public toilet; but after hours of fruitless search Enrique told us, reddening: "Too late . . . forget it, we don't have to look anymore." Since then we've called Moscow the town without toilets.

———

The flight to Havana was endless, and I was in a state of perpetual excitement, watching the infinite blue cloak of the Atlantic slowly pass before my window, and then feeling my pulse quicken at the final announcement that we were landing. Sure enough, under the plane's left wing the peninsula of Varadero appeared, its white outlines changing to ever darker blues as they stretched out to the sea. I remembered the words of Columbus upon arriving at the easternmost shores of Cuba: "This is the most beautiful land that mortal eyes have ever seen." Farther ahead was Matanzas, the town of my youth, where my parents still lived. I saw its port, its beach . . . *and yes, those small buildings around the park . . . my parents' place! . . . They're probably at the airport with Vicky. . . . Boy, what a feeling! I'm shaking all over.*

As the plane descended I felt myself finally growing calm. I had longed so much for this moment; at last I breathed in the moist air of the tropics and suddenly it seemed to me as if I'd left Cuba only a short while ago. I heard Vicky shouting my name from the balcony and looked up, confused, like somebody who'd just awakened. I couldn't even spot her among all the families and friends with outstretched arms greeting the arrivals.

After passing through Immigration Control we had a long wait for our luggage, so I walked up to the glass wall enclosing us and drew aside the curtain. There was Vicky in profile on the other side, next to my parents, standing on tiptoe to see above the heads of the crowd. I watched her silently for a few seconds through that transparent wall and suddenly, as if sensing I was there, she turned and ran toward me. There we stood for several minutes, separated by a few centimeters of glass that didn't allow us to speak or touch, looking into each other's eyes. A tear started rolling down her cheek, and I heard a voice from behind, drawing me out of my trance, "Excuse me, but it's prohibited to open the curtains. Please return to the waiting room until your baggage arrives." They checked my forty-five pounds of trinkets carefully as always, and I finally emerged from Customs, momentarily forgetting my guitar in my confusion.

The spectacle of arrival at Havana Airport was decidedly picturesque. It doesn't matter where you've come from or how long you've been away; when returning from abroad you're bound to be received by a retinue of family and friends eager to hug you passionately amid exclamations of joy. We were no exception and, between tears of happiness shed by my mother and Vicky, I could hear the exclamation—so friendly and typically Cuban—from someone nearby as I kissed and hugged Vicky: "Wow, what a squeeze!"

My father was then working in the Ministry of Culture at Matanzas, as director of the Department of Amateurs of Art, and in his latest car, a ramshackle Moskovich that could barely brake, we drove to my in-laws' house.

"What we have *here* is socialism, but what's in the Soviet Union is a lie," I told him at the first opportunity. I had returned so disillusioned with everything I'd heard before about that "great" country that I couldn't resist telling him how cheated I felt.

"What are you talking about?"

"Just what you heard. Their medicine is fifty years behind ours. Corruption is a way of life there, and the level of culture is so low that many asked us whether we'd come from Cuba by train."

"You're crazy—you know what you're saying. It's just your impression of certain individuals here and there. How can you say that the country most advanced in the world in space technology is more backward than we are?"

"I don't doubt their scientific progress. But I can assure you that such developments never extend beyond their laboratories and research institutes. The basic system simply doesn't work. The standard of living is incredibly low; sanitary and living conditions are atrocious. Alcoholism and adultery are epidemic, and family values don't exist. The supposedly revered veterans of the Great Patriotic War are rotting in the streets, subject to the worst misery and lack of care. Old women have to shovel snow in the early morning hours to gain barely enough to survive. And the military brass treat their subordinates in a despotic, totally humiliating manner. Many people openly profess racism, and the general population lives in total ignorance of the outside world, believing themselves to be the first and best in everything. It's all such demagoguery—an African can't even walk the streets peacefully without fear of being physically attacked."

"You know you sound just like the enemies of socialism. I have dozens of friends who've visited the Soviet Union and they have a very different impression than you do."

"Of course, they've been there on official visits, led around by Soviet authorities to model centers especially prepared for foreigners. But we lived with common, everyday people, visiting their homes and sharing the vicissitudes of daily life with them. I hope you never have to visit that country under the conditions we did."

"You're blind, my son."

"Dad, I'm the one who spent two years there, not you. I'm simply telling you what I experienced."

"I don't have to actually be there to know how it is. What I've read is enough for me—dozens of books on the history, culture, and development of the Soviet Union, which, thanks to socialism, went from being one of the most backward countries in the world to becoming the premier world power. I'd like to see if the United States would have managed to recover the way they did from the terrible effects of World War II."

"Okay, Dad," I said quietly, putting an arm around Vicky and pressing her close to me. I saw that I wasn't about to change his mind. After all, the Soviet Union was immense and I'd only seen a few of its remote southern villages. Perhaps what we students there said in fun was actually true—that the march of Soviet power had still not arrived in those parts.

That evening Vicky and I went on to Varadero Beach. She'd managed to get a reservation in the same place we'd spent our honeymoon. So off we went joyfully to relive in all its passion the beautiful time we'd shared there more than three years before.

Then we went to my parents' home and, after a week there, they drove us back to Havana in their car, together with my only nephew. We spent nearly the whole time laughing at his three-year-old's antics, and my father kidded him while driving, asking the kind of questions he'd already learned how to answer:

"Tell me, Faurito, are you a *verraco*?"

"No, Grandpa!"

"Then what are you?"

"A revolutionary!"

"And what else?"

"Militiaman, Pioneer, Communist," the boy declared, while we laughed in pride at having such a noble descendant.

After a week we returned to Havana, and for a short time we enjoyed studying together, as we had before, this time for Vicky's upcoming exam in biochemistry. By the time I returned from my next and final stint in the Soviet Union, she would only have one year left to finish her schooling. "When I return next year we'll order our first baby, if you like," I told her, smiling, and she hugged me in agreement. The day of my departure soon arrived but proved less traumatic than the first time, as I would be back in only ten months, the time it would take to learn to fly my first real jet fighter.

—

This time we were assigned to a base outside the village of Kushiovskaia. There the brand-new supersonic MiG-21Bs awaited us. Once we finished our theoretical studies we were assigned to instructors in groups of four; then we began flying that spirited, formidable machine, so like an unbroken colt in that it allowed not the slightest error in its handling.

One evening the chief of our squadron and the base political commissar came looking for me. They had served as instructors in Cuba and, charmed by the cordial treatment they'd received there, they were particularly friendly and hospitable to our group. They lived on the base with the rest of the flight instructors and professors, and since they were having a party that evening in one of the apartments, they had come over to ask me to join them with my guitar. It was my first invitation to a private party among Soviet officers and, as I followed them back with my guitar slung over my shoulder, I was filled with curiosity. When we arrived at the apartment, the wives of my hosts were seated behind a table full of sausages and other dishes carefully set out among bottles of wine and vodka. After I was introduced and took a seat, the first toast was made to me, followed by all customary attentions typical of Russian hospitality. And afterwards, between mouthfuls of the delicious foods they offered me, more toasts were raised: to the friendship between the people of Cuba and the Soviet Union, to the brothers fallen in battle so that we might enjoy moments like this one, to the health of our loved ones, and on and on. My hosts seemed sincere when they toasted the friendship between our peoples, and after a few drinks they didn't hide their admiration for Cuba and our leader.

"We need a Fidel to bring order to our country," the political commissar remarked after expressing his distaste for Brezhnev, so then we toasted the health of Fidel. I didn't enjoy drinking but was reluctant to offend them, so I simply pretended to drink a little with each additional toast. These two Soviet officers were speaking of my country with such affection and admiration that I felt happy to share that moment of genuine intimacy. This was unlike the corruption I had noticed in some high-ranking officers. I was pleased to find others for whom moral values, which had been so inculcated in us Cubans, came before material ones.

"The leadership is sickly, corrupt, because of this decrepit old man who hasn't finished dying," the lieutenant colonel, our squadron leader, concluded, his cold dissection of the Soviet leader filling me with amazement. What a revelation this was for me! Not only were they deprecating him, but they hated him! "That's why we need a Castro here," he added, and I noted the plural. How relieved I felt. I would finally be able to give a convincing explanation to my father: The system didn't work because of the man in power, not because of the system itself. Not everyone was corrupt. The majority continued being as idealistic as they had been in Lenin's time. This gave me hope and restored my confidence in the USSR. *They'll sweep away the evils that have been foisted upon them*, I thought with optimism.

We all longed for my distant country and sang together its best-known songs as I strummed my guitar. Then they began to dance, while continuing to gulp down huge quantities of vodka, exchanging wives between each dance. The squad leader wanted me to have a dance with his wife, but conscious of how drunk they already were, I excused myself, saying I was going to the bathroom. I had to find some inoffensive way of leaving that party, which seemed as endless as the supply of vodka they were willing to down. Coming out of the bathroom, which was located next to the kitchen in that tiny apartment, I was stunned to see the wife of the political commissar and the squad leader petting ardently by the sink. Confused, I went back to the living room, where their counterparts were repeating the kitchen scene on the sofa. This was certainly not a place I wanted to be, so despite their insistence that I stay a little longer, I left quickly under the pretext that I had to get up early the next day, forgetting my guitar in my haste.

Back in my quarters I threw myself down on the bed and stared at the ceiling. I'd felt so good in their company at the start; they'd given me back my faith in their country, which I'd all but lost. And now I returned to the mental shock of those last few minutes there. *I don't understand*, I thought to myself. *How routine does immorality have to become to make people feel they don't even have to hide it?*

—

One day we went for an excursion to the historical town of Volgograd, formerly called Stalingrad in honor of the great leader who had governed the Soviet people during their most difficult period. Somebody asked our guide why the name had been changed after the Communist party's Twentieth Congress, and the guide answered dryly: "Comrade Stalin committed grave errors in his cult of personality during the last stage of his life." We had a short walk through the town, which extended along the west bank of the Volga River, and then we went on to the main objective of our visit: the Mamaiev Kurgan Monument, dedicated to those killed in action during the heroic defense of Stalingrad and located on a promontory from which one had a magnificent view of the entire city. We began ascending the large steps leading to the top of the monument, impressed by the beauty of the gardens and fountains all about us. Eventually the stairs cut through walls of rock on which were carved the agonized faces of women and children, victims of the Nazi siege. Farther on was the impressive mausoleum set in a circular well in the ground with an eternal flame at its center. On its walls in golden letters were the names of the hundreds of thousands who had fallen in defense of the city, a battle that marked the turning point of the war. Walking to the beat of the funeral dirges that seemed to rain down from the sky, we entered the mausoleum, feeling transported back in time, to the point of smelling the gunpowder and burned flesh of the conflict that once transpired there. I looked up at those walls in silence, reading several names and feeling as if I knew them, imagining the faces and lives behind those simple letters. I looked at the eternal flame and thought about the tragedy and destiny of human beings. *It was fate that I was born in Cuba in 1956. And suppose I had been born here instead, well before then? I could very well have been one of one of these victims with their names inscribed on the wall up there, and it could just as well have been one of them looking up at my name now.*

We arrived at the top of the monument where the gigantic statue of the mother country was erected, holding in her right hand a sword nearly twenty yards long, expressing in her face the courage to die rather than to bend before the enemy. I gazed at her from top to bottom, awed to silence by the weight of her dead, of her burden of horrors . . . and I understood that we live in the past, still subject to its anguish though we never lived through it. We had no right to forget. Whatever we did, any sacrifice we made would be small compared to that of the fallen. With their lives they created this society for us, and I understood then that we are forever indebted to our dead.

—

We were completing our program of flight training when a notice arrived from the political section of the Cuban embassy. The screening of my application to be a member of the Young Communist Union had ended satisfactorily. In the letter of acceptance accompanying my membership card I received the following congratulations: *In recognition of the excellent results achieved in your studies, and of your exemplary revolutionary attitude . . .*

On the last day of our flights a solemn event took place out on the apron of the Kushiovskaia Airfield. With the resplendent MiG-21Bs behind us and under the Soviet and Cuban banners flapping sonorously in the breeze, the head of the base delivered the following speech:

"Brothers in arms: We congratulate you on the successful completion of the task assigned you by the Communist party and the people of Cuba. You are a bastion in the defense of universal justice, confronting North American imperialism head-on. We are proud to have taught you the past three years, and now that we've come to know you better we understand fully why the United States will never vanquish the Island of Liberty. Neither their NATO nor all their military technology will do them any good in the face of men like you. Weapons are worth no more than the man who puts them to use, and you as Cubans have demonstrated a worth far greater than the entire military strength of the United States."

The colonel's speech brought a lump to our throats. We had longed so much for this moment, we had overcome so many trials in that strange and sometimes hostile environment. We'd finally reached our goal and we were proud of it.

"Long live the Communist parties of Cuba and the USSR!" the

colonel concluded. "Long live the undying friendship between our peoples! Long live Leonid Ilyich Brezhnev! Long live—"

And our cheers resounded wildly, showing we were as ready as the jet fighters behind us to sacrifice ourselves to make a better world. We were warriors of the just cause. We were the pride of our people, and of our dead. We had finally graduated and were ecstatic to be going home. In Cuba, Vicky was waiting for me in hopes of never being separated again. My people were waiting too, and so was my covenant with the fallen, which was to inspire my life as an officer in the Cuban air force.

Chapter 6

—

On the Brink
of War

Upon my triumphant return from the Soviet Union, I was admired by family and friends alike. Vicky was in her last year of studies and wanted to end the year with our first child. After four years our tree would finally bear its first fruit. We spent the early days of my vacation on the beach, walking arm in arm along the sand each night, imagining the infant we longed for and loving it already.

A member of the Armed Forces Divisional Staff had been on hand at the airport to greet each pilot, presenting us with some letters of introduction and advising us to report to air force headquarters in thirty days. On the appointed day in November 1980 we all presented ourselves there, eager to find out where we'd be posted. Major Santos, inspector of the air force, welcomed us, adding, "Tomorrow at eight sharp we leave for Holguín, where we'll rehearse the swearing-in ceremony to take place the day after at the Mausoleum of the Second Eastern Front." He was referring to the site of Raúl Castro's former command post when he'd led the guerrilla fighting in the mountains of Oriente Province. The monument, established by our Minister of the Armed Forces, was a fitting stage on which to receive our epaulets designating the rank of second lieutenant.

"And now," Santos concluded while opening a slip of paper he'd extracted from his shirt pocket, "the bases to which you've been assigned . . . I warn you that no transfer requests will be considered, so join your units without any objections."

From the base at Holguín we were flown in Mi-8 helicopters to the monument, which was surrounded by the verdant ridges of the Sierra de Niquero. The landscape was majestic and inspiring, with our national flag waving among those mountains where our fathers had bravely fought. I'd been selected to recite the oath in the name of our group, so after the national anthem I took my place before my comrades, who were already kneeling solemnly on the ground, and began to read:

"I swear eternal loyalty to the fatherland and to the legacy of our martyrs."

And my comrades responded, each raising a closed fist as emphatic proof of his assent:

"We swear!"

"I swear to serve the cause of communism. . . ."

"We swear!"

"I swear to follow the orders of my superiors as my country's mandate. . . ."

"We swear!"

"I swear to be faithful to the trust placed in me by the Commander in Chief Fidel Castro. . . ."

"We swear!"

"Let the hate and scorn of my people fall upon me, at the cost of my life, should I ever break this oath!"

"Let it fall!"

That same afternoon, with the rank of second lieutenant emblazoned on our shoulders, we were flown in an air force AN-26 to Santa Clara Air Base, our final destination. The last rays of sunlight were falling as the plane landed after a shaky flight through turbulent, cumulus-laden skies. Colonel Cortés was waiting to greet us and escort our group to the "pilots' quarters," a group of buildings separated from the rest of the living accommodations at the base. The pilots' quarters comprised three parallel blocks of lodgings divided by well-kept gardens filled with roses, a dining room and club off at one end, and parking lot in front of the first block. Each room had four closets and a bathroom with a shower, four comfortable beds, a refrigerator, and an air conditioner imported from Japan—appliances available only to pilots on the base.

"These boys are too skinny," the colonel told the waitresses as he showed us through the dining room, "so feed them well." Then, turning to the corporal in charge of the facilities, who had accompanied us to our quarters, he added, "Nápoles, see to it that the refrigerators in their rooms are well supplied with snacks."

Nápoles was a man a little over fifty who had never risen above the rank of corporal, despite having fought in the mountains beside our country's leaders. Many of his old buddies had become generals, but Nápoles had remained a corporal, and his only responsibilities were taking care of the gardens surrounding each block of lodgings and changing the linens once a week. Apparently the party and the military command were both obsessed with maintaining the honor of their membership, and their entire organizational structures were accustomed to investigating the most flagrant cases of adultery. It was in this connection that Nápoles had been held back from promotion—for having refused to divorce an unfaithful wife. The day he was summoned before the party and military Counterintelligence, which presented him with proof of his wife's infidelity, Nápoles returned home and instead of keeping his promise to the authorities, he dragged from his house the silent witness of the crime—his mattress—and set fire to it under the astonished gaze of his neighbors.

The right of the party and Counterintelligence to meddle in our private lives was made evident from the very start, with my unmarried comrades receiving instructions from Major Felipe, chief of the squadron to which I'd been assigned: "When you begin dating a girl you must notify Counterintelligence immediately, and should you plan to get married you'll first have to wait for an investigation of her background to obtain the necessary permit."

He explained that the CIA was trying to gather classified military information by using pretty young girls to seduce our pilots. "Contact is prohibited with girls who profess any religious affiliation, or those with any relatives who've been detained for political reasons." All the aforementioned were automatically deemed to be potential enemy recruits.

—

Santa Clara Air Base was situated some six miles north of the town bearing the same name, and occupied about five square miles of a barren, stony terrain that is rather unusual in Cuba. The base extended westward toward a highway, which linked the city to another town farther north. Its boundaries were delineated by a kind of wall constructed with prefabricated slabs of concrete. On the side flanking the highway, the wall was dug under in certain remote spots to form pathways through which soldiers and local peasants passed freely. On the other side of the highway, but outside the base, was the "military community," a group of identical apartment houses where some of the officers from the base and other neighboring units lived along with their families.

One gained entry to the base through the Post 1 checkpoint, which had a rusty chain strung across it, with a red rag knotted at its middle. The soldier and officer on guard duty in the adjacent sentry box would raise or lower the chain, thereby monitoring the flow of personnel and vehicles. The pilots' quarters were located on the left, and half a kilometer down the road was headquarters, a four-story building fronted by a large plot of grass where an old Mi-4 helicopter and a MiG-17 were lying at rest like a pair of museum relics.

Behind headquarters was the parade ground, with its concrete grandstand, where we practiced daily drill. During one of our first infantry formations there our squadron chief admonished us: "You are pilots, the first to repel a massive enemy air strike. You must keep us informed of your whereabouts at all times, even on leave, so that you can be located in case of an attack. Those who live in Havana or other outlying cities will be allowed only four days a month as per the latest instructions from the Minister of the armed forces." Thus began our initiation as rookie pilots in a combat unit.

On my first takeoff I was astounded by the beauty of the island. Traveling like a swift bird, I veered from one end of its landscape to the other, my eyes caressing its lovely features: from those tiny islands of the north, which were spread out over the crystalline waters of the Caribbean like flecks of brilliant green edged in white reposing on a coral bed of a thousand colors; to the forested mountains of the south, which rose to meet the pale vault of the sky; to those soft-hued fields crisscrossed by hundreds of silvery roads, which ended in small villages with faded white houses. Thus I flew, in quick hops from coast to coast, feeling like the guardian of my marvelous island. Whoever tried to subdue her would first have to reckon with me, the jealous defender of her skies.

Hardly had we been a few days on the base when we were roused from sleep early one morning by the air-alert sirens. We dressed in seconds and ran to the bus, which was already waiting with its engine running. The driver rushed us to the hangars, where the planes were armed and ready. We younger ones were charged with excitement, while the older ones were talking and joking as if this were all the most natural thing in the world. With my breath and pulse racing, I climbed into the cockpit, navigating the darkness with the thin beam of the flashlight that hung around my neck and the further aid of my flight technician, who grabbed my hand and informed me, "Number six-eighteen ready, with two hundred fifty rounds, two heat-seeking air-to-airs, and a pair of radars."

I quickly flipped on the main switches while installing myself in the ejection seat and adjusting the parachute straps. As I switched on the navigation lights I heard a voice crackling over the radio:

"All Falcons, all Falcons, report squadrons prepared for take-off."

That's Command! Damn it, this is the real thing! I'd never even flown on a night mission before! *How close are those enemy planes to their targets?* I wondered. With the imminence of combat I found my legs were trembling a bit.

Thirty minutes elapsed, and all that one heard was the voice of one impatient pilot or another calling Command, and the invariable response:

"Hold position. . . ."

Evidently the U.S. Air Force fighter-bombers had yet to take off by the time of the alert. How had our leaders learned of the impending air strike? Most likely through operatives from State security who had infiltrated the very heart of the enemy.

From my cockpit with its open canopy, fighting off the insatiable mosquitoes that seemed bent on draining my blood, I saw the first glimmers of light cross the horizon. I'd spent three hours harnessed to a hard ejection seat and still no enemy planes had come.

Have the Yankees had second thoughts? I wondered.

The reason for our state of alert was the U.S. military decision to hold war games in the Caribbean, which included dispatching troops to Puerto Rico and deploying an aircraft carrier near Grand Cayman, just to the south of Cuba. Later we learned that High Command had considered such initiatives an ideal cover to mask a surprise attack on the island. We spent the entire day under the wing of our fighters dressed in full flight gear, having lunch there and receiving political instruction with the latest intelligence updates on the enemy.

Nearly ten years later I would discover that the U.S. government normally announces its military maneuvers with sufficient advance notice, but the Cuban command liked to keep such information from the public. Then, just beforehand, they would announce the U.S. troop movements as a secret strategy leading to a "probable invasion," and thus mobilize the people and the armed forces in defense of the Revolution.

For a month there was no letup in preparations for an imminent U.S. invasion. Every night we'd retire to an air-conditioned area reserved for pilots, leaving the planes under heavy guard. It was then that we'd see captains, majors, and even some lieutenant colonels slip away into the darkness, crawling through those gaps under the wall to spend precious hours with their wives and children. That time I spent in almost complete isolation from Vicky and my parents, who learned through the press about the danger of a U.S. invasion. The press reported that Ronald Reagan was planning to crush the island militarily for its continued defiance of American supremacy. And there we were, ready to show him that Cuba would prove to be a difficult stronghold to conquer.

There were no telephones on the base linked to the civilian network, so at night I would sneak off to town like the others, to spend a few minutes in a telephone booth talking with Vicky in Havana, nearly 180 miles away. Vicky thought she was pregnant and said she needed me, but duty kept me from her. And I tried futilely to transmit my love through the telephone wire, to give her courage; yet I was as dismayed as she was under the tensions of a war that never arrived but kept me from seeing her. A thousand times I thought of going to Havana regardless of the consequences, but the thought of an enemy air strike during my absence always dissuaded me. It would have been an unforgivable lapse on my part—who knows how many victims might have fallen under the bombardment of a plane that could well have been intercepted by me.

The state of alert was finally lifted. This time the Americans had decided not to invade, but we were kept nonetheless from visiting our families. With the lifting of the maximum state of emergency, we were told that a deputation from the Joint Chiefs of Staff was to arrive on a tour of inspection and we would continue to be restricted to base, working around the clock to update the backlog of paperwork, rehearsing on the parade ground a reception ceremony for the visiting brass and devoting what time was left to fulfilling the latest order from the Commander in Chief by manually excavating shelters and trenches in preparation for the impending war that President Reagan wished to wage with Cuba.

One morning when I was alone in my room getting ready for my shift on standby alert, I was paid a visit by Captain Yánez, head of military Counterintelligence at the base, who wanted to have a "very private" conversation with me. Although they had their office in a section of military headquarters, the men who worked for this branch of the armed forces enjoyed total autonomy. They were not subordinated to the air force command, but reported directly to the minister of the armed forces. They went about cloaked in an air of mystery, brashly entering and leaving the base on their motorcycles, dressed in civilian clothes with their shirttails hanging outside their pants to conceal the pistol they always wore at the hip. Their regulations were in notable contrast to those for the rest of the officers, who were required to wear their uniforms at all times while on the base, and who were not permitted to wear sidearms except during alerts.

Yánez took a seat opposite me, behind the table in the center of the room, took out a pad of notes, and, staring me in the eye, asked in confidential tones, "What do you think of the security organs of the State?"

"That they're necessary."

"That's all?"

"I think they carry out one of our more difficult and delicate jobs." *Why is he asking me all this?* I wondered.

"And about the men who do the job?"

I admired such anonymous heroes, and had learned that among the lists of martyrs of the Revolution there were many names, still guarded in secret, of heroes who'd died at the hands of the CIA without even receiving proper recognition from the people, who still considered them traitors.

"They're the most selfless of all. They can't even aspire to the respect and admiration of relatives and friends when they have to infiltrate the enemy.''

Yánez smiled, making a few circles with his pen on a blank page of his pad. ''We've studied your file. You're serious, intelligent . . .'' and he continued with additional superlatives, concluding, ''We want you to work with us.''

He'd hardly finished the phrase before I was imagining myself in the United States, infiltrated into the ranks of the CIA, radioing to Cuba the latest information obtained, just like the heroes from State security did in the TV serials I'd watched.

''What? Work with you?''

''Correct.''

''But I'm a pilot . . . my whole life's been as a revolutionary. I don't think I could infiltrate anywhere.''

''It's not a matter of that. We want you to collaborate with us in the protection of your comrades.''

''In the protection of—''

''Pilots are a priority objective of the CIA, and the United States would give anything to have just one of you defect with a MiG. Besides, it's impossible to control a pilot once he's airborne. Can you imagine what the CIA might pay to get a fighter pilot to drop a few bombs on Central Committee headquarters?''

''Of course. . . . I see. But what do I have to do?''

''Nothing, just keep in periodic contact with us. We'll give you instructions and you'll look out for the security of your comrades. We'll give you a code name.''

''But I don't have to hide to do it.''

''Discretion is important. At times the confidence others have in you is what allows you to find out about things.''

''I still don't get it. My comrades are totally trustworthy . . . aren't they?''

''Yes, but no one knows what could happen tomorrow.''

''Exactly. Anyone can become a traitor. But I don't have to hide to combat it, I would be the first to take action even before calling upon you people.''

''So then . . . you don't accept?''

''It's not that I'm refusing . . . I'll always defend the Revolution, but openly. To infiltrate the CIA is one thing, and quite another to spy on my comrades. I trust them; but if one of them ever betrayed us, you can be sure I'd be the first to act.''

''I think you don't realize. . . . eighty percent of the officers in the armed forces actively collaborate with Counterintelligence. Think about it; someday we'll have another talk.''

Yánez left as silently as he had come, but for many days I was struck by the details of my conversation with him, feeling disturbed without knowing why.

For a month and a half we couldn't leave the base, and finally I went to my squadron leader to request two days' leave, but the request was denied. That was when I decided I would go see Vicky no matter what. It would be difficult to discover my absence, given that I had no guard duty or flights assigned me during the next twenty-four hours; so I relied on the discretion of my buddies, who would cover for me as best they could. I awaited darkness to run for the wall and slipped away as anxious and gleeful as a child committing a prank, then I furtively swallowed up the mile separating me from the highway where I took anything that moved to get to town. From there I'd attempt to reach the capital, which had become difficult of late. What a surprise I'd give Vicky!

At last I arrived at the bus terminal in town, but there were no seats available, not even on the bus scheduled for the following day to Havana.

"Look over there, Lieutenant," the dark, skinny dispatcher kindly informed me, smiling at this stranger from his desolate ticket window, "there's a line for cars taking people to Havana."

Outside where he'd directed me was another skinny-looking character who looked me up and down mistrustfully, as if to decipher my intentions beneath the uniform, while I was asking the last person on line, "Are you going to Havana, friend?"

"Yes, on the first ride I can get."

Then the other character approached me, so close I could smell his breath, and told me confidentially, "I have a friend going there who charges thirty pesos. He's parked just around the corner."

"Sure, I'll pay—"

"Quiet, man, my friend's a doctor and isn't supposed to do this or they'll take away his car."

"Oh, sorry, I didn't realize."

He led me to the car, a 1970s Fiat, where two other customers were already waiting. We all paid in advance and got in without saying a word. As we left town the driver informed us, "I'm a physician and use the money to cover expenses for the trip. If any policeman stops us, tell him I'm taking you for free; otherwise I'm in trouble."

"Don't worry," we all assured him, anxious to arrive at our destination.

The fellow was one of the professionals who were allowed to purchase a car assigned by the State; but if he was caught using it this way the car could be confiscated. But none of that mattered to us— we were simply glad he allowed us to come along at a moment when it was impossible to find any other means of transportation. The trip proved to be quite an odyssey, since the driver panicked at the least hint that the authorities might be around. Never have I seen anybody obey traffic signals so carefully.

Finally we reached Havana. I went directly to Vicky's parents' house where, as always, the door was left wide open until it was time for bed. There was Vicky, seated forlornly at the same table where we had scribbled messages to each other during our engagement, her head now lowered in thought. I tiptoed quietly behind her to the old piano where she used to practice her lessons, and began to pick out a few notes of a piece we both loved. She raised her head as if waking from her meditation, her hands gripping the edge of the table, and with a shriek she jumped up and turned to face me. At first she stared at me with wide-open eyes, then threw herself upon me in a frantic embrace, trembling and sobbing as she cried to me, *"Papitoo!"* We stood there awhile, without another word, she weeping while I held her close, stroking her hair and whispering, "Yes, yes, I'm here. . . ."

Little by little she calmed down until she became quiet, resting against me, breathing softly. Then I separated her gently from me and, caressing her belly with the look of an accomplice, I asked, "You really think that you're . . . ?"

She dropped her head with a shy smile. "I'm not sure. I think so."

Whereupon I bent to kiss her belly.

That evening my mother-in-law's pots were fuller than usual and we celebrated my arrival with a delicious meal, amidst everybody's suggestions for names for the future boy or girl of the house. Then Vicky and I retired to the conspiratorial intimacy of the apartment where we lived. Soon I would have to return to the base. How we desired each other! And, caught up in our passion, we embraced each other, drowning in the tender innocence of love.

Asleep next to Vicky and exhausted from tension and nights without sleep, I began to dream. I was seated in a gray, windowless room, my officer's stripes ripped off my uniform. In front of me sat Cortés and three other colonels I didn't recognize. To his right sat Major Felipe, and behind me were about twenty young pilots, my comrades . . .

"Second Lieutenant, on your feet! Because you committed the crime of abandoning your post at a moment when your country needed you most, dozens of innocent victims perished . . . women, children, all fallen in a hail of enemy fire from a plane that *you* were supposed to intercept." He went on, reading off the names of the victims while flashing their pictures at me—almost all of them smiling children in their Pioneer scarfs. I despised myself.

"Your unauthorized absence under war conditions constitutes desertion and, in your case, a betrayal of your country." And solemnly facing the audience—who shouted at me, *"Traitor, traitor, traitor!"*—he concluded, "This military court condemns the prisoner to death by firing squad!"

At once a squad of soldiers bearing rifles entered the room, then led me out to the courtyard, where they ordered me to kneel down with my face against the wall. They drew to attention a few yards from me, aimed their rifles, and . . .

Little child, the one we've been waiting for, am I never to see you?

"Fire!" shouted the squad leader, but there was no sound. A woman's voice stopped them at the last second, calling me by name, and the soldiers looked at each other in surprise, as if they feared she would discover what was happening.

"Oré? Oré!"

I opened my eyes, raising myself slightly from the bed. It had all been a dream. . . . There was Vicky, one hand on her belly, standing by the ironing board with my air force shirt spread over it.

"What are you doing? Is it late? Why are you ironing that?" I asked disconnectedly, still half asleep.

"I wanted you to be able to leave with it nice and clean." As she spoke I noticed how pale she looked; her face seemed drawn.

"What's the matter, Vicky!" I said, jumping up from the bed to take her arm. "Don't you feel well?"

"I have a terrible pain. I didn't want to wake you, but it's getting worse and . . . I'm bleeding."

"But, what do you mean? We're going right now," I babbled as I dressed hastily, trying to figure out where to find a doctor at that hour. Vicky hardly complained, but in her worried expression I could clearly detect the physical and emotional pain that invaded her at the thought of losing the baby we already loved so dearly. "Don't worry, you'll see, everything will be fine," I told her, trying to encourage her.

We stopped a passing car and I spent the entire trip joking with Vicky, attempting to distract her. We quickly arrived at the maternity hospital, where a specialist with an immaculately white jacket and calm demeanor attended to Vicky immediately. I spent the next thirty minutes or more waiting tensely, wondering about the little thing at its birth, its face, its hands, its small half-shut eyes, its first smiles.

"Comrade."

"Yes?" The doctor's voice knocked me out of my reverie.

"Your wife is definitely pregnant. She almost had a miscarriage, but if she maintains complete rest during the following weeks she should be out of danger. She'll be out in a few more minutes."

"I'm definitely pregnant," Vicky confirmed to me, passing her right hand softly over her belly. With relief I kissed her, and we returned to her parents' house, overjoyed at how things had turned out, but also sad about my imminent departure for Santa Clara.

I didn't want to go back to the base until Vicky was decidedly feeling better, so I stayed the rest of the day by her side. That evening, however, on the return bus I was assaulted by the possibility of my absence being discovered. Arriving at the base by dawn, after staying away for thirty-six hours, I was quickly put at ease by my buddies, who assured me, "Don't worry, we spent the whole day yesterday closeted like idiots, and nobody even asked for you."

I breathed a sigh of relief and prepared to resume my duties at the base. Like others, I'd succeeded in visiting home without repercussions, but our virutal imprisonment on the base was becoming unbearable. Convinced of the guilt of our immediate superiors, we decided to make use of military regulations and claim our rights legally. We were then summoned to the office of the base commander, Lieutenant Colonel Eloy Fernández, a man of profound scruples and persuasive temperament, strict but good-natured with subordinates, and therefore highly respected.

"You may go in," the sergeant who served as the commander's aide-de-camp told us as he opened the door for us.

Timidly we eight complainants entered and were told to sit down. Commander Eloy smiled up at us from behind a desk cluttered with phones and an antiquated intercom, while Colonel Cortés—who, in a common practice for Cuban armed forces, was ostensibly of a higher military rank than that of his superior—was seated in one of the armchairs backed against the wall covered with maps and diagrams.

Eloy spoke first: "So you haven't been allowed to go home."

"It's almost a month and a half now we've been locked up here," Julito replied for us all.

"Why didn't you come to me earlier about this?"

Without intending to, we all looked at Cortés; but we didn't say anything, knowing that regulations prohibited us from challenging a superior directly.

"They spoke to me about it, Commander, but we had to prepare for inspection."

The discussion seemed to be headed in a different direction—not to the heart of the matter. I requested permission to speak.

"Our homes aren't close by, Commander. We all need at least two days to be able to visit our families. I think it's ridiculous for men at our age to have to leave the base on the sly, as I had to in order to see my wife. I don't want to do that again, in secret, feeling like I've committed a crime."

Eloy listened to my confession while looking me directly in the eye, and I felt better for having told him. I felt that Eloy was one of those men who admire honesty and abhor lies.

After hearing me out he smiled and said, "I think there's been a little confusion here. You should be able to go home but, of course, not all at once. You'll leave two at a time, married men first."

Wild with happiness, I went off to pack my things for Havana. This time I'd be able to spend more time with Vicky and even to visit my parents and my brothers.

—

It had been many years since all three of us brothers had been at my parents' at the same time. Young Orlando, who was then boarding at vocational school, had come for the weekend and Faure, now doing his military service as an ordinary soldier in an antiaircraft artillery unit, had also managed to get leave. A festive air reigned at my parents' home in anticipation of our arrival, and they had managed even to buy a small pig to cook from a farmer in the countryside. A friend who managed a nearby restaurant had allowed them to purchase a case of beer to complete the celebration. We all sat around the table conversing between beers and chunks of fried pork that my mother brought in from the kitchen, laughing at the latest adventures of my ever knavish brother Faure.

I wanted to have a word with my father in private, and with a nod I invited him to follow me out to the balcony.

"Dad, military Counterintelligence has asked me to work with them," I began, relating my conversation with Yánez, and my refusal to accept his offer.

"I think you did wrong," my father remarked.

"The pilots are the most trustworthy of all. Why should I have to spy on them covertly?"

"You're probably right about your comrades. But you don't know what fate has in store for all of us, or whether the Revolution might not need you in such a capacity in the future." And he added, "I have a friend, an old party leader, who just a while ago received a letter of recognition for his twenty years of service in State security. And he's a well-known leader, not a covert agent. What I mean is, if they've called upon you, it's because they wish to train you for the future."

I knew that my father had never worked for State security, nor had any military training whatsoever. But his view of the matter surprised me.

"The fact is that I refused, and now I'm worried."

"It's silly to be worried. They're observing you, and they'll have another talk with you when you least suspect it."

We returned to the table where my brothers were clowning together, and I joined in, laughing as well, happy to be with them, forgetting about all the days of tension on the base. But it wasn't to be the last time we'd be on the brink of war due to the threat of an imminent invasion.

—

Our lives were spent in a constant flurry of preparations for war with the United States, and we rookie pilots gradually gained confidence in the art of aerial combat and the use of weapons against ground and air targets. Our aerial maneuvers grew more complex and the precise conditions more challenging. An atmosphere of professional pride pervaded our efforts, as we prepared meticulously for our flights, developing that special competitive spirit that is usual among combat pilots, wherein each one tries to perform at his very best: to hit the target on the first run, to dodge the attack of a mock opponent, to lock on the enemy's tail and to fly, for the most part, with agility and grace.

As always, we spent most of the time restricted to base, for although the situation had normalized, a new order from our Commander in Chief decreed that at least 33 percent of the officers must always be present with their units, ready for immediate combat. That way every officer had the right to spend every third night on base; but since we, the youngest, lived elsewhere, we let those who lived nearby leave twice in succession, substituting for their shifts while we accumulated the four days necessary to go home each month.

During such standby periods we'd get together at the pilots' club in the evening to relax a little, watching television or just fooling around like one big family. Sometimes we'd sit outside under the trees near the parking lot. I'd bring my guitar and we'd sing some of the popular songs of the time, with Mario and Maujo usually enlivening things with their magnificent voices and their wonderful senses of humor.

But after the singing and joking died down we'd invariably end up discussing different facets of aerial combat. Each one would tell of his experiences during the most complicated exercises, and of the maneuvers he considered most crucial when going up against those F-14s, F-15s, and F-16s of the U.S. Air Force. As the joke went, if two pilots were talking about anything but planes, they were obviously drunk.

We flew almost daily, while new plans were carried out to accelerate the preparation of additional pilots. One day in May 1981 as we were completing a long string of flights, the sky began darkening with dangerous cumulonimbus clouds—a not uncommon weather pattern for Cuban afternoons in spring. The few planes still in the air were instructed to return immediately, for the airfield was about to be hit by a fierce storm. Mario, that jovial and magnificent singer from our group, was up in a trainer with Espiñeiro, one of the most experienced pilots on the base; Mario's part of the cockpit was draped, to prevent him from looking outside for bearings while he practiced instrument piloting. Planes were landing quickly one after another; but Mario, who was last, was told to go out farther and circle back blindly using an instrument approach for a landing, though conditions should have required his immediate return. Conscious of the danger facing one of our comrades, a bunch of us gathered around the speaker that broadcast radio communications in the cubicle belonging to the ramp engineer, and we listened with increasing anxiety to Mario's transmissions. Blind, and without being warned by his instructor, who was sitting behind him but who now had no forward visibility either, Mario calmly relayed his position.

"Nine-twenty-three, about to make my final approach," he reported calmly, probably unaware he might be entering those mountainous cumulus clouds threatening to crush him in their vertiginous growth.

"Distance fifty-five. Begin turn to left, banking thirty degrees." It was the flight controller directing his instrument landing.

"Nine-twenty-three, roger," Mario replied.

That was the last transmission we heard from him. The flight controller began calling him repeatedly, but there was no response. The small, brilliant dot of the plane on the radar screens, which until then had remained at least partially visible among the sparks of cumulus cloud, had now completely disappeared.

The alarm was sounded. Cortés ran to a fighter and took off in search of them, despite the fact that the storm was already underway; a helicopter manned by Search and Rescue also took off, while fire trucks, wreckers, and an ambulance raced to their positions at the end of the runway. We younger pilots stood in front of the shed where we normally received the day's flight instructions, our eyes glued to the sky, the truth beginning to dawn on us. Although we hadn't lived through such an experience, we knew full well it was impossible to make a forced landing in that type of plane. We could only expect the worst.

"Maybe they had time to eject," someone suggested hopefully.

After two hours of waiting, we finally heard the helicopter crew radio in that they'd sighted the wreckage and were preparing to land.

"The plane's demolished. . . . No signs of life."

Mario and Espiñeiro had crashed into the earth at an angle of 60 degrees and a speed of 660 miles per hour. Death had surprised them blindly, and they had been smashed to bits along with their fighter. In town Espiñeiro's wife and children were expecting him home, while in Havana Mario's mother was looking forward to her only son's monthly four-day visit. On the base a committee was hastily assembled, made up of the political commissar, the squadron chief, the head physician, and a nurse, to present the tragic news to their respective families once final clarification was obtained regarding the circumstances surrounding the accident. Devastated, we watched the committee depart on its sad mission.

In the evening Espiñeiro's family arrived at the base. A transport plane was parked at the apron, waiting to fly them to the funeral in Havana, along with the pair of flag-draped coffins containing a few bloody fragments from the plane and a guard of honor chosen from among the pilots. In Havana, our group acted as funeral cortege on the solemn march to Colón Cemetery to the heartbreaking beat of the funeral dirge. Upon our arrival at the Armed Forces Pantheon, both caskets were exposed to the sun for the final farewells.

"They died performing their duty as defenders of the socialist fatherland. Eternal glory to our martyrs!'' our base commander, Lieutenant Colonel Fernández, concluded with emotion, whereupon the air resounded with the firing of a gun salute followed by a solitary bugle call, which drowned out the desperate weeping of a mother and a wife.

When we departed, several floral wreaths had already been placed by their tombs. Two stood out from the rest by virtue of their size and beauty. On one was an inscription: FROM THE MINISTER OF THE ARMED FORCES, RAÚL CASTRO and on the other: FROM THE COMMANDER IN CHIEF, FIDEL CASTRO.

We returned to the base at Santa Clara, and I was called in to see the political commissar. ''You live in Havana not far from Mario's mother. Take this four months' salary to her.'' That was all he said.

''You're not sending anything else?''

''What more can we do?''

With nothing except the money, I went to see Mario's mother. After ascending a narrow staircase to an apartment in the Vedado District, I knocked at the door, which was opened by an unkempt woman in her sixties with swollen red eyes. She stared for a few seconds at the pilot wing fastened to my left shirt pocket and then, as if awakening, she looked into my eyes, exclaiming, ''Oh, my poor son! I still can't believe it—my son can't be dead!''

Never before had I found myself in such a difficult situation. I tried to say something to console her, but I was reduced to babbling.

She threw herself on my chest, saying in a voice that came from her torn heart, ''He was all I had. . . . How am I to live without my child?'' She sighed heavily, coughing and crying, convulsed by her pain, and still I could find no way to comfort the poor woman. I finally gave up trying to say anything and just held her in my arms, patting her softly.

''In him we lost a brother,'' I managed to tell her at last, in a voice that seemed more solemn than my own. ''He was our brother, and you can consider us as your sons.''

Mario's mother nodded her head as I spoke, and then, taking my hand, she replied in a maternal voice, ''Come in, my child, sit down.''

Only my mother called me ''my child,'' despite my twenty-four years of age, and the expression, coming from this woman's lips, had a heartrending effect, sharpening my pain for someone who was addressing me perhaps as she had the son she'd lost. We talked a long time about Mario, his joyful spirit, his musical talent, and his qualities as a pilot. She wanted to know the exact details of his death and I repeated the conclusions of the investigative commission: ''They flew into a cumulonimbus of enormous proportions, which hurled their plane to earth.''

''What's a cumulonimbus?''

I explained to her in the simplest way possible what I'd learned in meteorology classes about those treacherous clouds, which amassed vertically. Although she didn't look like she understood very well, she seemed to accept the explanation of the cause of the accident.

"I brought you Mario's salary for four months," I told her.

"I wanted to talk to you about that. I don't know if he told anybody, but he had a sweetheart who's going to have a . . . "

I knew who she was talking about. Mario had been going out lately with a girl from Santa Clara. We had seen her at the funeral, alone and silent, as if she didn't want to be noticed.

"She wants to end the pregnancy now that Mario no longer exists, but I begged her not to do it. There's nothing I want more now than a child from my absent child."

"Of course, I understand. Let me speak to the authorities at the base to see if they can arrange a pension for the child. Is that what you mean?"

"I don't know how to thank you, my child. She's a student and can't bring a baby into the world without a father."

"Leave it to me, I'll be back soon with some news," I promised her and kissed her on the cheek. Outside I felt a deep aching for this woman who could not escape her grief, helpless in the terrible solitude of her apartment. And without meaning to, I began thinking of Vicky and the child we were expecting.

I returned to Santa Clara and went to talk to the base's political commissar about the request from Mario's mother.

"This girl Mario was seeing has a reputation for going out with several men."

"And so?"

"And so nobody can guarantee this child is really Mario's."

"Well, how can you prove the contrary?"

"Why do you want to defend a woman of the streets?"

I found his question offensive, arrogant. I was disgusted with the *macho* attitudes of a great many of my superiors, and merely asked him, "Do you have any daughters, Comrade Lieutenant Colonel?"

The political commissar was perplexed, as if the question had come to him from another planet. He flushed and proceeded on the attack: "You're showing a lack of respect, Second Lieutenant."

"It was only a question, Comrade. In your hands is the fate of a being who has the right to live, regardless of who its father is. Please think of Mario's mother—for her the baby's the only thing her son left her before he died."

"All right, I'll see what we can do, but I promise you nothing."

"Thank you, Comrade Lieutenant Colonel," I replied.

I walked to my room, my lips parched, ready to drink a gallon of water, which always seemed to happen to me after a particularly disagreeable conversation. I threw myself on the bed with my boots still on, letting my feet hang off the bottom, worrying about what I'd say to Mario's mother when I saw her next.

———

Weeks went by and each time I visited Mario's mother I had the same news: "They're still waiting for a reply from divisional staff at general headquarters, but I'm sure they're going to grant a pension for the child."

One morning as we were preparing for the day's flights, I saw the political commissar walking across the apron and went up to him. Looking at me as though he suddenly remembered something, he said, "The staff cannot grant a pension for the child; there's not even one for Mario's mother. She's already received the four months' salary, which is all that's normally done in such cases."

I was dumbfounded by what I had heard. I couldn't understand. How was it possible to send only money? No letter, no gesture of kindness, nothing. The grieved mother remained there, alone, with no one to offer her help, if only moral support. That was how the political bureaucracy at divisional staff headquarters worked. I thought angrily, *Bureaucrats, insensitive, incapable. If the top leaders knew about this, things would surely be different! They had even taken the time to send wreaths of flowers to the funeral. But who's going to tell them?*

I was unable to fly that day. During the preflight examination the physician, who was a friend of mine, noticed that my pulse was rapid and my blood pressure slightly above normal.

"Did you sleep well?"

"Yes," I replied dryly.

"I think you're better off not flying today. Don't be angry at me, but you don't seem quite right today so I really should ground you."

"Whatever you like."

I wanted very much to fly that day, to have the tension of flight dissipate my feelings of impotence and growing indignation; but I didn't wish to contradict a friend who was determined not to allow it. I went to a bench near the pilots' cafeteria and watched the fighters take off and land, some of them conducting dive-bombing runs over a white target at the side of the runway.

A MiG-21 flashed the bright blue of its fuselage as it circled the airport to come in for the target. I watched it enter its dive from about 5,000 feet, silently, nearly inverted, searching for the proper angle of attack. Then it leveled its wings and fell from the sky, leaving behind it a thick, gray trail of smoke, which grew increasingly larger with its descent. It looked like a missile hurling itself down an imaginary line into the white cross of the target beside the runway. The MiG leveled out, having completed its dive at an altitude of 700 feet. Then it began to circle for a new attack, proudly displaying its identification number, the afterburner fire still visible in its tail, its deafening roar diminishing as it climbed.

It was one of the rookie pilots, Prado, a young man as modest in his behavior as he was skillful at flying. It was a pleasure to watch him maneuver, with those white clouds of condensation trailing off his wings as he banked under the effect of the g-forces. Prado returned for another dive and I watched him descend surely, beautifully. . . . The dive completed, he began to climb and banked to circle.

But just then somethiing inexplicable happened: The plane flippped over completely and, in an incredible manuever, descended in a circular trajectory, smashing into the ground and hurling thousands of pieces in the opposite direction. A dense smoke arose, forming a black mushroom, followed by an explosion. Prado hadn't had time for anything, not even to think about ejecting. It all took under two seconds from the instant the plane flipped over, and I couldn't believe it. It didn't seem possible that he was dead, someone who had been so full of life just a minute before.

We all started running in the direction of the wreckage but the ramp engineer held us back.

"There's nothing you can do there. Don't you realize he doesn't exist anymore? And there's still a danger of additional explosions. Stay here!"

We stood around in silent groups watching the firemen extinguish the flames that were consuming whatever vegetation surrounded the point of impact. Eventually a bus drove us back to the pilots' area. At dinnertime the waitresses were in tears once again at the loss of another friend in such a short time, but almost no one required their services, preferring to remain in thcir rooms instead.

Once again a commission was formed to transmit the bad news, and it went off on its heavy mission. Another funeral took place in Havana, and another young man was laid to rest in the Armed Forces Pantheon. Next to the tomb, when everyone departed, were two floral wreaths that stood out from the rest.

I took advantage of my time away for the funeral to go see Vicky, and also to pay a visit to Mario's mother. I didn't know how to tell her the bad news about the refusal to grant a pension for the expected grandchild. As I sat down beside her, she looked up at me sadly, saying before I could speak, "Don't worry, my child, the pension won't be needed anymore. The girl had a miscarriage while she was here visiting me."

I kept sllent for a minute, looking into her eyes and wishing to console her, but not finding a word to say.

"Don't trouble yourself about me," she added, "if I ever need anything I'll be sure to let you know."

I left bewildered, feeling, impotent at not being able to give solace to that woman. *Why does life have to hit some people so hard?* I

---

asked myself. *If a God existed there wouldn't be so much injustice in the world. Why was she deprived of the only thing she had?*

I arrived home distressed. The memory of Mario's mother wouldn't leave me. I saw her alone within the walls of her small, dark apartment, wasting away bit by bit from a sorrow she could share with no one.

"But what can *you* do?" Vicky asked me, preoccupied after I explained the reason for my mood.

"That's the worst of it, that I can't do anything. Who can return her son to her?"

Vicky regarded me silently, and I saw compassion in her eyes.

"Forgive me, my love, I shouldn't be telling you all this," I said, pulling her closer to me and stroking her belly, which had grown considerably.

"He'll be born in a month now," Vicky replied, putting her hand over mine and holding it against her.

"Does he kick?"

"Yes, a lot," she answered, smiling.

"Let me listen." I put my ear to her belly and listened there for a long time while she ran her fingers through my hair. Suddenly there was a movement as if something were skidding along the inside of her abdomen. I raised my head in surprise and cried out, "It's true—it moved, it moved!" Whereupon we began laughing, filled with happiness.

I returned to the base and that very first night the sirens sounded an alert. We pilots on duty all rushed to our planes and waited in our cockpits until dawn. Again it was the threat of a North American invasion. Days of extreme tension passed without my leaving the base, almost without communication with Vicky except when I managed to slip away under cover of darkness to call her from town.

One afternoon a soldier came to advise me that a pregnant woman was waiting for me at the entrance to the base, so without imagining who it could be, I followed him back there. As I approached the entrance, I saw Vicky with a package in her hands.

I quickened my pace, almost running up to meet her. "What are you doing here? What's happened?' Barely a week remained before Vicky was to give birth, so her presence there alarmed me in the extreme.

"I needed to see you, you've been locked up on this base for a good twenty days now. I brought you some whipped mammee and a flan I prepared this morning."

I was stupefied. The whip and the custard were my favorite delicacies, but that was hardly a reason for her to come all the way from Havana—a distance of about 180 miles. I glanced down to discover her leather sandal straps sunk into the skin of her swollen feet.

"Are you crazy, Vicky? Whatever possessed you to make a trip like this when you're about to give birth?"

"I had to see you," she replied.

I could just imagine her walking to the bus terminal in Havana early that morning, waiting patiently for an available seat, then arriving in Santa Clara and spending hours standing waiting there under a burning sun for the unpredicted local bus that would take her to the base.

"Shit! Look how swollen your feet are!" I finally exploded.

"Please don't act like this."

"You think it makes me happy to see you bringing these things here in the state you're in?"

"Please, let's not argue," Vicky pleaded once again, her eyes filling with tears, which made me ashamed at the rude way I'd treated her.

"Forgive me," I said, embracing her. "It's just that I'm terrified something could happen to you on such a long, uncertain journey."

We went together to the home of Vicky's cousin who lived in Santa Clara, where Vicky insisted I drink the mammee and eat the flan. As I did so she watched me, smiling, a gleam of satisfaction in her eyes.

"You like it?"

"Delicious," I told her.

The next morning we managed to find a taxi, whose driver promised to take her straight home.

"See you soon," I said before kissing her. And then when she was seated in the cab I added, "But please, don't do this again."

I returned to the base thinking about Vicky. I felt guilty about her trip, for not having gone to see her in so long a time, for the threat of war, which hung over us but never arrived.

Luckily my superiors hadn't discovered my absence this time, either, so I didn't have to give explanations to anyone. But one thing they *did* know: my wife was going to give birth at any moment. When the state of alert was finally lifted, I requested leave to be with Vicky at the birth.

"Impossible at such a time: There are already too many pilots away from the base," was the reply.

One evening I was called to the telephone to speak to our command post. They said they'd gotten word from air force headquarters that somebody had called in to say that my wife had been taken to the maternity hospital with labor pains. I couldn't sleep at all that night just waiting for sunrise to be able to request leave from my squadron leader. As always we assembled at seven-thirty on the parade ground behind headquarters, and from my position in formation I requested permission to address him. When it was granted, I explained.

"My wife's in the hospital about to give birth."

"So what?" Major Felipe retorted coldly.

"I'd like to be with her, that's all."

"We have no midwives here. The child will be born without any problem and you'll see it when you get a leave."

The reply stung me, with its harsh, humiliating tone, and for a moment I felt ashamed in front of my buddies, to be so weak as to demand repeatedly to be with my wife at childbirth. That night, the ninth of July 1981, I got another call from command post. Vicky's sister had informed headquarters in Havana that my wife had given birth to an eight-pound boy and both mother and son were absolutely fine. My comrades hastened to congratulate me, slapping me on the back and assuring me that I'd soon be seeing my wife and son. I went to my room and fell on the bed without undressing, my boots hanging off the edge as always when I wanted to give my thoughts free rein. And I took an imaginary journey to see them that lasted until dawn.

I was brought back by a few soft knocks at the door.

"Come in!"

The door half opened and Eloy peeked in. I jumped up quickly to stand at attention, but Eloy stopped me with a wave of the hand.

"I hear your wife gave birth. I came to congratulate you and to tell you that you've got two weeks' vacation."

"Thank you, Comrade Lieutenant Colonel!" I exclaimed, over-joyed. And in a few minutes I was already on my way to Havana, imagining my first encounter with this infant I'd already loved for so long a time: my son!

I arrived in Havana shortly after noon and searched around desperately for some flowers for Vicky. But in vain, and in the last shop I looked I was told that the flowers they received were destined solely for mortuary wreaths. Disappointed, I then made the rounds of the stores in search of a suitable present, but found nothing I could purchase without a rationing booklet.

At last, tired and sad as I walked to the hospital, I saw in a poorly kept garden before a house a single faded rose growing among the weeds. Jumping over the fence without the slightest thought about being caught stealing it, I plucked it and continued joyfully on my way to Vicky and my son.

When I entered the room, Vicky was lying in bed, attended by her mother and mine, whose backs were to the door. Vicky was the first to see me, and responded with an exclamation. I kissed both our mothers and approached her without saying a word, holding the flower behind my back. We looked at each other quietly and after I kissed her I offered the pale rose to her.

Vicky half-closed her eyes and, peering up at me with satisfaction, tilted her head and shook it gently from side to side as she held the rose close to her breast. She reached for my hand and squeezed it, frowning in a special way that meant thank you. Then she looked down at the little metal cradle next to her bed, saying, "Poor thing, they had to amputate a tiny fleshy protuberance he had on his left pinky."

The baby was sleeping peacefully on his back, his long legs outstretched and his arms resting on his chest, his right hand curled around the bandaged finger in a touching gesture as though protecting it.

"It must have hurt."

"It was very small—they tied it off with a string. I heard him let out a cry as they took it off. The doctor says he's the picture of health now, and there'll be no scar."

"Did you register his birth yet?"

"Yesterday, after the birth."

"What name?"

"Reyniel, like we agreed."

"Can I pick him up?"

"Of course. . . . I have to feed him."

As if he understood what we were talking about, Reyniel suddenly awoke, screaming his lungs out, and nervously I took him in my arms, rocking him awkwardly to quiet him down while Vicky prepared to nurse him. Our mothers were laughing together and when the boy finally seized Vicky's breast, with an appetite that seemed to me voracious, she burst out laughing and regarded me with mocking eyes.

"What's going on, why are you all laughing?" I asked.

"At your frightened face while you were holding a crying baby."

We all laughed as Reyniel suckled away desperately, his fingers clamped on to his mother's breast.

"This child seems to want to drink up all the milk in the world," I commented, happy at being a father and the husband of the tenderest mother I'd ever seen. I spent the rest of the afternoon in the company of Vicky and the baby, sitting next to her and holding Reyniel in my arms while he slept peacefully.

The next day I accompanied Vicky home. A group of neighborhood friends we'd known since our engagement were waiting at the curb to welcome the little one. And the three of us spent a marvelous vacation together without leaving the house. I watched Vicky nursing this little glutton punctually every three hours, after he'd give a strident signal of his hunger with the accuracy of a clock. And Reyniel cried, sucked, slept, defecated, and urinated in an unending cycle that we all shared with him, making him the center of whatever was done in the house.

Months went by and Reyniel grew vigorously, but I saw him no more than once or twice a month until some wonderful news arrived in May: I'd been assigned one of the new apartments just completed by the entrance to the base. I went quickly to Havana with the news, and after giving up our old apartment, we loaded a truck with our few belongings—clothes, an old repainted cradle, a mattress given to us by my in-laws, a chafing dish—and the three of us with Vicky's mother went happily to our new home.

—

And so we began our lives in that small prefabricated apartment, sleeping on the mattress placed next to Reyniel's cradle on the granite-tiled floor, Vicky spending long hours cooking with our makeshift chafing dish, while at the base I obtained a coupon allowing us to buy our own bed. Our life was a happy one despite its primitiveness: We didn't have even the most elementary furniture in our home. But we had our first opportunity of sharing most nights together, and I could now watch my son grow. At last the bed came and Vicky and I would put Reyniel on it and play with him, overwhelming him with kisses and caresses, to which he responded with a laughter that gushed forth like a spring of joy.

In the afternoons my greatest pleasure was to take the little glutton in my arms and lull him to sleep, whistling a gentle melody by Rachmaninoff while he looked at me smiling and gurgling, as if to say "Daddy." Then, overcome by the melody and sleepiness, his eyelids would begin to close; and initially he'd resist, staring up at me, before finally falling asleep. Then, very gently so as not to wake him, I'd put him in his cradle while Vicky looked on smilingly from the threshold of the door.

We were so happy in our cozy apartment, which we called our nest, that we hardly missed having a television or refrigerator, nor was I troubled by the wearying trips to the well of a neighboring peasant on my way home each afternoon, walking up the four flights with two gigantic buckets filled with water—water that almost never got to us the normal way. Each day began and ended with the same romantic joy, seeing Vicky and Reyniel sending me off to work and welcoming me back, waving at me from the balcony. On the few days I had off, Reyniel would wake us up by shaking the safety railing of his cradle until we took him into our bed. Then he'd smile with satisfaction as I took him in my arms, lying him on my chest while Vicky went to prepare his bottle, because it wouldn't take long for his smiles to change to tears, reminding us that his mood was dependent on his stomach's satisfaction.

One day while I was on guard duty the base commander came to see me. Entering the room where another pilot and I were waiting in our flight gear, ready to take off at a moment's notice from command post, Eloy motioned us to sit down and took a seat beside us. He asked after Vicky, the baby, the rest of my family, my state of health . . . and I realized he wanted to tell me something but couldn't find the right words. Finally he asked me to come outside with him, and we walked until we stood in the shade of a pine tree in front of the guardhouse. Then, putting his hand on my shoulder, he started to explain. "The war in Angola is taking an unexpected turn. The South African air force has made several incursions into Angolan territory and we don't have a sufficient number of pilots there. They've asked for reinforcements. Our base is to send two. Nearly all the oldest ones are there already; and of the younger ones only Pastrana, Isidoro, and you are ready for real combat." He paused and then added, "Isidoro's just been taken to the hospital with a case of hepatitis."

"When do I leave?"

"This afternoon a transport plane will take you and Pastrana to Havana. Tomorrow you'll leave for Angola. In a few minutes another pilot should be arriving to relieve you of your post. You'll then have a few hours to say good-bye to your wife and son."

Vicky burst into tears when I brought her the news and began pacing through the apartment, repeating in a low voice, "But why you?"

Pastrana and I were flown to Havana that afternoon. At air force headquarters they took some photographs of us to prepare passports immediately.

"Be here tomorrow at ten, ready to leave," the divisional staff officer told us.

Vicky accompanied me the next morning. In front of headquarters our group of pilots was assembling, prepared to leave in a matter of minutes for the war in Africa. Pastrana was with us the whole time, playing with Reyniel and joking with Vicky, who was making a huge effort to hold back her tears.

At a signal everyone began boarding a bus, which would take us to the airport. Reyniel had fallen asleep in my arms and I handed him to Vicky, giving him a last kiss on his soft cheek. We hugged each other with the baby pressed between our bodies, while I promised Vicky that all would be well, that I'd return soon. Vicky was trembling but didn't speak.

We finally separated and from the window I saw her holding Reyniel with one arm and waving good-bye with the other as a tear ran down her cheek. The bus pulled out slowly, and Vicky and Reyniel were becoming smaller, as the war insinuated itself between us.

Chapter 7

—

A n g o l a

Various outlandish anecdotes about this country in the African jungle served as our major amusement during the fourteen-hour trip to Luanda. The ferocious leopard capable of quartering two men at once before they had time to draw their guns; the death-dealing serpent "Three Steps," small and camouflaged, lying in ambush to bring instant death to the victim before he could take three steps; the parasites in the rivers and lakes that caused an irreversible and monstrous swelling of the genitals; the fly that deposited its larvae under a man's skin, which later would be crawling with worms. Our ignorance created the myth that everything was dangerous, so by the time we arrived in that beautiful land, we were afraid of the very air we breathed.

The plane circled over Luanda and through its windows we discovered the singular panorama of that city surrounded by a barren, copper-colored countryside as arid and rough as its imposing coastline, which stretched out before the infinite Atlantic. After landing we taxied around the international airport, among combat planes and helicopters reminding us of the war, toward the small terminal designated for Cuban troops entering and leaving the country. A euphoric group of Cubans dressed in civilian clothes like us headed in the opposite direction and crowded into the crude waiting room, where a captain of the so-called Cuban Military Mission in Angola asked for our passports.

"Climb on the trucks outside, which will take you to the reception center at Fotungo. Tomorrow you'll leave for your designated units," the captain told us as he collected our passports and threw them into a box, where they'd remain until we returned to Cuba. From now on the aluminum dog tags hanging from our necks stamped with our numbers served as our sole identification.

Our trucks got underway filled with soldiers in tourist clothes, passing first through the dusty streets of Luanda, which were inundated with troops in camouflage uniforms with AKM and Y-3 rifles slung over their shoulders, walking gloomily among the multitude of naked and dirty children busily playing, stomachs swollen by parasitosis. Fotungo was a 100 percent Cuban camp, which reminded me of those I was in during the School in the Fields from my school days; several rectangular buildings with asbestos ceilings sheltering the familiar cots with jute cloth stretched over the frame as a mattress. I climbed into my rustic bed and, tired from the trip and the tension at the prospect of the war, I tried to get some sleep. A group of soldiers returning to Cuba the next day and sharing the dormitory with us stayed awake drowning with animated conversation the anxiety of two years of dreams and plans reserved for that moment when they'd again be with their loved ones. And I was sleeping, sunk in the depths of fatigue without the voices of my comrades bothering me in the least, dreaming of being in that land fraught with dangers, when I felt gliding down my back a "Three Steps" serpent. I awoke with a cry and jumped to the ground from my upper bunk, confusing the animated talkers who regarded me with surprise when I pointed in the direction of my bed while exclaiming in terror: "A Three Steps, a Three Steps!" Which only made them laugh, and then I saw in the hands of the one who was lying awake on the lower part of the bunkbed a little wooden stick with which he was absentmindedly rubbing the jute on which I'd been sleeping, moving in a curve that had seemed to me the trail of a serpent.

Early in the morning we got on the transport plane that took us to our final destination—Lubango, a town with a magnificent climate, built just at the eastern edge of a gigantic meseta that rose to more than 6,000 feet above sea level, extending like a horseshoe of steep abysses around it and leaving the east open to the vast African jungle. To the south of the meseta, the desert of Mosámede, and to the west, after overcoming its almost vertical fall, a beautiful plain extending as far as the Atlantic coast. At the southern limit of the city, just at the edge of the steep, rocky headland of more than 1,000 feet of meseta, the statue of Christ looked toward the rising sun in the African heartland. It was in this relatively plain space, open to the east, that the air base was situated like a gigantic plate of asphalt and concrete, at the limits of which were the regiments of the antiaircraft artillery and supply depots. Behind the Christ figure, on the same summit of the cliff, was the radio-technical battalion with its radar installations ready to detect South African air incursions. A battalion of tanks housed in underground bunkers dug by hand in the midst of the jungle some fifteen kilometers (nine miles) to the south and the radio-technical units at Virey and Chibemba, out in the desert, formed with headquarters, which was situated at the eastern limits of the city, the bulk of the Cuban troops defending the region.

To these forces were also added the hundreds of teachers, nurses, doctors, and engineers comprising the Cuban civilian personnel. The latter lived in modern apartment buildings, which, bordering the asphalt streets of the city, gave the impression that Lubango was one of the most prosperous cities of Angola. Even so, at the time, the presence of hundreds of Angolan and Cuban troops carrying auto-matic rifles gave it a sad, desolate prospect, with no charm other than the occasional visits from tribesmen, who would enter the town on weekends dressed in their curious costumes.

The higher brass and the pilots were the only military personnel permitted to live in the city, and we occupied a lovely three-story house in the southeastern residential district, which most likely had once belonged to some wealthy Portuguese. The house was situated close to the railway link to the port of Mosámede, and at the edge of the tracks was a candle factory that blew its siren at five in the afternoon every workday to announce the end of the shift.

It was the custom in those days for the newly arrived to get their hazing by running for the cellar of the house when the factory siren blew and, to deceive them, somebody would yell, "Air raid!" to give the impression of a South African air strike. And we would all break into boisterous laughter at the expression on the faces of the recent arrivals. It was like looking at ourselves in a mirror, taking us back in time to the day we ourselves had arrived, to see that anticipation bordering on fear of a never-before-experienced bombardment.

The days went by and the war turned out to be different from what we'd imagined. Instead of combat, we spent our time awaiting the announced enemy attack, which, as in Cuba, never happened. But the isolated incursions by South African pilots on reconnoitering missions, who were detected almost always just as they were leaving our airspace, resulted in our spending various days in a state of total alert, sleeping in the airport's inhospitable underground shelter. In the meantime some of the higher brass were often out filling their suitcases with articles unobtainable in Cuba, and would only visit us long enough to inspect our rooms and toss at us a list of reprimands over trivial details, instead of making an effort to establish a bit of simple, human contact, so vital in a war, with the men under their command. Like them we lived in the city, and thus came to witness firsthand what ordinary troops assigned to the battlefield could not: their luxurious living quarters staffed by Angolan service personnel to satisfy their private needs, their parties, for which they squandered food that the troops were lacking, as well as the quotas of alcoholic beverages destined for the soldiers. It was a thoroughly corrupt way of life, the opposite of that of a revolutionary and a military leader. It was not uncommon to hear the pilots referring to their leaders as the "bourgeoisie," to express disgust at their behavior.

One day an engineer friend came by to bid us farewell, having completed his tour of duty and on his way back to Cuba. As I recall, he left us some copies of *Playboy* magazine, which he'd kept for a long time and which were later passed around among the shocked and curious pilots, who were amazed at the graphic nudity of the models and felt the excitement one inevitably experiences at the first sight of something prohibited. Those magazines were soon the favorite reading material of the group, who guarded them jealously and discreetly under their mattresses.

Not long afterward a Counterintelligence official showed up to search for the magazines, since some stool pigeon had informed him that the pilots were having ideological problems from reading publications that spread imperialistic immorality. An investigation followed, conducted by the political branch and Counterintelligence, in order to ascertain where the magazines had come from, and after many questions and self-criticisms, which we were all obliged to undergo for having succumbed to such immoral reading material, the magazines were confiscated and we were threatened with severe punishment should they ever again discover obscene material in our possession. The incident left us all with a disagreeable sensation of embarrassment, which we could not explain simply as resulting from the presence of the by-then infamous copies of *Playboy*.

October went by and we flew very little due to a radar malfunction. We were troubled by our lack of training for warfare, which might descend upon us at any moment.

On one of those useless days when we spent our standby alert seated around the table playing cards, the alarm suddenly sounded and the pair on standby alert was ordered to take off. Marrero and Ortiz, two of the youngest pilots, ran to their planes and took off immediately, while Ley and I assumed posts in the cockpits of two MiG-21s.

Hardly had we switched on the radio when we heard the voice of the flight controller at command post directing them to seek out some enemy South African fighters approaching from the south and instructing them to switch radio frequencies. The minutes of waiting in our cockpits passed interminably under a merciless sun. Then the voice of the controller crackled in our earphones:

"Three-twenty-six and -twenty-seven. Engine start, taxi, immediate takeoff!"

While the ignition cycle of the engines began, our faithful mechanics, always nervous about the impending combat from which we might not return, ran to strip the covers off the missiles and remove the parking blocks, then signaled us with an energetic wave of the arms that we could begin taxiing. We headed swiftly for the dusty taxiways, raising a cloud of reddish dust, which trailed us to the runway, where we hurriedly took off without even pausing to make a final instrument check. Barely had we left the ground when the flight controller instructed us to head south at an airspeed of 1,200 kilometers per hour.

The same old story, I told myself, remembering our countless attempts to intercept South African Mirage jets, which we could never catch, as we flew at very low altitude toward the heart of the desert, our canopies enveloped in a white stream of rarefied air due to our high velocity.

Then they ordered us to patrol the area, and with no further incident other than talking over the radio, we returned to the base when we had just enough fuel left to do so. After landing we taxied past the shelters housing Marrero and Ortiz's fighters, where we saw a swarm of mechanics and pilots gathered around them.

"They turned them into colanders," my technician told me when I opened the canopy of my cockpit.

"What did you say?"

"That Ortiz and Marrero were saved by a miracle. They were perforated like sieves by gunfire from the Mirages. I still don't know how they managed to—"

I didn't wait for him to finish the sentence but, waving him off the boarding ladder, where he was blocking my way, I jumped from the cockpit and ran in the direction of the two damaged MiG-21s. I heard Ley panting behind me as we arrived at the first MiG. Marrero was standing next to it, talking calmly with a group of comrades.

"What happened?" Ley and I asked him almost in unison.

Marrero stared at us, surprised that we knew nothing and, nodding his head in the direction of the plane, said in a subdued voice, "See for yourselves."

There was his fighter, like a wounded, faithful charger, with dozens of deformed aluminum strips protruding from its fuselage like pieces of skin stripped away by the impact of the explosions. We walked around the aircraft struck with horror at its wounds, as though it were a dying friend, until we arrived back at Marrero, who lowered his head in shame, saying, "They surprised us from behind."

"You're lucky you're still alive. . . . That's the important thing," was all I could say as I gave him a pat on the shoulder.

"Don't worry, you'll get your chance to even the score," Ley added, trying to lift Marrero's spirits.

From that instant our lives were jolted by an invasion of military brass arriving to investigate the incident, since it had violated standard procedure.

Marrero and Ortiz were young pilots without sufficient experience to be on their own during actual combat missions; yet they'd been designated as partners for standby alert in order to favor older pilots who'd been complaining about how often they were assigned that job. The head of the base, Colonel Bilardel, was demoted to lieutenant colonel and relieved of his command, and new regulations were made to ensure that younger pilots were paired with more experienced ones during standby alert.

It was painful now to see our formerly arrogant ex-commander wandering gloomily through the pilots' quarters to which he'd been forced to move, without anything to say to his former subordinates and with an expression of constant worry etched on his face. He had fallen into disgrace.

Meanwhile I continued asking myself, without understanding, why Ley and I hadn't been alerted by radio about the aerial combat our comrades had been confronting by themselves. Perhaps the pervasive paranoia then, for observing the rules of radio communication and not making information available to enemy listeners, was why the complement on duty at command post didn't inform us about this important fact, of which the enemy was certainly well aware.

—

Vicky remained for some time at Santa Clara, where she was unable to work because there was no spot open for Reyniel in any of the local day-care centers, despite her countless efforts and the preferential treatment she was supposed to receive as a result of having the head of family absent in the Angolan War. Finally, sad and disappointed at the lack of assistance, she went to live in Matanzas with my parents, who managed to help her find a day-care center for Reyniel and a job as a dentist.

We wrote almost daily, just as we had during my time in the Soviet Union, and once again I racked my brain composing ardent love poems, which I sent her to keep alive the flame that united us, striving to make her and my mother believe that I was not in any danger. She never stopped asking me to take care of myself, and told me that when she showed my photo to Reyniel, he'd get all excited, opening his eyes wide and waving his little hands. Then she would tell him, "This is Daddy," and he'd repeat, "Daddy, Daddy!" One day, as I was opening one of Vicky's letters, a sheet of paper caught my eye, with colored lines made by an uncoordinated hand. On the bottom was a brief note written by Vicky: *Daddy, this is my first work in nursery school. I love you very much, Reyniel.* An unbearable knot lodged in my throat, and a comrade who saw my eyes moistening asked me worriedly, "Bad news?"

"No, only . . . I just recieved the most important letter of my life."

At last we began flying again, and this time they put new training plans into practice to avoid repeating the mistakes that had led to the surprise attack against Marrero and Ortiz. From now on aerial combat exercises would be conducted spontaneously, without the mock enemy's informing his opponent beforehand about which maneuvers he should take to defend himself.

One day I was designated to direct landings from a mobile control tower placed at the beginning of the runway, and from it I watched Merino and Pastrana take off in a trainer plane behind Bober, an experienced pilot at the helm of a jet fighter. It was their mission to carry out a free-style aerial combat exercise.

"Three-forty, in zone five, requesting authorization to begin the exercise," Bober radioed in just a few minutes after takeoff.

"Cleared, three-forty . . ."

The routine followed, with MiGs taking off and landing before me, and then I heard the frightened voice of Bober over the radio, saying, "Three-forty-three, three-forty . . ."

Silence.

"Answer, three-forty-three, three-forty calling you."

A longer pause this time, and I had a presentiment that something serious was going to happen.

"Cougar, three-forty," called Bober to control tower.

"Go ahead, three-forty."

"Forty-three in trouble . . ." I heard the voice of Bober, hesitant, wavering terribly, "Aircraft forty-three has gone down. . . ."

An interminable pause followed, during which my mind traveled back to Cuba, Pastrana's young parents, Merino's wife and children. Other pilots in the air had access to the same radio frequency, but they didn't speak, nor did I, nor did the flight controller. It seemed as if we had all divined the worst, yet didn't want to face it.

"I don't see any signs of life around the explosion," Bober continued in a tremulous voice while my mind returned again to Cuba, remembering the day Pastrana and I met at air force headquarters for the departure to Angola, remembering how he had played with Reyniel, how together we had bid farewell to our families, how we had listened with astonishment to the outlandish annecdotes others told about this country during our flight.

The Search and Rescue helicopter took off, heading in the direction of the accident, and the last of the planes landed silently, our routine animation over the radio vanishing and each report from the returning pilots sounding stark and sad. Once the last of the fighters arrived, we gathered on the flight apron surrounding Bober as we waited for the helicopter to return. He told us what had happened, imitating the maneuvers of the planes with his hands:

"I was like this . . . making a pronounced turn at low altitude, and I saw them behind me simulating an attack . . . then I rolled the plane like this, downward, to circle in the opposite direction. . . . I looked for them again but I couldn't find them. . . . I continued to turn and then spotted the explosion. I think they stalled or they lost spatial orientation . . . they couldn't have had time to eject. . . ."

As Bober talked we listened, overwhelmed, observing the extreme pallor of his face and the unusual trembling of his hands, and we soon heard the helicopter already on its way back. The first to get out was Captain Romero, our squadron leader, who with rapid footsteps came over to us.

"It was horrible," he reported. "They smashed into the foot of a wall of jagged rocks one hundred and sixty-five feet high as they tried to come out of a free fall. They knew they didn't have sufficient altitude and they ejected, but it was already too late. The catapults functioned well enough, but there wasn't enough time. Merino's seat was the first to go, and his body continued the trajectory of the plane while the parachute began to unfold behind him. . . . His body slammed into the rocks at more than four hundred and eighty miles an hour, splattering him like a bird's egg smashed against the pavement. Pastrana fell with the aircraft; his seat started its separation from the cockpit just as the plane hit the ground."

Romero spoke in a daze, detailing the Dantesque scene, which allowed us to reconstruct events, as if he wished to alleviate the horror he felt by sharing it with us.

"When we landed we saw wild dogs carrying off some of their remains. We had to scare them off by firing a couple of rounds."

That night we held a wake at the officers' club for the remains of our comrades, and the following day we accompanied them to the transport plane that would take them to Luanda to be buried in the cemetery for Cuban troops. As we lifted the rustic coffins into the aircraft, a squadron of MiGs returning from Menongue made a low pass over us in a solemn farewell, and I thought of Pastrana happy and alive in those years that I knew him.

It was Saturday, December 8, 1982, and we all returned to the pilots' lodgings to drown the grief that possessed us in the alcohol that was used for the MiGs' radar cooling system. And I drank that mixture of alcohol and water, amid all of our anecdotes, numbing the pain with each swallow. Later someone suggested we all go to a party in the building for the Cobras, as the female nurses and teachers who lived there were called, so we marched off there together in search of a less nostalgic atmosphere.

It was there that I first became acquainted with some of the merits of being an internationalist father or mother—commanders and subordinate officers in combat fatigues competed on the same level for a woman's affections. A different world, totally removed from the one we'd left behind in Cuba, took shape before my eyes. There were couples there who acted like husband and wife, attending public events arm in arm, living together like families and at a certain hour of the afternoon sitting at opposite ends of the table to write to their spouses in Cuba, accomplices in a silent pact that they would not recognize each other once they returned home.

I recalled the images seen before on Cuban television, extolling the merit of the young mother who leaves her recently born child to go work on behalf of other peoples, or some military commander speaking in party meetings about the ethics of fatherhood, or about the famous woman doctor from Matanzas who liked to stroll through the park with her grandchildren. There they all were, showing not the slightest discretion, publicly sharing the romance justified by war. And I recalled the day we were reprimanded for the immorality of reading *Playboy*, and the years lived in the Soviet Union, trying to understand if what was important was what we did or what we said, and discovering ethics in words but not in conduct.

We returned to our quarters in the early hours of morning, and I couldn't sleep despite the alcohol. Staring at the ceiling, I searched for myself, lost in a world of mixed truths and lies, without finding myself. I asked, *Why pretend to be what we aren't?*

The answer came, *If we proclaim a morality that we violate later without the slightest bit of discretion, it's because we don't believe in it.*

Then why do we disparage those who say frankly they don't believe in that morality?

If at least we attempted to hide our sins.

No, my thoughts wouldn't permit me to sleep even though I was exhausted. I got up and went to the small lounge where there was a pile of old periodicals. Perhaps reading would help me to reconcile myself with sleep.

I selected a copy of *Granma*, the most important daily in Cuba, and the official organ of the party's Central Committee. There was not a single reference to events in Angola. It seemed as if the country was not involved in a war thousands of miles away. I was already setting it aside when an editorial attracted my attention: Armando Valladares, the dangerous terrorist imprisoned in Cuba, whom CIA propaganda had made into an unhappy, invalid poet, was to be freed at the request of the French government.

> *The Revolution is powerful and generous. If the French government wants to clean our sewer, let them! They can have the fake poet, but he will have to walk to the plane on his own two feet!*

Thus the editorial concluded, remarking that the supposed paralysis of the terrorist was faked.

—

The months passed, and despite the relative peace in which we were living, the pilots' vacations remained suspended, and some comrades had gone months beyond the date when they should have traveled to Cuba. First Lieutenant Alba, a good-natured close friend of mine, was one of the most severely affected, having been several times ordered back to his unit while he was on the point of boarding a plane home. Thus Alba lived in a constant state of anxiety to see his wife and daughter, and we would hear him in the night wandering sleeplessly through the house, muttering a string of obscenities over his bad luck.

At last the longed for day arrived when Alba was to leave for Cuba, and once again we gave him our letters so that they'd arrive more quickly at their destinations. A young doctor from Alba's hometown arrived to ask Alba a favor: Would he take a large suitcase full of clothes to the doctor's family? Noble as always, Alba agreed to the favor, but he was incensed to find out that the clothing came from United Nations' aid shipments to the Angolan people.

"What nerve!" he exclaimed upon learning of the habitual practice of many of our internationalist heroes, of trafficking in cigarettes, soap, and even cooking wine sold as whiskey to naive Angolans, all in fraudulent exchange to obtain articles unavailable in Cuba.

—

One night, Alba arrived with his eyes wide open in fright.

"Alba, what happened?" we asked.

"I saw a murder, a murder in cold blood!"

"A what?"

"A killing, man, and in cold blood. Look how I'm shaking," he added, hastily showing me his trembling hands, evidently under the effects of a powerful shock. Then he continued, "I went to the Soviet quarters, invited by some engineers . . . everyone in the apartment was drinking. . . . Then they invited me to the apartment across the way, where the colonel in charge of Soviet advisers in the south was drinking with an Angolan civil engineer."

"And?"

"The two began arguing over politics, but they didn't seem angry, just of different opinions. Suddenly the colonel pulled out his pistol and fired at the Angolan, hitting him in the forehead and killing him instantly."

"You're kidding."

"I swear!" Alba insisted, striking his chest with his fists.

"But just like that, for no reason whatsoever?"

"I ran out of there, and the guy started firing in all directions until he used up all the bullets, and then other Soviet officers went in and subdued him. They took him to the base. I think they've locked him up in the underground bunker where we were posted for our watch."

"Why there?"

"The Soviets don't want anybody to find out what happened, and plan to get him out of there early in the morning, before the Angolan police start investigating."

Early the next morning I began my standby-alert shift. Upon arriving at the bunker I noted that its entrance was guarded by a couple of corpulent Soviet soldiers. They let us go in without comment, and we saw the colonel assassin sleeping peacefully on one of our beds while two more men remained seated behind the table where we usually played cards. At mid-morning a Soviet AN-12 transport plane arrived from Luanda with food supplies for the Soviet troops, and when it was about to depart on its return flight, the Soviets put the colonel into a car, which conducted him to the head of the runway, where the aircraft was waiting with its cargo door open. Minutes later the plane was lost in the sky, carrying off with it the most important proof of the murder the Angolan police could ever hope to find.

The tedium of inaction and our tension over combat that never occurred began to relax the sense of precaution that had restrained us in the beginning; and we began to go into the jungle in search of adventures on the weekends. But it seemed that the famous African marauders had abandoned those neighboring outposts and we would return exhausted in the afternoons without having experienced the seductive excitement that danger produces.

I was unaware at the time that in Cuba Reyniel was crying disconsolately every night, and that Vicky and my parents were driven to desperation without being able to determine the cause of it. It was Amadita, a pediatrician friend, who told Vicky that the boy was crying because of his father's absence. And they kept the matter a secret from me so as not to torment me from afar, since they knew that I could not renounce the mission the government had sent me on.

One day we were called upon to strike positions of the UNITA troops, which had attacked various Cuban food-supply convoys. We were to destroy their airfield, built in the heart of the jungle and through which they were receiving supplies from South Africa, as well as their headquarters and supply depots serving the troops stationed in the area.

The brigade commander warned, "You'd better watch your tails. UNITA [National Union for the Total Independence of Angola] has succeeded in getting ahold of ground-to-air missiles, which they captured during a recent attack on Angolan forces. Furthermore, according to intelligence reports, you can count on sufficient antiaircraft artillery to repel your attack."

We took off before dawn without utilizing our radios in order not to invite enemy radio detection, and following our squadron leader, we flew just above ground level toward our objective. A very thin cover of mist blanketed part of the region when we reached the target, but obsessed by the possibility of having been detected, our leader preferred to exaggerate the poor visibility and return with our full the stony earth. And in my desperation I felt like the most impotent creature in the world.

"My daughter . . . my daughter . . ." he whispered, appearing to be delirious.

"They're coming, you'll see, we're going to get you to the hospital."

He took my hand again, but this time he didn't look at me.

"My little girl . . . I'll never see you again. . . ." he lamented, and I could no longer tell if he was coughing or crying.

I wanted to reassure him, but he no longer heard me. He died minutes later, as we were taking him to the hospital. I took the number off his dogtags to find out who this soldier was for whom I'd been a last friend. I wanted to meet his daughter, to show her a little tenderness when I returned to Cuba. But it wasn't possible. When I called the divisional staff of the military mission, they told me that any information regarding the dead was confidential. I explained my reasons, and they reiterated, "Don't be worried, the families of our martyrs will always be cared for by the Revolution."

—

After my tenth month in Angola I became tormented by the idea that Reyniel could forget me, that he might not recognize me and would reject me as a stranger when I returned. Four months had passed from the date I was supposed to have had vacation leave in Cuba, and even though pilots' departures had at last been permitted, they couldn't let us all go at once; thus I was awaiting Ley's return so that I might depart. He finally arrived at the appointed time, and I was waiting for him with my duffel bag on my shoulder, ready to leave. But first we had a brief conversation.

"Did you visit Pastrana's parents?" I asked him.

"Yes, I brought them his belongings," he answered, looking me in the eye and then, changing the expression on his face, he added, "You know? They went to deliver the news of Pastrana's death to his parents, but no one was home . . . so they left the message with the president of the Block Defense Committee."

I was speechless with astonishment at what Ley had just told me. He paused, letting out a sigh and shaking his head, then exploded: "What shits!"

"I can't believe it."

"Well, believe it."

Thinking indignantly about the bureaucrats at general headquarters in Havana, I boarded the plane that would take me to Luanda, and butterflies in my stomach continued bothering me during the three days I had to submit to preventative treatment against malaria before returning to Cuba. It was the same tickling sensation that had as-

saulted me since my schooldays whenever I was about to be reunited with my loved ones.

After landing I called Vicky from the military unit where we were housed while being tested for malaria, and when I arrived home, the whole neighborhood was out to welcome me. Vicky ran up to me first, crossing the street to throw herself around my neck, crying, and we remained in an embrace a few minutes.

Then my mother-in-law walked over to us carrying Reyniel in her arms, and he wrestled free of her and ran toward me, reaching out his little arms and calling, "Daddy, Daddy!"

I reached down and swept my child up into my arms until I was hugging him against my chest, and I felt his little hands pounding my back while he cried in my ear, "Daddy!"

Some neighbors were already wiping away their tears and I ran into the house, hiding my face in his little body, ashamed of my own tears, which I didn't want to be seen. There I wept in the arms of my family, as I hadn't done since I was a child; and Reyniel watched me tenderly, kissing me and wiping my tears away with his small hands, saying, "There, there . . . I love you so much, Daddy."

We went for that vacation to our favorite spot, and Vicky and I went out the first night to a cabaret. I drank so much that I suffered my only hangover. And I was so ashamed the next morning that I quizzed Vicky, wanting to know what I'd done the night before.

"I never saw you like that. But don't worry, you behaved very well. You spent the whole time talking about looking for some soldier's daughter . . . but you didn't know their names. Who are they?"

"I don't know," I answered, shunning the recollection of that poor dying soldier. "Probably I was remembering that Alba had asked me to visit his wife and daughter."

And the days passed swiftly at the beach, teaching Reyniel how to hold his breath underwater, the child filling our lives with happiness with that smile which only he knew how to give us. I returned to Angola at the end of the month, after witnessing Reyniel's innocent good-bye: a kiss and a smile, waving his little hand in the distance. Vicky looked at me sadly, saying only, "Come back."

—

Upon my arrival in Angola I found out that things had changed for the worse. A regiment of Angolan troops had been surrounded by UNITA forces in the region of Cuito Carnavalle, and they had many wounded and had run out of food and medicine. Eight of us pilots were then summoned to Menongue. There a Colonel Martínez Puente met us, and later that night he explained our mission:

"You'll strike UNITA's positions surrounding the Angolan regiment in order to keep the enemy pinned down for the amount of time

July came and we prepared to celebrate one of the most important Cuban holidays—the attack on the Moncada Barracks by Fidel Castro and a group of youths on the twenty-sixth of July 1953. An air show had been organized to celebrate the occasion, and from early in the day the people of the city began gathering in the stadium, over which there would be the parachute jumps and aerial acrobatics of the MiGs.

Roberto Hernández was the pilot designated to perform the stunt flying at low altitude above a landscape surrounded by mountains, and Ley and I were to accompany him to the airfield in order to monitor his flight from the control tower. On the way there Roberto chatted with us about the little time remaining for him to complete his tour of duty and return to Cuba. His wife and daughters awaited him anxiously in Camagüey, and he was looking forward to taking them to the beach for a few weeks.

From the tower we watched him take off and circle cleanly at nearly ground level as he swept over the stadium. He made one, two passes, then he began to carry out the sequence of vertical figures that he'd mapped out for himself—loop, chandelle, nosedive, reverse—and I watched the dot of the plane in the sky descending swiftly, nearly grazing the mountains as on his previous passes.

I think he's going to crash into those mountains . . . no, no, it's just an illusion of perspective because of the distance . . . no—no!

It wasn't an illusion; Roberto's plane had descended nearly grazing the headland of the plateau and struck against it almost at its base, exploding instantly. A cloud of gray smoke rose, forming the mushroom I was already so familiar with. We knew he hadn't had time to eject; he must have misjudged the last minute that he could pull out of the dive.

Ley and I looked at each other a few seconds without saying a word. Then he took the microphone he'd been holding and hurled it against the blackboard of the control room, now that there was no more pilot to speak to.

—

August began, and a group of pilots was summoned urgently to Menongue. A battalion of Cuban troops had been surrounded by thousand of enemy reinforcements from UNITA, against whom they were resisting heroically from the underground fortifications where they were pinned down, but the numerical superiority of the enemy was winning out and threatening to exterminate them all. Aerial support was essential until a battalion of tanks arrived as reinforcement. I remained with the bulk of the pilots in Lubango, following step by step the bloody combat in Cangamba, while the battle that at first they thought would last only a day was dragging on interminably.

The tank battalion was encountering hundreds of unforeseen difficulties on its route through the jungle, and the men at Cangamba fell daily under enemy fire despite the decisive role our airpower was expected to have through the constant bombardment of enemy positions.

I felt the need to be with my comrades in battle. This was the reason I was there—not to sit like a parasite in Lubango while others died. It kept me awake at night, filled with impatience, recalling the reports we'd received about some pilots shot down in their helicopter, whose multilated bodies were afterwards found by our troops. They'd been captured alive by UNITA, then murdered and their hearts and livers cut out later and eaten.

Our men poured out their heroism at Cangamba, and after the battle, which, incredibly, they won, the feats of the dead became legendary, like that of the medic who was blown to bits by a direct hit from a mortar shell as he crawled out of the bunker to reach the last of the wounded still lying outside.

It was October 1983 when my replacement arrived: First Lieutenant Morales, who had left his pregnant wife behind. I hurried to the airport to welcome him, and when I asked after his family, he simply told me with a sad expression, "I would have liked to be there when the baby was born." I was called to the regimental staff office, where they gave me the medal denoting Internationalist Combatant First Class . . . *in recognition of the more than forty combat missions in which you participated* . . . as it said in my letter of commendation.

I took the little plastic box with its gilded medal, tossed it into my pocket, and went off to prepare my small bag for the final return. I had completed my mission with firm commitment, and felt that the horrible experience of the war had matured me as a man. But even years later I would wake up at night seized by a nightmare: I saw myself once again back in Angola.

Chapter 8

Patriotic Posturing

The final months of my stay in Angola had been especially hard on my mother, who worked in the offices of the provincial government, which received the secret communications detailing the bloody combat and heavy losses of the war. My mother was consumed with anguish each time she found on her desk that envelope containing the lists of the dead.

After happily leaving our blood samples for the malaria test at the Havana reception unit, we boarded the buses that were to transport us to our respective provinces. But as luck would have it, two of the buses went out of commission and we had to manage with whatever we could find in the way of transport. The telephone lines were also broken, so I hadn't even been able to inform my family that I'd arrive in Matanzas via one of those autos that collect passengers illegally at a higher price.

While thinking of the happy surprise I'd give my family upon my arrival, I asked the driver to drop me off in front of the old building where my parents worked and I ran up the steps in search of them, eventually bumping into my father, who was walking down one of the corridors. He embraced me strongly in silence, then looked me in the eyes sadly saying, "The boy's in the hospital, but it's nothing serious. First let's go see your mother—she needs you."

We walked together to her office, and there we saw her, behind her desk, petrified before that envelope she feared to open. She had changed a great deal in those last months. Instead of her usual extroverted and happy self, I found someone forlorn and pensive, absorbed in private worries that she didn't wish to share with anyone. There she sat, without her customary smile, disheveled and sad. She had put on hardly any makeup to come to work, and she seemed not to care about the whiteness at the roots of her hair, which she'd so painstakingly tinted before. A sling of white cloth, carelessly knotted around the back of her neck, was hung tightly, supporting the arm which lay splinted across her chest, covered by a plaster cast extending from the shoulder to the beginning of her fingers, sadly inert.

Just a few days before, she'd been out walking, absorbed in her thoughts and holding Reyniel in her arms, when the scream of a passerby brought her back to reality with a start. She found herself in the middle of the street with a motorcyclist making a desperate turn to avoid her. There was no time for anything; she held the child with all her strength and felt the driving impact, which hurled her to the ground. From there she watched the unfortunate driver fall and roll several yards, caught under his cycle, while numerous pedestrians ran to help her.

"The child, the child!" she screamed without releasing him from her arms; and he, intact, but pale and disoriented, clung even more fiercely to the neck of his fallen grandmother.

The heroic motorcyclist was taken at once to the hospital, but my mother refused to follow him there, claiming she was fine. So great was her horror that something might have happened to the child! She examined him a thousand times, and a thousand times she thought of his father—her son—so far away. Only hours later did she notice that an acute pain was shooting through her arm. The doctor diagnosed a fracture.

Reyniel had emerged unscathed from the accident, but lately his nighttime anxieties had translated into fits of coughing and difficulty in breathing. The doctors had diagnosed pneumonia and put him in the hospital just a few days before. Since then Vicky hadn't wanted to leave the hospital, spending all her time at the child's bedside, refusing to take any break from her vigil.

They hadn't wanted to add worries to the ones I already had with the war in that strange land, and all the letters they sent me were self-censored by the family in an effort to keep the bad news from me.

My mother was lost in her sad thoughts, attempting to sketch in her mind the inhospitable conditions facing me, while I remained unaware of the sad events overwhelming her in recent days. She had no idea that I was on my way to her as she sat with her gaze fixed upon that envelope lying on her desk, frightened of opening it.

"Mom," I called to her softly from the doorway, feeling the pressure of my father's hand on my shoulder.

She turned her head toward us, and, lifting her good hand to her face, broke into a series of exclamations that burst tumultuously from her lips: "*Ay*, my little boy! *Ay*, I can't believe it!" And she threw herself upon me, drowned in tears. I squeezed her hard against my chest, and kissed her forehead and her wet eyes.

"My poor dear . . ." I babbled, my voice breaking.

"But why didn't you let us know? Look how you've made me suffer!" And turning to her comrades, who were now approaching, she exclaimed, "My boy's come! Look, my boy's come home!"

Anxious to see Vicky and Reyniel, we went together to the hospital. Quietly, we went up to the room where the boy lay, and what I saw from the doorway rent my heart. Reyniel was asleep in his crib, his breathing agitated, as if he was making a great physical effort, and Vicky was sitting in a chair next to it with her back to the door. She had her elbows resting on her thighs, and her face buried in her hands. Her back, curved over, contracted irregularly to the rhythm of a pitiful, quiet sobbing.

I sensed my parents discreetly withdrawing, and I contemplated Vicky in silence for a moment. How much I loved her! How much suffering I had caused her! I swallowed dryly, fearing that my voice had left me.

"My love . . ."

Vicky's body seemed to freeze, her back no longer contracting to the rhythm of her sobs. Slowly she lowered her hands from her face and slowly she turned around. Her eyes were wide open, and looked as inflamed as her lips. On her face, which was wet with tears, was an expression of disorientation and surprise. She was getting up slowly from her chair while she babbled wildly, "No . . . it's not true, it can't be!"

Something surged out of me in the form of a rattle in my throat, which would not let me speak with clarity.

"I-I'm here now."

We devoured the space between us and embraced, mixing our tears between desperate kisses.

"It's true, and I've come back forever."

We spent several minutes embracing without saying another word to each other. Finally her sobs subsided and she rested limply, very quietly, curled against my chest.

"Look," she murmured, turning toward the sleeping child, "he fell asleep only a few minutes ago. Last night he saw me crying and wiped my tears, saying, 'Mommy, don't cry, don't cry.' "

We stood beside Reyniel, watching over his sleep until he awoke. And then I took him in my arms, determined to deliver him from the unpleasant atmosphere of that hospital under reconstruction with its odors of cement and paint everywhere. We spoke to the young physician on duty and he agreed that Reyniel needed fresher air. That day we went to my parents' house, and the following day to Varadero Beach, where the sun, the breeze, and happiness cured the child in just a few days.

We lay on the beach, Vicky and I, and what we had lived through seemed to us an incredible nightmare, so happy were we now, contemplating Reyniel healthy and happy, digging with his little shovel and depositing the fine sand in the plastic pail he kept between his outstretched legs, mixing it with water, building who knows what fantastic castles.

The boy laughed more when I lifted him over my head to put him down again, rubbing my nose playfully into his belly. And he'd run off fearfully, between giggles, along the beach as I pursued him on all fours imitating a dog who wanted to bite his little naked toes, after his prank of escaping with the ball he would refuse to return to me.

Our happiness there was infinite, but not eternal. Scarcely had we relaxed a few days when I was called back urgently to the base. The United States forces had invaded the island of Grenada and an imminent danger of war hung over our country. For the first time Cuban troops, represented by a group of officers and enlisted men cut off at the island's airport, were facing North American soldiers.

Vicky had prepared a surprise for my arrival. With the savings she'd managed during my stay in Angola, she was able to buy a refrigerator, a simple table, and four chairs made from dowels used in construction. That had been possible due to the kindness of two of my mother's colleagues, who had supplied the coupons they'd received from the union to buy those particular goods. They didn't have enough money to do so themselves and decided to make a gift of the coupons to Vicky. We managed to convince a friend of my father's— the driver of a truck that transported goods to Santa Clara regularly— to help deliver the refrigerator, table, and chairs, and we set off immediately to make arrangements with him.

It seemed that the constant U.S. threat would once again deny us the right to our happiness. Vicky stayed at home with Reyniel, while I remained at my post with my comrades under the wings of our planes, gazing northward, searching the horizon for enemy planes, awaiting the North American invasion.

On arriving at the apartment, which for more than a year had been left empty, another surprise awaited us. Our neighbor Captain Allende, a pilot of the First Squadron, had been dishonorably discharged from the armed forces and had moved back with his parents in Camagüey Province. Military Counterintelligence had discovered that he was corresponding with an aunt who had abandoned the country many years ago and now lived in Miami.

For maintaining relations with the enemy . . . read the order expelling him.

This time the climate of war with the United States was to reach its highest pitch. From our shelters we heard, overwhelmed, the radio bulletins concerning events in Grenada. We listened to one report after another, without understanding why we weren't going to the aid of our brothers who fought so valiantly—and who were so outnumbered—against the troops of the U.S. Eighty-Second Airborne Division.

"We interrupt this program to bring you a special news bulletin," the radio newscaster announced in an emotional voice. "The last of the Cuban resisters in Grenada has just fallen before the invading North American troops, wrapped in the Cuban flag."

That was the final newscast on the subject, and I couldn't stop asking myself why they were sacrificing themselves while we remained at home, without fighting, just waiting.

Two, three weeks went by, and the U.S. attack never came. Gradually the details of the "bloody battles" engaging our troops in Grenada began to be known. The overwhelming majority had been taken prisoner by the enemy, and the legendary commander of the Cuban forces, Colonel Tortoló, had actually fled, seeking asylum in the embassy of "a friendly nation"—the Soviet Union.

Our Highest Leader organized the homecoming for the returning prisoners. One by one the planes arrived with their cargoes of defeated men. And one by one they were met by our Commander in Chief, who stood at the foot of the plane's ramp with outstretched arms. Later would come an investigation and its findings accusing of cowardice all those officers and enlisted men who hadn't died facing the North American troops in the manner described by the media.

"They deserve to be executed for treason against the fatherland," said the Minister of the armed forces in his analysis of the events, "but the Revolution is generous, and they will only be dishonorably discharged. They'll even be given another chance to cleanse their honor: by reenlisting to fight in Angola."

I could never fathom why they were obliged to commit suicide against such overwhelming superior forces while we sat safely at home. *Either we all fight together or we respect the decisions made by those engaged in combat. No one who was absent from the fighting has the right to demand suicide from those who were there,* I told myself each time I searched for an explanation for the humiliation suffered by those men after their return. That was the first time I had doubts about Our Leaders.

———

My squadron leader was sent to the Soviet Union to pursue advanced studies in military sciences, and I was appointed as his replacement. Thus began a new experience for me, that of being a military commander. The base commander at the time was Lieutenant Colonel Tarragó, an extremely insecure man who concealed his weakness by despotically imposing his will. It was a period in which war with the United States ceased to represent a threat and instead was converted into a form of paranoia, hardly letting us sleep. Some Japanese walkie-talkies were supplied by air force headquarters so that the squadron leaders could wear them and thus be reached around the clock. Those miniature two-way radios became for us the most unbearable electronic invention imaginable. We lived enslaved by those radio frequencies, which could reach us anywhere, bearing the shrill voice of our commander, who railed furiously, demanding our immediate presence at any hour of the day or night to discuss the most useless questions.

Our squadron, with its roster of instructors, had the responsibility of training the youngest pilots graduating from aviation schools in Cuba and the Soviet Union. We were to be flying with unusual frequency in a desperate schedule due to the rookie aviators, who had to be prepared as soon as possible to carry out real missions in case of war. The most dedicated sector of our troops were the men assigned to work on the ground, namely, the officer engineers and technicians, plus the soldiers who doubled as mechanics. They began their daily labor at 4:30 A.M., when they went out in the darkness to haul the MiGs up to the airport apron and prepare them for the morning's flights. When noon had passed, and the pilots had marched off to rest or to plan the following day's missions, the officers remained at the ramp awaiting the tractors, which never seemed to arrive, to haul the planes back to their hangars or repairing the continual malfunctions exhibited by the jets after each day's flights. I myself was in the habit of returning to the apron later in the day to share with the ground personnel their latest efforts at repairing those MiG-21s, which gave them one problem after another with each subsequent flight. Finally, when they marched off to rest, exhausted, they'd often find that they had no water with which to take a shower, or that the kitchen was already closed and they had to go to bed without eating. I was caught up in an unending struggle with my superiors to solve what seemed an impossible problem: providing sufficient water and food for the men.

The living quarters on the base had been built some ten years before, and once the air force moved in, it was discovered that under the ground floor and in the walls of those apparently comfortable dwellings there was no plumbing or sewage system whatsoever. The result was a complete farce, whose solemn inauguration had been presided over by the head of the Joint Chiefs of Staff—who had recalled in his speech the Revolution's constant preoccupation with the living conditions of its combatants.

From then on the top brass at the base found themselves plunged into a battle as exhausting as it was unending: to find the necessary appropriations to construct the plumbing and sewage systems. But the next echelon above did not have the resources for the project, and general headquarters did not seem particularly preoccupied by the succession of reports concerning sanitary conditions at the base. And the years passed, while day after day one would see officers walking in the evenings, newspaper in hand, toward the surrounding pine forest where they could attend to their bodily functions and afterwards wash themselves in the murky stream nearby. Then gradually, moved by growing desperation and the indifference of their Highest Leaders, the more than one thousand men who inhabited the base began to reduce the distance they walked to relieve themselves, and little by little excrement began to appear in the most unlikely places: behind the amphitheater, in wastebaskets, on the parade grounds, in the middle of the road traversing the base, even at the doorway of headquarters. Thus was inaugurated at Santa Clara Air Base its legendary Era of Shit.

And our commander kept calling us over his walkie-talkie each time he discovered with icy astonishment that the distance had been narrowed between his office and the deposits of excrement left in protest by disgusted combatants under cover of night. We squadron leaders would then rush diligently to Tarragó's side, to indulge with him and the political officer in the most absurd discussion about how to put an end to that anarchy of filth, which could only be resolved by greater respect for the troops, by giving them what they should have had in the first place.

And as had happened so often before in the face of unresolved problems, we resorted to holding futile open meetings daily with the troops to discuss ways of solving our problems—food, clothing, discipline. And our combatants spoke vehemently, conscious of who they were—exemplary men by all accounts: militants of the party and of the Communist Youth comprising more than 85 percent of the troops—all vigorously demanding that everyone exhibit the discipline and decorum of revolutionaries. And I listened to these fervent discussions, asking myself if it were possible that so much filth could have been left all over the place by the mere 15 percent of the combatants who were not yet deemed examples of proper sacrifice and conduct.

As squadron leader during that period of absurd war psychosis, I began to understand how men act under extreme conditions. These soldiers were young boys from seventeen to twenty years old, legally obliged to serve for three years, with monthly salaries that barely sufficed to buy two packs of cigarettes. Separated obligatorily from their homes and forced to live in humiliating conditions, they expressed their rebellion by being absent from their units and stealing any article possible for their private needs. And we commanders, along with military Counterintelligence, spent more time hunting deserters and thieves than studying the enemy lying in wait. Each day began with the disheartening news of some further loss of material: first it was the alcohol, which they would siphon from the tanks of the

MiGs' radar cooling systems; then the telecommunication cables linking the squadrons and the command post; then food from the supply depots, uniforms and boots, gasoline and auto parts, air conditioners from the offices, construction materials, laundry, cups, water basins—even the tank trucks for refueling the planes! And responsibility was placed on our shoulders, as direct commanders of the troops, for safeguarding such material, which was impossible to protect under conditions where men didn't feel treated like men.

At the same time desertions by soldiers increased, with many simply escaping in uniform from that small hell to return to the warmth of their homes, and we'd receive the most heated reprimands from the generals at headquarters, who put the blame for such disorder on their subordinate officers. Our Minister, Raúl Castro, second in command after Commander in Chief Fidel, had unleashed a war against military deserters, and we had to supply headquarters with a daily list of those absent from their units without permission. Thus soldiers were required, like prisoners, to muster three times per day so that some designated officer could take roll call. And commanders were eventually mobilized in their jeeps, with contingents from the military police under the command of Counterintelligence, to drive through towns in search of deserters, who were gradually filling up the military prisons.

The situation reached such proportions that the Minister decided to open the jails in the face of the unmanageable flood of deserters, and to resort to more persuasive methods of patriotic education to keep the soldiers at their posts. And our commanders understood that what was important was not the existence of deserters, but acknowledging that they existed, so as a result their communiqués to headquarters began to leave out any reference to deserters. It was the lie, arrived at finally, which pleased the leaders at the top as much as those below.

The expectation among officers of obtaining some material advantage, and the policy of rewarding them as a stimulus for work, was High Command's ultimate leverage to make its officers carry out their duties. Clothing, boots, perfume, electrical appliances, household furniture, and even automobiles were added to the list of scarce articles available for purchase only by those with the most outstanding records of service.

At this time Ley was one of our squadron instructors, and one day while we were eating lunch together with Vidal and Lombides, he mentioned that he'd like to return to Angola for his third internationalist mission, since that way he might receive the right to purchase one of those tiny Polish cars they sold to the most outstanding officers. We all had already undergone the experience of the Angolan war, and with such terrible memories of it we found Ley's obsession with possessing one of those cars unbelievable, especially to the point of sacrificing two additional years of his life in a war thousands of miles away, in such an inhospitable, dangerous place. And so we got the idea of pretending that the Minister had designated seven automobiles to be distributed among the pilots at the base. The rumor circulated until it reached Ley's ears, and we talked with the second commander of the base to have him make an arbitrary distribution of the autos, giving them to the youngest pilots, who had never been in any war. Then everyone began to wager who would be the fortunate ones to receive the right to buy one of those vehicles, and on everybody's list Ley's name appeared as one of the strongest candidates due to his seniority as a pilot and his two long internationalist missions in Angola. And each passing day saw Ley growing more excited, making plans for the trips he'd take in his car, and looking for spare parts for it, "in case something breaks down," as he explained.

One afternoon when we were preparing for our flights Lieutenant Colonel Carmenate came by with a list under his arm. After ordering all the pilots to take a seat in the large hall, he said, "The Divisional Staff Commission has just met to assign the seven automobiles authorized by the Minister for the selected pilots. I expect this will put an end to all the speculation on the matter."

He began reading off the names of the lucky ones, and with each name there was a feigned applause among our group, and the only one who didn't know it was all a comedy was poor Ley. Carmenate finished reading the last of the names, which turned out to be mine. Ley's name had not been mentioned, and he sat stonefaced as if he couldn't believe that they hadn't assigned him a car.

Holding back my laughter, I asked permission to speak in order to refuse my nomination.

"I believe there are other comrades who deserve it more," I started to say, making an effort to maintain composure.

"What do you mean? Who, for example?" asked Carmenate ironically.

"Captain Ley, for example."

"No way! No one debates the decisions of the Divisional Commission. You want the car or not?"

"In that case, no."

And turning brusquely to one of the youngest pilots, Carmenate demanded, "Lieutenant Mengana, you've been assigned the automobile in question. Do you accept it or not?"

"Sure!" Mengana answered happily, while Ley shot out of the room with a snort.

Knowing him as well as we did, we'd planned the flights for the following day so that Ley wouldn't be scheduled, since we realized he wouldn't sleep that night. The joke had gone off better than we'd expected, and we wanted with all this only to give Ley a lesson in what really mattered in life. It would never have entered any of our heads to spend two years in a war for the chance of owning a car.

The following morning at breakfast we were asking quietly if anyone had seen Ley anywhere, when we saw him enter the dining room like a locomotive.

"Look!" he said in a loud voice, halting in the middle of the room. His eyes looked bloodshot, and his face very wasted. Pointing to his eyes, he continued, "Look at my eyes! I haven't slept the whole night. It's completely unfair and I'm going to put in a complaint with the divisonal commander. If he doesn't respond, I won't hesitate to go to the Minister himself!"

He spun around on his heels and marched out of the dining room, slamming the door behind him. We all sat silently for a few seconds, until somebody broke the silence with a guffaw, while we others began to get concerned for Ley, because he was suffering more than we had anticipated. Later that morning we saw him approach the base commander, who finally told him the truth, and all of us surrounded Ley, laughing while he muttered something incomprehensible. The joke, which had been my idea, left me afterwards with a disagreeable sensation of cruelty and bothered my conscience. I didn't have the right to mortify such a good friend that way, but the saddest thing for me was to have seen him suffer so passionately for an object, to the point of being ready to go off to war to obtain it, leaving his family behind suffering in his absence. How much we had degenerated in uniform!

—

The life of constant tension and confusion led us to an excess of confidence in our human relations, and the personal tragedies of some were taken as comedy by others. The war had left its consequences like all wars, and many young soldiers who marched off to Angola suffered the infidelity of their wives who abandoned them or looked for a companion to ward off their loneliness. Then the organs of Counterintelligence would inform Command, and the latter would in turn inform the men when they returned, giving them the news of their wives' infidelities. Osmany the clown liked to yell at more than one comrade in such an unhappy state while he was boarding the bus among a group of pilots, "Cuckold, cuckold!" And he'd laugh brazenly while the other would make an effort to ignore him and show how he could conduct himself like a man of stone for whom the recent divorce had meant next to nothing. Then later Osmany also went off to the war in Angola, and his wife couldn't endure the solitude, so she got herself a companion. No one shouted "Cuckold!" at Osmany upon his return, but, ashamed of himself, he asked to be transferred to another base to start a new life far from those he had so offended.

One day during lunch they brought us news of the deaths of two of our comrades in Angola: Valle and Morales, the one who had been posted as my replacement. I remembered the day he'd arrived there, pensive and sad about the wife he had left pregnant. And I felt once more that my throat was closing, preventing me from breathing. Morales wasn't able to be with his wife on the day of her delivery. Valle, on the other hand, had gone off contentedly to that war as his last recourse to remake his life. Two years before he had been removed from flight duty and they had ordered him not to go near the planes. Military Counterintelligence had noticed that Valle was wearing a new pair of shoes of foreign make, whose origin raised serious doubts about the circle of his relationships. An investigation was conducted to determine the origin of those shoes, which turned out to have been a gift from his father-in-law, who had received them in turn from an exiled relative in the United States. The shoes therefore had come from the generous hands of an enemy, and Valle was suspended dishonorably from further flights for having accepted those comfortable shoes without having asked his father-in-law where they came from. For a long time thereafter he could be seen walking, taciturn and ashamed, turned into a pariah whom others avoided as the plague. He had fallen into disgrace. But luck was in his favor, and the tremendous need for pilots in the Angolan War made the top leaders change their minds and let him know indirectly that they'd permit him to "cleanse his honor as a revolutionary" by marching off to Angola. The day they let Valle know about the opportunity they were offering him, he could be seen leaping for joy and swearing that he'd never make another such mistake again. Valle was then once again accepted by everybody, and he went off to war contented to be no longer a pariah.

Upon my return from Angola I had been processed to enter the party, and I was admitted after the required investigations, which, in my case, after having been a combat pilot whose life had already been scrutinized in detail, was routine.

I called my father as soon as I received my party card to give him the news.

"Welcome to the family of Communists," he told me proudly. And he didn't hide the fact that his son, now a pilot, captain and leader of a combat squadron, was his greatest pride.

One afternoon while I was home resting before my night flights, I was visited unexpectedly by First Lieutenant Cepero, the officer from Counterintelligence who was in charge of the squadron.

"You're the squadron leader and we know how overworked you are," he began by saying. "You won't have much time for us, but we wanted to let you know we're interested in having you be a part of our ranks."

Several years had passed since they had approached me and I had declined. I recalled the conversation with my father, and even though I knew that my work as squadron leader took up all my time, I began to listen attentively.

"We thought you might not understand clearly what we're asking of you. It's not a matter of spying on your comrades, but of your establishing a working connection with us. No one knows what can happen in the future, or where you'll have to fight tomorrow. We think you have the right qualities to be working with us, and we only want to train you in case the moment arrives. . . ."

"I don't think I can do very much. My work barely allows me time to devote to my family," I began telling him, convinced that my responsibilities as a commander would take up all my time.

"The time we'll manage to arrange somehow. We're not going to sacrifice your job or your family."

"Then . . . on with it!"

"First you must choose a pseudonym, because we don't work with our real names."

I thought of Fidel Castro, the Commander in Chief, and I remembered his *nom de guerre*.

"Alejandro."

Then he took out a paper for me to sign, containing an oath of loyalty to Counterintelligence.

After I did so he added, "From this moment on, your pseudonym and your links with us are strictly secret. No one, not even your own wife, should know about any of this. Soon we'll arrange for your first interview in one of our safe houses."

This was turning out to be really interesting, similar to something I had seen before only in the movies or on television. In the early morning hours when I returned from my flights and found Vicky as usual waiting sleepily for me in the old easy chair, I whispered in her ear what had occurred that afternoon. She stared at me anxiously when I told her that they had asked for strict secrecy, including with her.

"Don't you worry, with you I will never have secrets," I said to calm her, but she couldn't hide her displeasure at this new activity that had infiltrated my life.

One Saturday on my way to the hangars where our squadron jets were housed I was intercepted by Cepero on his motorbike.

"What are you doing tonight?"

"I was thinking of staying home."

"We wanted to have our first interview with you at one of the safe houses."

All that seemed so ridiculous to me that I had to make an effort not to laugh. Cepero and I had an established work link, with him as officer from Counterintelligence assigned to the squadron and me as leader of the same squadron, for which we met openly at regular intervals. And now there was all this mystery, with safe houses. You'd think we were conspiring against the government!

He gave me directions to the house, and when he was sure that

I'd get there without fail, he added, "Check the front window. If it's open it means you can go in without ringing. If it's closed, continue on your way, and we'll see you another time."

"I got it," I replied, even more intrigued by such security measures.

"Lieutenant Colonel Tomasito wants to be present at the interview. He wants to personally congratulate you."

He was referring to the head of divisional Counterintelligence, and I understood that the interest in me came from higher up.

I told Vicky what was happening, and she said good-bye to me with a look that revealed that she was not at all pleased by my new connection. When I entered the mysterious "safe house," which turned out to be that of an ordinary family, I was led by the head of the family to a small room located in the rear. There, behind a small table on which sat two glasses of water and two empty coffee cups, Tomasito and Cepero sat waiting. They both got up to greet me with a warm handshake, as if we hadn't seen each other in a long time. Smiling, they invited me to take a seat and joked a bit before getting down to the subject of the interview.

"We wanted to congratulate you personally, and in the name of the Minister, who as you know is our direct superior," Tomasito began. And after thanking me for my cooperation and emphasizing the importance of my decision to join their ranks, they began to instruct me.

"Do you know what a mole is?"

"Well . . ."

"It's someone who obtains information by gaining the confidence of the source."

And they went on instructing me for a while about things I considered more a matter of common sense than special preparation, without delving into the "grand mysteries" of Counterintelligence that I expected to be briefed about. As we were finishing up the meeting, which I found rather boring, Lieutenant Tomasito became more serious and confident. Leaning over the table in my direction and speaking so softly that I could barely hear him, he began to confide while staring into my eyes fixedly.

"We need your help. You're the only person who can assist us in this matter." His expression clouded with a look of preoccupation mixed with pleading. "You're young, intelligent, good-looking . . ."

He continued, and I noticed that, as other times, flattery produced in me an automatic antipathy toward those who used it. He saw something in my expression that made him pause and then he added, "In our work at times we have to make use of our innate gifts. It's part of the sacrifice that Counterintelligence combatants make, however modest they may be."

"How am I to assist you?"

"You're Lieutenant Colonel Cordero's neighbor."

He was referring to my friend and former squadron leader, who at present was posted in the Soviet Union undergoing advanced officer training.

"That's correct."

"We believe that his wife is involved with certain elements disaffected with the Revolution."

"Really?"

"We think so."

He paused for a while as if measuring his words. I looked over at Cepero seated next to Tomasito, leaning slightly back in his chair with his legs crossed. His eyes had closed slightly and they gleamed with intensity, while an approving smile played on his lips, revealing to me that his commander was finally arriving at the real point of the meeting.

"We thought that perhaps . . . you might be able to seduce Cordero's wife."

What I had just heard left me astonished to the point of speechlessness. It seemed incredible to me. Marlen, the wife of my ex-commander, loved her husband and devoted her life to the education of her children and the care of her home. Whatever had prompted them to make such a proposition to me?

"We're sure you can get on intimate terms with her. You know, in bed women generally confide everything. . . ."

A sense of loathing began to knot my stomach.

"Marlen is a respectable woman who loves her husband," I started saying, attempting in my confusion to defend my friends' dignity.

"She's only a woman, and her husband's far away. In our line of work overcoming scruples is a necessary sacrifice. And this is what we're asking of you, the same sacrifice."

I knew that he had a wife and daughters and I felt the desire to ask him if he thought the same way about the women in his family. I made an effort not to explode, and swallowing the repugnance I felt for all I'd just heard, I spoke very quietly and slowly.

"I'm sorry, but I can't help you. For what you're asking me to do I feel more a sense of scruples than of sacrifice."

Tomasito listened to me, an expression of regret clouding his face.

"No matter, these things pass. You're only beginning, and it's normal for you to feel this way. In any case, think about it and keep an eye on her. Remember that Marlen is now one of our principal objectives."

The meeting ended in an atmosphere of coldness, which we all did our best to ignore. I headed home shocked and furious. So that was the mystery surrounding the organs of Counterintelligence! What lofty methods they had! What sacrifices their members made!

When I got home I told Vicky what had happened. She couldn't get over her astonishment as she listened, and I never, never got over the repugnance I felt about that meeting. From then on I always used my work as an excuse not to attend other meetings in those mysterious "safe houses."

—

One December afternoon in 1984 we were practicing combat formations with the rookie pilots when an alarm went off at the aerodrome. Alberto, my friend and neighbor, to whom I was distantly related, had crashed, along with Rabelo, the young pilot he was instructing, just before overflying the runway to make their final approach. A plume of black smoke rose in the distance, and I took a jeep with the chief of staff in the hope of finding survivors. They had inexplicably lost power and hadn't had time to eject. The plane had exploded on contact with the flat field, which was sewn with vegetables, opening a crater where the smoky remains of the aircraft lay. Fragments of bone, bloody shreds of skin, and hair lay scattered about the crater in a terrible scene.

In the dental polyclinic at Santa Clara, Vicky was attending Alberto's wife when the news of the crash arrived at the base. Both were terribly alarmed, and Vicky telephoned with the anxiety felt by wives in such cases. At the other end they informed her that I was okay—it had been Alberto who had perished. Feeling that her strength was leaving her and that she was about to faint, Vicky made an effort to control herself and asked for help since Alberto's wife was there with her.

"Get hold of yourself as best you can, and just tell her to go home," they finally told her.

Vicky pretended not to have gotten an answer, and Alberto's wife quickly got ready to go home. When she got there, a committee made up of the political officer, a physician, and a nurse were waiting for her at the door. A few days of sadness were shared by all, and then once again the flights resumed. Life did not stop.

One day when I returned, tired, walking along slowly while I caught sight of Vicky and Reyniel waving to me from the balcony, I saw a child of three running out to meet me with his arms held out, yelling, "Daddy, Daddy!" He stopped in his tracks just a few meters from me, and I saw his expression, at first happy, change slowly into a look of disappointment. He lowered his head, and turned on his heels, leaving me frozen behind him, caught in his mistaken gesture as if time had stood still, shattered by his innocence. It was Alberto's son.

Without our realizing, absorbed as we were in the constant activity of our jobs, which consumed all our time, months passed in which we hadn't visited our parents or even the entertaining cinemas and theaters where we used to go in the past. While I worked day and night without a break, Vicky spent all her energy in the slow daily effort to get to work, with Reyniel in her arms, and then make her way back home again.

Her odyssey would begin very early in the morning when she woke up the child, and then gave him his milk, dressed him on the run, and raced off with him in her arms to catch the only bus between the base and the city of Santa Clara. In the thick of a crowd of desperate commuters at the bus stop, Vicky battled to obtain a space on that bus, which always pulled up crammed with people. And she rode in the crowd, performing pirouettes to balance between brakings and potholes, holding Reyniel against her breast with one hand and gripping the handrail above her head with the other.

Vicky would always be racing against the clock to the nursery school where she left the child and then to her job, where she stayed until five-thirty P.M. On the return trip, the struggle to get onto the bus became even more fierce, with the desperation of all to get home early to their families. Finally she'd arrive home totally exhausted, only to find that the communal water basins were dry. Then she'd go back down to the patio of our good neighbor and he'd fill two pails with water, which she'd carry slowly up the stairs, drawing on her reserves of strength to vanquish the barrier presented by each floor she ascended. She couldn't count on my help, since I generally arrived home after eleven at night and would leave at five in the morning for my job as squadron leader, which sapped all my strength.

Many times when Vicky was dreaming of being able to go to bed early to relieve her fatigue, someone would knock at the door to remind her that the meeting of the Committee for the Defense of the Revolution, or of the Federation of Cuban Women, was already under way. And she would slowly descend the stairs, with a sleepy Reyniel in her arms, to listen to the latest discussions about the struggle to perfect socialist society, or to join in the study of the Great Leader's latest speech, just as they did at meetings of the Communist Youth and her union, which were held at her polyclinic after the day's work. And she wore herself out slowly in silence. She knew that a revolutionary dentist, and the wife of a combat pilot, had the obligation of devoting herself to the Revolution.

—

Little by little Reyniel was growing up, and as time passed we were spending less and less time together. I'd get home when he was already sleeping, and I'd leave before he even woke up. Saturdays and Sundays were the same as Mondays and Tuesdays in my exhausting schedule. Often our parents when they visited us on weekends had to obtain special permission to enter the base and stop by in the area where I was putting in my twenty-four hours of standby alert, which was nearly every other day. Sometimes Vicky would have to take the Sunday shift at her clinic, with Reyniel clinging to her skirt, while I remained at the base.

In the last days of 1985 the base commander summoned me.

"You've been selected to spend four years in the Soviet Union, where you'll receive advanced officer training," he told me, putting a hand on my shoulder. Although I still retained the worst memories of the Soviet Union and knew that I wouldn't be flying as much during that period, sacrificing my greatest passion for a long time, I was overjoyed at the news. For four years we could escape from that insane, grinding pace of continual sacrifice. Vicky had recently become pregnant with our second child, and the prospect of my simply being a student when the child was born made me doubly happy. I ran to tell her the news, which I knew would fill her with joy.

"I'll have to spend the next five months in Havana reviewing Russian and math before our departure. Will you come with me?"

Vicky leaped for joy and went immediately to phone her parents, who were euphoric at the news and readied a room for our impending arrival. We left for Havana the first days of February, and I began my preparation at the Military Technical Institute while Vicky and Reyniel enjoyed the constant attention showered on them by my in-laws, who were delighted to have them there. Each day I could sleep at home once again, and each evening the three of us would go to the seawall at Malecón. There, sitting by the sea on the same wall we'd gone to during our courtship, Vicky and I would guess about the sex of the next child while Reyniel ran about happily and attempted to fish with an old rod his grandfather had given him.

We lived during this period in a little room in Vicky's parents' house, in which we could barely fit our bed and Reyniel's crib, but we were extremely happy to have this cherished time to share with the family. Always before bedtime we would talk to Reyniel and I to the baby still to be born, while we caressed Vicky's round belly, running our hands softly over her stretched skin.

One morning as I bent over, searching for my shoes under the bed, I saw a glass of water sitting there.

"What's this glass doing here?" I asked Vicky curiously, and she answered me somewhat confusedly, "I put it there for myself in case I'm thirsty at night, so I don't have to get up."

"You don't have to do that. Just tell me you're thirsty and I'll get up and bring you some water." And I gave her a kiss, which she accepted somewhat pensively.

A few days later I found another glass of water under the bed, and I asked Vicky, "And this glass—what's it doing here?"

"So I don't wake you," she answered evasively.

"Are you sure that's the reason?"

Vicky lowered her head in embarrassment, and I saw she wasn't telling me the truth.

"It's that . . ."

I remembered having heard at one point about an old religious custom of leaving a glass of water under the bed to avoid misfortune, and in an instant I figured out what was going on.

"Who put it there?"

"It was Mom, but please don't say anything. She's only doing it so that the baby will be born strong and healthy."

"Of course I'm going to tell her that it's stupid to resign yourself to the influence of a glass of water. Instead, you should be taking vitamins more regularly and doing more exercises in preparation for the delivery."

I went to the kitchen to find my mother-in-law, whom I loved and respected like my own mother.

"María . . . was it you who put the glass of water under our bed?"

María seemed as surprised as a child caught in a bit of mischief.

"*Ay,* my son, don't be angry with me over that, because I'm doing it for the well-being of your wife and the baby she's carrying inside her. What harm does it do you?"

"A lot. It goes against my principles. If God existed there wouldn't be so much injustice in the world. And if people would only see that the solution to our ills is in using our own strengths, and not in believing in some divine will, they'd put up a better struggle to change things."

María seemed convinced by my reasons, and I went off to classes convinced of the tragic ignorance of so many unfortunates in the world who find the solution to their sufferings in something as transparent as a glass of water. The next morning I looked under the bed, certain that I wouldn't find the glass of water, but to my great surprise there it remained, adamant in its spot. I felt the blood rush to my temples and told myself, *What else can I do? I don't have the right to deprive my mother-in-law of her hope.*

Then I turned to Vicky, telling her, "You'll laugh, but please, just one glass. I don't want to find the whole table service filled with water under there by tomorrow."

Vicky jumped up joyfully, kissing me, and ran to the kitchen where my mother-in-law was preparing coffee. She returned in a little while, holding a cup of it in her hands, which, without my knowing why, tasted especially delicious that morning.

Before dawn one morning in May Vicky felt the beginning of her labor pains, and I accompanied her to the maternity hospital, bombarded by effusive comments from Reyniel, who didn't stop repeating, "Now my baby brother's coming! Now my baby brother's coming to play soccer with me!"

Vicky had spent the last marvelous months in Havana, without any problem with her pregnancy, attended like all Cuban mothers free of charge once a month by the wonderful collective of nurses and doctors from the network of polyclinics in the city. Our system of care for pregnant women was really quite good, and Vicky's diet was supplemented with vitamins supplied free of charge by the Ministry of Health.

By early morning Vicky still hadn't delivered, and I ran in search of flowers, which I hadn't been able to bring her when Reyniel was born. This time I had better luck and managed to get a wonderful bouquet, which I gave to her after the birth when they permitted me to visit. My mother had just arrived and kept Vicky company along with my mother-in-law in the room, which seemed to be the same one she'd been in when Reyniel was born. The labor had only taken three hours, and the baby boy, who weighed a little over seven pounds, had remained in the sterilized room for a few hours more, awaiting the departure of the first visitors.

Vicky was feeling very fit and decided to accompany me to the floor below to see the child, whom we named Alejandro, through the glass wall separating us from that room filled with cribs of newborn babies. The doctor, who was an old friend of the family, accompanied us there while Vicky supported herself on my arm. Lying facedown, with his head buried in the sheets of the little crib, lay a beautiful, energetic baby who still refused to turn his head to one side even after we called the nurse to adjust his head, frightened that he'd suffocate.

That day Reyniel was not permitted to see his little brother, so he returned to the house grumbling about doctors who prohibited children from entering hospitals. The next day we managed to slip him in, thanks to the help of a nurse, and he spent more than two hours contemplating his little brother with a tenderness that moved us all. In the future it was to be he, as older brother, who set an example to Alejandro, protecting him with as much dedication as his own parents did.

The day of my departure for the Soviet Union arrived. A process of changes had been started a few months earlier in that country, and its name, Perestroika, could be heard with increasing frequency. This time we were promised that following our first year of studies, we'd be assigned apartments in order to allow our families to be with us for the remaining three years. So with the hope of returning soon to get them, I left at the end of August 1986 together with eight comrades, on a voyage that would radically change our lives.

Chapter 9

—

Perestroika

The nine of us now on our way to the Soviet Union had been selected from among the youngest batallion commanders of the air force, the radiotechnical forces, and the antiair missile defense forces of our country, to receive advanced officer training, which would enable us thereafter to direct large military units. And although we had barely known each other beforehand, the last months of studies together in Havana had brought us together and established a wonderful camaraderie among us. We were traveling now, while animatedly discussing the harsh climate of the region, on a train from Moscow to Leningrad. We'd been met at the airport and seen to the station by an officer from the Tenth Command of the Ministry of Soviet Armed Forces.

"Make sure you don't miss your stop at Kalinin," the officer had warned us. "They'll be waiting for you there."

A crowd of impatient travelers jammed the platform as we got off the train, which they boarded hastily, thus leaving us alone on the platform when the train departed. It was then that a friendly man in civilian clothes addressed us:

"I am Colonel Kustiukov, in charge of your studies. Outside there's a bus waiting to take you to your hotel."

The hotel turned out to be an old but well-preserved four-story building close to the Volga River, which flowed through the middle of the city. The old woman seated behind the desk gave us a warm welcome and then, taking four keys hanging from a board on the wall, handed them to us, pointing out the numbers engraved on the attached tags.

"Those are your room numbers on the third floor. The showers are on the first, but we won't have hot water until sometime next week."

We ascended the wide granite staircase accompanied by Colonel Kustiukov, who led us down a dark hallway with a polished wooden floor, with twenty rooms off it. Kustiukov opened the door to one of them, and a torrent of light streaming through the large window at the back of the room delivered us from the uneasiness of the dark corridor. Before us was a room with perfectly square white walls, neat and clean looking, with a green Formica table standing at the center. On the table were a pitcher of water and four glasses carefully set upside down on an earthenware platter. Four unsteady-looking chairs were set around the table, and two rustic armoires of thinly varnished pine placed against the wall constituted the remainder of the room's furnishings, along with the iron bedsteads in each corner.

"This room should be occupied by three of you; the others hold two apiece," the colonel informed us, dropping one of the keys on the table. "You may distribute them among yourselves as you see fit and we'll meet back here in five minutes."

Three sets of bunkmates formed spontaneously and set off to leave their bags in their rooms, while López-Cuba, Cerguera, and I selected our beds indifferently.

"From now on, you are students of the Marshal Gregory Konstantinovich Zhukov War College, one of our most prestigious military institutions," Colonel Kustiukov began saying when the others had returned. "You will have remarked that you are living in the center of the city, outside the college limits, two kilometers away. You will commute to classes each day on your own, utilizing public transportation, which you'll pay for out of the salary you'll receive; the same goes for your meals. So be careful with your money since it is budgeted for that. You are absolutely prohibited from sleeping away from the hotel, and you must be back in your rooms by eleven at night. The 'grandmother' on duty is responsible for notifying the college staff immediately regarding any absenteeism among you."

As Kustiukov talked, I remembered the instructions Major Argatov had given us nine years earlier when we had arrived at the flying academy. There had been no changes in the style of dealing with foreign students, even when they were experienced officers. A change of tone in the manner in which the colonel was addressing us suddenly reawakened my attention:

"Things have changed since the advent of Perestroika. Before, beer could be purchased in the cafeteria on the first floor, opposite the receptionist's office. Now it's forbidden to consume alcoholic beverages in any armed forces facilities." And an expression of regret was etched on his face.

The college comprised some old buildings at the northern limits of the oldest part of the city, and its facilities had served from time immemorial for the academic training of military leaders, who in former times used cavalry instead of tanks for their shock forces. The solidly built stables, which had previously housed the cavalry horses, had been impeccably remodeled, and in their place comfortable classrooms and laboratories had been installed.

The college was made up of eight different faculties, which trained the future commanders of large military units. In the first seven were enrolled only Soviet officers, who studied the different specialties, including automated command systems for antiair defense, aviation, field command, and general headquarters, as well as the secretive system of antimissile defense, the Soviet version of Star Wars. The eighth faculty, for foreign students, was located at the north end of the college, near the gymnasium and the wonderful swimming pool hidden by an adjoining building. A complicated pass system, controlled by old men from the reserves and situated at different locations around the campus, permitted or denied access to the different areas according to the coding on the personal identification card of each student.

We foreign students took classes in groups separated by nationality from morning until two-thirty P.M., when we recessed for an hour to have lunch. Then we returned to classes and laboratories to continue our required individual study until seven-thirty P.M. An imposing group of colonels and generals with various scientific degrees and rich experience in commanding forces formed the core of professors, who gave us excellent instruction in the network of laboratories, command posts, and automated command systems housed in the academy, plus the diverse armaments set up in a large studies camp on the outskirts of the city. All the technical subjects, such as electronics, probability, and armament systems, as well as military subjects like operational procedures, were strictly classified. We students had valises in which we were obliged to keep all the maps, texts, and notebooks with their paged sheets. At the end of our studies each day, we would tie them closed with a string, covering the knot with a paste on which we pressed our individual seals before handing them back into the room labeled CLASSIFIED LIBRARY, whose door and windows contained iron bars. In this way the Soviets protected military secrets and prevented their being shared among the students, since the programs they studied were different, with access to information on the most recent models of armaments given only to the Cubans and members of the Warsaw Pact, while the Vietnamese and Mongolian students studied more antiquated versions.

We studied with great eagerness, feeling that we were resting from the continual grinding pace of work which we'd been used to in Cuba. And once more, after several years, we had the possibility of engaging in sports with regularity, for which reason we didn't take long, Cerguera and myself, in joining the college swimming team and working out in the early mornings before classes.

One day when once again there was no water in the hotel, someone suggested going to one of the public saunas known as *banhia*, and a group of us Cubans headed there to take a bath. We paid the modest fee at the entrance and walked openmouthed through the spectacle unfolding before us.

A dozen wooden benches with high backs over which were draped the clothes of the users, were spread one after another around the large salon in which some twenty sweaty, completely naked men were resting. Two old women moved about from one end of the room to the other, sweeping up between the men's legs all the birch leaves scattered upon the floor, without paying the slightest attention to their nakedness. We made our way to the back, and anxious but determined to pass the test we began to hand up our clothes until we were left as naked as the rest. That was when one of the old women heard that we were speaking a different language and approached, curious to learn where we came from.

"We're Cubans, Grandmother," we answered, addressing her in the affectionate manner normally reserved for the old women who worked in the different menial services of that country.

"Ah, you're the sons of Fidel Castro! Good boys!" the old woman proclaimed in a loud voice, and we were surrounded in an instant by a dozen curious folk, who welcomed us, establishing a cordial chatter which, embarrassed by our nudity, we interrupted quickly to enter the sauna with our ears reddening in shame.

—

The dreaded winter finally arrived, and on the city's museum tower, the electronic thermometer seemed to have frozen at $-49°F$. We ran to our classes and returned to our hotel wrapped up in as many clothes as we owned, even though there was no possible way to combat the horrible cold, which according to our good-natured, skinny Leyva, threatened to turn him to ice at any moment.

Vicky and I corresponded almost daily, and once again I wrote her impassioned poems on the backs of floral postcards, in which I praised her beauty and her virtues as a dentist, wife, and mother. Once again while poking through my things, I discovered little notes hidden by her before my departure in the most unexpected places among my books and equipment. *I love you* was all they said. This time she had stayed in Havana with her parents, and had already found work in a nearby dental polyclinic, while her mother remained at home taking care of little Alejandro as well as Reyniel, who had begun school and was already writing his name with mixed-up letters. Vicky told me about the children down to the minutest details, and I enjoyed reading it all, imagining myself there with them and picturing the various events she described.

Perestroika captured all our attention with its flood of new ideas, discussed openly, for constructing what they called a democratic socialism based on a society of citizen's rights. New, and each time more openly critical, programs were aired daily on television, struggling against censorship. We began to discover a society plagued with corruption, which bureaucrats were attempting to cover up. A talented new generation unknown until then began to appear on the cultural scene, demonstrating that they were always there but hadn't emerged until that time in order not to compromise their art with the system of stagnation established by Brezhnev. And we viewed those reforms with happiness, watching that society transformed little by little into a more open and courageous one in which corruption and vices that I'd seen nine years before were being publicly acknowledged in order to remedy them.

My younger brother Orlando was studying in the port city of Odessa on the banks of the Black Sea, and I decided to visit him one week in February, taking advantage of the winter vacation. I went on the long trip by train, sharing the small compartment with two economists from Odessa, who conversed between sips of vodka, and for the first time I heard someone speak of Stalin's crimes.

"But if it's true what you say about the millions murdered, why is nothing known about it?" I asked with open mistrust of my traveling companions, while I suddenly recalled some children's comic books that an old friend of my father once showed me. They had been published somewhere in Latin America, and they depicted Communists as some kind of bloody monsters.

"The truth will out sooner or later, and the day will come when they'll speak of it openly," the older of the two economists replied with certainty and a look of pity in his eyes.

"I'm not blind," I insisted. "I'm just relying on common sense and I find it hard to believe that one can hide the death of millions of people for so many years."

The man regarded me with an ironic smile, and he continued, using a finger to emphasize his words, "Obviously, it's not possible to hide such crimes. More than half the world knows about them. Except for people like you, who have only read the official versions of history. Suppose, just suppose, that what I'm telling you is true. Would the present Communist parties accept such facts as a blot on their glorious history?"

"And why not? Stalin was a man, not the party. He committed the error of allowing the cult of his personality, but from there to the crimes which you impute to him, there's quite a long—"

"That's okay, son. Just hope that the leader who still governs you doesn't turn out to be another Stalin who they expose after his death just like our own."

"Fidel is not Stalin! On the contrary, he's a simple popular leader. The only one in the world who waits for his athletes at the airport when they return to Cuba, and changes from his uniform to shorts to play basketball with schoolkids! No one has ever been so close to his people as Castro!"

"Enough!" the younger one interrupted, standing up in response to the heated tone of the discussion. And placing a hand on my shoulder he continued, "My dear Cuban: we admire and respect your people. Please excuse my friend. If anything is worthwhile, it is friendship among ordinary people."

He then took out the bottle of vodka, filled three glasses to the brim, and after handing one to the old economist and another to me, he lifted up his own, proclaiming, "A toast!"

I drank unwillingly what was only possible to get down in one gulp, and I saw that my interlocutor in the debate was smiling as he set his glass back on the table.

Then he turned to me, still smiling, and said, "You know? You remind me of myself when I was young. I was loyal and impetuous like you . . . until life obliged me to look elsewhere for answers. It was then that I started listening to Radio Free Europe."

I spent the week with my brother in warm Odessa, and felt immense pity for the foreign students who were obliged to live in subhuman conditions there. When I left, I understood that if my brother held out in his effort to become a hydraulic engineer, he'd become a man in the process.

Although I'd not been pleased by my travel companions on the train to Odessa, the words of the old economist kept hammering in my brain. Back in Kalinin, when I looked over at the old radio on the table, I felt the desire to turn the dial to the shortwave broadcasts to listen to the lies from abroad. But the presence of my comrades, and the possibility that they might take a dim view of it, held me back and made me give up the idea. Among the prohibitions drawn up in the orders from the Commander in Chief to the Cuban military was included listening to broadcasts from foreign radio stations. To do so could cost me a dishonorable discharge from the armed forces and a stain on my record that would follow me the rest of my life.

One spring day when we decided to walk back to our hotel, we saw a crowd of hefty men energetically pushing each other in front of a cosmetics shop. We asked one of them who was looking on from the sidelines what they sold there that was so special and he answered that it was a men's cologne.

"Why such a battle over men's cologne?" we asked, perplexed. And looking at us in astonishment, he flung his arms up in the air and then, dropping them to his sides in fury, exclaimed, "Because obviously, if there's no vodka, a man has to drink something!"

And we continued on our way, questioning the effectiveness of Gorbachev's measures to combat alcoholism. We had frequently witnessed, during the harsh winter that had just passed, men lying in the street completely drunk in the midst of a pool of vomit, in danger of freezing to death in a few hours while completely ignored by indifferent passersby.

One night in May as I was watching the most important news program on Russian television, I heard the newscaster announce that Brigadier General Rafael del Pino of the Cuban air force, along with his family, had defected to the United States in a small plane. The news left me frozen to my seat. I simply could not believe it. I'd known General del Pino from the time I was a cadet. His son Ramsés, who had fled with him, had been my buddy at aviation school in Krasnodar. Both were good men who were devoted body and soul to the Revolution. I racked my brains searching for a reason to account for del Pino's desertion, and all I could think of to explain the fact was that he must have been working for the CIA a long time, and that the whole of his exemplary daily conduct had been nothing but a sham to mislead us all.

—

At last the long-awaited month of July arrived when they were to give us the apartments we'd inhabit with our respective families upon our return to the Soviet Union. So with the keys in our pockets, off we went to Cuba, content to know that we wouldn't be coming back to the Soviet Union alone.

Vicky and Reyniel were waiting for me at the airport late that evening, lost as always among the joyous throng waiting to welcome relatives and friends. I was surprised to see how Reyniel had shot up in the eleven months I'd been away, and with him in my arms we headed home, as I was anxious to see the sleepy Alejandro. The younger of my sons was sleeping blissfully in my in-laws' bedroom when we got home late that night, and I took him in my arms to bring him to our room. Then the next morning, while Vicky and I were still talking in bed without having slept, Alejandro got up and, holding on to the crib bars, stared at us with curiosity.

"Look, Alé, Daddy's home now," Vicky told him, and the child smiled while jumping gently on the mattress and repeating over and over, "Daddy, Daddy, Daddy!"

I took him in my arms and set him beside me on the bed. With his first caress he tore out a handful of hairs from my naked chest, which made me jump up in pain, crying out, "You rascal! That's no way to treat your daddy!" Alejandro let out peals of laughter while yanking out hair from my scalp. From then on it was nearly impossible to get away from the little character, who followed me everywhere and insisted that I be the one to lull him to sleep, lying on my stomach when it was time for bed. Alejandro had been only four and a half months old when I'd left for the Soviet Union, and his attachment to me, as well as Reyniel's, was the result of Vicky's perseverance in talking to them daily about their "daddy" while showing them my photograph.

The officers from the Armed Forces Divisional Staff handling our transportation advised us before departure that we couldn't take more than forty-four pounds of baggage per adult, and twenty-two pounds per child. We struggled valiantly to make them understand that this wasn't a tourist flight, that we were moving abroad for three years with small children who needed a variety of things while away, but the answer we received was cut and dried: "Only the weight limit allowed."

On the flight to Moscow the children slept deeply, without an inkling as to the great changes awaiting them: the cold, the language, the culture. And I looked at them with compassion for their innocence. How hard these next years were going to be for them!

—

We arrived exhausted in Kalinin during the last days of August 1987. There we would be living in a rectangular ten-story building, which housed some two hundred tiny apartments, all identical and all accessed from the long, narrow corridors that traversed each floor from end to end. We would all be living there together with the families of Soviet officers, who occupied most of the premises. The apartments designated for our use had been freshly painted and, upon entering, we observed what had been given us as furniture: a sofa bed, two armoires of pressed wood, and a bed for the children, still packed in their cartons and waiting to be assembled. We spent the first night putting together each of those pieces of furniture while the children slept on some folded blankets on the floor. And by noon the following day we had arranged what would be our home for the next three years: some 400 square feet of space in which had been fitted a small room, a bath, and a tiny kitchen.

My whole previous experience in the Soviet Union had passed under the tutelage of the institutions at which I had studied, and I was surprised now to discover that I knew nothing about that society in which we were to integrate ourselves as one more family. And we descended into the street like blind people groping in the dark, searching for ways to resolve the problems of daily living in a world dominated by bureaucracy and restrictions.

Vicky and I didn't want our sons to feel isolated from the other children because of the language barrier, so as quickly as possible we took the necessary steps to enroll Reyniel in the neighborhood school and Alejandro in a nearby nursery school. They had to have their medical examinations prior to admission, and it was thus that we had our first experience with any medical consultation in a local polyclinic, housed within the thick, mildewed walls of a building constructed at the beginning of the century on the city's main thoroughfare. A young, ill-tempered nurse filled out the required forms and then indicated to us with an imperious wave of her hand that we should take our place on one of the wooden benches lining the corridor where dozens of other patients were waiting.

At last our turn arrived, and we were called into the consultation room. There a nurse stood with her back to us, fiddling with some blood samples in glass tubes, which she deposited in the wooden box set on the iron bedstead in front of her. To her right, in one corner of the room was a faded desk where a man of about fifty was sitting. A dark stubble of beard overshadowed his cheeks and heavy circles were drawn under his eyelids. His bloodshot eyes were lost in contemplation of the pen he held in his shaky fingers, which as he continued writing called our attention to the black grime under his nails. His dirty, unpressed white medical gown was unbuttoned down the front, and an old stethoscope hung from his neck, swinging from side to side like a pendulum over his chest. This was the doctor.

He looked up, regarding us with an imprecise stare, and ordered, "Have a seat."

I noticed then a mouthful of gold-capped teeth and caught the strong smell of alcohol on his breath. I felt like turning around and walking out, but where to go? Luckily it was only to be a physical exam, and the children had to have it to enter school.

I sat directly in front of him with Alejandro on my knee and began by saying, "Our children start school shortly and need to have a physical."

"I know, I know," he muttered while reviewing the forms which had been filled out by the nurse. And without looking up he asked, "You're Cubans?"

"Correct."

"Which is to say, you come from a Third World country where, we realize, the health facilities are not always the best, so we'll have to give your children a more careful examination."

What I was hearing from the mouth of this doctor seemed incredible. His country was nearly a century behind Western medical advances, which had already been put into practice in Cuba, and in spite of the truths that were coming to light under Perestroika, much of the population still thought that the Soviet Union was at the vanguard of man's scientific progress. I felt like telling him a little about health care in my country, but I knew it would make no sense to him, so I decided to remain silent.

"I will need a sample of their stool, just enough to send for an analysis to determine what parasites they may be carrying." And turning to the nurse, who was busy taking a blood sample from a child accompanied by her mother, he asked for two glass slides on which to deposit the stool samples, adding, "I'll take the samples. Undress the first of the boys."

Vicky and Reyniel had remained seated behind me, observing the coming and going of other patients attended by the nurse, and when I told them what the doctor had said I could see that they shared my sense of deep humiliation over the impending procedure. Vicky and I were busy helping the first of our sons take off his clothes with reassuring words when we saw the doctor take a box of matches out of his pocket. He took one of them by its head and was about to introduce the other end into the child's anus.

"But what are you doing?" I asked in indignation and alarm.

"Taking the sample."

"Don't you have a sanitary swab, with cotton?"

"Afraid not. Our budget is very small."

Once again I had a mind to walk out and forget the medical exam. But what about school? Without those papers the boys wouldn't be admitted. And the regulations were such that we couldn't try another doctor. This was the one assigned to the district we lived in.

We held the boy as best we could, talking to him all the while to calm him, while his tears—whether from pain or humiliation, we didn't know—tore our hearts out. Afterwards they proceeded to take blood samples with some very large syringes in rather dubious sanitary condition. And finally we marched home with our papers in order, but with a rather disagreeable sensation in our stomachs.

Months earlier I had read in the papers about the tragedy at a hospital in Gorki, where various children had been infected with AIDS by being administered injections with unsterilized needles. And after our recent experience at the polyclinic we quickly arranged for our parents to send us immediately from Cuba a sufficient supply of disposable needles and syringes, which were impossible to obtain in Russia. If either of our children needed additional injections or blood analyses, the doctors would have to use our syringes.

Classes began, and I returned home every night around eight o'clock to have supper with Vicky and the children in the confined space of the kitchen which barely held us all. Then we would retire to the only other room in the house, where we stretched out on the floor and played with the kids until it was time for bed. Then Reyniel would climb into bed, kissing us goodnight, and I would sit and watch the news on television while Alejandro would curl up on my chest until he too fell asleep.

Television had ceased to be a form of entertainment for the children, since political debates and educational programs for adults took up nearly all of the programming. The boys were continually irritated when they hurried in to watch the only cartoons broadcast for fifteen minutes in the morning before going off to school or in the afternoon when returning from their day, only to find the show interrupted suddenly with the announcement *To be continued . . .* flashing on the screen, in order to present the latest bit of news.

I, on the other hand, became more and more a prisoner of that television, which I'd sit watching till past midnight, so involved had I become in discovering more and better cultural talent, which until then had been underground.

One night, when I had supposed that Reyniel was already asleep, I heard him sobbing quietly. I went over to him and discovered he was lying facedown with the pillow over his head. He had his arms tucked under his chest and the irregular way in which he was breathing told me he was crying. I knelt down next to his bed and in a soft voice with my mouth nearly touching the pillow I asked him, "What's the matter, son? Why are you crying?"

"I miss Cuba, Daddy," he answered from his refuge under the pillow.

"Look, you don't have to be ashamed of crying. We all cry, children and grown-ups, whenever we're suffering about something." Then he rolled over, slowly uncovering his face, stared up at me with sad eyes, and wrapped his arms around my neck, breaking into uncontrollable weeping. Vicky stood at the foot of the bed and I could see the tears running down her cheeks as well. "Daddy, it's just that I don't understand anything they're saying at school! And the kids all laugh at me!"

I stroked his hair in silence, and when he had calmed down a little I began to talk to him.

"I know how hard it is for you; it's natural you feel the way you do. I'd like to go back to Cuba this very day, the same as you, but I have to study. At least here I can be with you every day, while back home I only got to see you every week or so."

Reyniel regarded me thoughtfully while I spoke, and lay his head on my chest once again when I paused a moment.

"One suffers a lot when there's no solution to things, but there is one for this situation," I continued, running my hand through his hair. "If you want, you can stop going to school, but then you won't learn the language and you'll be stuck in the house, ashamed not to be able to talk to the other kids. Anyway, the kids teasing you in school do it without realizing that they also don't know your language, which makes them seem a little stupid, don't you think?"

Reyniel smiled contentedly at my inane comparison.

"You, on the other hand, have the chance to learn their language, even though it means putting up with their ridicule for a time."

"That's what bothers me, that they laugh at me!" Reyniel complained furiously.

"Of course it does. But it'll be a lot different when you can put them in their places in their own language. Anyway, some solutions to our problems are good, others not. You've got a problem to solve now, and we'll back you up whatever decision you make, either way."

"Even if I decide not to go to school anymore?" he asked, surprised.

"Even if you decide not to go to school anymore," I answered firmly.

"Okay, let me think about it. Tomorrow morning I'll tell you what I decided." And giving us each a kiss, he wrapped himself happily under the covers and settled down . . . for sleep?

"And if tomorrow morning he tells you he doesn't want to go to school anymore?" Vicky whispered in my ear after we went to bed ourselves.

"I can't explain why, but I'm certain that he'll go."

"You're crazy. . . ."

The next morning Reyniel woke up with unusual gusto, exclaiming in a happy voice, "Mommy, give me breakfast right away, I don't want to be late for school!" while looking for his shoes under the bed.

In the kitchen, Vicky saluted me with a delicious cup of Cuban-style coffee while releasing her pent-up worry with a sigh, saying, "You gave me nightmares about it the whole night!" And she punched me gently with her fists in a gesture of feigned reproach.

Much to our happiness, in just a few months the children began to speak fluent Russian with no trace of an accent, which allowed them to pass for natives among those who didn't know who they were. The boys and I spent each day immersed in our respective schoolwork while Vicky fretted away in the solitude of that apartment. We wished for her to become involved in the outside world as well, and since the salary the school paid me barely gave us enough to live on, Vicky decided to accept one of the jobs that the nearby soda factory offered to the wives of the Cuban students.

The harsh winter had arrived and Vicky left early each morning for work while I dressed Alejandro with as many clothes as possible to protect him from the cold. Then I set off on my daily round with the children, starting with Reyniel's school and then continuing on to Alejandro's nursery school some five blocks away, pulling him along in his sled as we sang silly songs, which we made up along the way. We sang at the top of our lungs, gladdening our day, but not that of some of the aggravated passersby who begged us to be quiet—right in the middle of the street! But we were far too happy! For the first time I had the experience of helping my children get dressed, serving them breakfast, and taking them to school. For me it was more than enough reason to be singing happily each morning.

One day we were visited by a commission from the Cuban High Command. They had been charged with the task of explaining to us the "Process of Rectifying Errors and Negative Tendencies," which was being carried out in our country, led by Fidel. It was a kind of Cuban Perestroika whose motto, which had already filled hundreds of signboards all over the island, proclaimed: NOW WE'RE REALLY GOING TO CONSTRUCT SOCIALISM! Many who had devoted their lives to constant sacrifice on behalf of the Revolution began to ask themselves with stupefaction what it was that they had been constructing for so many years before.

During their visit they spoke to us about the Santa Fé Communiqué and the "vain North American hopes for a change in Cuba led by the younger officers in the Armed Forces." As for Soviet Perestroika, they reiterated the judgment of Our Highest Leaders: "It's a giant and we've no idea where it's going." This was the manner in which they spoke of the will of the people, which, without Gorbachev's intending it at the beginning of the process of change, had begun imposing itself more and more each day. In effect, the relaxation of censorship had provoked a sort of unquenchable thirst in people to learn the truth about their history, and each day more and more new documents revealing the crimes of Stalin and the reigning corruption under Brezhnev appeared in publications like *Literaturnaia Gazeta*, *Vzgliad*, *Moscow News*, and *Sputnik*.

Around this time the controversial party secretary for the Moscow region, Boris Yeltsin, had rudely criticized Gorbachev for the slow pace of reform and Yeltsin was isolated in the fashion of the Brezhnev period. The media were overcome with fear of the people and the younger officers in the Soviet armed forces with whom I was studying, and the appeal and indisputable popularity enjoyed until then by Gorbachev began to wane.

It was in that atmosphere of secret archives being opened to public scrutiny that I was able to read some of the documents from the trial of Beria, the feared head of the Cheka during the time of Stalin. Corruption, crime, sexual abuse, cases of torture, and experimentation with new poisons on suspected political enemies filled the pages, and reading such revelations horrified me. Such was the "heroic history" of Soviet socialism!

—

Vicky ran one of the machines at the factory and received for her work a salary of 120 rubles a month. She and the other Cubans working with her complained that they were not permitted to speak Spanish on the factory premises, and often they couldn't understand the jokes the other workers made about them in their presence.

"I have the impression they think of us as inferior beings," Vicky remarked to me on one occasion.

—

Each month we held a party meeting to review the academic progress of each of us; and Ramírez, who had difficulties with the language, never managed better than a satisfactory grade in Russian. Then all the criticism was directed at him and summarized in the log of the meeting. It disturbed me to watch Ramírez explain over and over that that was the best he could do. Daily relations between families were also subjected to analysis at party meetings. If someone preferred to spend his free time with his own family in the privacy of his home, that could be interpreted as a symptom of conflict with others. Why don't you visit your comrades? Why aren't your families getting together in your spare time? Thus even the affectionate relations among our families became a sort of party duty.

In those party meetings everybody had to speak, each one had to offer criticism and demonstrate some bit of self-criticism, express an opinion about someone or something. Whoever failed to do so would be judged as weak-willed and marked accordingly in the written evaluation of the proceedings. Thus the party appraised us in each and every aspect of our lives, right down to the last domestic detail. And nothing tormented us more than the eye of the party, present in the glance of every one of its militants, waiting in ambush to submit to public judgment whatever did not conform to the established norm. And nothing produced more panic in any of us than the idea of finding ourselves in the humiliating position of watching the collective point its finger at us while judging or presuming how we ought to be doing things in our own home.

We had a little stuffed crocodile we'd brought from Cuba as a sort of exotic present for a Russian friend, but then it happened that a certain Hungarian student came upon it one day while in the apartment for a few minutes and he became obsessed with the idea of possessing it. From that day on he pestered us with various offers in hopes of acquiring it, and one of his propositions was to trade it for a small Japanese-made radio–cassette recorder. We had never owned one, and in Cuba they had become so scarce that we never even dreamed of buying one someday. Now we were extremely taken with the idea of brightening up our apartment with something that would allow us to record our favorite music, not to mention to listen to the forbidden shortwave-radio broadcasts. So we happily agreed to the exchange and set our radio–cassette recorder proudly on the only spot available—the television.

We had committed a punishable offense as Cubans, since any exchange of goods—even among ourselves—was prohibited. Furthermore, all objects of capitalist origin provoked dire suspicions, and only something that some relative might bring back when traveling on an official mission was considered legal.

One day we were visited by one of the officers from counterintelligence who was stationed at the Cuban embassy and charged with keeping an eye on the military students in the region. Among other things, he referred with alarm to a group of Cuban students who had been dishonorably returned to Cuba for having purchased capitalist goods from some of the students from other countries. And he ended the meeting by giving a warning to those of our collective who might be tempted to commit the same error.

I returned home that day with the feeling of having committed a crime. Instead of playing with my sons like I normally did, I sat down in front of the television absorbed in preoccupations. I remembered Valle, who'd been benched from flying and converted into a pariah and I remembered my father the day he came back terrified from the place he'd taken his car to be repaired by a mechanic working privately on the side. I finally understood, after all those years, the reason for my father's fear! And with my eyes fixed on the wall, I watched as in a horror film the meeting at which my case was to be discussed. My comrades pointed to me accusingly as the villain who had blackened the honor of our collective and one by one they were calling for my immediate dishonorable discharge from the party, from the school, from the armed forces. I'd fallen into disgrace!

I told Vicky what had happened and was about to hurl the cursed radio–cassette recorder into the Volga River, when she insisted, "You haven't committed any crime to feel this way!"

And I began to realize she was right. How much I had degenerated during these years in the armed forces! I was honest; I'd always behaved honorably, and this time I wasn't going to allow myself to succumb to such absurdity.

My recent anguish had been caused by the ethic inculcated by Our Leaders, making us consider the simplest material aspiration as abominably egotistical. It was miserable to think that a revolutionary might covet something when millions of his compatriots didn't have it, and it was practically treasonable to purchase a capitalist product. The very laws of our country imposed this ethic, obliging its citizens to hand over to the government, for the common good, all dollars and other currencies they might receive from any foreigner. Hundreds of Cubans were now in jail for having wanted to "enrich themselves" with the scant dollars some Western tourist or other had given them either as a gift or in exchange for local currency. It was the same morality that had degraded us without our realizing it, turning us into wardens over everybody with the duty of spying upon one another and the right to know how much each of us had, in order to pass judgment upon one another. We were equally victims and accomplices in an absurdly egalitarian world.

Chapter 10

—

Oh, God ... ...
Forgive Me

That year's classes ended and I had to return to Cuba for a month for my annual flight practice. Vicky and the children were not allowed to accompany me, since they were required to remain in the USSR for two years before returning. "Please come back soon," Vicky told me with tears in her eyes. I knew that they would feel anxious during my absence in the midst of that setting, which, though not hostile, was certainly strange for them. I finished my flight exercises as quickly as possible and returned at once to the Soviet Union.

From the kitchen window Vicky saw the taxi pull up very early that morning and she ran downstairs to meet me, with Alejandro in her arms and Reyniel following behind.

"I thought you'd never come," she said, throwing her arms around me. "It's been so hard without you," she confessed, squeezing me tighter. Alejandro threw his arms around my neck and Reyniel hugged me around the waist. We stood like that for several minutes, quietly embracing each other at the entrance to the building. When we started back upstairs for the apartment I noticed that Vicky's right hand was bandaged.

"What happened to you?" I asked, taking her hand.

"I had an accident yesterday at the factory. I was trying to extract a bottle that had gotten jammed in the machine and a comrade accidentally turned it on."

"But how could she do such a thing? It might have mangled your arm," I insisted, horrified.

"Don't worry. Luckily, it was a small cut and only required two stitches, which they did right away at the hospital."

I let out a sigh of relief and we went up to the apartment arm in arm, happy to be together again. We still had a few days before classes were to begin and we took advantage of the time to go to the forest each day. We brought along a ball for the kids to play with, and we would cook an improvised meal over a fire while Reyniel and Alejandro would run happily among the trees. It was our favorite diversion in Kalinin.

The first day of classes Vicky woke up earlier than necessary. She was sitting on the edge of the bed, looking at her arms worriedly. I noticed a growing uneasiness in the expression on her face.

"What's the matter?" I asked, caressing her cheek. "Don't you feel well?"

"I didn't sleep well last night. I think I may have been food-poisoned."

I noticed then a reddish blotch along the arm, which she was still examining with attention. I wanted to take a look myself, and I discovered the same irritation was even more evident on her back and abdomen. Then I suddenly remembered that the day before we'd had some wild mushrooms for dinner which we'd bought from an old woman at the market. These old women would gather them in the woods, and the idea that Vicky might have eaten a poisonous one, picked accidentally by that old lady, terrified me. Luckily the children hadn't wanted to eat them.

"Let's go quickly to the war college hospital," I told her, convinced it was the best place to take care of her.

On the way Vicky began to feel worse. The welts were all over her body and her lips had begun to swell.

"I feel like I can't stand up. . . . My blood pressure must be way down," she told me, nearly fainting as we entered the small hospital.

Supporting her with my arm, we went up to the doctor on duty, a solicitous young woman who stood up quickly to attend to us. The minute she took in Vicky's state, she hastened to check her blood pressure. A look of concern darkened her expression as she listened carefully with the aid of a stethoscope to Vicky's pulse, and I was frightened to see that Vicky was about to pass out in her seat. I took her in my arms and lay her on the nearby hospital bed while the doctor ran in search of medication. She returned immediately with a syringe in hand and asked me to hold Vicky's arm while she looked for the vein, probing with her fingers.

"Her pressure's very low: sixty over forty. . . ."

I was silent. In scarcely a few hours Vicky had lost all her customary vitality. I watched her withering like a dying flower, and I suddenly felt like the most desperate man in the world. I wouldn't, I couldn't allow her just to die in my arms. I felt lost, demented, engulfed in a void of pain.

"I'm just injecting her with a stimulant."

I seemed to be hearing the voice of the doctor from far away. My world was reduced to nothing—nothing except Vicky lying unconscious on that hospital bed and myself, clinging anxiously to her arm.

"She'll recover in a few minutes, but you must get her to the regional hospital as fast as possible," the doctor explained. "She needs to be looked at by one of their allergy specialists. I'll give our ambulance instructions to take you there."

Vicky regained consciousness because of the stimulant and we set off in the ambulance, which turned out to be a sort of closed truck painted olive green, with two canvas cots hanging one above the other from the roof. I helped her settle in the lower cot, and I took a seat beside her, holding her hands in mine. Although she remained conscious now under the effect of the stimulant, larger and larger reddish swellings were covering her body. And I kept shouting, begging the soldier who was driving to go faster in that antiquated heap, which seemed to be making no more than thirty miles an hour.

The regional hospital was on the outskirts of the city, a modern seven-story complex that seemed to have been built quite recently. We went into the emergency room and asked for the help of an allergist.

While we waited Vicky showed me the hand she'd injured a few days before, remarking, "This is where they sutured the wound." Then she added, "I don't like the way they're taking care of their patients."

Vicky's medical knowledge caused her to observe with a critical eye what was going on around her, and something she had noticed during her last visit there had made her even more suspicious. The allergist finally appeared. She was a doctor in her forties, sober and unperturbable. She asked Vicky what she had eaten over the last few days and concluded she had been poisoned by the mushrooms. She gave her an injection and recommended that she be admitted to the hospital to be kept under medical observation.

"I'm not staying here," Vicky told her, upset by what she'd suggested.

I tried to convince her that she should stay, but it was useless.

"Ask for the medications, and if I have to receive any injections you'll do it for me at home." And with a look of pitiful entreaty in her eyes she added, "Please understand, I'm scared to stay here. I don't trust this place."

Although I worried about the wisdom of her decision, I preferred not to contradict her, and thanking the doctor, we returned to the apartment. But there things got worse. Overcome by the fear that hospital inspired in her, Vicky had lied to me about feeling better. And the swelling continued to get worse and worse. By midnight the effect was almost monstrous and I felt absolutely desperate, unable to do anything except take her back to the hospital that so terrified her.

"You must go even if you don't like it. Where else can we go?" I implored her in despair.

Vicky resigned herself, and when the boys were asleep I went to the apartment of one of my buddies and asked him to come stay at our apartment with them.

"Go and don't worry," Jiménez reassured me, hastily buttoning his shirt as he followed. "I'll stay with them as long as you need."

It was close to two A.M. when we got back to the hospital, but this time we found no doctor on duty able to attend her, which completely surprised us since we were used to Cuban hospitals where one could find specialists available around the clock. An old nurse filled out the forms required for admission and then, after much pleading, allowed me to accompany Vicky to her room. It was on the seventh floor, in the so-called Allergy Wing: a long, wide corridor with large rooms on either side. We followed her in silence halfway down the hall, stopping in front of the door to the room just opposite an office where the duty nurse sat nodding off to sleep.

"This is the room. The bed's the last on the left," the elderly admissions nurse stated brusquely and turned and walked away.

There were eight beds distributed in two rows at opposite sides of the room, and six patients were already lying there asleep. Vicky was leaning heavily on my arms and the sudden pressure of her fingers communicated her fear. Supporting herself with difficulty even with my help, Vicky made it to the last bed, which was set beneath a huge window. I had the sheets ready in seconds, and taking Vicky in my arms, I lay her gently in bed.

Her condition had significantly worsened in the last few hours. Now her skin looked like one huge welt, a sort of thick crimson mantle covering her entire body. Her face, previously almost childlike, had become entirely disfigured from the excessive inflammation of her lips, eyelids, and ears, which—with eyes filled with anguish—made her look horribly aged.

"I think my bronchial tubes are also inflamed," Vicky commented in a low, sad voice. And she added, drowning her words with her sobbing, "I don't want to die!"

And it was as if a glass world had shattered in my head. "But what are you saying? You're going to be all right!" But I knew I was lying, just as I knew she would take my soul with her. *Oh my soul! What power you hold, for even if I breathe, without you I feel I'm dead! . . . Don't leave me, Vicky, because my life will be gone without you!* I cried from the depth of my heart while I kissed her hands. Vicky sobbed, and freed a hand from mine to run through my hair.

"The children . . . my children . . . my poor little boys . . ."

"It's going to be all right," I repeated over and over. "Tomorrow the doctor will see you and you'll be better in no time." And I didn't know whether I was trying to convince Vicky or myself.

Everything had happened in less than twenty-four hours. Fate had vented its fury upon her with the utmost cruelty, and I had no idea how to fight against it. And for the first time in my life I felt defeated, without knowing what to do . . .

I stayed several more hours still, kneeling in silence next to her bed, and talking to her now and then in a whisper, trying not to disturb the other patients, while I wiped away the tears that rolled down her fevered cheeks.

"Calm yourself; be strong. Don't give up!" I implored.

"The children, you've got to take care of the children." Vicky hadn't forgotten that Jiménez had to leave fairly early for school. How much we needed our family at that moment, now, her parents and mine!

"I'm going. I'll get the kids to school and come right back," I replied solicitously, and kissing her hands passionately I left the room, leaving Vicky behind; and with her, my soul.

At home, the kindly Jiménez was nodding on the sofa, keeping watch over those two little beings who slept in tranquil innocence. I thanked my friend and sent him off with a squeeze of his shoulder. I needed to be alone. The room remained dimly lit from the kitchen through the slightly opened door. I covered the boys and kissed their foreheads. How innocent they were of what was happening.

Seated on the edge of Reyniel's bed, I felt exhausted, defeated. I stared at the floor and recalled the day I met Vicky, our first kiss, the first dreams shared.

How am I to explain that she has become the meaning of my life, the same as my children? What could my life possibly mean without them? What materialistic ideology, what Marxist philosophy could explain this emotion, which concerns existence itself? Where is the materialist explanation for why I now feel dead though I'm still alive? Where can I see it, touch it . . . this other me, which I feel departing from myself with her?

I got up slowly, with my arms hanging limply at my sides. I walked with difficulty, as if dragging an immense weight, until I reached our own bed. And I fell on my knees in a faint, staring up at the sky through the window. I clasped my hands together against my chest, and I cried out with words that were choked with tears.

"Oh, Lord . . . forgive me! How could I have ignored you my whole life? How could I have denied you when you've always been inside me? Please . . . don't take her from me! Give her the strength to live!"

And I doubled over, letting my face, which I had already covered with my hands, fall on my knees. I cried uncontrollably, as if with each tear I might finally clear my soul of so many lies inculcated throughout my life, until the first rays of the morning sun told me that it was time to wake the children. I washed my face and erased as best I could all indication of my pain before awakening them.

"Where's Mommy?" was the first and most predictable question they asked. But I was still unprepared to answer. "She had to go off to work a little earlier this morning," I answered confusedly and urged them to hurry. I had to drop them off at school and the nursery, and I didn't want to add to their worry by telling them of their mother's condition. Who knows what terrible things they might have imagined during the time they were there!

While Alejandro and I walked hand in hand, on our way to the nursery school, after dropping off Reyniel, Alejandro asked me, lifting his little face up to mine, his head not much above my knees, "Daddy, why aren't we singing today?"

"Oh . . . because my throat is a little sore."

"Then you whistle and *I'll* sing."

And he started to sing one of our improvised, nonsensical songs, while I forced myself to whistle along. But only one sound, like what one does when learning to whistle, came from my dry lips.

"Daddy, today you don't know even how to whistle!" he complained, and I bent over to pick him up and kiss him.

"You're right, but I'm going to sit you up on my shoulders anyway."

And I swung him up onto my shoulders while he exclaimed, "Hoooray!"

I left Alejandro at school complaining to me that not enough children had arrived at that hour to play with, and I ran off to the hospital. It wasn't yet eight o'clock when I arrived, and I went up to Vicky's room, ignoring the protests of the nurse on duty. Some of the patients were already up, combing their hair and putting on makeup with the help of little compact mirrors. I apologized for the intrusion and made straight for Vicky's bed. She lay with her back to the door, so I made my way around the foot of the bed to stand between it and the window. The rays of morning sunlight fell directly on her face and I saw with horror how terrible she looked. A dark bruise covered part of her forehead just above the left eye.

"You've got a bruise . . . what happened?"

"I had to go to the bathroom after you left. When I walked by the floor nurse I lost consciousness and fell and struck my head. I don't know how long I lay there . . . the floor nurse was sleeping over her desk. She doesn't even know it happened."

While Vicky was telling me this I felt the urge to scream, to go off and find the nurse to show her the consequences of her irresponsibility, to tell her what I thought of her stinking hospital.

Vicky read my thoughts, and taking my hand, pleaded, "It's not worth your getting angry. They'd never understand. It'll take them a long time before they can understand."

And I surmised that she was talking about the time it would take to undo seven decades of lies. All of the political questions that had begun to trouble me over the past few months I had shared with Vicky, and even though we had different points of view about our own country, we agreed that the seventy-one years of Soviet socialism had debilitated Russian society.

"Has the doctor seen you yet?"

"Nobody's come."

And I was filled with desperation. Vicky was getting worse and worse, and whenever she spoke she had difficulty drawing her breath. I took one of her hands, now terribly swollen, and when I kissed it I couldn't hold back the tears.

"No, no, please, don't cry!" And she also began sobbing.

That was how we passed the time until the moment we supposed the physicians must be arriving. Then I went up to the nurse, who greeted me with a scowl.

"And the doctor? We need a physician. My wife is very ill."

"All the doctors are in conference. As soon as the meeting is finished someone will come to see her."

I hurried back to Vicky's side.

"It's getting hard to breathe. My lungs are all inflamed."

I started to get up to go find a doctor, but the pressure of her hand held me back. She wanted to tell me something very important.

"I don't know if I'll be able to talk much longer." She was speaking so low I could barely hear her. "What's happening has nothing to do with having eaten mushrooms. I think I'm going into anaphylactic shock, a reaction to the tetanus shot they gave me in this hospital when I injured my hand last week. . . ." She paused to get her breath, then continued, "Before giving me the injection they checked me first by inoculating me with a small dose of the serum under the skin, to see if I had any reaction. But the doctor was in a hurry and didn't wait long enough. After they gave me the vaccination I noticed that my skin had become irritated around the spot they'd given me the test."

"Damn!"

"Forgive me. I've been so frightened I hadn't remembered."

I stood up, rubbing my forehead in terror.

"My left arm is in terrible pain—I'm afraid for my heart," Vicky confessed, and this time I couldn't contain myself. I stormed out of the room like a shot past the other patients, who looked up in astonishment.

"Where are the doctors?" I demanded from the nurse on duty, who was busy clipping her nails.

"I already told you they're having their morning meeting."

"I insist on knowing where they're holding it. It's urgent, damn it! Don't you understand!"

"Next-to-the-last door on the left," she replied, pointing down the corridor in the direction of the elevator.

"Come in!" a voice responded from the other side of the door after I knocked repeatedly.

There were five or six physicians seated around a rectangular table upon which were piled various medical files.

"Please, we need a doctor urgently. My wife is very sick!"

The white-haired man with a large forehead who sat with his back to the window answered curtly, "Comrade, can't you see we're busy with the morning's decisions? Tell your wife to wait." He seemed to be the chief physician.

"What do you mean, *wait*?" I demanded, closing the door behind me and going up to the indifferent physician. "Don't you understand that she's *dangerously* ill, that she could be dying?"

The world had again been reduced to nothing in my mind beyond its simplest dimensions: Vicky dying in her room, me, and that impassive doctor seated beneath the window. I don't know what he read in my expression, but before I reached him he had stood up and signaled one of the other doctors to follow him. "Come on!" And turning to me, he asked, "What room is she in?"

Seated next to Vicky's bed, the chief physician started questioning Vicky while the younger doctor wrote down the information in her file.

"Doctor," I interrupted, "my wife can barely speak. She's a dentist and she believes that she's suffering anaphylactic shock due to the tetanus vaccine she was given last week."

The doctor's face lit up immediately, and turning to his companion, he declared, "That's the key!" And he ordered him to hurry and bring back an intravenous serum to administer to Vicky at once. Then, turning to me, he informed me, "I'll have them give her an electrocardiogram immediately."

I stayed with Vicky until it was time to pick up the boys that afternoon. If I was surprised by the speed with which her condition had deteriorated, I was even more amazed at how quickly she began to recover. By the time I had to leave, the welts covering her body had almost completely disappeared and she looked alert and calm.

"She's out of danger," the doctor had told me a little after midday. "But she should remain a few days to watch her heart."

When they brought in the patients' lunch trays, Vicky and I observed with amazement that the aluminum plates, on which they served a repulsive-looking gruel as a meal, were covered with old, dirty grease stains. Vicky refused to eat and I didn't blame her. From then on, I told her, I would bring her meals that I'd prepare at home.

_____

I went off to pick up the children, overjoyed at Vicky's unexpected recovery. That night I explained to them that Mommy was sick in the hospital and that we'd soon go see her there, "Maybe after tomorrow." Then I gave them each a big kiss at bedtime, saying, "Mommy sends you each a kiss."

Each morning I'd get up early to wash their clothes in the tub and iron whatever they were to wear that morning. Then I made their and Vicky's breakfast. I spent the whole of each day going back and forth between the house, the hospital, the school, and the nursery. Cooking, washing, ironing, cleaning.

By the fourth day in the hospital Vicky seemed to have recovered entirely, but the physician refused to discharge her. The first electrocardiogram they'd given her, on that terrible morning when they'd finally diagnosed her, had revealed a worrisome anomaly in the heart. Now the doctor wanted to make sure that her heart was also back to normal. And so she and I began to escape from her room on the sly to spend the day seated on a park bench on the hospital grounds, holding hands in the wan September sun. One morning we discovered that the head physician was watching us from a window. When we came up we found him waiting by the elevator for us, and directing his comment to me in a tone of affectionate scolding, he said, "You spoil your wife too much!" And we all began to laugh. By then the doctors and nurses were already treating us with special kindness. "You're so much in love, you two," they would say fondly.

Reyniel and Alejandro would accompany me each evening so that the four of us might have dinner together on the benches of the little park, and no one any longer reprimanded us for it.

"Mommy," Reyniel interrupted one evening while we ate together, "Daddy cooks yummier things than you do."

Vicky and I laughed at the thought of my first serious culinary attempts.

One afternoon the chief physician called me into his office. He took out Vicky's file and explained to me the manner in which her sickness had developed. The vaccine against tetanus that they had given Vicky had been made from animal plasma. "The country still lacks sufficient human plasma to prepare enough vaccines," he commented in conclusion, and added, closing the file, "I'm terribly sorry."

"Tomorrow we'll do a final electrocardiogram, but it's just a formality," he said, shaking my hand in farewell. "Afterwards, you can take her home."

That night I cleaned and polished every object in the apartment. I felt proud at how I had left our old kitchen gleaming. The next morning I remembered I had to buy flowers before going to the hospital, and I started dressing before calling the kids. I noticed then that my clothing seemed much looser. I had barely slept during Vicky's illness and I'd lost about twenty pounds in the process.

We wanted to give the doctor something to express our appreciation, so I brought along with me the only present we still had in the house: a beautiful conch taken from the crystalline waters of Cuba.

Since we would eventually be going back to Cuba and I was afraid some complication might still result from her illness, I asked the doctor for a copy of Vicky's medical file.

"Generally we don't release the file in such cases. But I'll speak to the director of the hospital so that you can pick up a copy before leaving," was his reply.

We bid the kindly physician farewell with a warm handshake and stopped by the office of the hospital's director to pick up the file. There were records of all the results of the various electrocardiograms and the treatment administered. One thing caught our attention: the diagnosis read, *Acute toxicity resulting from an ingestion of mushrooms*. It was obvious that the director of the hospital didn't want it known abroad that they used serum obtained from animal plasma, without adhering to proper medical procedure in such cases.

We arrived home and as in romantic movies, I asked Vicky to close her eyes and I picked her up in my arms to carry her across the threshold. There we embraced in silence for a long while, happy to be back home together again. I ran a hand through Vicky's hair and then without thinking I said, "Thank God it's all over."

Vicky leaned back slightly to make sure she'd heard me, and staring at me in astonishment, remarked, "I've never heard you mention God before."

"And you . . . do you believe in God?"

"I've always believed," she replied in a quiet voice, as if she were afraid we might be overheard.

"You never told me."

"You never asked me. . . . And you?"

I didn't answer for a moment. Then I turned and walked over to the window. The sky was particularly clear that day.

Thank you, dear Lord, for giving me life, I thought without saying a word. I felt Vicky's arms wrap around my chest as she hugged me from behind.

"Forgive him, Lord," she whispered.

Chapter 11

—

History
Is the
Way It Is

Vicky remained in the house a few more days recuperating, while I reimmersed myself in my studies and my efforts to learn the truth about the political questions that haunted me. I became obsessed with reading the daily papers and magazines, which were reporting events in history that had been kept hidden until then, and I spent long hours each evening going through them and telling Vicky some of their revelations. One of those articles recounted the brutal manner in which the czar and his family had been murdered by the Bolsheviks, and reading it I felt transported back in time to witness a crime that filled me with horror.

In a meeting of the highest organs of power among the Soviets, the leaders of the October Revolution had decided to "execute" the entire royal family in order to demoralize once and for all the defenders of the monarchy who were still fighting against the young dictatorship of the proletariat. I read the report with growing dread:

It was already past midnight when the men charged with guarding the Czar and his family received the order to execute them all. The guards then marched resolutely—their bootsteps shattering the night's stillness—to the chambers where the royal couple slept with their children and ordered them out of their beds. And the children, still sleepy-eyed, were forced to descend those stairs, without understanding why the guards had wakened them. Then they were pushed into the cellar over the protests of their father. They finally reached the subterranean chamber without windows, and they felt beneath their naked feet the cold, rough floor in the same corner where their parents lay. Then they watched those men who had not said a word since awakening them draw their pistols . . . and they felt a bolt of thunder explode their still sleepy little heads. . . .

First they had had to watch their father being struck down; then their mother, drenched in blood . . . and now they no longer heard their own screams of terror as the pistols were turned on them. . . .

I read on, and I felt like I could see the horrified faces of those children murdered nearly seventy years ago. *In the name of social justice! What cause could justify the murder of a child? So that is the history of communism!*

Lenin, the idol who still remained laid out in Red Square, the genius of the century, the one who loved children so much, the absolute leader of the government at the time, was—a murderer. He had been my hero, the model of self-sacrifice, of modesty and simplicity, the man who was always inspired by love. Now I saw him as *the* person responsible for the crime against those children. But it wasn't only Lenin. The heroes of the Great October Revolution whom I'd been taught to worship—they too approved of the crime. And how many other crimes? *And wasn't it a crime to have kept hidden from me the real history of my heroes until today?* I asked myself. *Why had they done it? By what right?*

They had hidden and distorted the facts, presenting Stalin as the most tireless defender against fascism and the supreme artist of its defeat. Now I was discovering that the highly touted Socialist Republics of the Baltic were not conceived by the will of their peoples, but had been the result of a secret pact between Hitler and Stalin, which had permitted the latter to annex them to the Soviet State.

"The great leader who had commanded the epic of the Soviet people against fascism," Raúl Castro had just called Stalin in the latest of his speeches, the same Stalin who had congratulated Hitler when the German troops entered Warsaw; the same who murdered thousands of officers from the Polish army in the Ukraine; the same Stalin who now was accused of the murder of more than forty million Soviets—twice the number of those the country lost in the Second World War!

My thoughts raced on: *And Zhukov, the illustrious marshal who four times was decorated hero of the Soviet Union and whose name graced my war college? I suppose Zhukov, the most important mili-*

tary chief of the Soviet Union during that period, had no inkling of the murder of those Polish officers? Nor did Rokossovsky, Budenny, Vorosshilov, or all the other Russian generals whose feats we are now studying in our classes on the art of war?

First came the crimes of Stalin, of Beria, the shadowy head of the Cheka. Now, those committed by other important figures from the more recent past under Brezhnev. The giant Soviet State, the vanguard of civilization, had been constructed upon the corpses of millions of victims. And never a word, a book, anything that might reach my hands so that I could make my own judgment!

Each magazine, each newspaper, each parliamentary discussion broadcast over television constituted for me a revelation of the evil of a world in which I had believed to the point of having been willing to die for it. I read, and with the pain came the outrage against the kind of enslavement of my consciousness that had been imposed through ignorance and lying since my childhood.

I couldn't help but think of the young soldiers facing death in Angola while considering themselves heroes defending universal justice. They had died with the conviction that what they did was right, like modern Quixotes sowing justice in their path, when in reality they were defending the legitimacy of a crime of which they too were the victims.

But the guilty ones were also men, those who blinded themselves for the sake of power, I thought. *In theory, communism continued to offer the best alternative for a just society. Then why hasn't it functioned?*

So I began to question the theory created by the genius of Marx, Engels, and Lenin through the simplest of reasonings. My thoughts ran thus:

Communism presupposes a solution to the injustices that have dogged humanity because it redistributes the wealth among all in a fair manner . . . And the source of the wealth? Let's see: We take all the wealth and technology that capitalism has accumulated and we hand it over to a country steeped in misery like Angola. Does it solve the problems of that people? Definitely not. The most probable outcome is that with the passage of time they will have consumed the wealth and the technology will remain unutilized.

Then wealth is what is created, not what is consumed. Why then were such peoples as the Germans and the Japanese able to recover from the effects of the Second World War and now count themselves among the greatest economic powers on the planet, while the Soviet Union—so rich in natural resources—finds itself sunk in poverty?

It would seem that wealth is, above all, the result of a combination of a work ethic plus savings, cultivated over the centuries by certain peoples; and of a system that stimulates economic development by offering freedoms to its citizens. Peoples will therefore become wealthy to the extent that they are free and forge their own work ethic.

I spent the days in torment, searching for replies to the increasingly anguished questions that entered my mind, obsessed with the need to learn the truth. One night when Vicky was observing me with growing preoccupation, she commented persuasively, "You're going to drive yourself crazy if you continue like this. . . . What can you do?"

"I don't know. I feel as if I haven't lived my own life."

"But you have to resign yourself to it."

Vicky wanted to rescue me from the world of internal suffering into which I'd been slowly sinking since I'd started to learn about the crimes committed in the name of communism.

"It's that it's not in my nature to accept things the way they are!"

"But you can't change history!"

Vicky didn't understand that I'd begun to feel myself absolutely betrayed, used for the worst possible ends.

"Right, but I refuse to live with lies! I refuse to accept the idea that in Cuba the same sort of thing is going on this very minute."

"Perhaps in Cuba things aren't that way."

"Maybe, but I'm not certain. I don't know what the so-called counterrevolutionaries think; I've never been able to listen to them. The same way I didn't know what had happened here until now! I just hope that, who knows how many years from now, I don't end up learning that in Cuba they committed the same sort of crimes!"

Vicky ran her fingers through my hair.

"I just don't want to see you tormenting yourself."

But I wasn't really listening to her. There kept hammering in my head passages from the recently published interview with Armando Valladares, that "dangerous terrorist" freed in 1982 at the request of the French government, and who now was United States ambassador to the U.N. Commission on Human Rights. Twenty-two years in prison, ten of them naked in a tiny punishment cell, eleven hunger strikes protesting ill-treatment, torture—such were the recollections of that man about Cuba. I couldn't believe it!

I stretched out beside Vicky, pretending to sleep, but one question hammered in my brain: *Could what Armando Valladares says be true?* I felt Vicky trying to nestle against me, and I put my arm around her. *From now on nothing is ever going to be the same*, I thought with apprehension.

—

One afternoon when I arrived home Vicky was waiting for me in a state of total indignation.

"The chief of personnel at the factory got sick, and the woman who took her place has paid us higher wages."

"And?"

"We thought it was a mistake, but it wasn't. They'd been cheating all of us Cubans the whole time until now. The worst of it is that there's nothing we can do about it. Who's going to defend our rights?"

We both saw that they were obviously discriminating.

"We can live off what I earn." I told her as a way of putting an end to the humiliation she had suffered. And that was the last day Vicky worked in the factory.

—

Winter had arrived and once again I was pulling Alejandro to school on his sled, amid the same cacophonic songs and the same protests from passersby. Reyniel took pleasure in the winter that we had never had in Cuba. Each afternoon on the way home from school, he joined the gang of kids skating and playing hockey on the small rink constructed by our neighbors in the courtyard of the building.

One morning when we were waking the children to get ready for school, we noticed blisters had broken out all over Alejandro. We took him to the doctor, who confirmed our suspicions: He had a case of chicken pox. Vicky stayed home with him, while I went off to classes convinced that the disease would run its course in a week, the same as would happen with Reyniel soon after, since he'd never had it either.

In a few days Reyniel also came down with it, but as opposed to Alejandro, his symptoms were more acute. The blisters on his skin were larger and more numerous, and the itching he felt seemed unbearable, making him more and more irritable. Our preoccupation increased seeing Reyniel worsen each day, and we felt really desperate when we noticed the spots appearing in his throat.

We hurried once again to the doctor's, and he explained to us that the disease, normally of short duration, could sometimes be fatal if it invaded the digestive tract. And he immediately filled out a referral to have the child admitted to the hospital for infectious diseases. It was already late in the afternoon when we got off the streetcar and I carried Reyniel in my arms down the long street to where they'd told us the hospital was.

"Here it is," Vicky said, stopping in front of the entrance about halfway along the crumbling, moldy concrete wall that flanked the pavement down the length of the block. A bronze plaque at the entrance read REGIONAL EPIDEMIOLOGICAL HOSPITAL, with an arrow to indicate the path to follow through an evergreen grove on the other side of the wall. It was a walkway that had obviously seen better days: two twisted, rusty lengths of wrought-iron fencing lay toppled in the grass and overgrown with weeds dried out from the winter. Debris, rusty tin cans, and scraps of cardboard were half covered in snow, making us think we'd come the wrong way, when we glimpsed through the foliage an old yellowed building. We continued our weary march until reaching a turn in the walk, which led out of the grove to the entrance of the hospital, an old, dilapidated mansion overrun with vegetation. Two crows poked around in the snow under the wreck of an old truck that lay abandoned in the courtyard, and I felt Vicky clench my arm in fright as they spread their wings noisily in flight.

"It's here?" Vicky asked with a preoccupied look while surveying the desolate scene.

"I think so, unfortunately."

We mounted the few wooden steps of a crumbling portico, avoiding the broken boarding, which threatened to trap one of our legs. We called out at the front door.

"Come in!" The voice echoed unpleasantly from within, and we turned the latch and pushed the door, which opened with a groan.

An elderly woman still wearing her gray kerchief and high winter boots came out to meet us. "What can I do for you?" she asked gruffly.

"Our boy is sick. . . . We have a physician's referral."

The old lady reached out and snatched the paper from my fingers, and read it with an expression of doubt in her eyes, as if inspecting a possible forgery. Then, without looking at us, she muttered while disappearing through a doorway, "Take a seat and wait. I'll call the doctor."

We took the only available seat in the small parlor: a decrepit wooden bench. And there we awaited the arrival of the doctor, absorbed in mournful silence while Vicky took Reyniel's temperature again with a thermometer she'd brought from home. Some energetic footsteps sounded beyond the doorway through which the old woman had disappeared, and we waited expectantly.

A blue-eyed young man with trim beard and reddish hair appeared in the doorway. A white doctor's robe, carefully buttoned, covered his clothes, and a pair of thick-lensed glasses sat unsteadily on his nose by one stem whose lost screw had been replaced with a brass paper clip. Twined among the fingers of his left hand was a carefully folded stethoscope.

"Good evening!" exclaimed the doctor in a youthful, energetic voice.

"Good evening," we answered almost in chorus as we stood up to greet him. Reyniel was still in my arms, and since the moment we passed through the gloomy walls surrounding the hospital, he had fastened himself to my neck, refusing to let go.

"You're Cubans, aren't you?" he asked with evident delight in his tone.

"That's right, Doctor."

"I was in Cuba for two years," he began telling us, and I felt tremendously relieved at the thought that this man was familiar with other horizons besides those of his own country.

At least he knows that this shambles is a far cry from the world's best hospital facilities, I thought to myself, relieved that this physician would at least be aware of the sad aspect of the place and make an effort to reassure Reyniel.

"You know, I was simply fascinated with your country. And medicine is quite advanced there."

Reyniel turned around then, leaving his hiding place between my neck and shoulder long enough to remark, "In Cuba everything is better!"

We reddened in embarrassment, but the doctor agreed, smiling. "You're right, son. In Cuba, everything is better!" Then he turned to us and said more seriously, "As you can see, conditions here are quite terrible, and medical practice, archaic. In this same hospital you have—isolated from the rest of the world, thrown together like excrement—those with leprosy as well as those with syphilis, gonorrhea, and other venereal diseases."

A chill ran up my spine. "Our child is only suffering from a very bad case of chicken pox," I began explaining to the doctor, but he interrupted me with a smile.

"Don't be alarmed. Here all patients are isolated from each other. Chicken pox is a very contagious disease, and this is the only hospital where they treat serious cases."

"But he's a child. You know what sort of hygienic conditions exist here."

"I told you not to worry, he won't be in contact with the other patients." Then he added, turning to Reyniel in a friendly manner, "Now, my boy, let's have a look at you!"

He examined Reyniel carefully, then declared, "He ought to stay in the hospital. . . . I'll bring you personally to one of the rooms we have for children." Then, turning to the desk, he took a flashlight and a gigantic key from one of the cubbyholes, adding: "Follow me!"

Night had already fallen when the four of us left the building, and we followed the doctor along the narrow path, illuminated by the doctor's flashlight, that led to the rear courtyard.

"Careful going up the steps. . . . The stairs are all falling apart here!" the doctor warned us, pausing at the bottom of the few wooden steps leading up to a door with a huge, rusty padlock.

The doctor carefully preceded us, and we heard the padlock give way with a piercing squeak.

"Go ahead, please," he motioned from above after switching on the light, which illuminated the frightened expression on Reyniel's face.

"Daddy, I don't like this place," he whispered fearfully into my ear.

"Me neither . . . but first let's have a look at the room. You have to get better here."

We proceeded up these stairs with the same care to avoid breaking a leg, went through the doorway, and entered a small room furnished with an iron bedstead, a chair, and a little table also made of iron.

"Here the boy will have total privacy," the doctor explained while spreading both arms as if to encompass the entire room.

"You mean just the child?" I asked, disturbed by the reference made in the singular.

"Of course, no one is allowed to stay with the patients. We have a fine staff of nurses on duty to see to everything."

"But we're not about to leave our child alone here! You have to understand." I couldn't help insinuating to the doctor with my tone of voice exactly what I thought of the place.

"All right, we'll make an exception in your case since you're Cuban. We'll allow one of you two to remain with the boy the first night," he relented finally, and pointing then to a small black button attached to the bed, from which emanated two electric wires that extended up the wall to the ceiling, he added, "If you need anything during the night, you only have to press the button and the nurse on duty will come immediately. Tomorrow I'll come by to see how the boy is doing. Good night!" And he turned on his heels and vanished into the darkness of the courtyard.

We were now alone and I had no idea how to discuss with Vicky, in front of Reyniel, either my impressions or the course of action I wanted to take. I merely made a gesture to her suggesting we get out of there, and I received a reproachful stare as an answer. I knew what Vicky wanted to tell me. In the hospital, at least, there ought to exist the medications and equipment necessary for any emergency. What could we do at home if Reyniel suddenly got worse? Where could we go? Inevitably we would have to be admitted to this same hospital.

Vicky calmed Reyniel as best she could, putting him to bed and covering him with the blanket. She afterwards took the little iron chair next to the bed and told me, "I'll stay with him, don't you worry. . . . You look after Alejandro."

The boy had spent the entire day at nursery school, and there was less than half an hour to pick him up before the place closed. We had thought of asking the wife of one of my buddies to do it for us, but how? In the entire apartment house, where they had some 200 apartments, there did not exist a single telephone. Instead, we called the nursery, alerting them that I'd come by at the last minute.

Alejandro greeted me with a scolding when I arrived. "Daddy, I don't like you to come for me so late!" And I had to listen to the string of protests our beloved little tyrant regaled me with all the way home.

That night Alejandro slept curled up against me like a little pup while I counted the hours that remained until morning so that I could hurry back to that infernal place where I'd left Reyniel and Vicky.

"Today you come pick me up early, Daddy. Understand?" Alejandro insisted when I dropped him off at the nursery.

"Today I pick you up early. Daddy promises!"

On reaching the hospital I saw that the padlock was once again hanging from the door to the room in which Vicky and Reyniel had spent the night, and I felt my heart wrench. I mounted the steps in one leap and was searching for any note left on the door when I heard Vicky calling to me from inside.

"Is that you, Oré?" she asked, frightened.

"Yes, it's me. Why's the door locked?"

"I don't know, someone must have done it while we slept," and she let out a sob.

"Daddy!"

I heard Reyniel calling, followed by his own sobbing.

"Daddy, I don't want to be in here!" he continued to cry from the other side of the door, and I felt my vision clouding and my lungs struggling for more air.

Vicky finally spoke up again. "Last night his fever got very high again and, no matter how much I pressed the button the doctor showed us, nobody came. And on top of that they locked us in!"

"Get away from the door!"

Vicky knew what I was about to do.

"We're out of the way," she replied, then continued trying to persuade me not to. "Maybe the nurse who has the key is already up."

But it was too late. The screws holding the hinge from which the padlock hung had already given way and the door flew open, letting the morning light fill the damp room. The three of us hugged each other, and we stood silent a few minutes just clinging to each other.

"I couldn't even give the poor thing an aspirin," Vicky explained, her eyes swollen with crying, "not even an aspirin. I had to bring the fever down with wet towels of cold water. Luckily it seems to have subsided a little."

"We're leaving," I answered once and for all.

"But just walking out?"

"Just walking out. I think we can do better for him at home."

And we wrapped up Reyniel as warmly as we could, while he started laughing in spite of how he felt, overjoyed at the prospect of leaving that inferno. He stood up on the bed, opening his arms and asking me to carry him, and when I picked him up he whispered, kissing my cheek, "I love you so much, Daddy."

As we walked along the path leading back out of the hospital a group of patients walking through a clearing in the wooded grounds, wrapped in their tan dressing gowns, stared at us with surprised curiosity. They seem to have lost nearly all their hair and their faces and arms were dotted with suppurating sores. We passed by them in silence, just a few feet away, and they also contemplated us in silence, raising their arms and slowly waving them back and forth in a mournful, definitive farewell. And when we reached the bend in the pathway, we paused to look back. There they were, motionless and silent, with their sad eyes still fixed upon us. We lifted a hand to also say good-bye, and they answered our farewell with dreamy smiles on their faces.

Luckily Reyniel's condition quickly improved after just a few days under our care, and we had the good fortune never to have to visit a Soviet hospital again.

—

The spring of 1989 arrived, and we anxiously counted the days left before our departure for our vacation in Cuba. Perestroika had given us a new awareness, which made us examine with a more critical eye whatever was happening around us, and little by little we started to question more earnestly an increasing number of the stereotypes upon which we had been raised. Thus the until-then tedious classes in Marxist-Leninist philosophy and dialectical materialism had been converted into open debates in which the professors saw themselves as more and more vulnerable to the arguments expressed by their students.

Our professor of missile technology was a decorated veteran of the Second World War. Founder of the Soviet Missile Command, Colonel Telux was liked and respected by all, in spite of his being thought of as a man devoted to the cult of Stalin. One day when we were commenting in our classes on the decision of the Congress of Deputies to have a monument built in memory of the victims of the Stalinist purges, we asked our beloved professor his opinion on the matter.

"I know you think I'm an admirer of Stalin because I'm not in the habit of talking about the changes which today are shaking the foundations of our country," the colonel began in a barely audible voice while staring over our heads. "I'm already past seventy. My whole life has been devoted to fighting honorably for my country, for the party. During the war, when I climbed out of my trench for the attack on the German positions, I did it crying out, 'For the fatherland, and for Stalin!' Today I can only feel loathing over it, knowing the millions of victims of his dictatorship. But only today, under Perestroika, have I been able to know it. It's like suddenly realizing that my whole life, of which I have always been proud, has in fact been spent in a world that makes no sense. . . ."

The colonel paused for a long moment, seeing how hypnotized we all were by what he was saying. He swallowed dryly, then went on in a broken voice, "I wanted to live it over again. But as you can see . . . we don't have two lives, and as for this one, I don't think I have much left. And I wouldn't want to spend what is left of it . . . wading through the manure."

When Colonel Telux finished, a total silence fell over the room. It seemed as if we'd all been turned to salt by his words. How terrible I felt for my professor!

No, I will never accept seeing myself in your situation sometime in the future, I vowed to myself. *If no one will tell me the truth of my country, then I'll find it out myself!*

—

A new wave of information about the "mysterious West" swept over the media, and we watched with acute interest the first newscasts transmitted directly from the United States, West Germany, and the United Kingdom by journalists from Soviet television. We began thus to understand the workings of the democratic systems of such countries, and the role played by the different institutions of power. "Congress," "Senate," "House" were words that took on significance for the first time with us. And events that before would have gone unnoticed in our scheme of things suddenly took on enormous importance for us.

This was the case with the United States Congress veto of the new president George Bush's choice of Senator Tower for secretary of defense, which was the best proof we could have had until then of the way in which the power of those governing is limited in democracies. That example was enough to make me ask myself whether the most democratic system in the world, as our own leaders termed the Cuban system, would be capable of rejecting any of the nominations or designations for high office made by our own Commander in Chief. The answer, obviously, was totally unfavorable to Fidel Castro, who personally compiled the lists of nominees for membership in the Central Committee, Secretariat, Political Bureau, Council of State, and Ministerial Council and for the positions of deputies, ambassadors, party secretaries, and presidents of the Popular Directorate in the provinces, university rectors, and even some hospital directors. Obviously the "all-powerful president of the United States," as Our Leader called whoever happened to occupy the White House, did not remotely have the powers that he himself wielded.

In our country ministers were appointed and removed without explanation to anybody. An army was sent to Angola in the greatest secrecy, hidden even from our deputies, who never received an accounting of what happened in the war. And the income and resources of the country were arbitrarily disposed of at the whim of our leaders. I had always believed in the honesty of our leaders, blaming our ills on intermediate functionaries whom I saw as opportunistic.

The repercussions of Perestroika in Cuba could be seen in the inauguration of the Process of Rectifying Errors announced by Fidel in 1986, and many of us interpreted it then as a positive step that Fidel was taking in the fight against bureaucracy, corruption, and opportunism.

What fools we were!

Now, on the contrary, Our Leader struck down with the stroke of a pen the laws passed a few years earlier that permitted peasants to sell part of their harvests privately and laborers and artisans to work on their own. He announced, moreover, a ban on Soviet publications, which were previously sold in Cuba, and announced an absolute censorship of all Soviet material arriving on the island.

"We have absolutely no use for such garbage," he had declared recently on one of those videos marked "Secret" in which they recorded his interventions during the meetings of the highest levels of government, and which we now received ad nauseam from the military attaché in Moscow.

It was on those videos that we saw Fidel call Gorbachev a traitor and level his most injurious attacks on figures like Yeltsin and other humanists highly respected by us, such as Sakharov.

History is the way it is, not the way we want it to be, I told myself, condeming the actions of my leaders. *They're simply afraid of the truth.*

Chapter 12

—

Enemies

of the

People

One day we received some news that alarmed us all: Arnaldo Ochoa, the most brilliant of the Cuban generals, had recently been arrested and was under investigation on suspicion of drug trafficking to the United States. For some time now Fidel had made reference in various public addresses to the fact that the United States—in a campaign of lies orchestrated by the CIA to discredit the Revolution—was accusing Cuba of complicity in drug trafficking. At the time, accustomed as we were to the notion that our country had its borders rigidly controlled and free of narcotics traffic, we believed Our Leaders. And absorbed as we were in the political upheaval generated by Perestroika, we had already forgotten the matter of American accusations about the Cuban traffic when news came of the arrest of General Ochoa. From that moment on, the newspapers we received from Cuba a week or so late became the focus of our attention. With each day's editions came new revelations implicating a group of high officials from the Ministry of the Interior, who in complicity with Ochoa had collaborated with the Colombian cartel by facilitating the transhipment of cocaine via Cuba to the United States. The greatest corruption scandal involving the decadence of the Cuban Revolution was now being revealed.

When it finally came to trial, far from accepting the official version of the scandal, I questioned it with arguments prompted by history and common sense. Just prior to the opening of the trial, General Leopoldo Cintra Fría, who had been a subordinate of Ochoa during the Angolan War and now was commander of the troops remaining since the peace treaty was signed, had insinuated in a letter published in the principal dailies that Ochoa's treason could only be exculpated by death. My attention was drawn to the words *treason* and *death*, leaving no doubt in my mind that Ochoa would be executed for a crime that, according to the existing penal code, was punishable by a maximum sentence of fifteen years' imprisonment. The validity of the evidence against him was, to say the least, questionable.

The trial began, for which the accused were given defense lawyers appointed by the State. Following the proceedings as reported by the official press, I seemed to be reading an exact reproduction of the minutes from the trials of Bukharin and other prominent Soviet leaders who were murdered by Stalin. It was simply impossible to differentiate between the allegations of the prosecutor and the defense. The same language, the same accusations of treason—what else could one expect except the death penalty? As the height of hypocrisy, Ochoa had been tried first by a so-called honorary tribunal composed of generals, among whom figured Efgénio Amejeira, rehabilitated recently after having been punished for using drugs and committing immoral behavior.

Ochoa was one of the youngest Cuban generals and was deemed an honored commander and highly influential within the armed forces. He was considered by those who served under him during the war in Angola to be a kindly officer, independent-minded and with a strong personality. His oft-repeated praise for Perestroika was no secret to anybody; nor was his sharp criticism of the deterioration that had taken hold of Cuba. His views were known and shared by many of the men now returning from Angola, and Our Highest Leader—ever perspicacious—swiftly realized how dangerous such men might become with time.

The audacity to think for himself and divulge his thoughts had cost this remarkable general his life. And Our Leader, eager to prevent other military leaders from cultivating independent, critical thinking, did not hesitate to create an unconstitutional tribunal which incorporated nearly all the top military commanders and thereby compromised them with the political crime he had engendered. In that way, far from conspiring, they would become his elite guard, since any change in Cuba would lead to their own trials for the crime committed.

I watched the unfolding of the trial, predicting its outcome, and each day's session only confirmed my suspicion of political intrigue. I understood then that my life would not in any way follow the course drawn for me by the Historical Leaders of the Revolution. All that I had available to me to confirm the betrayal to which I'd been subjected were history and common sense—not a single living witness, not one piece of evidence of repression instituted in my country. But wasn't my own ignorance a form of proof; the fact that we were forbidden to seek information, to read foreign publications, to have any contact with our relatives in the United States?

In the midst of all this one thing was becoming very clear to me: I'd given the best of myself to the cause laid before me by my leaders—I'd believe in it sincerely—and from now on it would be impossible for me to pretend loyalty to something for which I no longer had any respect, or to follow those in whom I no longer believed. Each night I lay awake with tormented thoughts of the future. What to do? Accept things as they were? Let some time pass and then look for a manageable way to get out of the armed forces? And my honor, the dignity I felt I possessed and which allowed me to hold my head up? How would I explain my silence to my children in the years to come? How could I accept their being indoctrinated the same way I had been? They would also grow up obsessed with the struggle against imperialism, grow up without God, without any right to childish fantasies, without Christmas, and I would perhaps end up by watching them march off in a few more years to another unjust war. No, that would be an unpardonable crime.

And if I spoke the truth? If I condemned what I saw and talked to my children of God, of Christmas and the Epiphany? If I taught them to search for the truth about the world no matter how difficult it may be and to form their own judgments? I'd certainly be prevented from accomplishing my task. I'd be accused of being an agent of the always-implicated CIA and thrown in jail, or shot, like Ochoa. The result would be then to have my children turned into pariahs from whom all would flee as if they carried a contagious disease, and they would receive special attentions from my government with the aim of "cleansing their heads of the poison inculcated by their traitor father."

Plot to change things? Obviously the attempt to put an end to all the infamy would be legitimate. But how? One doesn't plot in order to die, but to triumph. My comrades in Cuba seemed to think very differently from me, or at least pretended to. This wasn't the moment; the conditions didn't exist.

It was then I understood the meaning of the word *totalitarianism*: In Cuba it would be impossible to organize clandestine cells, hold secret meetings, travel anonymously, print pamphlets. All the country's institutional structures belonged to the government, were controlled and politicized by the regime, devoted to its defense. Print the truth? It was impossible to obtain a printing press and its possession was illegal. Write to the newspapers? Only "acceptable" views were published. Move to a hotel? They were only available to foreigners with hard currency. Cubans were accorded the right to register in hotels only as an incentive awarded by the State-controlled unions. Lead a clandestine existence? Impossible. To eat in any of the few existing restaurants one would have to devote all of one's time to waiting on interminable lines with no time left for conspiring. And the rationing card system forced one to purchase food at specified stores in the neighborhood. Hide in some friend's home? They wouldn't have enough to feed you, and the Block Committee would inform State security of the presence of a "stranger." It seemed that the only way the system could collapse would be a palace coup or a spontaneous popular uprising, at least for the time being.

And I understood more, I understood the reason for the people's support of the Revolution. Each citizen of Cuba saw himself ensnared one way or another in the ranks of innumerable organizations whose principal task was "safeguarding our socialist conquests" and "struggling against the enemies of the Revolution." At six years of age one became a Pioneer; at fourteen, a member of the Committee for the Defense of the Revolution, of the Federation of Young Cuban Women, or of the selective Union of Young Communists. With matriculation in high school one militated in the Student Federation for Secondary Education; or the Student Federation for University Education, if one was admitted to college. In the labor sector one was inevitably drawn into the state unions and the territorial militia forces.

Whoever refused to join such organizations would be considered an enemy of the Revolution, would never study in a university reserved exclusively for revolutionaries, would be given the worst and lowest-paid employment, would be ostracized by the rest of society eager to demonstrate loyalty to the Revolution, and finally would never have access to a single one of the basic necessities, which were offered by the unions as a stimulus to their most outstanding members.

Not even our wives, who had traveled abroad only as our spouses, escaped such surveillance despite their now being so far away from Cuba. Every month they had to attend obligatory meetings of the Union of Young Communists and the Federation of Cuban Women for political instruction.

And the cult of personality of Our Highest Leader? It was promulgated from childhood, and it no longer passed unnoticed with my new perspective on these things. We had brought first-grade reading material from Cuba with the idea of teaching Reyniel how to read and write Spanish. Vicky had started teaching him the alphabet, using the first reader. When I came home one afternoon I heard them reciting together: "F like Fidel . . . R like Revolution . . . S like smile . . . ," followed by the sentence: "Look at the smile on Fidel in Revolution Square." Vicky was so intent upon Reyniel's learning his ABCs that she hadn't really noticed the content of the book's mes-

The author at fourteen months.

Above: *The author and his inseparable brother Faure, in their years of boarding school and mischievousness.* Right: *The author's family celebrates, in 1966, the first birthday of the youngest brother, Orlando.*

Vicky at fifteen.

Sweethearts stroll along the
Havana Malecón in 1976.

Above: *The USSR, 1979. The author with his classmates and the instructor, at the Air Force Academy.* Below: *The USSR, 1980. The author during a training flight at the Air Force Academy.*

Left: *At the Angola War, 1983, a pilot friend and the author.* Below: *Angola, 1983. Whiling the long hours of guard duty at the cockpit of the MiG.*

Havana, 1981. Reyniel, the firstborn, being held by the author.

Vicky and the author; Santa Clara, 1984.

Reyniel, Vicky, and Alejandro in 1986. This picture came with the author on his first flight to the United States.

The USSR, 1987. At the Marshall Gregory Zhukov War College.

The Lorenzo family at Kalinin, the USSR, 1988.

The group of international graduates from the Marshall Gregory Zhukov War College, the USSR, 1990, together with their instructors.

New York, January 25, 1992. The author rallies for the liberation of his family during a street demonstration.

The author at the office of the Valladares Foundation, during the campaign to free his family.

Above: *May 1992. From left to right: Armando Valladares, Elena Diaz-Verson Amos, Mr. Ronald Quincy, the author, and Mrs. Coretta Scott King.* Right: *July 1992. First day of the hunger strike in Madrid.*

Above: *View of the road where the rescue took place.* Below: *The rock and the transit post that were not in the landing plans.*

October 7, 1992. Virginia and Azul, on their first trip to Cuba, meet Vicky and the boys.

Above: *December 19, 1992. Picture taken by Kristina of the author, in Marathon, minutes before the rescue flight.* Below: *Picture taken by the author: Vicky, Reyniel, and Alejandro, sixteen minutes after the rescue, during the flight to freedom.*

Above: *Photo of the author taken by Vicky shortly before landing in the United States.* Below: *Vicky is the first one to land in Marathon; here she embraces Kristina.*

At a hotel in Miami, the first day of freedom, together with Elena and Kristina.

February 19, 1993.
The maid of honor
and the best man
accompany Orestes
and Vicky at their
wedding before God.

sage. That night we revised the remaining text, substituting other examples for each letter. We simply couldn't endure it!

Quite possibly society as a whole detested the system that forced it to live that way, but that was impossible to determine. Pretending loyalty to the Revolution was the only possible way to survive.

How blind I'd been until now!

I might plot on my own to appease my conscience, then rot in a cell or fall riddled with bullets from a firing squad but take my honor with me. But my family, my children? What evils would they be left to face alone? To what would they be subjected in the name of the fatherland?

Enough of all this demagoguery, which has only brought tragedy to our people! The fatherland is the sum of the interests of all families, and I must begin by defending my own family's! I told myself— considering for the first time the possibility of defecting. I decided to speak with Vicky about it.

One afternoon I asked her to take a walk with me to the Volga River, a half mile from our apartment house. The existence of some system of auditory surveillance in the building might have spelled dire consequences for the things I had to say to Vicky. We stretched out on the sandy shore and watched Reyniel and Alejandro playing in the small park in front of us. I took Vicky's hand and, brushing off the sand on it, I asked her, "Do you realize what's happening?"

"You mean to you?"

I nodded my head.

"Of course . . . you hardly sleep anymore!"

"I can't sleep now, and I won't be able to survive tomorrow if I have to live a lie in silence."

"You frighten me. At times I think you're going to do something crazy. Please think of our sons."

"It's you and them I'm thinking of above all."

"Love!" she exclaimed, hugging me tightly. "It's just that when I first knew you you always said first the Revolution and then the family. How happy you make me now!"

"Good, good. The fact is you've always been what's most important to me. Before I used to think that we'd all live to be proud of the sacrifices we'd made."

"Yes, but I'd never heard you say it."

"I've been thinking about defecting . . ."

"What?"

". . . remaining in Canada when the plane stops for refueling."

Vicky first stared at me in astonishment, her eyes wide open. Then a smile of complicity formed on her lips and, shaking her head from side to side, she murmured, "You really have gone crazy."

"Hope is called insanity nowadays?"

She smiled again. "But how are you going to do it, whom will you go to at the airport?" And she added with a warning, "You don't speak English." Vicky leaned her head back again on my shoulder, murmuring, "Canada . . ."

"I know it'll be very hard in the beginning, but if the system there is the way I think it is, it's worth a try. Just imagine, Vicky. We'll learn English together while the boys are in school. We're enterprising, I know we'll be able to find some kind of work."

Vicky listened to me while absorbed in her own thoughts. Then she looked into my eyes and, to my surprise, appeared more convinced than I had hoped for.

"All right then, but we wait till the return trip, after our vacation."

I couldn't hold back the smile of happiness on my lips.

"You didn't understand what I meant. I'm talking about doing it next year, after I've finished my studies."

"And why not this year?" Vicky asked with a disappointed expression.

"This is a radical decision. Although I don't have the slightest hope that change could still happen in Cuba in the time remaining for me to finish my studies. Besides, I want to complete the studies I've undertaken. The knowledge may prove useful in the future."

"In the military?" This time Vicky's expression showed real disappointment, and I realized that she also had hopes that I would put an end to my military career.

"No, of course not. But perhaps in some university."

"Let's hope things change and we don't have to do it," Vicky concluded, lowering her eyes, and I realized we'd have to think hard about it. The prospect of starting a new life in a country where we didn't know anybody involved so many unknowns.

Reyniel and Alejandro came up to us, arguing, and as usual we had to sort it out and make peace between them. Then all four of us headed back hand in hand, to the rhythm of one of Alejandro's improvised songs, as well as to Reyniel's complaints about his brother's horrible pitch.

—

When August came we left for vacation in Cuba, enveloped in a euphoria of happiness at the impending reunion with our loved ones. At the news of our arrival my father hastened to Havana with my mother and brothers, and after we all embraced each other with great emotion he asked me to come outside to see something.

"Look, it's got yellow plates now," he said pointing to the Soviet auto he had used for work all these years and which now displayed the yellow license plates reserved exclusively for private vehicles. It had already been his for all practical purposes, and he had maintained it as well as he could with the hope that one day they'd allow him to buy it and thus have free use of it.

In previous years, when Vicky and I were living at Santa Clara and he would visit, he was pained by the conditions in which we lived and the terrible difficulties Vicky experienced almost daily while going to and from her job. I realized that he would have liked to help us at least by lending us that official car he utilized for his work; but unlike others my father would in his nobility never conceive of allowing his children to use something that belonged to the State for their private ends.

Now he was showing it off to me with its new yellow plates and patting me on the shoulder. He added with evident pleasure, "It's yours—you can use it whenever you wish."

I knew quite well my father's sense of honor and the dedication with which he had devoted himself to the so-called work of the Revolution. He had lived his whole life immersed in the most understandable humility, refusing opportunities for wealth and privileges that the positions he occupied might have brought him. His life had been that of a romantic idealist, and now I was filled with pity at the thought of how difficult it was going to be for him when the moment for facing the truth arrived.

During the vacation I made a few attempts to share with my father some of the indignation I felt for what I considered to be a betrayal of myself, of him, of all the Cuban people. But I ran up against his preconceptions, which were difficult to overcome by simple conversation. He needed actual experience, the undeniable truth of events, which I could not offer him with mere words. His attitude brought back to me the memory of dear Colonel Telux, and I decided to respect his peace.

During the month we spent in Cuba, other high officials were arrested and condemned to long prison sentences. Among them, the all-powerful minister of the interior and the chief of State security. They were accused of the unlawful use and distribution of government property and of "capitalist aberrations." All the crimes that were imputed to them in the trial were also being committed daily by the Highest Leader, who administered the property of the State at his own whim.

—

On the way back to Moscow we made a fuel stop in Canada, and while we sat in the transit lounge waiting to board the plane again, I noticed Vicky looking longingly through the plate glass window . . . toward the street.

"Next time," I promised softly.

The last year of study began and we anxiously continued to watch developments in Cuba. The execution of General Ochoa and the jailing of the principal officials of the Ministry of the Interior was followed immediately by a thorough purging of the lowest echelons. Thousands of students being educated in the Soviet Union were recalled to Cuba, and the bilateral accords governing educational exchanges were suspended. They began to refer to youths contaminated with the virus of the truth as "Perestroikers." We were sent a video in which Our Highest Leader attacked them as self-seeking traitors, which dampened completely the remote expectations we still had of changes in Cuba.

It was autumn when the wave of revolutionary changes swept through all of Eastern Europe, taking the world by surprise, and we shared unreservedly the jubilation of our German friends over the fall of the Berlin Wall. This event created a truly ridiculous situation for us all, inasmuch as until very recently we had had to begin our presentation of the decisions we made during war games with the well-known refrain: "Because of the threat represented by the NATO bloc to the socialist countries . . ." And now it turned out that one of these socialist countries had been integrated into that camp, making the German officers with whom we studied part of NATO's forces.

"So *you're* the threatening enemy," we would chide them affectionately when we met between classes.

Barely a few weeks had gone by since the Congress of Rumanian Communists, during which television had broadcast images of the delirious masses cheering, *"Long live Ceausescu!"* when the latter was deposed by a popular uprising. And I watched events in Rumania with the growing realization that that was the only way it might be possible to bring about a change in Cuba. But Castro, prescient as always, had anticipated events by eliminating factors and people that might have brought things to a head.

The German officers left for their winter vacation in February 1990, anxious to cross the fallen barrier that had once been the Berlin Wall and see with their own eyes what was once the other side. East Germany had been the socialist country with the highest standard of living, and I waited anxiously for the return of my German friends to hear what they had seen of the other side, supposing that it was still possible that they might bring me disheartening news about capitalism, which now seemed to be the best option for civilization. My friends finally arrived and one day when I found myself alone with them in the cafeteria, I asked Mattias, "So, what's your impression of the other side?"

Mattias looked me up and down as if I had come from another planet.

"What do you mean, what impression? I was enraged."

"Enraged . . . you hated the West that much?"

"No, my friend, enraged at discovering how I'd been duped for so many years."

With the arrival of spring I was devoting all my energies to finishing my diploma project. General Boris Ivanovich Popov, who held the chair in tactical aviation, was to be my director in preparing the defense of my project. The more we worked together, the more I got to know that man, who had first seemed so unapproachable and now showed himself to be communicative and caring, taking pleasure in our collaboration on my project. Little by little a sincerely cordial relationship blossomed between us, and more and more frequently our conversations would turn upon political matters.

One day when we were discussing the situation in Cuba, he told me, "Fidel has betrayed all of you, son, just like Stalin did to us. Don't allow them to tarnish your life."

"You can be sure I won't," I replied, and we never again spoke of Cuba, or of how I was going to avoid their tarnishing my life.

Another day the general presented me to his aide-de-camp, a stocky, powerful-looking man with typical Russian features.

"Private Alexander Nikolaievich," he introduced himself. He saluted smartly and stepped forward, extending his hand.

We shook hands, and then the general continued, "Alexander is a fantastic draftsman and wanted to help you with the preparation of whatever diagrams you will need for your diploma defense."

Sasha, as everybody called Alexander, began working with me on the complicated schematics I had sketched out on various sheets of paper, which he now elaborated on with great skill on the large sheets of poster paper I'd utilize during my defense. As we worked we'd talk about different things, and he turned out to be a humble, good-natured person, completely devoted to his family, and a pious Christian who had been obliged for many years to keep his religious faith a secret.

One day I told Vicky about my new friend, whom I wanted to invite to dinner along with his family. I wanted our families to get to know each other, and to thank him in this way for the generous help he'd given me. On the specified afternoon Sasha arrived with his wife and son, and the customary bottle of vodka under his arm. We served some typical Cuban dishes, which fascinated him, and we watched the children happily playing together, when we noticed that the bottle of vodka on the table had sat practically untouched. At which point Sasha confessed to me, reddening, "I brought the vodka because it's customary . . . but I'm not much of a drinker either."

We were also invited to dine at his house: an apartment of sorts in a building near the river that had the look of a fortress constructed centuries ago. There they shared the bathroom and kitchen with their neighbors, finding privacy only in the confines of their bedrooms. Sasha and his wife turned out to be extremely hospitable people who reminded me of the peasants found in the works of the greatest

Russian authors. As soon as we entered his home, we were lavished with abundance and joy. Svieta cooked exquisitely and, through her, we discovered a delicious Russian dish previously unknown to us. When we praised it she explained that they had inherited certain recipes from their grandparents, and that they only ate dishes that they themselves prepared from products grown on their relatives' farm. Then Sasha stood up and rolled back the carpet from the center of the room to lift open a kind of trapdoor that led to a small basement. And despite my protests to the contrary, he started taking out sausages and other foodstuffs carefully stowed away, which he insisted we taste. And we laughed Sasha exclaimed, "Now tell me . . . what do you think of real Russian food?"

I felt such respect and admiration for my friend, who was so proud of his family, his beliefs, and his culture. It was a time that filled us with hope for the future of that country. We were fortunate enough to get to know some of our neighbors better, as well as the retired head of our studies program, Colonel Kustiukov—who all dedicated themselves to their families with sobriety and devotion in a society that each day seemed more decadent. But I will always think of my friend Sasha as the most genuine Russian of all those I knew.

—

Winter had gone, luckily not a harsh one that year, and we finished up our classes and all the necessary preparations for defending our diploma projects. So on that May afternoon of 1990, on which we were to celebrate the Soviet victory in the Second World War, we Cubans decided to set out earlier than usual on a walk. As our group of officers strolled along the avenue bordering the river, delighting in the first rays of sunshine in many months, we saw a group of people crowding around the entrance to an establishment selling alcoholic beverages. Realizing that they would be opening for the occasion, we decided it would be nice to buy a few beers to celebrate the end of classes. It was nearly an hour before the little place would open, so we joined the line of impatient customers. The majority of these were old men and women who today were proudly wearing the medals they'd won in the war, and I regarded them with profound respect, reading the inscriptions on their ribbons and imagining the feats they'd performed in battle for the glory of their country. And as I glanced at each medal pinned to their ragged clothes and read the inscriptions— *Medal of Valor . . . of Meritorious Combat . . . Wounded in Battle*—I was overcome with a feeling of shame at the inevitable comparison that occurred to me: ourselves, young and handsome, with impeccable military uniforms; and these people, so poor, so ragged, so forgotten.

As the hour finally approached for the shop to open, other customers began arriving. Then when there were just a few minutes to go, a gang of tough youths showed up, determined to go in first.

They suddenly charged the crowd of waiting veterans and pushed their way to the front of the line. The old people protested against the insolent behavior of the youths, who laughed at them and told them to go back home where they belonged. Already some of the youths had managed to reach the door of the establishment, while others were pushing their way forward by slamming the terrified veterans over the head in a rude, gladiatorial display. Even we were getting shoved back and forth by the onslaught of youths, coming from all directions. One veteran demanded respect for his medals and was answered by a blow on the head. That was the final straw for all of us, who could no longer stand by passively and watch. Without thinking I shouted, "Enough! Show respect for your veterans!"

At the same time our group charged the entrance in full force, punching any of the youths who happened to get in our way, until we cleared a path through which we asked the veterans to pass. The old people broke into applause at our actions, which had surprised everybody, while the impulsive, headstrong youths looked on with stupefaction from the safe distance to which they'd retreated. We didn't know if it was our accent or our uniform that commanded their respect, but whatever it was we were happy it worked, because they certainly had the numbers and the physiques to flatten us like mosquitoes. As we left the place we walked right by them, and we noticed that some of them lowered their heads.

—

An official from military Counterintelligence who was stationed in Moscow had recently arrived and, in an unusual procedure, visited each and every one of our apartments on one pretext or another. I knew he hoped by such visits to examine the manner in which we lived and to detect any articles that might betray some special relationship with the German, Hungarian, and Polish officers, in order to determine the degree of contagion we suffered from the strains of freedom rocking Eastern Europe. He would also take advantage of the opportunity to question each of us about the opinions the others had expressed on the subject of political changes. I realized then that we were objects of suspicion and fear to our leaders.

I had openly criticized the trial of General Ochoa and the policy of censorship applied in Cuba. And even though I trusted in the discretion of my buddies, I couldn't be sure that one of them might not inform Counterintelligence of my opinions. That would have been sufficient reason to have me sent back to Cuba with my family on a flight in which passengers would not be permitted to disembark during the stopover for refueling, and once back home I would be subjected to careful scrutiny. Over the past few months I had also noted that a number of the letters I'd sent to my parents seemed to have gone astray. Now with the visit from that Counterintelligence officer, I realized that they must have been checking our mail as well.

It was obvious that Our Leaders were worried about their own men, and I decided to write a letter to my parents, but in reality for the analysts in Counterintelligence. I carefully embroidered into it the old, nauseating platitudes about anti-imperialism so that they would judge me to be free of bad influences. And I found the ideal pretext for it in the latest brouhaha sent up by the Cuban newspapers over the latest U.S. military exercises to be held off Cuba at the end of May. I wrote, *The imperialists had better think twice before committing any aggression against my country! Because even if I'm not there right now to defend it, I'll fight against them wherever I happen to be!*

—

All that remained was to finish our final exams, go through our graduation ceremony, and take the leap into the unknown that I'd proposed to Vicky the previous year. I took a Russian-English dictionary out of the college library, and paged through it, memorizing the words I'd have to say to the Canadian police at Gander Airport: "We're Cubans and we don't want to continue our flight. We need your protection." I also began to instruct Vicky, on our trips to the little beach along the river, as to the manner in which we should do it, but each time I brought it up she'd become very serious and completely aloof. I realized then that something was wrong.

"What's the matter? Why won't you say anything?" I asked her over and over worriedly.

And she'd answer with pleading eyes, "Please . . . I don't want to talk about it now."

And I'd let it pass, day after day, seeing her pensive, hesitant.

One night I whispered into her ear a reminder that the moment was approaching and we should be prepared for it. Immediately, she broke into sobbing.

"Please, don't say anything more about it. It's driving me crazy!" she implored.

Vicky was going through one of the worst moments in her life. I realized that the nearness of events had caused her to reflect more seriously upon it—and that she had changed her mind!

I took her in my arms and held her close while I begged her in a whisper to calm herself.

"Let's walk to the river, we have to talk."

Seated on a bench in a park where the children enjoyed playing, I turned Vicky's face toward me to see her eyes, which seemed to have fled to infinity.

"What made you change your mind?"

"My parents. . . . They'll be waiting for us at the airport. . . . Can you imagine what will happen?"

I understood that the year she had spent without seeing her mother and father had weakened her resolve. The last time they had watched us leave they had tears in their eyes while exclaiming: "At least this time it's only for a year!"

Vicky wasn't ready for any good-byes that might be permanent.

"Your comrades will walk out of the airport yelling at them, 'Scum! Vermin! Your children are traitors!' And you can be sure the crowd always gathered there will commit some act of repudiation. . . ."

"I don't think they really would. Those acts of repudiation are never spontaneous. They're organized by the government."

But she wasn't listening to me.

"Can you imagine my parents in that kind of situation? My mother would have a heart attack. It would kill her." And she broke into tears again. "Forgive me, I couldn't endure it! I'm not ready yet!"

"It's not a matter of waiting until later. This is the only opportunity we're going to have. You know we'll never have another occasion for all four of us to be traveling abroad."

It was simply a fact that in Cuba there seldom existed the possibility of anyone's traveling abroad with the entire family, not even most diplomats, who were required to leave part of their families at home. We had been an exception, and the opportunity would likely never be repeated.

I felt sorry for Vicky, and sorry for myself and my sons. What poor creatures we were, hostages to the system because of our love for our family!

"Have you thought of the children, of their future? Don't you think we'll feel guilty seeing them grow up in a lie, watching them go off tomorrow to some other unjust war from which they might not return?"

"I don't know, I don't know! . . . And have you thought of how it could be if in Canada tomorrow we find ourselves thrown out on the street without a penny to buy milk for our children?"

The question suddenly revealed to me the hazards of such an undertaking, and I realized with horror that Vicky might be right. I knew I could convince her to take the leap, but it was a leap into the unknown. And if she *was* right? If once we were in Canada nobody helped us, and our children began to cry for food, which we couldn't provide?

"I can't really say. All I have is faith, nothing more," I said, defeated, tormented that I couldn't convince her that I didn't see it that badly. We'd be free! What more could one want?

"I only know that going on like this I wouldn't survive, that I'd begin to die, little by little—"

"Please don't say that!"

"I can't lie to you. Freedom is something you carry in your heart, and I've found it in mine. If I can't exercise my freedom it would be like slowly dying . . . without dignity, without honor . . . ashamed of my existence."

"But think of your parents, of your brothers."

"I do think of them, but above all I think about our sons. They will be subjected to a crime about which I couldn't even speak to protect them."

"It's because you're here right now that you think this way. When you get back and see your parents and your brothers you'll see how it'll all be different."

Poor Vicky! How innocent she was! It pained me already because I knew what the future held in Cuba; I already perceived the tragedy that would befall the family. But she didn't see it yet.

"All right," I began by telling her, already exhausted by the collapse of my dream, "we won't talk about it again. We'll go back!"

Vicky's mood clearly improved from that moment on, and I hid as best I could the already unbearable despair that would remain with me for a long time to come.

—

Graduation day arrived and we were splendidly dressed for the solemn proceedings, which would take place in the courtyard of the war college.

After we were lined up in formation in the courtyard, standing at attention as we listened to the address given by the commander of the college, Reyniel suddenly broke out of the ranks of families attending the ceremony and raced across the parade ground shouting at the top of his lungs, "Dirty rats! What are you doing? Stop it, you dirty rats!"

The more than one thousand faces assembled there now turned to watch Reyniel running to fight off a group of other boys who were trying to remove some baby pigeons from a nest, which, curiously enough, had been built in the mouth of one of the old cannons enshrined there as museum pieces.

"*How embarrassing!* Do you see what your son's doing?" someone behind me muttered, lightly tapping my shoulder.

"Of course I do, and it's the proudest thing that could have happened to me here today!"

Once the ceremony was over we marched past the podium in a final review. In a few more days we'd be leaving for Cuba and I'd once again resume my duties as a military commander. We paraded to the measured strains of a military band, and I reflected that this was the first time I was marching in retreat, to where no hope remained.

Chapter 1 3

—

A   D o o r w a y
O u t   o f   H e l l

"Attention!"

The voice of our chief of staff, Lieutenant Colonel Teddy Rodríguez, crackled over the loudspeakers, rebounding with a deafening
echo off the dormitory walls to the other side of the parade ground.
From my place on the podium I observed the various troops assembled for that Monday morning reveille of August 1990: four fighter
squadrons, the aerotechnical support batallions, communications,
security—all standing perfectly aligned in block formation. Rodríguez
turned on his heel and, lifting a hand to his cap in a military salute, he
began to deliver the order of the day to the base commander, who
stood next to me on the podium.

"Comrade Lieutenant Colonel Cordero, the units participating . . ."

Cordero listened to the report and, with his right hand also held
in salute, he greeted the troops:

"Good morning, Comrade Officers, Subordinates, Sergeants, and
Soldiers!"

"Good morning, Comrade Lieutenant Colonel!" thundered the
voices of the men on the parade ground like a dissonant chorus weary
of a thousand rehearsals.

Then the political officer spoke, filling the troops in on the latest
"Yankee imperialist ploys against Cuba." Finally, Cordero presented

me to all the assembled units as the new second commander of the base.

The news of my promotion to second-in-command reached me shortly after our arrival back in Cuba, and I had received it without much excitement. There was no longer any responsibility I could fulfill with real interest. I would gladly have renounced my commission in the air force to serve in some lesser capacity a government built on lies. But how? It would have certainly been interpreted as a betrayal of the party, of the armed forces, of the Commander in Chief.

Cordero, a friend of many years, was now to be my immediate superior. He had finished his superior command studies in the Soviet Union two years earlier, and had acted as second-in-command of the base at Santa Clara until his recent promotion to base commander. Now I was listening to him present me as the officer who would take over his previous duties at the head of these troops, among whom I noticed many familiar faces and others completely strange to me, having been assigned to the base during my four-and-a-half-year absence.

A few days earlier, while driving with Cordero in his car, I listened as he railed against the enemies of the Revolution who, emboldened by events in Eastern Europe, were criticizing its accomplishments: "Many false revolutionaries are now hoping to use the situation . . . and the Revolution must crush them without hesitation."

"You think there's no vice or corruption in our society?" I asked him while watching him drive. He kept silent, and I continued, "If you had officials actually betraying their people, the best way of protecting their positions would be to accuse anybody who criticized them of being an enemy of the Revolution, don't you think?"

Cordero continued to drive in silence, and I understood then that he preferred the empty glory of his position to coming to terms with his conscience. What a temptation it was to tell him that those very people he was defending had once proposed to me that I seduce his wife! But I preferred to keep quiet. I knew he'd never believe me, anyway.

I started my first day on the job, and already I had to cope with basic housing problems for my family for which, however, there was no adequate solution to be found. Due to our prolonged absence, the wooden window frames in the kitchen and bedrooms had rotted out completely and now threatened to give way and plummet four stories to street level. It was obvious that they should be replaced to avoid a serious accident, but replaced with what? Even though the apartment belonged to the base, there was no one charged with its maintenance and repair, nor any place to buy wood to rebuild the frames. What little in the way of raw material existed was earmarked "for the works of the Revolution."

Only one alternative presented itself: to take some of the wood stored in the brigade warehouses, or in those of the nearby construction company, and have the carpenter on the base do the job in his spare time. It was Cordero who'd actually suggested the idea when he saw the state of our windows. He himself had had to do the same thing two months earlier. And this was the problem, so very simple in appearance, which now dogged me: I didn't want to do it—I didn't want to ask for wood from the neighboring construction company, or to take it from the base's supplies, or to solicit the private help of a carpenter who figured in the ranks of my subordinates. But how to buy the materials? Whom to see?

Each time I returned home in the evening Vicky would point out the danger such windows represented to passersby.

"There's nothing I can do," I would reply bitterly.

And then she would point out her own helplessness. "How are we going to live without windows? We won't have any privacy whatsoever. . . . How will the boys sleep when it rains?"

"We'll deal with it the way any simple, honorable family would."

"But how do you think people deal with their problems? Are you blind? The State won't sell you even the most ordinary items, and so everybody just takes whatever they need to survive from the companies they work for."

Vicky was absolutely right. I saw myself caught now in the following predicament: either I succumbed irreversibly to that subtle mode of corruption imposed by the system by having a talk with the construction company so that they'd give me "some scraps of wood" and asking the carpenter at the base to do me the favor of rebuilding my windows in his free time, or I and my family would live with the gaping holes in the walls left by fallen windows.

Of course I had to choose the former. The foreman of a team of construction workers, whom the Highest Leader had personally congratulated a short time ago on her excellent work, agreed to supply me with some "discarded" pieces of lumber. I also had a talk with the carpenter, who willingly installed the new windows. But an unpleasant sense of shame lingered in me for a long time after.

If I had to do this to solve such a simple problem, what wouldn't the highest government officials be capable of doing to manage their own needs? I kept asking myself, and I was overwhelmed with disgust. Our leaders had endeavored to construct a society overrun with fine revolutionary slogans, but corrupt to the core. That mode of enforced corruption imposed by the system itself was just another method of demoralizing and debilitating the ones who served it, making them continually suffer a guilty conscience that must be expiated by more and more sacrifice.

In the four and a half years I'd been away, some changes had taken place on the base. From a single regiment of jet fighters, the base had enlarged to house a brigade, which had under its command additional security, communications, and aerotechnical support battalions. Construction had also been completed on the magnificent bunkers for housing the latest squadron of fighters. We were now awaiting the swift delivery of MiG-23 BNs to be shifted from Havana, and construction was nearly finished on the more than one dozen bunkers built for the protection of personnel in the event of a North American bombing.

Nevertheless, the same eternal problems continued to plague the daily lives of the troops. Each day at the end of a work shift, officers and enlisted men could be seen heading off in the direction of the nearby woods with newspapers under their arms.

One day as I inspected the recently completed personnel bunkers with the engineer in charge of their construction, we were repelled from the entrance of each shelter by the stink of excrement the troops had left there.

"I hope you never have to dive in here during an air raid," the engineer remarked humorously, referring to the brigade's personnel.

"I hope you never have to live under the conditions these men are living in now," I replied without further comment.

Hounded by the same old problems, these men found themselves in an even worse situation due to the termination of Soviet aid, known in Cuba as "just and mutually beneficial commercial exchange." Meat, eggs, milk, and other products had been eliminated from their diet, and they had to work off-hours in makeshift gardens to assure themselves of a minimum to eat.

Our country, with its exceptionally fine climate for agriculture—in which it was possible to grow two or even three harvests a year—now found itself heading irremediably toward widespread hunger. The government easily could have alleviated the scarcity of food simply by permitting the peasants to work the land on their own and be free to sell their crops. But this would have inevitably brought economic independence to the peasants, to the thousands of workers who would have headed for the countryside in search of better pay, and to additional thousands of small businessmen and intermediaries who would have arisen to sell country goods in the cities. And moreover, people's living standards would be determined by their dedication to their jobs, not by their unconditional loyalty to the regime. Who then would attend the manifestations of revolutionary fervor, the weekend volunteer work sessions, the territorial militia troop exercises, the massive gatherings in Revolution Square to adore the Leader? Where would be the masses to demonstrate their support for Revolution by their participation in such activities? Most likely busy with their new jobs, which would offer them real economic incentives.

It would have been impossible for the government to control like a flock of sheep those now economically independent men and women who would pose a real danger to the extent that the well-being of their families would depend on their own efforts and not on the infinite charity of the State. Such men and women would thus have to be permitted to speak their own minds on political matters. And Our Leaders clearly understood as much, given their prescient instincts for self-preservation, which compelled them to speak rather of the impending privations provoked by the Soviet Union's betrayal and the United States' commercial embargo.

New and mystifying definitions like "Extraordinary Period of War in Times of Peace" began to be repeated incessantly at the time by the machinery of government propaganda. More than 200 directives personally penned by the Highest Leader were issued from his desk, establishing privations to which the populace must submit in order to confront "this difficult period in the face of North American imperialist threats." Every man and woman in the country saw him- or herself plagued by the notion, disseminated through all the militant organizations, that the United States intended to conquer them through starvation, and a new slogan was soon being repeated everywhere: "Resist, Resist, and Resist!" Once again they were appealing to the pride of a young nation, inciting it with a lie in order to keep it subjugated, and very few were still capable of understanding, in the midst of such fevered hatred toward the United States, that no commercial embargo could be blamed for the absence of agricultural products that the country itself was capable of growing in abundance.

Every means of communication had been brought to bear on the campaign, and I found myself shocked by the blindness that overcomes people in such circumstances and of which I had been a victim myself in the past. But now I had returned from the Soviet Union with the virus of truth in my brain and I questioned everything, discovering with horror that the tragic holocaust, visited upon other peoples in the past, could be glimpsed now in Cuba's future.

———

Little by little our life returned to its rhythm of five years earlier. Vicky finally began work in the same dental polyclinic in Santa Clara, faced the same vicissitudes on her daily commutes to and from her job. A new day-care center, built near our apartment, had at least freed her from traveling in that always overcrowded bus with Alejandro in her arms.

Meanwhile I'd started flying again and instructing the younger pilots. My standby alerts were not spent any longer at the foot of a plane but at the head of the complement on duty at our joint command post and that of the Anti-air Missile Brigade, with a frequency that sometimes reached two or three times a week. There in front of the radar screens and mock-ups of the aerial situation, I'd meditate sadly on my family's circumstances and the terrible future that hovered over my country.

We'd inherited on loan a telephone belonging to a friend who'd departed for his advanced training, and Alejandro got into the habit of sitting on the bedroom dresser to await my call. The boy had gotten used to my daily company during the years of study in the Soviet Union, and he now refused to eat dinner before talking to me.

"Mommy, why does Daddy have to always be on duty?" he'd ask with evident annoyance.

One day when I was passing his day-care center, I heard a siren and immediately saw the children running to the underground shelter constructed beneath the school courtyard. They were being trained for the day when the North Americans would bombard Cuba. That night when I got home, I heard Alejandro mentioning the inevitable war with the evil Americans, and the way he was going to defeat them. I looked at Vicky and burst out, "I can't stand it!"

Vicky lowered her head and walked off to our bedroom, while I stayed, playing with the boy.

—

It was December 1990, and the imminence of a war in the Persian Gulf was the constant theme of discussion among my comrades at the base, who got their information from the latest issues of *Granma*. A manifestly euphoric sympathy for Saddam Hussein was expressed in the Cuban press at the time, which emphasized the high level of combat readiness among Iraqi troops to confront the North Americans successfully. All my comrades were busy praising the Iraqi lines of defense, calculating the tens of thousands of casualties the U.S. forces would suffer during the first day of combat. I was astonished at the blindness with which men of superior military training viewed the probable development of the Gulf War.

It was then, on various occasions in the dining hall, that I got into discussions with my comrades—Cordero, Méndez, who was the political officer, and Teddy—expressing in all sincerity my strictly professional opinion.

I told them that I thought it was obvious that the concentration of supplies and forces orchestrated by the United States and its allies would allow them to engage in a prolonged and independent action against Iraq. The months of waiting and international pressure on the Baghdad regime had also permitted them to conduct an exhaustive surveillance of the exact positions of Iraqi troops and armaments with the most advanced visual and radioelectronic means possible. It was not difficult to imagine therefore that the evident air supremacy and the long-range capability of their "smart" weapons was going to allow the allied troops to strike the Iraqi positions with impunity and, aided by powerful radioelectronic jammers, to neutralize the Iraqis' defense systems, cut off their supply lines, and destroy the bulk of their armaments. By the time the ground assault was launched, the Iraqi troops would be completely demoralized and the advance of the allied ground forces would be unstoppable.

Such opinions drew the attention of Counterintelligence officers, who began to ply me indirectly with more questions about events in the Persian Gulf, searching for any signs of sympathy on my part for the North American forces bivouacked there. They sent me more than one "mole" to elicit such sympathies from me, of the sort they'd spoken to me about years earlier when they had tried to recruit me for the same job. I simply limited my responses to the most general terms of professional evaluation. Then they went off apparently to present their findings to their analyst-superiors, while I made up my mind to exercise greater care in expressing my opinions, or I was going to pay dearly for them.

—

On Monday mornings Cordero generally reported to divisional head-quarters and I had to take his place at morning reveille in front of the brigade. There I would hear the order of the day while looking over the sad, exhausted faces of those young enlisted men, who had to endure the added burden of duties provoked by the latest "North American imperialist threats against Cuba" and the "betrayal by the former socialist countries of Europe." I'd scan their mournful faces, reading the boredom they felt at listening to the same business every day—and it seemed as though I was being asphyxiated by the repugnance I felt for those political precepts meant to keep them in ignorance.

Each passing day brought home the truth of the prediction I'd made to Vicky prior to our return: I felt like I was dying. I'd lost hope, and I was drowning in the sea of lies surrounding me. I watched our children come home to talk about the "war against the Yankees," and I felt guilty and ashamed of myself for not being able to tell them that no such war existed unless the Highest Leader provoked it. I would return home each day and lose myself in thought while sitting in front of the television, which I'd been accorded the right to purchase upon my return from the Soviet Union. And there I'd sit, consumed by the anguish that was slowly killing me. I no longer played with the boys and I barely spoke to Vicky. Only one thought hammered inside my head uncontrollably: *My honor; what's happened to my honor? What's happened to my dignity as a human being? Where is my pride at saying whatever I think? I'm a coward. . . . I have to explode, even if it costs me my life. Death is preferable to living a lie.*

Vicky would observe me from the kitchen doorway and ask me all the time, "What's the matter?"

And each time I would answer her, "Nothing."

The days passed and I grew more and more sullen, feeling myself of the Revolution had given way to a total absence of scruples in obtaining hard currency.

If all the properties of Cubans had previously been confiscated under the pretext of social equality, now they were selling hotels to foreign investors, who refused to admit native Cubans and expelled black workers from their former employment in a kind of apartheid against Cubans.

Such was the prostituted destiny the Revolution had offered my people!

One of the things that our Highest Leader had most often repeated during the years that brought him to power was that Cuba needed such a revolution to put an end to its prostitution.

"Before the triumph of the Revolution, Cuba was the whorehouse of the continent," he had said on various occasions.

Although I hadn't lived through that epoch, I harbored no doubts about the existence of endemic prostitution in prerevolutionary Cuba. But now our prostitutes were engineers, graduates, professionals who plied that trade out of a desperation at the misery they'd been reduced to, in exchange for an invitation to dinner, to dance at a discotheque, for a cake of soap, some perfume, an article of clothing. Our prostitutes now were the least expensive and the most cultivated in the world!

The next morning I handed over the keys of the house to the representatives of the tourism company who were there to meet me, and I headed back to Santa Clara with the sense of being a man without a country. *Only for the time being, because I'll find one for my family—where there are rights and a sense of propriety, at least about themselves!* I told myself, now convinced that my next solo flight was going to be to the United States.

Vicky and the boys ran down the stairway to meet me as soon as they saw me getting off the bus from up on the balcony where they'd been anxiously waiting. We'd spent a whole week without seeing each other, and now Reyniel and Alejandro were noisily interrupting each other to register their mutual complaints and fill me in on the latest details about their school week. The four of us spent the remainder of the afternoon playing on the living room floor, and when it was time to turn in for the night, I whispered to Vicky, "On the first flight I make . . ."

She curled up to me, laying her head on my chest, and slept that way the entire night.

The following morning I apologized to Reyniel and Alejandro, who accused me of always working on Sundays, and I left early for the command post to go on duty for what looked to be the last time in my life. In the afternoon Vicky and the boys made a surprise visit. They'd left the house some four hours earlier, to have time enough to wait for the bus and stand on line for pizzas at the officers' club. Now burning up inside with the misery of my inevitable death and the ensuing family tragedy. *Either I say what I think to the four winds or I blow out my brains to protect Vicky and the children with my silence.*

One night Vicky posed a different question: "Tell me, is there another woman in your life?"

"Are you really that stupid not to know what's happening to me?"

I'd never spoken that way to her before.

Vicky broke into uncontrollable weeping while making an effort to keep the children, who'd just gone to bed, from hearing her.

"I know, I know! . . . I'm the one to blame for what's happening! I shouldn't have—" she confessed, sobbing.

I stood up and took her in my arms. It pained me to have spoken that way. I didn't consider her to blame for what was going on. Nothing like this would have been happening if we hadn't been victims of a tyranny. I kissed her cheek, which was wet with tears, and spoke very softly in her ear, in case there were hidden microphones in our apartment.

"You're not guilty of anything, Vicky, and I don't blame you in any way whatsoever. But I can't take any more. I prefer death to remaining silent, allowing them to indoctrinate our children, making them live out their lives denying God, making them believe that loyalty to their leaders is more important than anything."

"Then go, go away!" she whispered finally, tightening her jaw and digging her fingers into my shoulders.

"What do you mean, go away?"

"Do it, in a plane. I'd rather that than have you do something really crazy."

"I'd die before I'd ever abandon you."

"But we want you alive. . . ."

"Don't even think about it."

I consoled myself as best I could that night, but the idea she'd suggested began to hammer in my brain from that day forward, with greater and greater insistence.

In the last days of December I got word that the dentist at the base had asked to be transferred to another unit closer to where she lived. Thus there opened the possibility for Vicky to work there, avoiding once and for all the exhausting trips to the city. Vicky received the news with jubilation and immediately presented her application to the directorial board of the armed forces medical services. In just a few days she was accepted to work at the base's medical post. That reason for ephemeral rejoicing made us forget a while the tragedy under which we lived.

It was the last day of the year and I was on duty at the command post, when Vicky and the boys arrived around eight o'clock at night.

They had come to spend New Year's Eve with me, momentarily alleviating my unhappiness with the surprise of their presence for the evening. Vicky had brought along a small dish wrapped in paper.

"It's a flan I made today . . . to celebrate the arrival of the new year with all four of us together," she told me simply, and I understood that it was all she could do. In any case I could think of no more divine manna for our celebration than that simple flan.

We brought in the New Year of 1991 in the small waiting room at the command post with the boys asleep in our arms, and I couldn't help gazing at them with pity. We had not a single toy, not even a little tree, not a single distraction—nothing appropriate for their age to give them. What they taught them to celebrate in school was the triumph of the Revolution occurring on the first of January thirty-two years ago.

After the first weeks of 1991 had passed, an inspection committee arrived from general headquarters with the task of verifying compliance with the directives of the Commander in Chief regarding the "Extraordinary Period of War in Times of Peace." They wanted to see how well we were managing to grow vegetables on the base, to cook with firewood for the troops, in effect, to see how soldiers and officers were holding up in the nearly subhuman conditions in which they found themselves, eating foods as exotic as they were disgusting, which were now included in their diets in order not to capitulate to the North American embargo. Such was the case of the famous, indigestible "grapefruit rind steak."

"Tonight's the welcoming dinner for the committee at the officers' club. Be sure to bring Vicky," Cordero had insisted shortly after the inspectors from general headquarters had arrived.

We showed up and took our seats at one of the tables where we hosted the guests. Cordero, the political officer, and the chief of staff did the same at the remaining tables, and I could hear plainly their comments regarding the outstanding results our brigade was achieving with respect to the application of the Commander in Chief's directives.

Then the waiters began to serve beers and bring in the platters of grilled pork, served with yucca and rice with black beans—the traditional Cuban dish of which millions of households all over the country had been deprived for a long time already. I thought about what our soldiers must be eating at that moment and, staring at the meal set before me, I felt I couldn't touch it; a knot of repugnance lodged in my throat, preventing me from eating. Vicky eyed me silently and seemed to share the same sentiment because she didn't touch her plate, either. Then one of the inspectors turned to me to remark through a mouthful of food, "Major, you'd better eat. You don't see an opportunity like this every day!"

I felt like vomiting, but I must have managed to conceal my real feelings, since everybody seemed to believe me when I excused myself, saying I wanted to get a little fresh air because I didn't feel very well.

Vicky left with me, following in silence out to the tree-shaded patio of the club.

"You couldn't take it, right?" she asked me, taking my arm with both hands.

"It's more than I can endure. I can put up with all the scarcities we have to endure: water, food, transportation, even the lack of matches and plain candles when there's no electricity. But this life of swallowing one lie after another—I can't stand it!" I exploded, punching a tree trunk with my fist.

"You terrify me when you get like this. One day you'll commit some insanity and we'll lose you. You have to go away."

I lowered my head, remembering the conversation we'd had, and the many times the idea had hammered in my head since then.

"I've been thinking about it since the last time we spoke."

Her eyes widened in astonishment, and she asked simply, "When?"

"I don't know. . . . I've been thinking about how to do it with you and the children. I've even tried to learn to fly some of the helicopters under my command now, but the restrictions on flights due to the shortage of fuel has made it impossible—"

Vicky leaned her head on my chest and began sobbing while she repeated, "Oh, my God, I'm to blame. I feel like something terrible's going to happen to you."

"Don't talk that way. Calm yourself, please!" I begged her, holding her at arm's length as I continued to talk to her as softly and calmly as possible. "We're in a situation I can no longer deal with unemotionally. I no longer sleep, I hardly play with the kids . . . I've changed so much that even they've begun to notice and to complain that we no longer do the same things together that we used to. I feel like I'm dying because I feel I have no honor, putting up with all this garbage."

Vicky continued sobbing, her eyes wide and staring at me.

"Get hold of yourself, please! I'm only trying to reason with you. . . ."

"Okay, okay . . ." she murmured, nodding her head.

"The way things are, either I say openly what I think, or I commit the folly of attempting to take matters into my own hands. At least then I'll have the satisfaction of saving my honor, even if it costs me my life, but you and the boys will then have to suffer the consequences of my rebellion for the rest of your lives."

"Oh, no, please!" she started begging me, struck with horror.

"I told you I'm only trying to reason out the alternatives with you. Calm yourself, I'd never do a thing like that."

She seemed reassured and I continued. "The other thing I could do to give myself peace is put a bullet through my head—that way nobody would ever bother you and the kids."

Vicky looked up at me in horror. "But the children, and me? We'd die of unhappiness without you."

"I'm asking you to be calm! First listen to me! I could never think of abandoning you, in any case. The only alternative left is to escape, but it looks like it'll be impossible to do it all together. I don't know how to obtain a boat, a launch, anything capable of making it across the Florida Straits with us aboard. Besides, the surveillance that pilots are subjected to would make it impossible for us to board a boat together. I could only do it relatively easily in a MiG, but the three of you would be left behind, and that's what I can't accept!"

"But it's preferable. I know you're going to explode at any moment, and that would be the worst of possibilities for us all. Do it!"

"I just don't know. Maybe you're right . . . but let me think about it some more. What's certain is without the three of you I wouldn't be able to live in any case!"

Vicky embraced me again, crying. And I remarked to her gently, "You're the most tearful woman in the world. If anyone comes out here they'll think we're having a quarrel."

She smiled and hugged me tighter, saying, "I love you so!"

"I love you, too. We won't talk any more of this, especially in the apartment. I'll give it some more thought . . . and I'll talk to you when the time comes."

Chapter 14

—

I ' l l   N e v e r
G i v e   Y o u   U p !

One day the base was shaken by scandal: the captain in charge of chemical services and the most experienced radar navigators had been arrested by Counterintelligence on charges of slaughtering cattle and selling the meat. From the earliest years of the Revolution there had been a law prohibiting the slaughter of cows, in order to increase the size of the country's herds. Yet they continued decreasing over the decades, as did the amount of meat people were allotted through the rationing system. And now, desperate for want of food, various officials had begun to slaughter cows they would capture in the mornings, slaughtering them in the very pasture in which they found them, dividing the meat among themselves and later selling off the excess.

A witch hunt without precedent was then unleashed upon the base. Officers from Counterintelligence took away the suspects and kept them isolated for days on end under constant interrogation in order to learn the names of everyone involved, including those who bought any of the meat. Each day the number of detainees increased, including some of the officers' wives; and nobody talked of anything else in the neighborhood community, waiting to see who'd be next to be taken off by Counterintelligence.

When they summoned our friend Osiris to interrogate her for having bought two pounds of meat, the scandal reached its climax, since it implicated the first of four pilots, which made Counterintelligence officials extremely uneasy. Osiris was the wife of Major Roberto Tompson, leader of one of the fighter squadrons, an Angolan War hero, and one of my dearest friends. From that moment on, they were subjected to a campaign of intimidation by Counterintelligence to drag out of them a confession that Tompson had known about his wife's purchase of the meat so that they could make an example of him.

The new head of the division's Counterintelligence, Lieutenant Colonel Ernesto Cordero, had given immediate instructions that Tompson not be permitted to fly as long as the investigation was under way.

"To keep him from trying something crazy," Counterintelligence commented, suggesting the possibility of his defecting to the United States for such reasons.

They think so little of our men as to suppose they'd abandon their country just to escape punishment! I told myself while I watched them conduct their investigation, remembering the reasons why defecting had already crossed my own mind.

One afternoon I asked Vicky to accompany me to Roberto and Osiris's place. They were going through one of their worst moments and they needed moral support.

"Whatever the circumstances may be, we want you to know that we're the same friends as always," we told them, and I caught a glimpse of appreciation in Tompson's eye amid the preoccupations overwhelming him, for he'd fallen into disgrace.

Osiris explained to us that she'd simply bought some meat somebody had offered her a few months ago because her little girl had been sick with a high fever and she had had nothing to feed her. Tompson had been on duty at the base at the time, and had been so busy the remainder of the week that he'd barely managed to come home long enough to sleep. She had never mentioned what had happened, considering it unimportant, and she was now choked with guilt at having caused her husband to be suspended from flying.

Their family now faced the tragic consequences of a minor event converted into a crime by an absurd system. And it pained us to see in our friends' faces that expression of helplessness and insecurity, as if they were wondering in agony, "And now what's to become of us?"

One day in early March, Lieutenant Colonel Ernesto Cordero and Lieutenant Valdés came to see me at the command post. They had remembered two important facts for their investigation: that I was a collaborator with Counterintelligence despite my being virtually an inactive one; and that I was on intimate terms with Tompson and his family. They began the conversation by inquiring about how my family was and other ridiculous questions, and then they broached the subject that had brought them there.

"We know that now you're even busier than before, but we need your help to settle a matter of the utmost importance," Ernesto began by saying while Valdés stood beside him smiling. He had that same glint in his eye that Cepero had had during our meeting of so many years before when they had asked me to seduce the wife of Cordero, who was now my commander.

"It has to do with Tompson. We want to protect him, to maintain his prestige. But to do so we need to know for certain if he was or wasn't aware that his wife had bought that meat."

So that was the most important task of this organization that had been created to fight against the shadowy CIA. I felt like I was living in the time of the Stalinist purges. What similar intrigues were now being hatched by the upper reaches of power against those who had ceased to please our Highest Leader?

"What do you want from me?" I asked, making an effort to control a grimace of disgust.

"Tompson is your friend. We know that he and his wife trust you and Vicky."

Valdés grew more and more excited as his commander continued—and, as with the first time, we finally got to the point.

"We want you to visit Tompson in his home and see if you can pick out some object that could be easily substituted."

"I don't understand."

"We need to plant a bugging device in his house to listen to what he and his wife are saying. We figured you could help us by casually taking some small article out of the room whose absence they wouldn't notice and delivering it to us to prepare it. Or you could describe something to us that we might be able to replace."

Twice they had asked me to help them solve a difficult problem, twice they had asked me to betray my friends! Such was loyalty to the Revolution, built upon the betrayal of those dearest to one! Bastards!

"I'll see what I can do, but you should know that I'll be leaving in two days for Havana and Varadero," I replied, determined never to comply with their request.

They went off, and once more I was left filled with repugnance. How much more could I endure?

I returned early to the base, since Cordero was on vacation and it was my job to inspect the troops in his place that Monday. Just before mounting the podium at the base, the Chief of Intelligence handed me the latest order of the day regarding the enemy, which I was supposed to comment upon to the men assembled for reveille. The document said that the 101st Airborne Division of the U.S. Armed Forces was returning from the Persian Gulf in a state of total combat readiness, and that some fourteen thousand troops were parachuting on North American soil from the planes that were bringing them home, euphoric with victory.

"In the unipolar world which has emerged with the disappearance of the Soviet Union, nothing will prevent the United States from committing aggression against Cuba with impunity. That makes us think that the enemy is preparing to launch a surprise strike against Cuba with the troops and materiel returning from the Persian Gulf,'' the report concluded.

I completed my reading of the text realizing that I wasn't capable of repeating it in front of the men assembled on the parade ground, and I returned it to the Chief of Intelligence asking him to read it instead. An expression of surprise and doubt was reflected then in the eyes of Méndez, the Political Officer . . . It was customary for the Commander to transmit that level of information to the troops. I'd put up with the most reprehensible lies, but to have to recite them to these overburdened men was beyond my capabilities. No, I'd had enough.

I hadn't stopped thinking for a moment about some way of fleeing with Vicky and the boys, ever since the last time we'd talked about the matter together, but it was clearly impossible to do it with them.

And if I escaped by myself in a MiG during one of my practice flights? Vicky could pretend that she had no idea, that way they couldn't punish her.

Others, like General del Pino, had escaped with part of their family. As for the rest of the family he'd left behind, like his mother, they'd forced them to repudiate him to the Cuban media—calling him a traitor to his country, to his people, and to his family; regarding him as worse than dead. That was how the repressive system functioned, exploiting the psychology of the masses to convert a setback into a victory. A person considered a traitor by his own family could serve to galvanize the populace around the leaders of the Revolution.

The method was simple: the leaders would come, loyally and generously, to the assistance of the abandoned relatives, accompanied by the greatest hoopla. And the people, ever magnanimous with those who suffer, would open their arms to those suffering the humiliation of a traitor among their number. The media would manage the rest: That was the real family! The one made up of our people and our Highest Leader!

Thus del Pino's defection had been turned into a triumph.

Those relatives forced by circumstances and fear to make declarations against "the traitor" now saw themselves caught in the web spun by the media; and terrified that the multitudes expressing their affection for them might also consider them to be traitors, they felt too morally vulnerable to ask permission to leave the country and be reunited with their loved one.

Fidel and Raúl Castro had devoted their lives to cutting a noble image in the press and repeated incessantly in their public statements that no one was held in the country against his or her will:

"Those who want to leave . . . let them go!" the Minister of the

---

211

armed forces had pronounced in his latest speech before the principal military commanders.

The Commander in Chief, for his part, declared to a foreign journalist during an interview broadcast over national television, "We're not to blame for the ones who can't leave—it's the United States' fault for refusing to grant them visas. On the contrary, our doors are always wide open."

All that Vicky would have to do is pretend to be shocked at my departure; and then, shielded by the grief and the trauma that my desertion had produced, abstain from any declaration against me to the press and refuse to accept the privileges offered by The Leaders of the Revolution. That would allow her to have the temerity necessary to ask to leave the country once I obtained the proper North American visas.

Little by little, a new and desperate plan was taking shape in my mind, filled with risks, but it was the only alternative possible.

And if they refused to permit Vicky and the children to leave, even though I manage the visas? Then I'll turn to the foreign press, and Vicky can do the same with the correspondents from other countries accredited in Havana. The publicity would be so adverse for them that they'd have to let them leave immediately.

When I finished my shift on the day after Cordero and Valdés's visit, I asked Vicky to go for a walk with me and the boys to a nearby stream. We took two soccer balls we'd brought back from the Soviet Union, and with the pretext of going out to play a bit, off we went just as evening was falling. The next day I'd have to go to Havana for a week to receive basic training for the MiG-23 BNs that had recently arrived at the base, and on my way back I'd have to pass through Varadero to hand over the house that had served as a vacation retreat for the pilots to one of the new companies for international tourism run by retired military officers. That was the reason for my taking the rest of the afternoon off.

The children were now playing animatedly, up to their ankles in the stream, tossing their balls into the stream to splash each other amid happy laughter, while Vicky and I watched them from a nearby rock where we sat.

"It seems the only possible way of doing it is for me to escape first in a MiG."

"When?"

"The first opportunity after my return from Havana. But you're going to join me one way or another very soon after."

Vicky stared at me with evident curiosity, saying, "How will we manage it?"

And I explained to her my plan for dealing with the campaign that would descend upon her after my defection. Then I asked her, "Do you think you can manage it, bearing up under all that?"

"I think so. . . ." was her reply.

"You can't give them the slightest indication that you were aware of my intentions to leave, or all the weight of their vengeance will fall upon you."

"I'll do the best I can. They'll never drag a confession out of me, even if they threaten to kill me."

"I don't think they'd ever torture you physically. The system doesn't work that way."

"How do I explain it to the children?"

"You will have to take them immediately out of the environment in which we live so that other children aren't able to throw in their faces that their father was a traitor. Go live with your parents in Havana; they'll be happy to have you there with them. Tell the boys that I've been temporarily transferred to another base—to the Soviet Union—whatever occurs to you. But take the time needed to tell them the truth when the initial investigations have died down."

"It's going to be very tough."

"I know, which is why I want to be sure that you can handle it."

"Of course I can."

"Another thing: you have to take for granted that every word you say at home is being heard by them. Don't hesitate to do a little thinking out loud, railing against me for what I did, the first moment you have to be alone after they give you the news. That'll help make them believe that you really knew nothing."

"I understand."

"If all goes well, I'll call you by telephone from there, asking you to forgive me for never having told you anything. Once you've heard from me, go to the U.S. Interests Office and apply for visas for you and the children. I'll be doing the same thing at the other end."

"And if the United States refuses to give us visas?"

"I'll return to face the consequences."

Vicky stared at me in horror.

"If there exists no refuge of liberty for us in this world, then I don't think life's worth living. . . . It's a risk we have to take."

She lowered her head silently, knowing that we really had no alternative.

"We have to have faith," I added. "If we do things right, we'll gain the necessary time for me to obtain the North American visas. Once we have those in our hands, they can no longer keep you here in the country. It would cause an international scandal if they took you and the children as hostages while proclaiming their humanism. I don't think they'd dare."

"Nor do I . . ."

We both sat in silence for a while, watching the children romp and play as the sun set slowly behind them.

"I think they'll let you and the children leave quietly to avoid the embarrassment."

Vicky smiled with a gleam of hope in her eyes that I hadn't seen in many months and then declared, "They won't have any choice. How long do you think we'll be separated?"

"I don't know; it depends on how long it takes to obtain visas from the United States. If at that point they don't let you leave the country, they'll see the scandal I'll raise on your behalfs!"

How innocent we were then! How mistaken we were regarding the sensibilities of the international press and the reaction of the Cuban authorities!

I left the following day for Havana, not without first going by to see my parents, who readily lent me their car to use for my needs. I attended classes at the Technical School of the Air Force, and I noticed in my movements about the city that the same automobile was always behind me. What before had never drawn my attention now absorbed all my interest because of the tensions overwhelming me at the thought of my approaching defection.

One afternoon as I was returning to the house of my in-laws with the fateful car following behind, I decided to continue on my way to the busy area of the Rampa, wanting to see if I really was being followed. I parked in a space left a moment previously by a car pulling out, and I saw in the rearview mirror that a man in a checkered shirt was getting out to follow me on foot while the driver went looking for a parking space. I walked up to a group of people waiting on line for an ice cream cone, and I observed the driver joining the other fellow at the end of the same line a few minutes later. It was clear they were following me, and that they were also suffering the consequences of the economic crisis. They had only one car for the job, and couldn't even change it from one day to the next.

Why were they following me? Had Cordero reported something concerning my doubts about those who didn't want to accept criticism from the people? Or had Méndez informed them about my way of thinking with respect to the war in the Persian Gulf?

From my place on line I observed my pursuers obliquely while remembering the incident of the report and the opinions I had expressed concerning the Gulf War. *Maybe Méndez informed them of suspicious attitudes on my part. Maybe Cordero . . . I don't know, but I'll have to watch out or I won't have the chance to put our plans into action*, I told myself, annoyed that I'd now have to wait out the long line of people ahead of me to have my necessary ice cream.

I drove back to my in-laws and the next day I returned to Varadero without noticing them following me, at least not so obviously.

Varadero was one of my favorite places, not so much because of its beauty but because I'd spent so much of my childhood there, running along its beaches while attending its swimming school, lying in wait for *kawamas*, which came ashore at night to deposit their eggs in the sand. It had changed a lot, that magnificent beach resort, which was now reserved almost exclusively for foreign tourists. I learned from friends that, with the growth of the international tourist trade and the conditions of poverty pervading the country, hundreds of youths had prostituted themselves, trading their bodies for the most ordinary consumer products with the evident complicity of the authorities, who had no wish to trouble a tourist spending his dollars in Cuba.

I wanted to see with my own eyes this world I refused to believe existed, and that night I went for a walk through the streets of my beloved seaport. New restaurants had opened up everywhere, with notices posted that they were reserved exclusively for foreigners. I went into one of them to ask for a glass of water and I felt turned upon me the humiliating glance of a waiter who warned me, "I'll give you the water, but you'll have to realize this place is strictly for foreigners."

"Sorry, I didn't know," I answered, turning around and heading for the door.

"Hey, comrade, your glass of water!" I heard over my shoulder.

"No thanks . . . I think I just lost my thirst," I answered without looking back, and hurried out of the place.

Even my country they take away from me, I said to myself, pained, as I hurried along the street on that revealing stroll through a new world created in my country by the hand of that Revolution once called "by the humble and for the humble."

A group of cars surrounded by passersby up ahead caught my attention and I went to see what was going on. A blinking sign announced EL CASTILLITO DISCOTHEQUE at the entrance to a building constructed to look like a medieval castle. More than a dozen young girls wearing tight, short skirts to highlight their charms were standing at the entrance. They were chattering loudly among themselves, gesticulating with their arms, until some tourist pulled up in one of the automobiles with blue plates, which only foreigners could rent. Then they all flocked around the car, besieging the driver with proposals for him to invite one of them into the discotheque. The tourist eyed his aggressive admirers with an expression of shock and delight, until he took one of the girls by the arm and hurriedly entered that world of diversion that only tourists could gain entrance to. Several police officers observed the scene from where they stood beside their patrol car on the other side of the street, "to make sure things don't get too rowdy," as I was told.

I made my way back to the pilots' vacation house feeling bitterness enter my soul. I had spent several years of my life studying on scholarship in this Varadero I no longer recognized. The romanticism here they were with their precious cargo of crisp pizzas and an infinite amount of joy, which the children expressed at once again being at work with me. Vicky, on the other hand, couldn't hide her preoccupation.

"Do you know when the next flights are yet?" she asked, as though afraid to hear the answer.

"Wednesday," I stammered, recalling the phone conversation I'd had with Cordero a few hours earlier regarding the flight schedule. "Luckily this week I won't be tied to the command post, so I can be at home with the children."

Vicky was pleased at least that we would be able to be together when the moment arrived. The last few weeks there had been no water either at the base or in the block of apartments, for which reason Alejandro's play group had been closed, and women with small children were excused from work for the time being.

We dined on those pizzas which seemed so delicious to us, and then when the moment came for them to leave Alejandro began to cry.

"I want to sleep here with Daddy!" he complained as Vicky took him by the hand to head back home.

I tried to explain to him that children weren't allowed to sleep there, but my voice faltered and I had to excuse myself and leave the room so they wouldn't see the state I was in. Vicky swallowed dryly and found the courage I was lacking to insist upon their leaving and somehow convinced the boys to follow her without further fuss.

The next day I again went directly to the base and locked myself in my office. I unfolded the map which included the southern sector of the United States and I made the necessary calculations with a navigational ruler for a flight to the Boca Chica Naval Air Station at Key West, from the various points in the region where we were accustomed to flying. I memorized the data without leaving any trace on that map, which differed from those normally used for flights in that it included the southern portion of the United States, and I took various secret documents I had in my drawer back to the office where they were kept.

I want to be free. If they accept me they'll have to do it without conditions, I decided, conscious of the fact that if I took a few of those documents along I might be better received.

I was just leaving general headquarters when Cordero and Valdés caught me at the door.

"Let's go to my room. We want you to see a videocassette that the office of the Minister sent to all commanders," Cordero told me with a grave look while Valdés walked beside him, smiling.

We got to his room and found the chief of staff and the first navigator of the base already waiting, curious to know what we were about to see.

The tape began with an explanation of the latest activities against Cuba by the CIA, and it showed clippings already aired on national television of supposed diplomats from the U.S. Interests Office in Havana placing messages in secret drops. Then it spoke of "certain officers from the armed forces who had offered to collaborate with the CIA." The tone of the voice-over grew shrill when commenting on such traitors. Footage taken by a hidden camera showed a group of journalists from the armed forces' magazine *Verde Olivo* sitting around their office telling jokes that ridiculed the personality of the Highest Leader. Next came the case of the colonel in charge of naval war communications who had "dared to criticize the Commander in Chief." That was also the crime of Captain Jardinero, commander of the guard at the military hospital of Santiago de Cuba. The final case recorded on the tape concerned a captain-professor at the Military Technical Institute of Havana, who had written to the party Directorate and to the institute confessing that he believed in God and asking them to allow him to continue at his post since he saw no conflict between his religious beliefs and his commitment as a soldier to defend his country. His trust in Our Leaders had led him to take seriously the recent campaign undertaken by the government to invite men and women with religious beliefs to join the party. He didn't realize that this was just another ploy to give the public the impression of change.

While the tape was being played I noticed Valdés watching me with attention, especially when it spoke of "those who'd fallen into the traps set for them by the CIA."

So I turned to him, saying, "The Minister's message is clear."

"I'm pleased you understand," he replied as if giving me a warning.

In forty-eight hours I'll be so far away that you'll no longer be able to see me as one of your potential victims, I retorted silently, and, asking Cordero permission to leave, I walked out of the room.

When I got home, even though we didn't speak of the matter, Vicky couldn't hide the nervous state she was in. The next morning took us by surprise, coming so quickly after we'd gone to sleep. It would be our last day together.

"There's no coffee, but I can make you tea," Vicky told me in a sad voice.

"No thanks, I don't think I could drink it." And giving her a kiss, I went off to the brigade.

I spent the morning inspecting the squadron areas and visiting the men, to whom I wanted to bid a silent farewell. I felt a deep respect for and appreciation of those men, and I was tormented by the thought that the following day they would think I'd betrayed them.

Someday history will put the real traitors in their places, I thought in consolation as I watched them preparing the planes for the next day's flights.

Chapter 15

—

The First Day

Now she was distractedly observing Alejandro from the kitchen doorway as he sat on the living room floor, moving from one side to another with those small fighters he held in his hands, flying across who knew what fantastic zones.

Poor little thing, she was thinking, *so innocent of what's happening.*

"Errrrr . . ." Alejandro continued, mimicking the sounds of flight as he lifted those little airplanes I'd carved out of wood for Reyniel before he was born.

It was him, she told herself, remembering the last MiG to take off that morning while she was walking to the market with Alejandro to get their ration of bread and milk. *Did he make it? Has he gotten there safely? Why the total silence? What if they shot him down! Oh, God, how long am I to suffer the uncertainty?*

A knocking at the door made her turn in fright.

Dear God, is it them? I'm scared.

She walked up to the door holding her breath, and noticed her hand trembling as she reached out to open the door.

"Who is it?" she asked fearfully.

"It's me, Mom."

She swung open the door with a sigh of relief. She'd forgotten that it was lunchtime and Reyniel would be home from school.

"What's the matter, Mom?"

"Nothing."

"You look pale."

"I wasn't expecting the knock at the door. You scared me."

"Really?" And a mischievous look came over his face. "Whoo-whooo!" he said, raising his hands as if to catch her and leaping toward her to frighten her again.

"Enough games, now, you need time to have your lunch," Vicky told the boy and went back into the kitchen.

In a little while she came back with two plates of rice, each with a fried egg on top.

"Alejandro, put the planes down now and come have lunch with your brother," she said as she arranged the settings and placed a glass of water beside each plate. The children ran to take their seats, and she took her seat beside them in silence.

I have to get hold of myself. If it'd been them, they would have noticed how nervous I am. . . . Why do my hands have to keep shaking so? she thought while watching the boys eat.

"What about you, Mom, aren't you going to eat lunch?" Reyniel asked suddenly.

"I ate a little while ago. I was hungry. . . ."

She lied, and they both looked at her strangely because they knew she liked to wait for them to all have lunch together. But they didn't say anything.

They've suspended the flights, but no one's come to tell me anything! I have to get hold of myself or they'll realize as soon as they look at me that I know! Vicky looked at her watch again. *He told me it wouldn't take more than twenty minutes to make it there. Did he manage?*

—

Far away, at the southeastern tip of the United States, a group of people began to gather around the recently arrived Cuban air force MiG-23.

"She says she's Liene Johnson, an official from the Federal Bureau of Investigation," the sergeant said, translating what the woman who'd just got there was saying.

Only a few minutes had gone by since I'd jumped to the ground from my cockpit to ask for asylum from that affable colonel who had then offered me his hand in welcome. He was now moving from one side to the other, giving instructions to his men, but his gesture of kindness had dissipated the last remnants of fear I'd harbored about this country, which I'd been taught to fear as a pit of injustice, racism, and oppression. I turned to the FBI official who'd just arrived and I smiled timidly, nodding my head.

"She wants to know if you're carrying any weapon or drug with you," the sergeant continued as interpreter.

"This is all I have with me," I replied, starting to take from my pockets the billfold in which I carried my driver's license and my identification as a major of the air force, along with cigarettes, lighter, and the photo of Vicky and the boys—which I couldn't help glancing at again before surrendering to her.

The recollection of Vicky trimming that photo the night before with a pair of scissors, and of my sons sleeping as I gave them a good-bye kiss, occupied my mind for a few seconds.

"It's your family?" she asked, looking at the photos, while an unbearable knot tightened in my throat.

"My wife and my children."

"You have a lovely family," she remarked, returning the photo and the other articles as she looked up at me again.

At that point no translation was necessary: she saw the uncertainty in my eyes regarding my loved ones, and I, an infinite compassion in hers for which I'll be forever grateful.

"Will you accompany us, Major?"

This time it was the colonel who spoke, indicating the open door of the automobile.

"Of course," I replied through the sergeant, while still turning an instant to explain something to the armament specialists who were attempting to de-activate the MiG's twenty-three-millimeter cannon by extracting the ribbon of projectiles stored in one side of the fuselage. Then, picking up my flight gear, I got into the car, which the colonel drove to the control-tower building. There a lounge, equipped with a coffee table flanked by two easy chairs and a couch as well as several telephones, served as our refuge from the unbearable heat outside.

"Have a seat," the colonel said, gesturing toward one of the easy chairs as soon as we came in. "Would you like a Coke, a hamburger?"

"No. . . ."

"You prefer a sandwich?"

"Thanks, but I don't feel like eating."

"A coffee, then?"

It was the only thing I could have taken. My stomach seemed to have become paralyzed by the surge of emotions taking hold of me. "Yes, please."

The colonel asked someone to bring in coffee for everybody, while the official from the FBI took a seat opposite me with her little notepad in hand.

"Do you have relatives in the United States?" she asked in a very soft voice and with that look of compassion still in her eyes. *I must look in pretty bad shape!* I thought.

"Yes, several aunts and uncles, and cousins."

"Do you know where they live, do you have phone numbers?"

"I just know that one aunt lives in Miami, but I don't know her address or her phone number."

"No other information that might help us locate her?"

"No. I believe her son Charles is an officer in the air force."

223

"What did you say his name was, your cousin?"

"Charles . . . Charles Armenteros."

She wrote it down in her notebook and went to the phone.

"Your coffee, Major."

It was the sergeant who'd been acting as my interpreter who now held out a cup of steaming coffee.

"Oh, thanks very much." I felt touched by the affability of those men and women whom I'd been taught to see as terrible enemies.

A woman with blond hair and large green eyes had come into the room, and she turned to me after a brief word with the colonel.

"I'm Linda Harrison, from U.S. Immigration Service," she said in perfect Spanish, extending her hand. "May I take a photograph of you?"

"Certainly." I got up to stand against the wall.

"Major?"

It was the FBI official, who was calling me to the telephone.

"I've got your cousin Charles on the line."

What she had just said completely astonished me. She'd found Charles in those few minutes, with barely any information about him.

"Hello, Charles?"

"Yes. . . . You say you're my cousin? What's my father's name?"

He wanted to be sure I really was his cousin.

I talked to him for a few moments, in which he was clearly overcome by emotion. I had to calm him. He wanted to come immediately from the air force base in Texas where he was stationed, to see me, embrace me, help me.

"Hold on," I tried to reassure him, "I'm in the hands of good people who will tell you what the situation is."

He finally understood and I handed the phone back to the FBI official, who continued talking with my cousin in English. Then I glanced around the room where a number of people were busy on the telephone, while others were scribbling away in their notebooks and still others going in and out of the room, creating an atmosphere of constant activity.

Am I the cause of all this commotion? I asked myself worriedly, noting that this was the first instant in which nobody was talking to me. Then I felt a desperate desire to smoke, and I turned to the sergeant who spoke Spanish. "Excuse me, Sergeant. Is there somewhere I could smoke a cigarette?"

"There's an adjacent lounge for smoking. I'll show you."

Another sergeant and a black enlisted man who were sitting behind a coffee table stood up to welcome me.

"I'm leaving you in good hands, Major," the first sergeant told me as he withdrew, leaving me for the first time without the assistance of an interpreter, "I think you'll manage together."

"Wife? Children . . . ?" the soldier asked me.

"No comprendo. . . ." I said, lifting my hands.

"Fa-mi-ly?" he repeated.

"Ah, familia! . . . Sí, esposa, y two *niños,"* I replied, gesticulating with my hands to try to make myself understood.

Then he took out his wallet to show me a photograph of his wife and daughter. The sergeant and I did the same with our own loved ones, patching together a curious dialogue in which we managed to understand each other even though they were speaking in English and I, in Spanish.

"Don't worry," the soldier told me. "Everything will be okay."

"Como?"

"Wife, children, you . . ." He continued, pointing to my family in the photo and to me. And then, intertwining the fingers of his two hands tightly, he said, " . . . all together, soon . . ."

The sergeant and I exchanged lighters as a remembrance, and the soldier offered me a can of Coke that he'd just brought in. I didn't feel like drinking but I took it thankfully, feeling a flush of embarrassment as I tried to figure out how to open it. We were already saying good-bye when the soldier took his squadron insignia from his pocket and offered it to me as a memento of our meeting. I wanted to return the gesture but I realized with humiliation that I had only what was sewn on. He sensed the reason for my awkwardness and, looking at me with sincere sympathy, pointed to the reverse side of the emblem, repeating what he'd written there in his own hand:

"Welcome to freedom."

I took his hand, squeezing it hard, and with a knot of emotion in my throat that made my voice falter, I said to my black friend in Spanish, "Thank you, friend. You have no idea how much those words mean to me!"

I'd just had what seemed to me to be the most touching moment of that long day.

"Major, permit me to introduce you to two air force intelligence officers who've just arrived. . . ." It was the first sergeant returning now in the company of two men.

"Captain Sánchez," said the youngest, stepping forward to shake hands.

"Rodríguez," the other said, "Welcome."

"I see you both speak Spanish. . . ."

"We're Puerto Rican," the captain replied amiably, and added, "You think we might talk for a minute, Major?"

"Of course." And realizing I would have to answer quite a few questions, I took a seat with them around an adjacent table.

Captain Sánchez was about to begin by taking something out of his attaché case when I noticed on his watch that it was already three P.M.

What's happening with Vicky and the children?

—

For a while Vicky had been standing by the window, observing the front of the building through a crack in the venetian blinds, and she felt her heart stop as she saw Cordero, Méndez, and Cortés get out of the jeep that had just pulled up to the curb.

"They're coming!" she murmured in fright, and ran into the bathroom to look at herself in the mirror. "I have to look okay!"

After lunch Reyniel had gone back to school, and Alejandro had lain down for a nap, leaving her once again absorbed in the uncertainty produced by that silence descending over the base since the last MiG's takeoff. She'd observed through the blinds an unusual amount of activity among the neighbors returning from the base. They were gathering in little groups in front of the building, and they seemed to be discussing something in whispers, as if afraid of being overheard, amid the oblique stares they directed up at our apartment. It was obvious that they already knew, but they couldn't say so to her. *Why can't they tell me?*

She had cried while watching Alejandro peacefully asleep, asking God if I were safe and sound far away from there. And she feared her tears would give her away when they came to give her the news and to interrogate her. Several times she'd gone to wash her face in cold water, making what felt like a superhuman effort to control her emotions.

She was tormented by the question as to why, despite their knowing what'd happened, they hadn't come to tell her yet. She felt as if she were being asphyxiated, to the point of hysteria, by that silence, which hovered about her as though plotting against her. In her anxiety she'd gone down to see Miriam, the wife of Lieutenant Colonel Pedro Díaz, one of my closest friends, in hopes that she might tell her something. Also there was Marlen, Cordero's wife and personal secretary, who had just returned from the base. But both of them had behaved very nervously in her presence and had avoided all conversation referring to the base.

And now at last they were coming.

She thought she heard them knocking at the door and she came out of the bathroom rubbing her cheeks. She took as deep a breath as she could manage and, holding it, opened the door. Before her stood the three men from the jeep whose faces were so familiar. An unaccustomed paleness characterized Cordero's expression, and Vicky decided to take the initiative. "What's the matter, has something happened?"

They stared at her without replying.

"What's wrong? Tell me! Is my husband dead?"

"Something worse . . . he's alive," Cordero finally began to tell her with a mixture of fear and anger in his expression, "he's landed in the United States!"

A shock of joy seized her whole being. *Thank you, Lord! He made it!* she said to herself, but she exclaimed aloud, "Whaaat?"

"He landed in the United States. I only hope it was a mechanical failure . . . and that this is not some treason," Cordero replied dryly, and Vicky understood that that man, a friend of so many years, was no longer my friend—not mine, not hers, not the children's.

Perhaps he never was, she thought, realizing that from then on he would be motivated by his instinct for self-preservation, putting the greatest possible distance between himself and them—now that they'd fallen into disgrace.

She felt alone, terribly alone, faced with the entire unpredictable machinery that was about to descend upon her. She wanted to cry, to cry.

"I can't believe it!" she exclaimed, and she collapsed into the chair where I used to sit at the table when we would have meals together. Then she covered her face with her hands and gave full vent to her desperate need to cry, which she had held inside until that moment.

They waited in silence standing around her, witnessing that sobbing, which was not feigned; then a thought suddenly assailed her: *His parents . . . I have to break the news to them. Who knows what they might tell them!* And she got up to go to our room.

"What are you doing, Vicky?" Cordero asked.

"Calling his parents. I have to tell them what's happened."

"No, you mustn't do that. We'll inform them later."

"But why later?"

"Don't worry about it, we're investigating right now. We'll tell them eventually, but it'll have to wait."

Cordero spoke like someone giving instructions, no emotion in his voice, saying only what was absolutely necessary.

"Don't do anything for the moment, we'll be in touch with you." And without another word he marched down the stairs, followed by his companions.

Vicky went back to her seat, and sensed that she was going to have to keep to herself whatever emotions might take hold of her. She had prepared herself to confront that moment, but the painful uncertainty about how long we'd have to go without seeing each other, and her own doubts about whether we would ever manage to see each other again, made her feel desperate. She needed compassion, someone who at least would say to her, "I'm sorry," but that someone hadn't appeared.

"I'll stay with you in the meantime. . . ." It was the voice of Marlen behind her, who'd come from her apartment just across from us to sit with her. And Vicky felt that at last someone had come to give her succor; but Marlen simply took a seat, watching her in silence as she wept on. Not one word, not one phrase of consolation from somebody who'd been her friend and neighbor, nothing. Only her fleeting stares, fixed on the hands covering her face as she sobbed.

Is it genuine, or is she pretending? Vicky asked herself, feeling that stare fixed upon her. *Was she really my friend before all this? I don't know . . . but if she does feel pity for me she's unable to express it.*

Alejandro suddenly woke up, and luckily Miriam had just come up from her apartment. She scarcely said a word to Vicky but her look was filled with compassion and Vicky noticed with gratitude that she too had been crying.

"I'll take Alejandro with me to play, and Reyniel too when he gets home from school. Don't worry about dinner, I'll cook it for them," Miriam said at last, taking Alejandro with her and Vicky felt infinitely grateful for that courageous gesture from her friend.

Marlen and she were left alone together once more: Vicky, with her face in her hands, rocking back and forth like a pendulum in her chair, perhaps hoping to burn up with that movement the anguish and anxiety produced by such waiting for the unknown.

After a while Marlen finally spoke. "You were always a slave to that man. He never loved you, and that's why he didn't hesitate to betray you. . . ."

Does she really feel that way? Is she that frightened already of her intimacy with me?

She felt like vomiting even though she hadn't eaten anything since the previous day, and without replying to Marlen she ran into the bathroom. Her stomach also ached. How terrible it was all turning out! What unbearable pain despite her having prepared for it!

How I miss my parents right now! When will they allow me to call them? We must get out of here as soon as possible! she thought to herself while suffering unbearable intestinal cramps. She sat by the sink, leaning her elbows on her knees and her head in her hands, not wanting to return to the living room to face the scrutinizing stare of someone who'd once been her friend.

What's happening to him now? Are they treating him well? She let her imagination fly, conjuring up in her mind that country that we'd been taught to consider as hell, and that had become our hope of freedom.

———

At Boca Chica I was being inundated by a flood of delicately posed questions from the armed forces intelligence officers.

"What made you change your ideas?"

That was one of the many questions they'd asked me, and it was one that I didn't expect would have been for them the most important. Although I knew that the United States' systems of optical and radioelectronic exploration, as well as their espionage services, would have obtained for them exact findings regarding the position of Cuban troops and armaments, I'd still anticipated a host of questions on the matter. In fact, however, after completing a brief biographical sketch of me, those officers from air force intelligence seemed more interested in the reasons that had led to such a radical turnabout in my life and the psychological process of my evolution than in Cuban military secrets.

"I couldn't answer that in just a few words, nor even mention a deciding factor. . . . I was a dedicated Communist. I never acted from favors or privileges, but from convictions. I would say that the truth—history, pure and honest, which had always been concealed from us, plus common sense—led me to decide. I never felt discontent or frustration over what I was discovering because I had nothing material to lose by the fall of communism . . . only indignation, irritation at discovering I'd been used, betrayed . . . at having acquiesced in living amid all that, at having lost my personal dignity, the integrity essential to go on living."

"And do you think you'll find that here?"

"I don't think the United States is a paradise, nor did I come here to switch sides, since I'll never adhere blindly to any dogma, leader, or party organization. My whole life's experience has been sufficient to make me prefer death to falling into the same traps. I only bring the hope of finding here the truth I'm searching for: my right to keep myself informed, to make my own judgments, to choose and speak what I think. I hope to God I find this . . . because if it isn't that way, I think life won't be worth living."

Captain Sánchez would stop writing on occasion, pausing to stare fixedly at me while he listened. Sometimes I got the impression that I was talking too much or that they didn't understand me. Then I'd pause and ask them if I should be more specific.

"Not at all. Talk, just say whatever comes to mind," they would invariably reply.

And so I continued, talking and talking, feeling that infinite pleasure at being able to say—for the first time!—everything I was thinking.

"And when was the actual moment you changed your ideas?"

"There was no precise moment. I told you I acted out of convictions, and one by one I had to admit to myself that they were false. From The Leaders of my country and their system of governing to the Marxist philosophy itself in which I had been educated. It was not enough to realize that communism didn't work in Europe, I had to prove to myself that it didn't work ever in any country at all, and why. I had to be sure I wasn't simply acting in an egotistical manner or betraying the helpless victims of the kind of abuses prevalent in the world. I had to prove to my own satisfaction that communism would never resolve the injustices that still exist, but would only aggravate them further.''

"What are your immediate plans?"

"To be reunited with my relatives here, obtain visas for my wife and sons, learn English, and find a decent job to support my family.''

"Do you think you'll find a good job?"

"I don't mind starting at the bottom. I have confidence in myself and I know things will work out.''

My questioners were listening attentively when someone called Sánchez and he stepped out for a minute, only to return immediately with two men in dark suits to whom I was introduced.

"These men are officials from the FBI who've come to also have a talk with you.''

"I'm Rubén," said the younger one, extending his hand.

"My name's José," the other, tall and thin, in his early fifties, introduced himself.

"I see you men also speak Spanish.''

"I'm Puerto Rican," Rubén explained relaxedly, "and José's Cuban; so we're all in the family.''

He'd perhaps spoken in that way to win my confidence, but the idea that they thought I'd be more sympathetic simply because of their being Hispanic disturbed me.

"It's nice that we can do without a translator, but I don't see anything special about your being Puerto Rican or Cuban.''

"You're right about that, at least to begin with.''

Rubén didn't seem older than thirty-five. He was wearing loafers nearly hidden by the cuffs of his trousers, and his hair shone with some product that allowed him to keep it combed carefully back. With delicate hands, and with the air of a refined dandy, Rubén gave me the impression of being someone who had recently graduated from his advanced training and was now caught up in the bureaucracy of an office, very far from a man seasoned by experience in the field.

"We want above all to welcome you," Rubén continued, while José remained silent. I responded simply with an appreciative look while nodding my head. So much obsequiousness on his part embarrassed me. "And also to ask you a few questions.''

I saw that another, different round of informal questioning was to begin, if one could thus call that session of questions and answers at our improvised gathering. And since the concentration of adrenaline in my blood didn't allow me to feel the slightest bit tired, I readily acquiesced to answering all their questions.

"First, middle and last name? Date of birth? Schools where you studied? Address of every place of residence from birth? When did you enter the air force, the party? Positions you held?" Rubén asked and José recorded, compiling another brief rundown of my life.

"What made you come? When did you decide?"

They were more or less the same questions I'd already answered. Then Rubén asked, "Any other organization or group you were a member of?"

"Well . . . I also collaborated with military Counterintelligence."

Rubén's expression changed and he gazed very seriously at me. "You didn't tell me that before."

"And why should I have told you that before?"

I noted a kind of insinuation in the way he'd made that remark, like somebody catching a criminal in the act. But I was no criminal. I didn't consider myself a dog now begging for clemency, and I couldn't help the way I'd answered him, staring right back just as seriously at him. I'd never acted with base motives and had nothing, therefore, to be ashamed of. I'd never accept being treated that way and I wanted him to know it.

"You're right, there was no reason to tell me beforehand," he finally admitted with a smile.

We were interrupted at that point by the arrival of the immigration official who'd interviewed and photographed me hours earlier. She was carrying a canvas bag and smiling.

"Everything's fine," she started by saying, as she held the bag out to me. "Here you'll find some clothing and whatever else you'll need for the first few days. And here's twenty-five dollars. You'll need it."

"Thank you very much," I replied embarrassedly, shaking her hand, although I felt the words were inadequate to describe the impact upon my heart of that touching gesture.

I took the money and I couldn't avoid staring at it with curiosity before putting it away. I'd never seen dollars before, those dollars I'd learned since childhood to consider repugnant, the same ones that could send you to jail if you had them in your pocket in Cuba, unless you were part of the upper hierarchy.

"It's time for you to be going," Sánchez began, having just come back in. "There's a plane outside waiting to take us to Homestead Air Force Base. If you wish you can wash up and change before leaving."

"No thanks. I prefer to do that at the other end."

Now we were heading for a place I'd only known as one of the targets I'd studied at the military academies. Night had already fallen and I still hadn't asked them what they planned on doing with me. *Why bother?* I thought to myself. *My fate's in their hands in any case.* Then, just as we were about to board the plane in the company of the FBI officials, the sergeant who'd been my Spanish interpreter came up to us.

"I just wanted to come and say good-bye, Major. I've brought you this book, which I read a while back. It was written by an exceptional human being, and I know it'll be helpful to you. He talks about the Cuba you don't know."

I shook his hand warmly to thank him and read the kind dedication he'd inscribed on the first page. On the cover was the face of a young-looking man with a resolute expression in his eyes—it was Armando Valladares, and the title was *Contra Toda Esperanza, Against All Hope.*

Finally I'll be able to hear the voice of this man whom my government called a "terrorist," and who was freed while I was away in Angola, I thought to myself with the intention of reading it in one sitting.

We boarded the small two-engine plane and flew to Homestead in silence. A mantle of lights blanketed the horizon to the north when we circled the base to land.

"That's Miami," Rubén remarked upon seeing me stare out the window, filled with curiosity.

"I never imagined it was so big," I answered, astonished at the immensity of that city known as "the political capital of the Cuban exile community."

"Part of its growth is due to the Cubans who've emigrated since 1959," José added.

And I was overwhelmed with nostalgia to recall the beautiful Havana that was now deteriorated into such a ruin. *How would our capital have been now if our country hadn't been governed for so many years in the manner it has been?*

The plane parked after landing next to a building with large windows and a roofed passageway extending several feet out to the apron. The pilot opened the side door of the plane and then Sánchez asked me to go out first. A red carpet extended from the foot of the ladder, and two soldiers stood in profile at the end of it, holding their rifles at solemn, ceremonial attention. Beyond, the commander of the base stood waiting. They were receiving me with military honors!

I felt embarrassed by such attention, and I stepped forward in confusion, deeply touched and forgetting even my military protocol by not saluting smartly. Such was the power of their chivalry before an enemy who was surrendering! I finally saluted the two soldiers first, once again forgetting protocol, and they responded confusedly by offering me their hands. I was so disoriented!

"Welcome," the commander told me when I reached where he stood, "it's a pleasure to have you as a guest."

We climbed into the automobiles waiting to drive us to the two-story building where I'd be staying, as Sánchez had explained to me during our flight. There we all proceeded, led by the commander of the base, to a large room furnished with sobriety, in which they had a small table, a sofa, some easy chairs, a refrigerator, and a television.

"Here you can make yourself at home," began the colonel in charge of security at the base, who'd just joined us. Then, opening another door, he showed us the bathroom and then the bedroom, furnished with the biggest bed I'd ever seen. Our hosts then departed, while the officials from air force intelligence and the FBI remained a few minutes more.

"Here you have plenty of food to eat whenever you wish, Major," Rodríguez, who'd been quiet almost the whole time, explained while opening the refrigerator and a small adjacent cabinet to show me their contents.

"Thanks, but I still don't feel like anything."

"But you should eat. . . ."

"What would you like for breakfast tomorrow?" Sánchez interrupted.

"I don't know, usually I just have coffee."

"But you ought to eat something. Tell me if you'd like to have anything special; for us it'd be a pleasure."

"Thank you, but—"

"We only want to see that you're—" Sánchez insisted, and my face began to flush with embarrassment.

"All right, I'll have some fruit, or some juice."

"Now you're talking, man."

Sánchez made a note of it, and we sat in front of the TV, which someone must have turned on because a Spanish station in Miami was broadcasting news of my arrival just then. The newscaster spoke about the photos taken of the MiG-23, which had already been moved to a hangar at Boca Chica Naval Air Base, and she mentioned my name and military rank, but was mistaken by four extra years about my age and about some hamburgers she suggested I'd eaten with evident appetite upon my arrival.

"Nothing further from the truth!" I exclaimed as I listened to her, and my interrogators broke into laughter at my reaction.

The newscast ended, and they got up to leave. But first Sánchez had another word with me.

"They'll be two armed soldiers guarding the door," he said while indicating it with a finger, "but that's only for your protection. You're free, and you've only to tell us if you wish to leave."

"We'll be back in the morning and put you in contact by phone with your aunt in Miami," Raúl added, and they all departed, wishing me a pleasant rest.

I went into the bedroom and began slowly to unpack on the bed the contents of the bag I'd been given by the immigration official, with the intention of taking the bath I desperately needed. I had no intention of eating, even though I hadn't touched any food the entire day, and I knew that I wouldn't be able to sleep. I just wanted the next morning to come, and with it those officials whom I'd gotten to know and whom I felt now completely dependent upon, like a boy. I was setting out things one next to the other, but I no longer distinguished them. My mind had wandered far away, to Vicky and the boys, to my parents and my former comrades.

—

It was already seven at night and Vicky had not received any further communication from Cordero following his instruction that she wait at home. Since then she'd been spending most of the time on continual trips back and forth between the living room and the bathroom, subject to those terrible intestinal cramps. Now she was silently appreciative of Miriam's kindness in taking them to her apartment to feed them and distract them as much as possible.

Luckily everybody had shown discretion about keeping from the children any knowledge of what had happened. And Vicky noticed that her neighbors were already staring at them with infinite compassion, as if their father had suddenly been carried off by death itself.

A group of girls who were undergoing a year of training at the base before enrolling in the military institute had been sent to stay with her for part of the afternoon when Marlen had to go off somewhere. They had stood about with terrified expressions on their faces, without knowing what to say, while Vicky was consumed with anxiety while waiting as Cordero had asked her. Now at least some of her closest friends were gathered there, come to be with her in her grief, seated in silence with a mixture of anxiety and sadness etched on their faces, as if I'd suddenly died, like other friends in times past, from one of those not infrequent accidents that befell combat pilots.

One neighbor came up to the apartment, which was now full of silent guests, and asked Vicky to go into the bedroom for a moment with her.

"They're already broadcasting news of it on American radio," she whispered into Vicky's ear, referring to a broadcast over Radio Martí, the U.S. government station transmitted to Cuba, which many listened to in secret.

Then Vicky picked up the telephone to call my parents while murmuring all the while, "I won't have them finding out about it over the radio. It would be too terrible for them. . . ."

"Hello?" It was the voice of my younger brother at the other end.

"Orlando?"

"Yes . . ."

"It's Vicky. Are your mother and father there?"

"Yes . . . something wrong?" Orlando had noticed the strange tone of Vicky's voice.

"Yes. . . . Your brother landed his plane in the United States, today, sometime around noon—"

"*What?*"

"He went off to the United States. . . . Tell your—"

She couldn't finish. Orlando had hung up the phone and then run into the kitchen to my mother with his hands clutched to his temples.

"*Ay*, Mom, Mom! What a disgrace, what a disgrace!" he cried suddenly with a look of tragic horror on his face.

"What's happened, son? Tell me what's happened!"

It was Wednesday, and like every Wednesday when I was flying, my mother had thought about me more than usual, always anticipating that something terrible might happen to me in those airplanes that frightened her so. My father had already gotten up from his seat in front of the television, and he rushed to Orlando, only to see him in the grips of that species of insanity that was making him repeat over and over the same vague phrase while pressing his hands to his temples: "What a disgrace, what a disgrace!"

A sudden pallor came over my father's face as he stood next to my brother without saying a word, while my mother kept hitting Orlando on the chest, yelling, "Oré, Oré! What's happened to Oré? Tell me!"

"He's not killed, he's alive. . . ." Orlando finally began to explain, coming out of his hysteria.

"What happened then!"

"He flew to the United States!"

A complete silence descended upon them, while my mother stared at Orlando wide-eyed, as if she couldn't fathom what she'd just heard.

"It isn't true," my father finally reacted.

"Vicky just finished telling me so," Orlando replied, this time without shouting.

Then my father ran to the phone to call Vicky, but the line was busy.

Vicky was talking to her younger sister in Havana.

———

"Aurora, Oré's . . . gone," Vicky began telling her in a halting voice.

"He's left you? I can't believe it."

"No, no . . . he's gone to—"

"It doesn't matter, sis. If he's leaving you, you can move here and live with us."

"No, Aurora, he's not leaving me."

"I thought it strange for him to be doing that."

Aurora never lost a chance to anticipate crises before hearing what they were.

"He flew off to the United States in his plane—"

"Did you say *the United States*?"

"Yes."

"*Ay!*" And Aurora broke into uncontrollable sobbing, which prevented Vicky from telling her anything more.

———

In Matanzas my father was still trying urgently to get hold of Vicky, but the line continued to be busy.

—

This time it was Cordero who was on the line, telling her that a delegation from Counterintelligence had just left Havana and was on its way to interrogate her. Vicky felt a chill run through her body, realizing the motive for their guarding their silence while they made her wait.

They didn't want me to be preparing for this meeting, she thought, hanging up the phone, and immediately she heard a knock at the door.

The first to enter was Lieutenant Colonel Ernesto, followed by a group of strangers.

"We need to ask you a few questions and search the house. . . . We still don't understand how your husband could have done what he did, and we need to look for any evidence—"

"Please sit down," Vicky asked them, gesturing to the chairs that my comrades had given up in the presence of such visitors.

"No, we'd rather have a talk with you at Cordero's home while they search the place here."

"All right," Vicky answered, traversing the short space which separated our apartment from that belonging to Marlen and Cordero, who was already coming up the stairs on his way back from the base.

He waited until the last minute to let me know, Vicky thought, as she saw him arrive five minutes after having called her on the phone.

They'd barely stepped into the apartment when the telephone rang and Marlen picked it up. "It's for you, Vicky. It's your in-laws," Marlen told her as she handed her the receiver.

Vicky gave an inquiring look to the recent arrivals from Havana, and the one who seemed to be in charge indicated with a nod of the head that she should answer the call. My father couldn't believe what he was hearing and asked to speak to Cordero, who in a few sentences quickly explained what had happened. My mother and my younger brother stood next to my father while he was talking to Cordero, and they noticed the extreme pallor that returned to his cheeks as he listened. He placed the receiver slowly back on the telephone, at the same time murmuring the last words he would utter for some time: "My son's broken my heart. . . ."

Then they all understood that the story was true.

"That boy must have gone crazy! How could he do such a thing?" my mother exclaimed, adding, "He had to be crazy. . . . Who knows what kind of torture they're subjecting him to now to make him tell military secrets!"

Orlando took the keys to our father's car then in order to go find our brother.

"Faure, Faure! Oré's gone off to the United States!" he told him, bursting into his house with excitement. The two of them embraced in tears at the tragedy as soon as Faure understood what had happened, and they wept with grief as if I had died as they drove back to my parents' house. A funereal atmosphere hovered about the family home from that moment on and for some time to come.

———

At Santa Clara, Vicky faced the deluge of questions that the officers from Counterintelligence posed to her in Cordero's apartment. Other officers, meanwhile, ransacked our apartment, searching for evidence that would expose my "ties to the enemy"; and they hid a number of listening devices around the apartment to monitor Vicky's activities. They didn't realize then that Vicky had already definitely decided to leave for her parents' home the following day.

"Did you hear your husband make any critical remarks lately about the Revolution?" the investigating officer questioned her while leaning toward her as if expecting the most scandalous reply as an answer. Before beginning his questioning, he had set a small leather bag on the table, doing it casually as if he carried the thing everywhere with him. Now Vicky heard emanating from the bag the clear whisper of a rotating audio cassette recorder, revealing the ridiculous manner in which they were taping the conversation.

It's better they think I don't know, she told herself.

"No," she replied. "He normally came home and played with the kids, or watched TV. But he didn't talk to me about politics. . . ."

"And the Commander in Chief? Did you ever hear your husband criticizing him?"

"In no way . . . he would never do that—"

"And when he listened to the Commander in Chief's speeches . . . what sort of expression could you see on his face?"

"Actually, the last few times the Commander in Chief spoke, he was on standby alert at the base."

"Understand, we need to discover the reasons for which he betrayed the Revolution, betrayed the Commander in Chief, betrayed you—"

"I don't understand it myself! I can't think of any reason, and I'm going crazy trying to understand why—"

At this point somebody knocked at the door. It was one of the men, who'd already finished searching the apartment. He whispered something to the chief investigator and, turning to Vicky, said while pointing to her, "The neighbor's just come upstairs with the kids. . . . They want to see her before going to sleep."

Vicky ran out immediately and calmed the boys, telling them that she was helping Marlen with something. Miriam promised to keep an eye on them while they slept, and Vicky returned to answer more questions.

"You didn't notice anything strange about your husband's behavior lately?"

"I don't know what you mean by strange. He seemed to have the same things on his mind he always did regarding his work."

"Did you notice him going out lately without telling you where?"

Do they really think that the CIA bought him off? she asked herself for a second, understanding where the line of questioning was leading. "It would've been impossible. When he wasn't working on the base, he was on standby alert. We've barely had two weekends together in eight months."

"And in the Soviet Union? He never traveled to Moscow to meet somebody?"

"The times we traveled to Moscow we did it together, including the children. I never saw him with any strangers there."

"Who were his friends in the Soviet Union?"

"The Cuban group and a subordinate officer from the war college."

"You noticed nothing strange in his intimate behavior . . . in his sexual comportment, for example? Did he act differently?"

Vicky understood that they were attempting to appropriate the most tender moments of our relationship, beautiful, among other reasons, for being so intimate that they were shared with no others.

They think that he'd be or not be Communist to the extent of his success or failure in his personal sexual relations?

The voice of the investigating officer shook her from her meditations: "I mean . . . you haven't noted any symptom of homosexuality in him?"

Vicky realized then what they were looking for—the real reason for the lengthy interrogation and the searching of our apartment. They knew well enough that the CIA could never recruit her husband because, even if they had wanted to, the opportunity had never presented itself to do so. They knew as well that no one had induced him to fly to the United States, and they understood that he had acted as a result of his own ideas. They were actually looking for something else.

The man who had now turned traitor was a loyal son of the Revolution, someone who had consecrated his entire life from childhood to it as an idealist. If his house was barely furnished, it was precisely his modest way of living and his unlimited dedication to service that provided the foundation for the authority he had among his comrades. Then how to explain to these men her husband's desertion? How could they be told the real reasons that had led him to commit such an act? Obviously they couldn't. Then they needed some fact, some evidence, that would allow them to build a campaign to discredit his image before those who'd been his comrades. They needed something, even if it were only a declaration against him by someone who knew him better than anyone, by his wife. . . . *They'll never get such a thing from me.*

"Never," Vicky began by telling them. "You all know him very well and can see well enough he's not a homosexual. Our relations were always beautiful. We've been happy from the first day to the last."

"We knew you would answer that way," the interrogator remarked with disappointment.

"But what other way could I answer?"

The man looked at his watch and, standing up, put an end to the interview. "We'll keep in touch with you." And as he was about to leave, he added, "Oh, I forgot! A psychologist is coming from Havana to take care of you. Your husband betrayed you, but the Revolution will see to it that you and the boys are well taken care of." Then he left the apartment, followed by his retinue of intelligence agents.

Then Vicky turned to Cordero, who still remained seated in the living room. "Tomorrow I'm leaving for my parents' house. I'll be back another day to collect our things and hand over the key to our apartment."

Cordero stared at her with obvious signs of worry in his expression. "You should stay here for a while until the investigation's been completed."

"They can ask me whatever they want at my parents' house in Havana, because if I stay here one day longer I think I'll die of anguish."

"Think about it. In any case I'll see if there's a car available at the base to take you to the bus station tomorrow," Vicky heard him say as she was going out the door in the direction of our apartment.

She checked the boys, who were sound asleep, and thanked Miriam as she said good-bye. How much she appreciated Miriam's quiet support! Then she ran to the phone and called a neighbor of her parents, from whom she learned, to her relief, that they'd already left Havana to join her.

They'll be here by morning. At least I won't be alone.

Then she called my parents' house and asked my brother Faure if he'd be able to come pick her up the following day in my father's car. She didn't have the strength to face who knew how long a wait for a bus at the terminal.

"Don't you worry, I'll be there before midday," Faure promised her readily.

She went back into the bedroom and watched the boys in silence. It was nearly three in the morning, and she knew she couldn't sleep.

How will I explain all this to them? she asked herself while glancing at the disorder of the room after the search. *I'm sure they're listening to me*, she thought, remembering my warning and the advice I'd given her when we had gone over the plan of my escape. Then she sat on the bed and, staring at the ceiling in anguish, she exclaimed for the ears of those spying on her, "*Why*, my love? Why did you do it? How could you abandon us like this, *forever*!"

Then she scrutinized for the last time the details of those four walls that had been our amorous refuge for so many years, caressing them with her stare, bidding them good-bye forever.

Chapter 16

—

Waiting

"Officers, Sergeants, and Soldiers . . . Comrades, yesterday morning we suffered a betrayal . . ."

The men and women mustered on the parade ground listened to the voice of Cordero echoing over the loudspeakers in a graver tone than usual. Before dawn their battalion commanders had summoned them in an unprecedented manner to conduct a "repudiation meeting," which would be held simultaneously at all other military units in Cuba. A sense of collective shame provoked by the crime committed by a member of the great family to which they belonged devastated everyone. They listened to the words of the base commander with heads bowed, sharing in the humiliation which from that day forward would mark them as combatants from the unit that engendered a traitor.

". . . and we are gathered here to express our repudiation of someone who pretended to be our brother in order to one day stab us in the back with the knife of treason. . . . Down with the traitor!"

This time Cordero's voice sounded particularly emotional, hoarse.

"*Down!*" the multitude of combatants repeated with fists in the air.

"There are traitors who are capable of selling their souls to the devil for money, but imperialism had better know—and imperialism had better know it well—that all the money in the world could not buy a single one of the combatants who stand together here today!" Cordero continued, becoming more and more exalted as he spoke.

"Imperialism sometimes deludes itself with traitors: the pusillanimous and the cowardly who are incapable of facing the economic difficulties imposed upon us by its commercial embargo. . . . They believe, these North American imperialists, that we will all end up betraying our fatherland. But they're roundly mistaken. . . . Here are a people and an armed forces ready to die rather than fall on their knees before them!''

And he concluded, pounding his fist on the concrete podium upon which rested the microphone:

"Eternal hatred to the traitor!"

"Hatred!" the troops replied.

"Death to the traitors of the fatherland!"

"Death!"

"Socialism or death . . ."

"We shall be victorious!" finished that chorus of hundreds.

Then Cordero withdrew a few steps back to allow the political officer to approach the microphone.

"We also wish to express by this act of repudiation . . ." Méndez began in a measured voice as he gazed from left to right at various units assembled in formation, ". . . the fact that, more than ever, we trust in the brilliant guidance of Our Commander in Chief. That we will never falter in our trust, and that we will know how to cleanse with honor the filthy betrayal which took place in our ranks. . . ."

All then lowered their heads once more. To have betrayed the trust of the Commander in Chief was doubly humiliating.

Méndez had paused to take a breath, and now, raising his voice as loud as he could, he proclaimed the slogan learned by all from the earliest primary school grades:

"Commander in Chief: For whatever it be, however it be, wherever and whenever: . . ."

"Tell us!" all of them replied with one voice.

—

At home, Vicky was getting ready for the departure, in the company of her parents, who had come to help her. Miriam had met them on the stairs and the exclamations of sorrow, which Vicky heard, announced their arrival. The boys had awakened delighted to see their grandparents, and now they begged Vicky to let them go out and play downstairs. But again and again she refused. A friend had come up early to warn her that a group of children had gathered downstairs just outside the building in order to yell at Reyniel and Alejandro that their father was a traitor, in a kind of spontaneous act of repudiation, and since then she'd done her best to keep them up in the apartment. In the confusion that still overwhelmed her, she had also lied to them when they had first asked where their daddy was, telling them he'd been called on standby alert. And she hadn't been up to explaining to Reyniel clearly the reason for not letting them go to school that day.

Now the moment had arrived to give them a more logical explanation of events, and she asked them to sit down and listen carefully to what she was about to say.

"Pay attention. Uncle Faure is on his way here. When he arrives we're all going to go with him."

"Hooray! To see our cousins!" Alejandro exclaimed, excited as always at the prospect of taking a trip.

"Daddy had to go to another base to work there for a long time, and so we're going to go live with Grandma and Grandpa in Havana."

"Hooray!" exclaimed Alejandro all over again, who at four years of age didn't seem to like very much where he'd been living.

"But why didn't Daddy say good-bye to us before he went, Mommy?" Reyniel then asked with a very serious expression.

"He had to leave at night and didn't want to wake you boys. But he spoke to you and kissed you while you were sleeping."

Vicky attempted to explain to them what they would be doing from now on and why when they were interrupted by the arrival of Faure and his wife, Isabel, from Matanzas. There were no words of greeting. Seeing Vicky standing before him, Faure broke into tears, throwing his arms around her, while Isabel hugged both of them from behind, also crying. Never had there been so many tears in our family, never in our lives had a member of our family died. The boys, who looked on in astonishment at what was happening, ran up to their mother as well, hugging Vicky around the legs in a natural reaction.

"Mommy, why are you crying? Why is everybody crying?" Reyniel asked with tears and fright visible on his face.

"It's that your father's gone away for a long time . . . and it upsets me to leave our home . . . and we're all sick about it!"

The children watched as the grown-ups sat down, having finally gotten a hold of themselves. And now they were discussing which belongings they'd be taking and how they were all going to fit into that little car, when a knocking at the door interrupted the conversation. A young woman with chestnut hair and sad gray eyes, wearing her everyday uniform with first lieutenant stripes on the shoulder, appeared in the doorway.

"Hello. I'm Magalis, the psychologist from the Ministry of the Armed Forces. I've come to assist you."

"Come in, please," Vicky told her, offering the seat my brother had vacated for the newly arrived guest.

"No thanks. Is there another place where the two of us could speak alone?" asked the impromptu guest, pausing in the middle of the room to size them all up briefly.

"Okay . . . in the bedroom."

They went into the room Vicky had shared with me for the last time just two nights before, and they sat together on the edge of the bed facing the dresser whose drawers guarded all of our mementos.

"I'm deeply sorry about the way your husband has betrayed you. . . . We know how hard this must be for you, and I've come on behalf of the Ministry of the Armed Forces to help you."

Vicky listened in silence, recalling that Cordero had called her much earlier that morning to inform her that another bus with more investigators had arrived from Havana before dawn and that they wanted to speak to her. Luckily he had called her back to say that only the psychologist would see her; the other arrivals had no interest in speaking with her. Now this young officer was there conversing with her in the sweetest possible tones.

"First of all I want you to recount your whole lives together from the first time you met. What was he normally like with you, with the children? Did he often go out by himself, did he drink? . . ."

And Vicky began to tell her our life at the same time as she showed her the pictures in our family album, as the psychologist insisted on her doing. Vicky knew that this psychologist had been sent for other purposes, in order to uncover evidence of possible intrigues that was needed to weave a campaign of slander against me. But in spite of that, the recounting now of our lives so filled with love and happy moments helped her to open her heart, drowning her words in a restrained, intimate weeping.

"He always loved me. He was a wonderful father and always very affectionate to the boys, very attentive to his parents. . . . All of that you already know, and I can't tell you anything more. At home, at work, in the neighborhood . . . he was always the same person. He never had a taste for drinking, and he had no interest in going off to find any diversion elsewhere. Every free moment that work left him he'd hurry home to spend it with us . . . and our vacations always started at his parents' home. His only hobby was scuba diving, which he did with his brothers whenever we visited them. I can't understand why he did it!" Vicky confessed amid sobs while the psychologist listened in silence.

"Vicky? Are you going to be much longer? If we don't leave soon we'll have to be on the road at night." It was my brother talking on the other side of the door, urging her to get going. He'd seen the state of fear and depression Vicky was in when he arrived, and, more than worrying about whether or not they'd be on the road when night fell, he simply wanted to get her out of that place, which had clearly become a torment for her.

"Yes, we're coming," Vicky answered, standing up, and the psychologist did the same while assuring Vicky that she'd visit her often in Havana.

"It'll be easier for me to be of help to you there, since I live in Havana," she promised as she left.

They were all just about to leave when Marlen came in to ask Vicky to come with her for a moment to her apartment. There, seated in one of the living room chairs, was Lieutenant Valdés from base Counterintelligence.

"Is it true you're leaving, Vicky?" he asked, standing up and with evident preoccupation.

"Yes, right now in fact . . ."

"That's why I've come. It's necessary that you remain a few more days."

"I'm sorry, but I can't stand to be here another second. Everything around me just reminds me of him, and I don't know how to distract the boys. I need my family and I'm going."

"But listen . . . we need your help! We don't have any evidence, we don't know what happened, nor why he did it. We need to clarify matters, and only you can help us—"

"I don't know what else I could tell you; I know as much as you people do. I'm sorry, but I'm going. It wouldn't be good for the children to remain here, either."

"Send them to your brother-in-law's, and you stay here a few more days."

"I won't be separated from them during a time like this. You can all come to Havana if you wish to see me."

Valdés looked very pale. He hadn't expected such obstinacy from Vicky about leaving, and he saw himself losing his only opportunity to come up with something that would free him from blame before his superiors. He had been assigned to the base to prevent such things, and he knew that the Highest Leaders would hold him responsible for not having discovered the plans of a traitor. My whole file, containing even the most insignificant comments I might have uttered at one time or another and recapitulated there in the testimony of some informer, would be utilized henceforth as evidence against him. It would serve as proof of their having acted negligently, of their deserving to be punished with the mistrust of their leaders, who from then on would block their advancement in their careers, or even the resuming of them. Perhaps he knew that while the Highest Leaders knew only too well my reasons for deserting, they could never explain that to the people or to the military. And it wasn't so unlikely that, as a result of the investigation now being carried out by his superiors newly arrived from Havana, who would also be interested in washing their own hands of guilt, his own name might end up being included in the list of "negligent and irresponsible officers" who had permitted my escape.

Now the pallor of Valdés's face evidenced the fear that was overtaking him as the inevitable approached. He had fallen into disgrace.

"You've got to understand, Vicky! We still don't have anything; we've found nothing . . . not one reason to explain why he became a traitor!" And dropping the normally peremptory tone with which he addressed people, he implored Vicky, almost in tears, "Please, I beg you, Vicky . . . stay a few more days!"

Vicky regarded him with pity, perceiving the panic overtaking that man, whom everybody on the base feared, and who now was acting on his own account to save his own neck. But she was in no better a situation, and now there was no way of keeping her there, short of arresting her. And that, she knew, they wouldn't do. Nothing would be gained by it except to make her seem in an even worse situation in the eyes of the other pilots. Better to attempt to gain her confidence and see if once the initial shock was over they might convince her to construct some sort of calumny. In case they suspected her of complicity, the best way for them to find out about it would be to keep her under surveillance while letting her believe she'd tricked them. In any case, they'd always have her under their total control.

"I'm sorry, Valdés, I couldn't stay even if I wanted to. It's all been too much for me and I haven't the strength."

"Shouldn't we get going?" It was my brother who spoke now from the doorway, where he'd come in search of Vicky.

"You help me make her understand. Please," Valdés continued, repeating to Faure the same things he'd said to Vicky.

"Don't you see the state she's in? Don't you realize that she's been sick with vomiting and diarrhea since yesterday from the shock she's suffered? She needs the tranquillity and support of her family! You people can go to see her in Havana."

Perhaps Valdés wanted to arrest her and attempt to drag confessions out of her, but he wasn't the one making the decisions anymore. Those were in the hands of a special group reporting directly to the Minister of the Armed Forces, who had recently arrived from Havana.

—

I'd spent the night with my eyes glued to the ceiling of the comfortable quarters given me at the Homestead Air Force Base, thinking about Vicky and the boys, about my parents, my brothers, my friends, about the impact my defection was to have on all of them, and the manner in which Vicky was to deal with the dangerous questions they'd put to her. It seemed like an eternity since I'd seen her and the children, despite my having bid them good-bye less than twenty-four hours ago. And now the uncertainty over the amount of time we might have to go without seeing each other gripped my heart until I felt I was going to choke.

In my sleeplessness I'd started to read the book by Armando Valladares, and the description he gave of the crimes committed from the outset of the Revolution seemed to me to be an atrocious exaggeration. So I'd tossed it aside with disappointment, convinced that such episodes, told with passion and not with truthfulness, simply nurtured the thesis, so popular among left-wing intellectuals, of a Revolution victimized by the calumnies of the United States government.

I was thus absorbed in thought when I heard the door of the adjacent reception room open. It was Sánchez, who'd come by very early, quietly so as not to awaken me, only to be surprised at seeing me emerge from the bedroom dressed in new clothes.

"Good morning. I didn't think you'd be up so early," he confessed, greeting me with a smile.

"I didn't sleep very well. . . . My wife and my sons were on my mind. But I'm happy you've come this early; I couldn't bear the solitude."

"I've brought something for you," he began, reaching into his attaché case. "It's a pocket Bible. I know what it meant to you to find God. This one's divided into three hundred and sixty-five readings, so that you can read something each night before going to sleep."

That man had started the day with a gesture that touched me profoundly, making me feel like more of a human being.

"Thank you, Sánchez. You've given me what I needed most," I commented while paging through that Bible I held in my hand, the first Bible of my whole life. "I've also got something for someone," I told him as I went into the bedroom to find my flight suit. "Do you think it's possible to find the soldier who gave me this insignia?" I asked while holding up the reverse side of it to show him the dedication and the signature of the soldier who'd given it to me the day before at Boca Chica.

"Yeah, I think I can find him."

"I wanted to get this flight suit to him as a remembrance of our meeting each other."

Sánchez took a seat and we talked about things in general until someone knocked at the door, bringing breakfast: an ample tray of various fruits, toast, butter, juice, and coffee.

"I feel very badly, Sánchez," I told him, staring at the tray, "but I'm afraid I can only take some coffee."

"I understand, don't worry about it."

A few minutes later Rubén and José arrived, dressed once more in their dark suits. Rubén was the first to talk after we greeted each other.

"I have a surprise for you," he told me as he walked over to the telephone and took a piece of paper out of his pocket. "I'll dial your aunt's telephone number so you can talk to her. You can tell her you're with us, but I ask you not to tell her where you are."

My aunt hadn't seen me since those Christmases we celebrated together when I was three or four years old, and now she seemed so excited and happy that I was here. She told me how the TV cameras from the local television station had marched into the place where she worked to ask her countless questions, to which she'd had no answers, and that an imposter had been on television claiming to be my older brother. She also wanted me to come live with her.

"Well, I don't know, probably."

"What do you mean, probably? Your father is my brother and you just better come live with me."

It was that same affectionate, authoritarian tone of my peasant relative who'd abandoned the fields of Zaino nearly half a century ago. In spite of having spent more than three decades in the United States, she had changed less in her family culture than had my own father in Cuba.

"Try to understand, I can't be sure. I still haven't talked to my mother's sisters. I still don't know if I'll find a job somewhere else. . . . I don't know anything!"

"All right, that's fine. Tell me where you are and I'll come see you right now."

"I can't, Aunty, I'm . . ."

"They've arrested you? Look, I'll go get you a lawyer right away—"

"No, no, Aunty," I interrupted. "I'm not in jail. I'm fine and with good people."

"Then why can't I come and see you?"

"It's only for a short time. You have to understand, what I've just done affects the already difficult relations between governments. They have to investigate."

"Who're you with there?"

"The FBI."

"Oh, I see. They already called me. How are they treating you?"

"Very well, with great respect and consideration."

"I want to see you if only for a minute, to bring you some money."

"No-o-o, it's not necessary. I told you I'm all right—"

"You're sure you don't need a lawyer? You have rights."

My aunt evidently needed more information in order to appreciate the situation in which I was in. But her last words filled me with emotion. It was the first time in my life that anybody spoke to me of my rights.

"Probably, but I assure you I don't need a lawyer." I told her, laughing this time, and she seemed to calm down.

When I hung up the phone I stood there pensively a few seconds, moved by the conversation with my aunt, to whom I felt as close as if we'd never been separated. Something in her way of talking had particularly impressed me: her independence in speaking out, her courage in questioning, especially since she was questioning the FBI.

Freedom goes this far here? I asked myself emotionally, when the voice of Rubén once again caught my attention.

"How's your aunt—everything all right?"

"Yes, she just wants to see me right away."

"Don't you worry, you'll see each other soon."

"I understand."

"Meanwhile, we want you to have the best possible time. If you like we'll take you on an excursion tomorrow to see the city."

We spent the morning and part of that afternoon chatting informally as if we were friends getting to know each other amid anecdotes about our lives and discussions about the most disparate subjects such as sports, the war in the Persian Gulf, music, and life in Cuba and the United States. I understood that through those informal discussions I was being scrutinized as part of a thorough investigation of my case. Yet it didn't trouble me; rather I was enjoying their company as casual friends in a country where I hadn't yet even gotten together with my relatives.

Nevertheless, I felt nervous excitation at the magnitude of the change and the natural preoccupation with the fate of my family. By the start of the afternoon I was plagued by uncontrollable yearnings to burn off some of my excess energies, so I mentioned it to Sánchez.

"Would it be possible to go out walking or jogging a bit?"

He smiled at the request and standing up, replied, "Absolutely. I could use a bit of exercise myself."

Minutes later we were walking briskly along the edge of an artificial lake at the base, burning off a little of that adrenaline that kept me from sleeping. As we walked, my attention was drawn to various families of the personnel at the base who were strolling hand in hand along the lake. And I recalled my former life in Cuba, the life still led by my comrades. Access to Cuban bases by relatives was permitted only very rarely for certain political celebrations taking place on the premises.

That evening Sánchez brought a supper prepared with taste and delicacy by the staff of the military club.

"They've prepared it as a special welcome," he said, smiling as he lifted the cover off the tray adorned with a flower set in a tall, thin pottery vase.

"I feel overwhelmed by all your kindnesses," I remarked with a bit of embarrassment, feeling that for the first time in days my stomach was showing signs of hunger, and I ate with gusto while we sat watching television.

—

That night I had a terrible nightmare: I was on an endless desert of salt, already old and wasted, with my skin cracking from the sun and thirst, wanting to make my way toward a hill behind which Vicky and the boys appeared to be yelling to me for help. And I was dragging myself up the hill now, bleeding from the lacerations in my flesh, feeling the fine salt swallow my arms and legs, preventing me from gaining ground. . . . And then I no longer heard their cries but saw the silhouettes of two hyenas fleeing across the horizon. I woke up soaked in sweat and looked at my watch. I'd barely slept twenty minutes, just enough to suffer that nightmare.

In the morning Rubén and José came by with another very young official, all dressed casually for our excursion into the city. I sat in the front seat next to the driver, ready to take in that impressive city I'd seen from the plane—the main refuge for Cuban exiles. The huge highways, the modern cars of so many makes and models, the unexpected tolls, all caught my attention like new data to be incorporated into a totally unused part of my brain. But more than anything, it was the grass that astonished me—hundreds of miles, millions of acres carefully cultivated and cropped at the sides of the roads, in the yards of the houses. Now that was something that had never before entered my imagination! In all my years of service at the Santa Clara Air Base we'd never even managed to cut all the grass bordering the runway to avoid the flocks of birds that came to eat the seeds and thereby jeopardized takeoff and landing security. And never in my life had I seen a highway with mowed lawns on either side.

Our tour included Miami's Calle Ocho, center of Little Havana, the geographical heart of the Cuban exile community. A group of senior citizens were gathered in the open air on the patio of a curious club that excluded minors under sixty. Stopping by the fence, I watched them playing dominoes and discussing the enslaved passion of their lives: Cuba. In each one of them flowered a dream: returning. And seeing them, I felt the grief of more than a million Cubans forced to leave their homeland because they were not able to live there with dignity.

On our way back we stopped at a shopping mall, and contrary to what my friends expected I wasn't impressed by all the products I saw there, for me it had been enough to see the mowed grass. But the dozens of families walking around there with their children in hand reminded me of the contrasting emptiness in my vision of any similar place in Cuba or the Soviet Union, where such sights were lacking. Rubén insisted we go into a store, and he practically forced me to try on some sneakers.

"So you're more comfortable when you go jogging," he told me when he handed me the bag containing them.

When we were heading back I tried to get some idea of my fate. "How long do you think I should be staying with you?" I asked Rubén, turning to look at him in the backseat, where he was staring distractedly out the window.

"I don't know. . . . I couldn't say for sure right now. Perhaps a week or two, maybe three. I'm not sure." He spoke hesitantly, pensively, while scratching one knee with his right hand. Then, looking up at me, he added more animatedly, "But don't worry, it

won't be for very long. For the moment we want to be sure th
life wouldn't be in danger off the base. Dozens of agents fr
Cuban secret service might very well be looking for you at thi
to settle accounts, and we wouldn't want them to succeed."

"I see," I commented, thinking that they also needed the ti
check whether I really was who I said I was, if my story was
They also had to protect their country's security.

"For the rest we'll do our best to make it as comfortable for
as possible," he concluded, giving a slap on the knee he'd b
scratching.

"One more question: What will I have to do to obtain visas ;
my wife and children?"

"First wait until you've legalized your situation in this counti
. . . then do whatever anybody does. With that we can't help you."

"I understand."

I spent another two weeks with those officials, whom I ended up
appreciating as real friends, until they concluded their investigation
and my MiG was returned to Cuba. They'd allowed me to talk by
telephone almost daily with my relatives in Miami, New Jersey, and
Texas, but not to see them; and now they were saying good-bye to
me, telling me I was free to go wherever I wished. Before me opened
up a world of relatives and newfound friends who were ready to help
me with what had already been an obsession even before I'd left
Cuba: to be reunited with Vicky and my sons.

———

In the house of each relative I visited I was received by welcoming
relations, including second cousins whom I didn't even know existed,
but who treated me as if I'd grown up with them. Such was the Cuban
family tradition, preserved by these people over so many years and
transmitted to their children born here, while being almost forgotten
in Cuba because of the imposition of an ideology that deprecated
family values. Every one of them who came up to me had something
to give me, including inevitably money, which they assured me I
needed to make a start. All that they insisted I accept seemed very
little to them, but each time I felt myself reddening with embarrassment at their generosity. Over time I discovered a deep solidarity
among the Cuban exiles with those who escaped from the island,
receiving them with particular affection and helping them in every
way possible from the very first moment.

For several days I tried in vain to talk to Vicky, and the lines of
telephone communication with Cuba turned out to be extremely
unreliable. I spent dozens of anxious hours next to the telephone,
listening to the solicitous telephone operator, who received the same
reply from the computer to her insistent efforts: "All lines are busy."
Exactly a month had gone by since Vicky and I had last seen each

other and I felt myself going crazy for lack of news, when one early morning the operator managed to put the call through. I'd called the home of some neighbors, and I felt choked with desperation during the minutes that it took them to advise Vicky, terribly frightened they might cut off the call.

When Vicky opened the door to the insistent knocking at that unlikely hour, she found her dear neighbor standing there before her, very pale, her eyes wide open in shock.

"Oré?" Vicky spoke breathlessly from the distance she'd run to get to the phone.

I wanted to speak to her, but the words stammered out in an unintelligible groan: "My love . . ."

"Oré . . . ?"

Vicky could barely speak either, and we were both the victims of overwhelming emotions, which prevented us from uttering another word over that line occupied now only by uncontrollable weeping.

"How are you all?" I finally managed to say in a trembling voice.

"We're okay, but very sad. . . . The boys don't know what's actually happened."

"My love . . . forgive me for never having told you anything." It was the first thing I had to say in order to protect her.

"But what happened? Why did you go away?"

"I can't explain it to you now, but I want you to know that I still love you the same as always. Forgive me."

Vicky was weeping at the other end. She had to let me be the one to speak, but I was barely able to. I paused once again to regain my composure. Then I said, "I couldn't tell you about it. . . . I just want to know if you still love me too."

"My life . . . !" Vicky broke into sobs.

"Vicky, my love . . ." And I was also sobbing like a child, uncontrollably.

"Don't cry like that, my love!" she begged me amid her own tears from the other end, without our being able to help ourselves.

"I just want to know if you love me."

"Of course I love you! I don't know what you've done, but I'll go on loving you forever!"

"Are you willing to come with the children to join me?"

"It doesn't matter to me where you are. There or in the middle of a desert, or in the Antarctic . . . we want to be with you. We need you so—"

They were her final words. Our conversation had been cut off, but we both already knew that from that moment on we would fight for our reunification.

—

Since Vicky's arrival in Havana the psychologist had been visiting her two or three times a week, always going over the story of our lives, always asking about different details in that investigation disguised as assistance that never seemed to be ending, always repeating that I'd betrayed her, that she ought to start a new life.

Two weeks had transpired since my flight to the United States, and the children were already attending a new school, when Vicky made up her mind to travel with my brother to Santa Clara to see to the transfer of her rationing cards, collect our remaining belongings, and hand the key to our apartment over to Cordero. The trip took them nearly twenty hours because of the constant breakdowns of that truck they had rented, paying the equivalent of four months' salary, and now they were carrying everything downstairs under the cold stares of Marlen and Cordero, who seemed to be looking on indifferently through the open doorway of their apartment, as if they meant to display in that manner their frank disgust.

Such was the fear of intimacy with that family in disgrace that a former friend who had been traveling by car to Havana a few days earlier had refused to take along the fan Miriam asked him to return to Vicky.

"Are you crazy? I'm not looking for trouble," he had answered her coldly.

Vicky still had the opportunity to see her most loyal friends during that short visit, who surreptitiously recounted to her the latest comments that were circulating from mouth to mouth within the military community. Some said that I'd escaped to the United States because I was implicated in a case of illegal slaughtering of cattle; others, because she had surprised me with one of my lovers; and still others, because I was involved in a network of illicit trafficking, which had been uncovered by the police. No one who knew me believed such things, but it became clear to Vicky that, given the impossibility of fabricating a campaign against me, the organs of propaganda had decided to feed the people puerile rumors to cover the real reasons for my desertion.

Vicky and the boys were now part of that family of eleven members who lived huddled together in the small three-room dwelling belonging to her parents. Her sister and her brother had married in the last few years but had had to continue living there with their spouses and children for lack of a place to go. They all helped Vicky and the boys in every way possible, but inasmuch as she and our sons were accustomed to leading independent family lives, they felt terrible each day they remained in those crowded quarters, which didn't go unnoticed by the special group investigating our case.

After our phone conversation Vicky had told the boys the truth about where I was, and to her surprise Reyniel had taken the news very well, saying, "At least he's not in the Soviet Union. The United States, now that's a good country!"

The last month spent in Havana had been enough for him to gather, with his nine years of experience, why the kids of his own age, silent witnesses to the humiliating inequality between Cuban and tourist, would reply when asked what they wanted to be when they grew up, "Foreigners."

It was already evening on that day when the psychologist arrived at an unaccustomed hour, asking for the first time whether she'd had news of me, and Vicky realized she already knew about our extended conversation of the night before.

"I spoke to him on the telephone," Vicky started telling her in a soft, measured voice, ready to defend henceforth the right to have our family reunited regardless of political considerations.

"Really? You don't actually think you matter to that traitor!" the psychologist exclaimed, interrupting her immediately.

"He told me he loved me and asked me if I still loved him as well," Vicky continued, as if she hadn't heard her.

"But you wouldn't be crazy enough to sacrifice yourself for that man who's already shown you he doesn't love you."

With her eyes lost on some point on the wall, Vicky continued to ignore her while commenting, "And I know that we can't live apart—"

"Don't be a fool, girl. You're still young and beautiful. You have a future ahead of you . . . you're not going to sacrifice yourself for a man who doesn't really love you—if he did, he'd never have done such a thing. But the Revolution is generous with you and your children, even if he's a traitor. We're here to help you start a new life, to reintegrate yourselves in society, so that you'll watch your children grow up in a healthy world, free from violence and drugs."

"You people don't understand. Neither of us can live without the other."

"You're mistaken. You think that because very little time has passed for you to begin to understand things. . . . In fact I'm bringing you some good news today."

Vicky then stared at her with sincere doubt in her eyes. What good news could they possibly give her?

"The Revolution has decided to provide you with a spacious home right here near your parents, and to offer you a position as dentist at a nearby polyclinic."

What Vicky heard left her dumbfounded: A spacious house for her and the children in the center of Havana—when she knew of thousands and thousands of professionals with decades of outstanding service to the Revolution who lived in the worst overcrowded conditions in deplorable lodgings, which many times collapsed, causing numerous fatalities? And so many others who raised families living separately because of not being able to find even a single makeshift roof under which to sleep? A position as dentist in a polyclinic here in the city, when other thousands of doctors and dentists who lived in Havana had to work for years in the countryside because there was never a place for them here? Obviously they had listened in on our conversation, and wanted now to deflect her with offers that any other person could only have dreamed of.

Vicky returned her gaze to that point on the wall where she had previously fixed her stare and continued, unmoved, her recounting of our conversation. "He asked me if I was willing to join him."

"You told him to go to blazes, didn't you?"

"I told him we were ready to join him, wherever it was. That it didn't matter if it were at the Pole or in a desert, but that we love each other. The boys love their father, and all three of us want to be with him."

"You don't know what you're saying. . . . They'll never let you go to him."

"Why not? I'm not an enemy of the State. I'm only a wife, a mother. My sons can barely comprehend politics and only wish to be with their father. Why can't we be reunited with him?"

"Because he's a traitor—"

"And they're going to punish *us* for that?"

"No, on the contrary. We're offering you the best that the Revolution can give you."

"We don't need anything. We only want to be with him."

The psychologist lowered her head and remained silent for a few seconds. Then, taking a breath and shrugging her shoulders, she said with mournful resignation, dropping her shoulders once more, "I knew you'd say that to me. I understood from the very first day."

She stood up and slowly walked, head lowered, toward the door. Then she turned back for a second before leaving, and looking at Vicky, told her, pointing with a finger, "Think about it . . . they'll never let you leave."

Vicky had spent part of the day trying unsuccessfully to reach the U.S. Interests Office by phone to initiate the steps necessary to obtain visas for her and the boys, following our plans to do so once I'd called her. At last she managed to talk to someone, a day later, who gave her an appointment.

"You should wait until your visas are approved before undertaking the necessary steps with the Cuban authorities for your departure. We'll contact you as soon as we have a reply."

—

In the United States, meanwhile, I'd started to exercise the customs and beliefs that had been denied me since childhood. One Sunday, excited as a child, I prepared myself to attend mass with my uncles, aunts, and cousins. I'd been baptized by my parents at birth, when in Cuba religious beliefs still weren't a shameful onus to those who practiced them, but this was the first time I'd passed through the portals of a church fully conscious of the fact. It was my first mass. I sat beside my family, confused at not knowing what to do at each moment. I didn't know the hymns or the prayers, nor how to leaf through the Bible in search of a psalm, but a powerful force burned in my entrails at the first songs of the chorus. I felt it inside me where it always had been, although they denied it to me; I felt it in the others gathered there, in everything. And I cried in silence because I felt love, felt myself a man, all too human.

Little by little I was discovering through my family and their friends the history of horrendous crimes committed by the Cuban leaders in the name of the Revolution, overcoming my skepticism in the face of so many proofs. Photographs, videos, testimonies by victims, and even by some of those persons mutilated by the kind of torture in prison that Armando Valladares had described in his book, all that provided me with the clearest evidence about a Cuba whose existence I had only intuited after living under Soviet Perestroika. Only then did I pick up Valladares's book once again, realizing with horror that the magnitude of the crime was even greater than that narrated by him.

I also learned of men and women, civil and military functionaries who had escaped the island at different moments, whose families had been kept hostage in Cuba since then, prohibited from leaving despite their having visas from a number of other countries. Many of them had dedicated all their energies to denouncing such a crime to the world, and had almost always encountered deaf diplomacy and an indifferent press on the subject, able to count only on the help of independent human-rights organizations, which were generally ignored by their governments.

I realized then, horrified, how ignorant and naive Vicky and I had been to think that they would have to let her and the children go under threat of being viewed by international public opinion as holding hostage innocent women and children. And the obvious danger hanging over their heads, the fact that their future might be dictated by persons who despised them, filled me with terror. Now they knew that Vicky wanted to join me, and I no longer doubted that they were capable of doing anything to make her say the contrary. She and the children were completely at their mercy, and only the swift granting of visas would give them some protection by way of their being accepted as refugees by the United States government.

One of my cousins advised me to call the State Department and attempt to speak to somebody in the Office of Cuban Affairs. Without knowing anybody there—without any personal recommendation whatsoever—I called at the end of April, identifying myself in the only way that might make possible someone's helping me:

"I'm the pilot who flew the MiG-twenty-three from Cuba on the twentieth of March," I told the person who answered the phone, and seconds later I was speaking to a Ms. Vicky Huddleston, who agreed to see me with evident interest. My cousin Paul Gómez offered immediately to take me to Washington, D.C., in his car, and after an entire day on the road, dirty and exhausted, I arrived at the imposing offices of the State Department. Ms. Hudleston showed a genuine interest in hearing from my lips the reasons why I'd decided to abandon Cuba, and seemed especially sympathetic when I started telling her, with tears in my eyes that I couldn't hold back, about Vicky and the children.

"Calm yourself," she pleaded solicitously, "I promise I'll do whatever's possible."

From that moment on I spent the nights awake by the telephone, hoping to talk to Vicky at least once a week, each time expecting her to give me the news that she'd gotten the visas, each time telling her that she'd be receiving them shortly to keep her spirits up.

The psychologist had continued visiting her two or three times a week, insisting over and over that she start a new life, that she accept the house, the new job, that she forget the traitor, the man who'd traded her for imperialism's dollars.

And now the boys were also anxiously awaiting their visas, asking Vicky every night before going to bed how much longer it might take to receive the necessary papers to go where Daddy was. And over and over she told them not much longer, still nurturing the tenuous hope that they would let her leave with them once she had the visas. It wasn't until June that the long-awaited news came: "We've got the visas now. This very day the U.S. Interests Office delivered them to me. . . . Tomorrow I'll begin the necessary steps for emigration."

I had avoided making any declaration to the media, following the advice of friends and relatives who felt that my silence would encourage the goodwill of the Cuban authorities, and I had withdrawn to the city of Orlando to keep my distance from circles in Miami concerned most with the Cuban question and to devote my time to studying English, which I did tirelessly in order to be able to find a job as quickly as possible.

All that was left to do now was to await the reaction of the Cuban authorities.

—

The day after receiving the visas Vicky went to the immigration office of the municipality to request permission to leave the country. The offices were located in an old colonial house with a large entryway where various people with tired expressions sat on benches lining the walls. Vicky asked where the end of the line was, and someone looked up to point a finger toward the interior of the house. A dozen or so people were scattered about the different benches in that room, which might have been the waiting room of a dental polyclinic if it weren't for the high, dark counter at the back. On the left wall was a gigantic poster of the island of Cuba in vivid colors, and across it the phrase I'M HAPPY IN THIS LAND. Other paintings with even more beautiful landscapes of the island were hung here and there among placards reading I'M STAYING, I'LL BE FAITHFUL, SOCIALISM OR DEATH.

"Next!" came the call from the young girl in the uniform of the Ministry of the Interior, shaking Vicky out of her reverie.

"Fill out these forms and bring them back with birth certificates and four passport-size photos of each one, plus one hundred fifty pesos in postage stamps," she told her, holding out three packets of forms after listening to Vicky without looking at her.

Vicky felt her heart leap for joy and ran to get the children to have their pictures taken. *I can't believe it. It's all turning out to be so easy*, she told herself jubilantly as she hurriedly walked the two miles home to get the children. She didn't have the patience to wait for the bus.

It took her two days to have photos taken, obtain the birth certificates, and purchase the stamps. And two nights to fill out those forms, which reconstructed their entire lives question by question: Why did she want to emigrate and who awaited her abroad? Organizations in which she militated, dates, positions, relatives abroad and their reasons for emigrating, relatives punished at any time for political reasons, and relationship to them; the list went on and on.

It was dawn by the time she filled in the last answers, and with nervous haste she returned to the Office of Immigration. She knew she wouldn't be able to sleep, and she wanted to be the first to enter as soon as it opened.

The woman behind the counter reviewed the documents with an expression of disapproval on her face.

"And your job release?" she asked without looking up.

"What release are you referring to?" Vicky inquired with a presentiment that things were not going to be as simple as they had seemed.

"Don't tell me you don't know. You're a dentist, and as a professional you have to bring a document from the Ministry of Public Health authorizing you to leave the country."

"I don't understand. . . . I don't work any longer."

"You still need a release from the Ministry of Public Health."

"But I don't have any idea . . . what am I supposed to do?"

"How should I know? Go to the provincial office of the ministry in the province where you worked to ask for your release."

Vicky felt her hopes being dashed for the moment. She'd have to go to Santa Clara to ask for the necessary document.

"Is that the only thing I'm missing?" she asked, frightened that she'd end up with the same scenario on her next visit.

"No. You must also bring a clearance from the Technical Investigations Department regarding your husband."

"Where do I find that department?"

"Write it down," the woman said, handing her paper and pencil.

Vicky wrote down the address, and, thanking her, hurried off to obtain the clearance.

"When did you say your husband left Cuba?" the woman asked from behind her desk, which was adorned with a plaque that read INFORMATION.

"In March . . . "

"Of this year?"

"Yes."

"I'm sorry, but the data we have on emigrants only goes up to 1989."

"But what am I supposed to do? I don't understand."

"How did your husband leave?"

"In a MiG-twenty-three."

"Oh! My goodness . . . In that case his file is never going to arrive here. They know that very well, so you go back and tell them that there's no file here, nor will there be one, on your husband."

Vicky returned home then, wondering whether that wouldn't be an insurmountable obstacle. In any case she was still lacking her release as a dentist, and she asked her father to accompany her on that intolerable trip to Santa Clara.

Vicky had sold my belongings and with part of that money she was able to pay the month's salary to get seats in one of those autos making illegal trips to Santa Clara.

"Let's hope your job release arrives shortly," remarked the amiable woman who typed out the document request forms at the Provincial Division of Public Health.

"Excuse me, you mean I can't take it with me right now?"

"I'm sorry," the woman began to explain, the first to do so with a certain kindness, "but the forms have to be approved by the ministry at the national level. Once they do that, they send it directly to Immigration. You should wait until you hear from them directly at home."

Vicky and her father returned to Havana without saying a word the whole way. It was midnight when they arrived, and they discovered Reyniel and Alejandro asleep in the living room.

Their grandmother lamented to Vicky, "They barely ate their dinner tonight, and they didn't want to go to bed until you got back."

Vicky kissed them both on the cheek, and they woke up, asking together, "Did you do it, Mommy? When do we go to Daddy's?"

"There's still a bit more," she answered, leading them to the mattress she shared with them, suspecting bitterly that still more difficulties would arise on the path to our reunion.

The following morning she returned to Immigration.

"My release is being sent here by the ministry," she explained to the same woman behind the counter, with the hope that they would let her know if that was all that was still needed for them to grant her the passports and permission to leave.

"And the clearance on your husband?"

"The Technical Investigations Department says that they only have files going up to 1989."

"How did your husband leave the country?" the woman asked then, for the first time looking Vicky in the face.

"He left on March twentieth, in a MiG-twenty-three."

The woman then opened her eyes wider and knit her brow in a frown. "But in that case . . . you realize . . . it's a very special case. Wait a moment." And she disappeared through a door. Minutes later she returned, accompanied by a major from the Ministry of the Interior.

"You say your husband is the pilot of the MiG who betrayed the Revolution in March?" the major addressed Vicky with a penetrating stare.

"Well, yes, the one who left in March . . ."

"You should know that it's not up to us to decide in such a case. Only High Command can make the decision."

"How will I know the decision?"

"We should receive an answer in a few weeks."

"I understand." And thanking them, Vicky this time walked slowly out of that room filled with lovely landscapes that millions of Cubans had bid farewell to with the eternal nostalgia of the emigrant.

Magalis the psychologist began to come to the house almost daily while Vicky awaited an answer, always insisting that I'd betrayed her, that she start a new life, that she accept the comfortable house in the Vedado District, the coveted employment. Vicky listened to her with the same lost look as always, recounting with some enjoyment the various anecdotes of our lives once again and saying how deeply we loved each other. And Magalis kept insisting, insisting, even though she knew that Vicky wasn't about to change her mind.

Scarcely had they arrived back in Havana when the neighbors let Vicky know that they'd noticed the presence of strange guests who were sitting in front of the tenement day and night watching and methodically taking notes on whatever people were coming and going there. And Vicky would smile each morning when she took the children off to school and saw one of these strangers get up nervously from his habitual seat on the porch steps of the house across the street to follow her surreptitiously as if she didn't see what he was doing. It didn't matter where she went. To pick up her quota of rations at the market or to the immigration office, they invariably trailed after her. And she'd smile while walking, asking herself how long that ridiculous surveillance would last, and wondering how a country could not be in a state of total degradation if it was wasting so much of its resources on spying on thousands and thousands of persons who, like her, represented no peril—other than a moral one—to the government.

Her new position in society, as the wife of a man who had escaped from the country, slowly revealed to her the true feelings of dozens of people she'd known since childhood and whom she'd never suspected of opposing the system. It was through them, and the experiences they related to her after she'd won their trust, that she began to learn about that other Cuba, silent and concealed under the mantle of revolutionary fervor, which survived at the cost of daily struggles on the black market, which listened furtively to foreign radio broadcasts, and which prayed every night for the end of ignominy and the return of hope for the country.

At the end of two weeks' waiting, Vicky returned to see the disagreeable woman at the Immigration counter.

"We still have no reply. Wait at home until we send you a telegram," she told her without looking up.

For three more weeks Vicky kept visiting the municipal immigration office, ignoring their requests that she remain at home until she received their telegram; and this time, the last, the woman actually looked up to eye her insolently while telling her, "Your request to emigrate has been denied."

"But why?"

"Well . . . don't you know? Because your husband is a traitor, girl!"

Vicky felt her anger, her impotence, and her grief clawing at her heart, making her breathe faster.

"But that's him. . . . What can you be accusing us of?"

"Of being his family."

The woman turned away, and taking up a pencil as if writing something else, put an end to the conversation.

"I still don't get it," Vicky insisted to reclaim her attention, "the Commander in Chief and the Second Secretary of the party have said repeatedly in their speeches that anybody who wants to leave the country can leave."

The woman replied then, still staring at the papers she was pretending to fill out, "That's generally speaking, but not in the particular instance of a traitor."

"They never made exceptions when they said it."

"Look here, girl. Don't you realize that the Ministry of the

Interior has a directive prohibiting the emigration of any relatives of traitors?"

"I don't believe in such a directive. The constitution of our country says I can leave whenever I want, and there's no law that can abolish that right."

"Well look: there's a directive which refuses to allow you to leave."

"Can I see this directive?"

"No, it's verbal." And looking over Vicky's shoulder, she nearly screamed: *"Next!"*

It had been a month since Vicky had received those visas, which she still held as her hope for salvation, but she now felt all the weight of a system that not only prevented her from exercising her rights, but that avoided confronting her by forcing her to deal with bureaucrats who had no authority to make decisions.

No, I won't sit still for it, she told herself over and over while pacing back and forth in her room and thinking of the next move to make.

Luckily we'd been able to talk by phone two more times without the call being cut off, and I was kept abreast of the details of her efforts.

With each passing day the boys became more and more aware of the reality of their situation and silently despaired that we would ever be reunited again. One night Vicky had heard some faint sobbing through the door to the bedroom and, opening it, she found Alejandro cowering against the wall. In his hands he was holding a photo of me while talking to it, as the tears rolled down his cheeks. It upset the boy to be surprised in this act of intimacy, and on seeing the tears filling his mother's eyes, he confessed, sending a chill of terror up Vicky's spine, "Mommy . . . my heart can't stand it anymore."

Reyniel no longer liked to play as before, and his always smiling face had now become serious, bewildered, even though Vicky never caught him crying. He kept watching his mother in silence, seeing how she suffered from having her hopes crushed one after another, and then he would tell her, "Mommy, please, don't be sad."

Then he would go to bed, suffering his first bouts of insomnia at age ten and his first cough, which accompanied him from then on like a nervous tic wherever he went.

I wanted to bring the matter into the open, publicly accuse the Cuban government of punishing my family for my own actions; but friends, relatives, and even Vicky asked me to wait until all possible avenues had been exhausted. I then wrote dozens of letters to the chancelleries of the various Latin American countries and of Spain, asking them to intercede with the Cuban authorities in favor of the release of my family. But inured to the terrible truth of the world, which was brought home to me daily by the free press in the United

States, I nourished small hope of a genuinely human effort from governments that normally turned their backs on even more horrendous crimes.

Vicky then wrote to the Commander in Chief, the Minister of the armed forces, the chief ideologue of the party, the minister of the interior, the national director of immigration, the historic commanders of the Revolution, and she delivered each of the letters to the respective offices of the government concerned. Then a month later she received a telegram from the national Directorate of Immigration, and she rushed to the place with the hope that her letters had had an effect. It was located in a complex of residential homes whose owners had emigrated after the triumph of the Revolution. A fence had been put up around the complex, leaving only one gateway through which to enter, guarded by a soldier.

"Go ahead, and ask for Lieutenant Colonel Manuela," he told Vicky, returning her identity card and the telegram, which he'd carefully perused.

A young woman accompanied by a son and a daughter, who couldn't have been more than seven or eight years old, waited silently in that small anteroom—this time with no counter—to be summoned to the interview for which they'd been asked to present themselves. Vicky greeted the woman quietly and took a seat on one of the three benches installed there, without their exchanging another word during the moments they shared under that roof. A flurry of doors opening and closing, and of officials coming and going through that small anteroom, distracted them until the woman with the two children was finally called. Then Vicky heard the nasty voice of another woman behind the door, drowning out the weeping of the woman who had been waiting with her, shouting, "Your husband is a traitor! You're someone we'd never permit to leave, never!"

"But if other people can leave," the mother of the children begged amid the sobs Vicky now heard clearly, "then why not us?"

"Such cases have been authorized at the highest level. But not you. He's a traitor! And none of you will ever leave here!"

Vicky listened, and a knot of desperation tightened in her throat. Now it was her turn to confront this rather attractive-looking woman with her hair freshly done up, wearing lieutenant colonel's stripes on her shoulders, who was busy leafing through some documents without even bothering to look up at the person she had had sitting in front of her for several minutes already.

A young woman with captain's stripes seated behind the desk to the right had instructed Vicky to sit there quietly until the other officer attended to her.

Finally, the lieutenant colonel put aside the file she was perusing with a dismissive gesture and, leaning back in her chair, addressed Vicky with her head to one side and an excessive note of calmness in her voice, as if enjoying looking at some repulsive creature. "Victoria, I don't know why you wrote to this office, because the response already given you by Municipal Immigration will never change. Your husband is a traitor, disaffected with the Revolution."

Vicky listened in silence, watching how that woman began to gesticulate and impart to her words an increasingly violent tone for which there was no justification whatsoever.

"What you have to do is grow up, girl! Stop being such a fool and begin a new life. Accept the house the Revolution so generously offers you; take the job they're telling you. . . . What your present attitude will get you is harm to your children instead of helping them. How can you want to go join a traitor?"

Vicky had listened in silence, feeling rage at not being able to control the tears running down her cheeks, seeing through a mist of tears that woman gesticulating and shouting louder and louder. She finally felt something explode inside her and, jumping to her feet like a coiled spring, she screamed as loud as the other: "My husband's no traitor! I can't see him that way! He's my husband, the father of my children, the man who loves me and whom I'll love forever! Look at things as a mother sees them."

The lieutenant colonel stared at Vicky in bewilderment, then sat back in her chair without another word.

Then the captain at the adjacent desk spoke in a more conciliatory tone. "You have to understand, girl. . . . In cases like yours they can't let you leave. How would that affect the other pilots in the air force?"

Vicky nearly broke out laughing. That was the first acknowledgement she'd heard by a government official that military officers and functionaries were virtual hostages, though many of them didn't suspect as much.

"Listen to what Captain Zonia's telling you," Manuela insisted now in a more courteous tone of voice, "there are simply cases that can't be authorized because of the connotation they might have. . . . Maybe after a few years, depending on the attitude he demonstrates abroad and you here, you'll be permitted to leave."

Vicky seemed not to understand and gave her an inquiring look.

"I mean, if he makes no declaration to the media against the Revolution, and you accept the house offered you and start to work normally . . ."

Vicky smiled then, realizing the meaning of what they were saying. To agree to that, she knew, would mean to live without hope of ever seeing each other again.

"And one more thing," Manuela added as a final thought. "Whenever you want to speak to us, come back. You just have to tell the sentry at the gate who you are."

Vicky went home convinced that they were ready to go as far as possible to keep her and the boys from leaving the country, but she still held on to one final hope: Her letters to the highest leaders of the Revolution had still not been answered. She would wait a little longer before beginning an open battle for our right to live together as a family wherever we wanted.

It had been a while since she'd seen my parents, so she decided to go to Matanzas with the boys, who were now on vacation, in hopes of providing them with some distraction to mitigate the anxieties assailing them. They didn't have a toy in the house, or a place to go walking outside of the decrepit zoological garden they already knew from one end to the other. Not even the television helped to distract them, since normal children's programs had been suspended for economic reasons.

Arriving in Matanzas, she was shocked to discover how thin my parents had grown. Suffering the painful loss of their eldest son, they still nurtured the hope that he would resurface, building him up in their imaginations as a probable agent from Cuban intelligence who was infiltrated into the heart of enemy territory on an extremely confidential mission. Vicky listened as they hinted at such dreams, and was moved by the resourcefulness with which parents steeled themselves in their grief to salvage their son when they were unable to comprehend the reality of the world around them.

"I know it's hard for both of you . . . but you have to face the truth for your own well-being," she told them, and watched my father go off to his room, where he remained for some time, hiding his grief at the harsh reality before him.

I'd thought a great deal about my parents, especially about my father, and I understood how terrible that truth would be for him, how guilty he would feel for his son's tragic fate, and his own. To dream up stories like a child protected him from his own conscience, whereas to open his eyes to the crushing reality would signify the negation of his entire life. He wanted to go on living, and to feel that his life had had meaning, so he retreated into an unreal world built upon the idealism with which he had always acted, without perceiving that the very ethics of honor he had inculcated in me had inspired me to break with the Revolution.

A surprise awaited Vicky and the boys upon their return to Havana: two telegrams from the offices of the second and third heads of state, two similar replies after that long silence:

"Received your letter. Your case being analyzed. Await reply."

C h a p t e r   1 7

—

L o v e   W i l l
T r i u m p h

It was the last days of August 1991 when I was able to speak to Vicky again and learn the story of her meeting with Lieutenant Colonel Manuela and the telegrams received the previous day. The latter had rekindled our hope, and we decided to wait in silence a while longer.

Perhaps the chancellery of one of the governments I wrote to has interceded with the Cuban government for them, I told myself with a glimpse of hope in my heart.

But Vicky had to spend another anxious month of waiting before being visited by a mysterious woman who asked her to report the following morning to the offices of Raúl Castro, in the seat of the Council of State, where she'd be given the final decision on her case.

At last our pleadings have touched his soul, Vicky thought as she listened to her.

She spent that night without sleep, amid continual trips to the bathroom, overcome by intestinal pains, which assailed her each time she was confronted by the uncertainty of their fate, determined by the supreme will of those men. She felt weak, and she asked her mother to accompany her to the group of governmental buildings located behind the celebrated Revolution Square. She felt her heart palpitating when the sentry standing at the entryway, armed with an AKM rifle, opened the glass door for them and pointed toward the Bureau of Information.

A gigantic vestibule with shining marble floors opened before their eyes, lit by ostentatious lamps which heightened the beauty of the plants and furnishings and the unusually elegant attire of the people working there. Vicky and her mother felt silenced by such opulence as they had never imagined, and with slow, nervous steps they proceeded to the counter that read INFORMATION.

One of the women behind the counter greeted them with a smile and, after making a brief call to the office of the Second Secretary of the Party, asked them to wait a few moments.

"Good morning. I'm Magalis Chacón, assistant to the Minister of the Armed Forces. Will you follow me, please?" said a woman of short stature and elegant dress who finally came over to where they were waiting. "You'll have to wait here," she added to María when the latter got up from her seat with the intention of accompanying them.

Vicky followed her to a tiny office barely accommodating a desk piled with telephones, three easy chairs, and a personal computer, which caught her attention for being the first one she'd ever seen in her life. Another woman who was waiting there stood up to introduce herself.

"I'm Melba Chávez, assistant to the ideological chief of the party."

"Well, let's sit down," Magalis ordered, adding, "Victoria, Comrade Raúl Castro was unable to welcome you personally, occupied as he is at the moment with other tasks, and he's asked us to attend to you on his behalf. The same is true for Comrade Carlos Aldana, whose assistant is here to join us for our meeting."

Vicky saw that those men had delegated the matter to their assistants because they didn't have the courage to face the injustices they themselves were dictating. She leaned forward in her chair then, focusing all her attention on what Magalis was about to tell her.

"We want you to know that your case has been examined by the Directorate of the party and the Armed Forces Command. And the decision they've asked me to transmit is"—Magalis paused for a second, and Vicky felt her pulse pounding and a chill running through her body—"well . . . that your husband can come back."

"What are you saying?"

"That's right, your case has been studied, and we think that he acted on an impulse, from momentary feelings. We want you to inform him that the party and the government are giving him a chance to come back."

"But what do you expect? That he'll come back to be put on trial?"

"Well . . . it will be taken into consideration that he hasn't made any declarations against the Revolution."

Vicky comprehended now that she and the boys had been taken

as hostages. The government was hoping that the anguish caused by our indefinite separation would make me come back sooner or later, and then they'd be able to put on a show-trial for treason before the rest of the armed forces with a double purpose: to demonstrate the repentance of the traitor, and to give an exemplary warning by executing him immediately. The precedent set by General Ochoa, and other cases of military officers who were rumored to have been executed in secrecy, could hardly make her think otherwise.

"But don't you understand that we don't want him to come back. The purpose of my letters was to find out when we can join him."

"Never!"

Vicky felt terribly fragile, insignificant, impotent. Her life and that of her children depended, had always depended, on the absolute will of the men who governed the country. Neither the law, nor any judge, nor the constitution itself could ever contradict the will of those individuals who governed their lives at a whim.

"This is unjust. The boys are suffering, they need their father."

"The one guilty for their suffering is the one who didn't hesitate to betray them. What you need to do is take the house and the job we're offering you and start a new life as an exemplary mother. How can you wish to take your children to such a corrupt society, plagued with drugs, prostitution, injustice, and more vice than anyone could conceive of?"

A man with colonel's stripes on his shoulder had just entered the office without either asking permission or knocking at the door, and was listening now in silence to Magalis.

"I'll never do that," Vicky began to tell her, feeling her voice struggle between impotence and indignation. "The only thing we need is to live as a family with him, it doesn't matter where it is because we'll know how to educate our sons. . . . I'll wait whatever time is necessary, even if it's the rest of my life, but we'll be reunited."

"In that case," interrupted the colonel, who had been listening in silence until then, "you should know that the Comrade Minister of the Armed Forces said that if your husband had the guts to leave with one of my MiGs, maybe he has the guts to come back and get his family."

Vicky turned then to face his arrogant stare, thinking what she dare not say: *It's your Minister who should have the guts to face up to his own crimes instead of sending you people to do it.*

She stood up slowly then, with barely the strength to do so, but satisfied for the first time at not giving into tears. No, they'd never again see her tears! And telling them good-bye, she left in search of her mother. They walked home in silence, Vicky tormented by the thought of her children waiting for her filled with hopes that they would soon be leaving to meet Daddy. "Because Fidel and Raúl really are good," Reyniel had told her when she kissed him good-bye.

Now she felt herself toughening, ready to face with dignity and love as her only weapons the powerful system that threatened to crush them. *Enough already of waiting in the dishonorable silence they impose upon us!* she told herself while standing in the bus crowded with passengers. *From now on we'll go to church even if they interpret it as an act of rebellion. God will bring us together in spirit, even if we're now separated by insurmountable barriers. And I won't hesitate to speak to diplomats and foreign journalists to denounce our plight and ask for help.*

The children received the news in silence, without shedding any tears. They had also gotten tougher, and they gazed at their mother securely when she promised them, "I don't know when, but don't you ever doubt that we'll be reunited with your father."

Reyniel was lost in his thoughts, his face very serious, while he stared at the sky through the window.

Alejandro's only comment was, "Mommy, why are those men so bad?"

The psychologist showed up the next day, curious about the children, and Vicky remembered that a friend had told her that the psychologist had visited the school, inquiring about the boys' behavior, wanting to know whether they saluted the flag, participated in patriotic ceremonies, or spoke of their father.

"You know how boys are and the harm this business is causing them," Vicky said, looking at her firmly. "From now on they'll attend church with me and find in God the faith and hope which has been taken from them here."

"But are you crazy? Look how you live. You'll never get to leave here. You should take the house, that kind of opportunity nobody ever gets. I myself have to live with my parents."

"I don't need anything."

"But why are you going to destroy your life for a traitor? He's a young man, I'll bet . . . he's probably already found some rich, attractive young girl to share his life with."

Vicky turned to her then with pity in her eyes. She sighed, and putting her hand on the dauntless psychologist's arm, she told her compassionately, "You make me so sad, Magalis."

The psychologist appeared not to understand, and she opened her eyes with real interest.

"How many years have you been married?"

"Five years," answered the psychologist in confusion.

"It saddens me that you haven't known real love in spite of all . . ." The psychologist listened in stunned silence. She didn't know what to say, and Vicky continued, while slightly pressing her arm, ". . . that you haven't been loved as I have, that you haven't experienced it as I have. Love isn't negotiable and nothing will make me renounce him. I also know that he'll wait for me all his life if necessary."

The psychologist lowered her head and then looked up as if wanting to say something, but the words stuck in her throat as she repeated confusedly, "I, I . . ."

She fell silent once more, then she stood up slowly and headed for the door.

"Good-bye, Vicky," she said without turning around, and she never returned to help Vicky begin a new life.

—

Only in October was I able to talk to Vicky again by phone and learn the story. That was our only means of communication besides the few letters that some Cuban might boldly agree to take with him to mail from another country when he went abroad. I had also sent various letters to Vicky at the beginning, but frustrated by their constantly being intercepted to prevent their reaching her, I finally gave up writing further.

I had kept silence, burning with the certainty that they'd never let them leave, given the evidence of other cases I was gradually learning about, and now I received the green light from Vicky to start the public campaign for our right to live as a family.

"It'll be hard," I warned her when we talked. "From now on all the coercive machinery of the system will be turned upon you and the children. They'll watch you day and night, looking for some way to implicate you in the slightest transgression to put you in prison. . . . Until now they wanted to convince you, from now on they'll want to destroy you. Don't go out of the house, because any of their stooges may try to provoke you on the street in order to lock you up for the crime of public scandal. Don't trust anyone who offers you the chance to participate in internal dissidence. You're simply a mother, a wife who's fighting for the reunification of her family. Even less should you think about trying to leave the country illegally; don't trust anybody who offers to help you that way."

All this I told Vicky hurriedly, fearful they would cut off our call and I wouldn't be able to give her the necessary advice. I'd received enough information about the face of the regime that I hadn't known when I fled the country, and I saw clearly now what they were ready to do to force her to submit.

They would never lock her up for wanting to reunite her family, since they always committed their crimes under the mantle of a justice they called revolutionary. They realized that the example of her fighting for her family's reunification would end up weakening the authority of the government by winning the sympathy of more and more people; so they had to destroy her example, but using other reasons for doing so. They wouldn't hesitate about setting the most

"You're their only help or protection," I told the tens of thousands of Cubans I knew were listening. "The only thing I ask you is that you offer them spiritual solidarity in these difficult moments, human warmth. . . . No one has the right to arbitrarily divide a family."

Our Leaders never tired of repeating in their public interventions that in Cuba anybody who wanted to leave the country could do so freely, and I knew that many Cubans, unable to hear other voices, believed it. If the people drew close to Vicky and the children, there would now be a double reason for the government to refrain from openly repressing them.

We had anticipated the Cuban government, from now on it would be more difficult for them to commit any treachery against Vicky and the children.

We were about to conclude the broadcast when I repeated to Vicky those words filled with faith, which I had uttered to her a long time before:

"This is a struggle of truth against lies, of love against hate . . . and love will triumph!"

—

The same night the program was broadcast in Cuba, Vicky's parents' house was inundated with visitors, some arriving discreetly and others openly, to offer their help. They brought prayers, food, money, and above all, their concern. Days went by and Vicky had not a moment's rest from the constant stream of visitors. Some of them from other provinces took advantage of traveling through Havana to come by. And from then on there was no lack of anonymous peasants or fishermen who would bring something or other for her and the boys to eat. Two old women from the distant province of Camagüey offered their warmest prayers, another sent the children some toys she'd guarded over the years, and even poems inspired by their plight began to arrive. A group of ten mothers from Havana wrote a letter to the Highest Leader, which they made public through the foreign press, asking for the immediate release of Vicky and the boys. Not a day went by without some voice raised in protest somewhere in the country, through phone interviews with journalists abroad, against the abuse of their rights. In fact, the sympathy awakened by the courage with which they defended our right to live as a family touched even lesser functionaries in the government with whom they had to deal in their daily struggle. And far from being repudiated by those people, who were increasingly choked by economic deprivation and political control, my family often enjoyed their consideration and respect.

Without wanting to be, Vicky became a popular figure, constantly being stopped by people who affectionately greeted her, many of them—to her surprise—well-known revolutionaries. On food lines she would end up blushing at the insistence of those in front of her that she pass to the head of the line, and groups of kids from the neighborhood spoke of fighting any crowd that might show up there for the purpose of organizing some act of repudiation against her and the boys. No sooner had a new "observer" been posted across the street or another inspection conducted by State security, which had already informed the Block Defense Committee that she was a "dangerous enemy," than someone would come by the house to let her know.

At the same time she had to contend with undercover agents sent to induce her to participate in activities that would serve as a pretext to arrest her. Despite my warning over the radio heard by those who came to help her, to the effect that those who offered to sneak her out of the country wouldn't be acting as friends, there were those who offered to arrange for her escape, to which she would answer that they would only leave the country when the authorities permitted, knowing that instead of putting her aboard some boat they would be handing her over to State security.

I managed to talk to Vicky and the boys after the first radio transmissions, and I was crushed by the innocent worry that tormented Alejandro.

"Daddy, you don't listen when I send you kisses over the radio," he told me without my understanding very clearly what he meant. Afterwards, Vicky explained to me that when the boy would hear me on the radio, he'd run up to it, hugging and kissing it as if it were me.

One day Paul brought me the phone number of Armando Valladares, the man the Revolution had slandered, calling him a terrorist in order to torture him for twenty-two years because of his ideas. After his release from Cuba, he became the United States ambassador to the United Nations Commission on Human Rights, and now he was putting his passion and experience to work for the defense of human dignity through the foundation that he'd created in his name.

"I think he might be able to help you," Paul remarked, handing me the number.

Armando immediately offered to help, and we both agreed that continual public denunciation was the only way to protect Vicky and the children until we obtained their freedom. He himself had been freed only because of the international pressure on the Cuban government, provoked by the extensive campaign of denunciations carried out around the world by his wife.

"We have to take the campaign everywhere, and I think the first place to start should be Washington," he told me, suggesting we knock on the doors of congressmen, senators, and diplomats, and at the same time offering me his house in Virginia as a place to stay while we did it.

From then on I stayed in constant communication with him and

Kristina Arriaga, executive director of the Valladares Foundation, who immediately went into action using the network of contacts they'd already established with human rights organizations around the world.

As the year drew to a close, the first Christmas arrived that I was to experience in freedom. Christmas trees, traditional carols, and Santa Claus began to make their appearances everywhere. I received my first gifts, which friends and relatives regaled me with like a little boy, and for the first time in my life I went to a toy store in search of gifts to give. On every shelf I saw a dream, an expression of childlike imagination, and I felt dismay at the absence of my own children, deprived of their childhood, of their dreams, of their presents. I wandered like an insane straggler during those days, from house to house, feeling the emptiness in my soul that nothing could fill, consumed by the anguish at the hateful punishment my sons were subjected to.

Twelve chimes announced the arrival of the new year at the house of a friend, and parents and children embraced each other while I went out on the balcony to talk to my own, looking up at the stars.

"You have to be strong, Orestes. Sooner or later they'll be with you again." It was the voice of my friend behind me, who preferred not to embarrass me by looking me in the face, in case I was crying.

"You can be certain of that . . . sooner or later. These will be my last Christmas holidays without them," I answered without turning around, clenching my fists and taking as deep a breath as I could, while I felt his consoling hand on my shoulder.

Two or three times a week I participated in the programs of the Voice of the Foundation, inspired by the support of the men and women who worked for the Cuban American National Foundation. One afternoon the four North American owners of the broadcast station came by and, when they heard from Ninoska the story of my family's plight, they asked her and me to step into a small office with them. There we all joined hands, quietly forming a circle above which rose the voice of one of the owners in the first prayer I ever heard in English—"Lord, hear the prayer of thy children"—and we were all overcome with tears of love as he concluded. That day the children of the people I was taught to hate were praying for my children. No, I'd rather die than allow my sons to be indoctrinated in that same diabolical hatred!

With our radio programs we'd obtained the support of the Cuban people in Miami and on the island, but it wasn't sufficient to generate the climate of pressure that would force the government to allow Vicky and the boys to leave. We needed the moral support of everyone—men, women and children, family people—who would be disposed to write a letter to the Cuban authorities asking for their release. I felt convinced that if we succeeded in flooding the governmental offices with hundreds of thousands of such letters, my family would be granted permission to leave for fear of the publicity that their case was receiving. But how to reach the people, how to make them know what was happening in order to gain their help? I didn't have the money to do what was necessary. When Paul and I tried to pay for the first printing of flyers with the photo of Vicky and the boys that I'd brought with me on my flight, a friend who was also helping me with the campaign for their release picked up the expenses.

At the end of January 1992 a group of artists and intellectuals denying there were any human rights violations on the island met at the Jacob Javits Convention Center in New York to spread goodwill regarding the Revolution and raise funds for the Cuban government. Thousands of Cubans were mobilized from all over the United States to disseminate the much ignored truth about Cuba in the streets of Manhattan. Paul and I flew to New York in a plane chartered by the Cuban American National Foundation, bearing the first twenty thousand flyers of Vicky and the children donated by our friend Armando Muñoz. Dozens of volunteers and friends distributed them while others marched through the streets carrying huge posters friends had made of the same photo. Friends from other countries endured the freezing wind blowing in front of the Javits Center as they heard the testimony of dozens of victims. I had my first opportunity there to speak openly to a gathering, and I couldn't help shedding tears of emotion at the freedom exercised in the country where I now lived, where its detractors were now assembled in a convention center protected by the police.

It was at that protest that I met Janet Weininger, another who had suffered the blows of the Cuban authorities. For eighteen years she'd struggled tirelessly to obtain the return of the remains of her father, a U.S. pilot shot down during the Bay of Pigs Invasion. But the Cuban government demanded payment of $35,000, which she didn't have, in exchange for her father's body, wishing to profit at the cost of her right to bury on her own soil the person she held closest to her heart. She was married, moreover, to an F-16 pilot the same year Vicky and I had had our wedding, and her children were of similar ages to our own, making us feel especially touched by each other's stories. Possessed of extraordinary energy, Janet wrote to the principal newspapers around the country and set up meetings with influential personalities to ask their help in obtaining freedom for Vicky and the boys.

At this point the Weininger family home became a kind of coordinating center for the campaign, where we'd meet each day to discuss the next steps to be taken. I could barely make myself understood with my rudimentary English, but the sincere concern of that family captured my affections forever.

By then the majority of Miami's Cuban community was familiar with our struggle, and hundreds of hands were extended to help us. Not a few friends made me blush with shame when they put money in my pocket to help me with my campaign. One day I asked Paul to have reproduced at a studio owned by a Cuban couple a limited quantity of photographs of Vicky and the children, which I had money to pay for, and when I came back later to pick them up, there were hundreds of extra copies for which they refused to charge me. It turned out that the owners of the studio had endured a similar separation in the sixties when the husband first arrived from Cuba. With time Bertha and Benito Filomía ended up more or less adopting me as a son whom they protected and cared for with real compassion.

One day I was given the phone number of Álvarez Andrade, an officer from State security who'd recently escaped from the island and wanted to talk to me. I called him at once and learned that he'd worked at the general headquarters of that feared organ of repression until the moment he defected.

"I know of important plans against you and your family, but I don't want to talk about it over the telephone," he told me, suggesting that we meet directly. I immediately arranged to go see him.

In a very low voice, as if afraid of being overheard by anyone else, Álvarez told me that a team from military Counterintelligence reporting directly to Raúl Castro had come up with a plan to assassinate me; he had found out about it because they needed the cooperation of agents from State security where he worked to be able to carry it off. According to Álvarez, a team of psychologists assigned to the case had concluded that before long I'd be so distressed at the impossibility of obtaining the release of my family that I'd be open to returning to Cuba if they promised me a pardon. Cuban agents abroad would therefore approach me in such a way as to have the suggestion come from me, and they would then prepare for my secret repatriation, killing me during the trip. Then in Cuba the government would circulate the story that I'd been a Cuban agent infiltrated into the heart of the enemy with an important mission, but had been assassinated by the CIA working with counterrevolutionary organizations in exile in Miami when, after being discovered, I attempted to return home. A photograph of me would be displayed from then on in the Hall of Martyrs, in State security, and some school would be named after me. Even Vicky herself, heartbroken at my death, would end up accepting the house, the job, and the car they would now give her as a gesture by the Revolution on behalf of the family of one of its most recent martyrs. The revolutionary press would take care of the rest, and nobody would give any further thought to the reasons why a man with a clean record, a genuine son of the Revolution, would choose to break with it.

One night a friend of many years who habitually traveled abroad because of his job called me from Mexico.

"I wanted you to know about the terrible situation Vicky and your sons are in, without the slightest chance of being allowed to leave the country," he began by telling me, then to make me feel responsible he added, "I know that sooner or later you'll regret what you did, since you're the one who's to blame for the mess they're in." And I realized that our friend had ceased to be that when he concluded, "Only, I wanted you to know that should you decide to return I can serve as intermediary between you and the authorities in order to have you pardoned."

I knew then that this was the first direct message I'd received from the Cuban government.

"Thanks," I replied, "but I prefer to die rather than betray my children." I never got another call from him again during the many trips he continued to make abroad. What would have been the point?

Paul and I had finally gotten enough money together to rent a car and spend a week driving to Washington and New Jersey to coordinate the efforts of the Valladares Foundation and the group of enthusiasts represented by my family there, together with Vicky's various relatives with whom I'd also made contact. We spent two days at the home of my aunt and uncle in New Jersey, sufficient time to meet dozens of people eager to shake our hands and make a contribution to help carry our effort forward. There for the first time I learned the real reasons why my uncle and aunt had been forced to emigrate to the United States when I was eleven years old. And I couldn't get over the pain and indignation of realizing that the damage inflicted by the Revolution on the very heart of our family had been hidden from me all those years.

They lived modestly in a small apartment in West New York, but without debts, despite their having arrived here with two small children and no other wealth than their willingness to work. It was that right found in the United States, to live decently by the fruit of one's honest labors, which had been denied the people of Cuba for so many years, and which had provoked the exodus of nearly 20 percent of its population.

My aunt Fela was a wonder of kindness and honesty, virtues still as fresh in her as when she and her eight peasant sisters first emigrated to Cabaiguán in 1950. Short and heavy, talkative and energetic, she'd go around the apartment being everywhere at once. And how I suffered under her delicious culinary tutelage, pursued by her at every turn to taste something more ambrosial.

"Eat, my boy, eat. Look how skinny you are!" she'd tell me when, after gorging myself, I complained that I couldn't eat another bite.

They had organized their own group of volunteers to initiate the campaign in the Northeast, and each day Uncle Raúl visited dozens of commercial establishments, where he left pamphlets which he and my aunt had had printed up, while his son William sent hundreds of faxes and letters to prominent personalities soliciting their support. Meanwhile Paul and I were practically spending more time in the car than not because of the constant traveling to and from interviews with the press and with personalities, visits to schools, churches, and synagogues. In Washington Armando and Kristina were waiting with a tight schedule for us to complete, despite our exhaustion.

Armando invited us to his home, which was blessed by the shouts and laughter of their three precious children, who raced around our legs while we were talking. Their squeals were like music to my ears, at the same time filling me with longing for my boys. And it wasn't long before I was on the floor playing with those happy little characters, who called me uncle and stole my heart. Martha and Armando told us about their lives, about the battle waged by her around the world to obtain his freedom, and he took us into his library to show us the tiny pieces of paper on which he had clandestinely smuggled out to her passionate love poems while he was held in a tiny punishment cell.

"In spite of the tortures, they never got me to hate them," Armando said of his torturers, while I listened, horrified, to his description of the tortures to which he'd been subjected.

We saw Kristina the following morning, and she took us to the various appointments she had set up in Congress. She met us on the sidewalk, offering her hand while introducing herself with "I'm Kristina."

She had a childlike face and lively brown eyes that were constantly moving about as she talked a mile a minute, like someone forever in a hurry.

"Your tie is horrible," she added after I greeted her, and I didn't know what to say, since I'd never before given much thought to how my ties should look.

We briefly went over the schedule she'd meticulously prepared, and we spoke about what strategy should be followed in approaching that world of politicians, which was totally unknown to me.

She finished by explaining, "The tie also counts," shedding light on her particular interest in what I was wearing.

In Congress we followed Kristina from office to office, astonished at her ease and mastery at dealing with people there, and at the kindness with which we were received in each office without anybody asking us for personal identification or proof of our appointment.

In a short time Armando and Kristina had managed to get various senators and congressmen to agree to sign a letter directed to the Cuban government soliciting the release of Vicky and the children. And if I didn't obtain their release with it, at least it offered them considerable protection against possible reprisals because of the reaction they might produce on Capitol Hill among those now interested in the case.

One more undertaking was made possible at the last minute, thanks to a friend of Kristina's. Wayne Smith, ex-head of the U.S. Interests Office in Havana, who maintained cordial relations with the Cuban government and often traveled to the island, agreed to receive me. I'd scarcely sat down when Smith started talking to me in perfect Spanish, criticizing the policies of the U.S. government toward Cuba.

"I've come here to ask your help in the case of my wife and sons. It's all I'm concerned with," I told him frankly, avoiding any discussion of a subject about which we wouldn't agree. Was the United States to blame that the Cuban leaders had committed the worst crimes in betraying the people and the Revolution that had brought those leaders to power?

Such was the attitude of not a few intellectuals who, tormented by the horrors of the world, continued believing in a genuine revolution as the means to ending such horrors. The same had occurred with the crimes of Stalin and Mao, which now shocked the world, and the same was now being repeated in Cuba, with those who preferred to justify the existence of a tyranny from the comfort and protection of the democracies in which they lived, instead of informing themselves and confronting the truth with courage.

Smith finally heard me out. All that I asked him was that on his next trip to Cuba he might intercede with the country's authorities, asking them to allow the departure of a woman and two innocent children for humanitarian reasons.

"Don't call me, I promise you I'll bring back a response from Cuba," he told me while taking down my telephone numbers. I thanked him and left the office asking myself if he really intended to do what he said. Smith traveled to Cuba several times thereafter, but never called me.

Whenever I was disappointed by someone's not helping us, Kristina usually reminded me that the way was long and difficult, but not impossible.

"This is only the beginning," she'd tell me while handing me a list of more organizations and personalities to contact. "We'll have to work very hard, but we'll finally do it."

—

At the end of the month the U.N. Commission on Human Rights was scheduled to meet in Geneva, where I was accorded the chance to speak through the Association for Continental Peace (ASOPAZCO), to plead for international help to convince the Cuban government to release my family. Armando and Kristina took the opportunity to give me letters of introduction to various ambassadors and heads of delegations they'd gotten to know during their years of working there.

Meanwhile, Vicky dared to challenge the government once more by writing letters to foreign dignitaries, which she handed in to the various embassies in Havana.

If we manage to present the case before the United Nations, they'll have to let them go, I told myself, overcome with excitement while working day and night recording cassettes of testimonies by Vicky and the children, which I thought to distribute there as proof in case the Cuban delegation denied the existence of the case.

With a ticket donated by the Cuban-American National Foundation, I went off to Geneva filled with illusions, while enjoying for the first time in my life the freedom to travel without having to wait for anybody's permission to do so. I was met in Geneva by Mari Paz Martínez Nieto and María del Valle Álvares Guelmes, whom I didn't know but who, through the efforts of Armando and Mas Canosa, had put their organization at my disposal to arrange for my speech before the Human Rights Commission, and who covered all my expenses during my stay. Mari Paz was a petite Spaniard with jet black hair and eyes who overflowed with energy and talent in the struggle she waged for respect for human dignity. A sincere, courageous woman, capable of changing things by her actions, she was feared for her outspokenness, and she'd been beaten by the head of State security when they had expelled her from Cuba barely minutes after her landing at Havana International Airport, where she'd come to investigate openly the violations of human rights on the island. Valle had come from Argentina, a twenty-seven-year-old filled with dreams for a more just world, and now devoted his energy and talent, like Mari Paz, to the organization defending the rights of so many others.

They, along with Luis Zúñiga, a former political Cuban prisoner with whom I shared my hotel room and the tales of the tortures he'd suffered in Cuban prisons, were my collaborators in the battle I was undertaking before the eyes of the world. Together we prepared the speech I was to deliver, adding the names of other families in the same plight.

The first day I attended the meeting of the commission, I was surprised and outraged by the intervention of Vilma Espín, wife of one of the Castro brothers who had arbitrarily assumed the right to divide our family permanently. She talked during her intervention about the rights of the child, and the exemplary manner in which Cuba respected them, provoking my nausea at her words. At the end of her speech, in which she condemned "Yankee imperialism for the hunger and wretchedness of millions of children on the planet," she said she preferred to see such children killed by the effects of a nuclear war rather then see them victimized by the hunger that now plagued them.

I never imagined I would hear such an atrocity at the United Nations. The members of the Cuban delegation ran through the corridors of the hall applauding furiously and ridiculously to produce an effect of contagion in the assembly, and I felt horrified at the apathy with which those present regarded a clarion call to world holocaust.

"I address this assembly and the international community to demand help to put an end to the plight which my wife and children are now suffering, taken as hostages by the authorities in my country," I began reading in a nervous voice before those diplomats who wandered from one end of that hall to the other, which before I'd thought to be a model of order and discipline. In a few words I recounted the way in which they were forced to live, mine and other families separated arbitrarily, under constant fear and uncertainty, knowing that their lives depended not on laws but on the will of men who despised them.

And as I concluded, calling out the names of the victims and those who held them captive, I was interrupted by the insistent banging of a fist by an infuriated head of the Cuban delegation on his table. Not even in the United Nations did they manage to behave with decency! What could one hope for then in Cuba?

The period of the commission's sessions ended, and a majority approved the naming of a special United Nations representative to investigate the situation of human rights in Cuba. After the vote the head of the Cuban delegation spoke, attacking with gross epithets the countries demanding respect for human rights on the island and declaring that they would never permit a representative of the highest international organization to set foot in the country.

—

I returned to Miami disappointed with the results of my trip because of the impunity with which the Cuban authorities acted even before the United Nations, which was riddled with bureaucracy and scorned by governments who ignored its decisions, violating the rights of millions of people throughout the world. They'd calculated my state of desperation well, and I found myself besieged by Cuban agents pretending to be exiles who offered me their services to go to the island for Vicky and the boys. So confident were they that I'd fall into the trap that they offered me everything from frogmen and sophisticated electronic equipment to the collaboration of supposed clandestine networks operating in Cuba. I'd seen enough through the experience of a few unfortunates who'd gone fully armed to the island with the crazy idea that they could liberate it with their rifles, only to be met at their landing spot by coast guard units who'd been alerted beforehand. Then the Cuban government would mount, based upon that tiny incursion of armed men landing as expected, yet another propaganda campaign accusing the CIA and the Cuban community in Miami of terrorism. The existence of an outside enemy once again would serve as a pretext to repress any internal dissidence and to exacerbate the nationalist spirit of a people blinded by disinformation.

Several months later, a Cuban agent who'd infiltrated the hierarchy of an exile organization decided to defect and collaborated with a local television station to tape with hidden cameras and microphones one of the meetings during which he received instructions from a Cuban intelligence officer accredited as a diplomat to the United Nations in New York. He then provoked a scandal explaining how the Cuban government itself had provided him with funds to finance some of those illegal paramilitary operations carried out by exile groups against Cuba.

There were other individuals who also wanted to "help" us with different ends in mind. One day I was invited by a group of wealthy businessmen who offered me a Bell helicopter to rescue my family, which of course thrilled me, since I trusted them. But my dream soon went up in smoke when they asked me to pay for it by assassinating Fidel Castro during one of his public speeches in the open air, using the same helicopter.

"We'll furnish you with enough money for you to be able to hide forever with your family anyplace in the world after you've done it," they told me to close the deal.

"Thanks, but I'm not the man you're looking for," I replied, and I never saw them again.

Each passing day made me more convinced that the Cuban government, fearful of the younger officers in the armed forces, would never permit the release of Vicky and my sons, and that sooner or later I would have to go get them myself. But how? I needed first of all to find the means, and then to elaborate a plan, which somebody I completely trusted could deliver to Vicky in Cuba. But I had neither. And the people I trusted couldn't travel to the island.

—

In the meantime Janet had managed to contact a group of prominent Cubans living in Atlanta who invited us to visit them to seek support from prominent personalities living in the area able to intercede with the Cuban leader. There we were unable to reach Ted Turner of CNN, whose assistant replied in a short note that he couldn't be of help. However, we did receive very essential support from Coretta Scott King, whom we weren't able to see directly since she was away at the time, but who sent a strong letter to Fidel Castro asking for the immediate release of the children and Vicky. The letter from the widow of the North American who'd struggled so hard for civil rights in the United States was ignored by the Cuban government the same as countless others. And once more I felt convinced that no action of that kind was going to obtain results.

One day Armando asked me to accompany him to the home of Elena Díaz-Versón Amos, director of the foundation and founder with her late husband of the American Family Life Insurance Company.

"She can help you a great deal, and she insists on meeting you," Kristina informed me, observing that I wasn't very enthusiastic about the idea.

Actually I found it extremely unpleasant to think that anybody should see me as someone looking for a handout in order to obtain his family's freedom. What else could Elena think of a stranger coming to her house with such a problem?

"Thanks, but it's not money I need, but rather people who comprehend and fight along with me," I told Kristina with the frankness that characterized our relationship.

"Don't talk that way; you don't know Elena."

They finally overcame my obstinacy, and now I was flying in a private plane Elena had sent for us, even more uncomfortable at the prospect of meeting her. In Columbus, Georgia, we were met at the foot of the boarding ladder by a woman dressed with taste and simplicity who introduced us with a smile one by one to her companions and demonstrated boundless energy as she moved about, giving instructions all around. We got into the waiting limousine with her and set off immediately with a police motorcycle escort. Then she confessed, looking at us with the playfulness of a child caught in the act, "This isn't my car. It's the only limousine in town. And I borrowed it from the funeral parlor!"

Then she broke into delightful laughter like a child enjoying her prank, and we all joined in. En route to her home, she seemed to take pleasure in every turn of the road, telling us the history of that town, which she loved with a passion, and bursting with candid delight each time the police sounded their sirens at the local intersections.

Elena lived in the penthouse of a seven-story building next to the offices of her company, which dominated the entire city with its imposing height. When we entered the vestibule of the apartment with its floor of shining marble, she took off her shoes with a sigh of relief while explaining, "Oh, how I love to walk barefoot in the house. Take off your shoes as well, if you wish."

Surprised by the liberties I was being asked to take in a place I'd never before visited, I followed the examples of Kristina and Armando to enjoy the refreshing coolness of that floor in my stockinged feet. It took only a few hours to get to know Elena, and already her candor had so captivated me that I felt myself laughing as I hadn't done in a long time. Every object in that flower-filled apartment bore the mark of her character.

Elena had always been passionately attached to the man who had become her husband in their adolescence. His death the previous year seemed to have left an immense void in her soul.

She wept at the details of the plight in which Vicky and my sons found themselves, and she wished to speak to them by phone and write to them as if they were part of her own family. From then on, she never ceased striving to obtain the intervention of people who could help us, whether from churches or schools, or among the numerous congressmen and senators she knew. Among these was Ms. Coretta Scott King, who received us in her office at the King Center and expressed her willingness to help us in any way possible to attain the reunification of our family.

She wrote to Ted Turner, once more asking him to call Castro and take advantage of their having met in Cuba to ask for the release of my loved ones. Again there was no reply and we decided not to insist.

In Cuba, Vicky received the only reply to her countless letters to personalities abroad. Madame Danielle Mitterrand, the wife of the French president, wrote that she lamented not being able to help Vicky because she wouldn't be able to obtain a U.S. visa for them. Evidently she hadn't understood what Vicky was asking, and so Vicky wrote to her again, explaining that she had already obtained the necessary visas and simply asking her—on her upcoming visit to Cuba, which had already been announced in the official press—to take advantage of her meeting with Fidel Castro to ask him to allow them to leave the island for humanitarian reasons. The second reply from Madame Mitterrand was more succinct: "I'm sorry, but your husband obviously took Cuban military secrets with him to the United States, and I wouldn't be able to intercede for you."

Other persons, however, restored my faith in an overwhelmingly just and noble world. Such was the case of the young Brandon Scheid, a student at George Washington University and intern at the Valladares Foundation, who spent hours in the office of the organization coming up with new strategies for our campaign. He wrote to the press, to politicians, religious leaders, artists; modest and generous, he seemed possessed by a kind of obsession to attain justice in the case, to help, to be useful. Jokingly I used to call him the most powerful weapon the United States had against its detractors, whereupon he'd stare at me, apparently unable to fathom the idea that a part of the world existed whose goal was to paint his country as the kingdom of egoism and fratricide.

On my return to Virginia I was invited to lunch by a Cuban who wished to help us, having been involved since his adolescence in the cause of human rights. Frank Calzón was the representative of Freedom House in Washington, and had at his disposition a wide network of relationships with Congress and the American press that would permit us to give new energy to our campaign. Frank had been one of the organizers of the campaign to free Armando, and honestly felt that if we managed to put sufficient outside pressure on the Cuban authorities they would agree to free Vicky and the children.

As in the case of the months I'd spent in Miami, a group of Cuban families from Virginia now spontaneously adopted me, looking after me attentively to the point of not letting me have a moment's rest between invitations to dine and spend time with them so I wouldn't feel alone. Armando's home by then had turned into my second home, and I used to visit him often to partake of that delightful mayhem with their children, driving Martha crazy with the commotion resulting from having another child to contend with, as I'd get down on the floor to join the kids in playing with the dog. Then Martha would eye us from the kitchen, and call out without making any distinction, "Time to eat, kids . . . it's on the table!"

Now five rascals vied for her scandalized affections in the house: three children, the dog, and I. And when sometimes Armando or Martha noticed that I wasn't playing as usual with the others, they'd asked me worriedly what was wrong.

"I love the horseplay with the children," I'd tell them, while looking on sadly as they played without me, "but sometimes the silence of my own kids is louder than the noise yours are making."

It was already June, and thousands of postcards in various languages with the photo of Vicky and the boys had been printed by the Valladares Foundation and Freedom House, to be given to people interested in sending them to the Cuban authorities. Frank Calzón had even managed to publish an article on the case, and now, with a group of volunteers from Of Human Rights, he was managing a campaign of letters and postcards to Queen Sofía of Spain, for her to intercede with the Cuban leader during his upcoming visit for the Summit of Heads of Ibero-American States in Madrid. For the occasion I'd managed to contact, with the help of Mari Paz, the president of the Junta de Galicia, who also maintained very cordial relations with the Cuban government and had been honored with the highest official Cuban decoration quite recently. The Junta had managed to obtain the release of various political prisoners through their diplomacy, and I was overjoyed to receive word that the president of the Junta had written the Highest Leader asking for the release of Vicky and the children on humanitarian grounds.

It'll be difficult to refuse him, I thought, hoping that Fidel Castro would finally accede to the request of someone he called a friend of Cuba. But I was mistaken.

At this time my father-in-law had been invited by his sisters in New Jersey to come visit for humanitarian reasons, since it had been over twenty years since he'd seen them. First he obtained the temporary visa from the U.S. authorities. His sisters had already paid in dollars the exorbitant price charged by the Cuban government for travel documents and the plane ticket, which could only be purchased from an agency that passed on the hard currency to the Cuban government. All that remained was for him to get on the plane.

I lived then in a state of anxiety produced by my illusions—I'd already bought some tasty *puros*, the food he liked best, for that man whom I revered as much as my own father. My little apartment warmed to the celebration. How happy I would be to embrace him!

—

In Cuba, Gerardo was now getting ready for the trip, excited as a child about to receive a great present. He had everything, documents, ticket—all was ready. The following morning he would go off to the airport.

In a few hours I'll be with my sisters, and see him, he was thinking, feeling his pulse quicken with anxiety. No, he wasn't going to be able to sleep that night.

Someone was knocking at the door, and he ran to open it. *It must be someone else with a letter they want me to take to a relative,* he told himself, recalling the visits throughout the day from people asking him to mail their letters in the United States. It was the most typical way of sending letters to relatives there, and the safest.

"Good evening," said the unknown young man standing at the door. "Gerardo Rojas?"

"Yes."

The man took out his wallet and, opening it, let Gerardo see the card with a green diagonal stripe and three large letters stamped on the edge of it: DSE. Gerardo felt a chill. What could State security want with him? The man silently put the card back in his wallet while Gerardo waited expectantly, his eyes wide open and his breathing quickening.

"I was asked to inform you," the stranger started to tell him, while looking over Gerardo's shoulder into the house, "that you cannot travel."

Gerardo felt his throat tighten, and with a voice strained by the effort he asked, "But why not? If I have everything, ticket, documents . . . there must be some mistake."

"I've already told you, so don't pack your bags . . . or you can unpack them right now if you did. You can't leave the country, and you know the reason. Your daughter's husband is a traitor!"

Gerardo returned to his bedroom, dragging his feet. He stared at the small suitcase opened on his bed—and began to cry. It was the first time he'd done so since the death of his father many, many years before.

—

The Madrid summit was to begin at the end of July, and I decided to go there with the intention of carrying out a hunger strike to draw the attention of the heads of state and the press gathered there.

Perhaps the public embarrassment of seeing himself in the role of a tyrant who sequesters women and children might force Castro to let them go, I thought, placing all my hopes on the impact a hunger strike could create. But we needed to come up with the necessary funds for my journey. A friend I had met through Armando, who had arrived in these lands from the Cuban countryside more than thirty years ago—but who still maintained the fresh candor of a peasant—plunged into the task of obtaining the money needed from among the members of Casa Cuba. Nelson Lima and his family looked after me as zealously as Armando and Martha, both families ever preoccupied at what the desperation that sometimes assailed me might drive me to attempt in the face of so many failures. Once, overwhelmed with frustration, I'd sworn I would go get Vicky and the children myself, which filled them all with horror. From then on Nelson insisted that on weekends I go hunting with him or that we visit his friends in the country together. I soon realized he was doing this to keep me from going into a depression that might lead to some catastrophe.

Preparations for the hunger strike turned into a sort of collective suffering, especially on my part, as I saw myself becoming the victim of the extreme overattentiveness of those who loved me and offered myriad suggestions to avoid anything going wrong during my fast.

"You have to take vitamins"; "You have to stop smoking as of today"; "You have to eat well in the meantime to build up your reserves of energy" were some of the countless suggestions I received on every side from morning till night.

Elena began to come by with some regularity, and we would always get together at her Washington home to discuss the latest projects involving our campaign. Now she was deeply involved, together with the churches in various countries, in organizing a chain of prayers around the world for Vicky and the children. She animatedly showed me the prototype of a card bearing their photo, on which she asked people to join her in prayer. Then as the day approached for my departure to Spain, Armando, Kristina, and I were invited to join her for dinner. They were busy watching me eat with the hearty appetite they had lost just worrying about me, when Elena exclaimed, pointing to me, "If this hunger strike business isn't over with soon, we're all going to die of hunger except him!"

Armando was the only one to understand and gave his full support, since, with his own experience of eleven hunger strikes while in Cuban prisons, he knew nothing untoward would happen.

"The most important thing is that you be in good health when you begin the strike," he would tell me. "And you'll see nothing bad happens. The hunger is the only thing that's terrible, but it lasts only the first two days. After that you lose interest in food, and you even feel a certain sense of well-being."

I knew that I could hold out for the week intended, but the idea of enduring a more and more insistent hunger as the time passed didn't thrill me in the slightest.

"Don't you worry. In less than two days you won't feel the least desire to eat anything," Armando repeated, drawing on his experience.

The day of my departure arrived, and with the money collected from over a hundred contributors I set off for Spain, concentrating all my hopes on this attempt. I'd talked with Vicky before leaving, and had managed to convince her to go about her life as usual, even though she wanted to accompany me with a hunger strike of her own.

"It'd be absurd for you to do something like that in Cuba. There's no press there capable of reporting on what you'd be doing. I need you strong and healthy," I'd told her.

Reyniel, for his part, read me a letter he'd written to the Cuban leader:

"You who are good to children, I know that when you receive this you will let us go to our Daddy."

And I swallowed bitterly, not having the strength to make him understand that his illusions were in vain.

In Madrid, Mari Paz and Valle were waiting for me, more alarmed than my friends in Virginia.

"You're crazy. Spain is very different from the United States. A hunger strike here will have no impact whatsoever," they told me over and over, trying to convince me not to do it.

"On the other hand, we can organize meetings with the press which all the visitors will read. That'll create a real impact."

I had arrived a few days prior to the opening of the summit of the heads of state, and I took advantage of the fact to give various interviews with the help of Mari Paz and to appear on the popular radio program hosted by Encarna Sánchez. Months before, our family had participated in one of her radio broadcasts—I, from Miami, Vicky and our sons, from Havana—by telephone. Now she'd managed to make telephone contact from her studios with a neighbor of Vicky's and had the conversation broadcast live. Vicky and the boys made a dramatic appeal to all Spanish families to write letters to the Cuban chief of state during his visit, and Encarna gave the address of the office of Mari Paz at the close of the program.

I'd prepared a crude documentary of eight minutes showing images of the Cuban Leader and his brother declaring in public that no one was kept in Cuba against their will, juxtaposed with other images taken from the Canadian footage of the boys explaining that they felt like slaves who couldn't be reunited with their father. No one would agree to air even a fragment of the material I had put together with such difficulty, and, convinced that only the hunger strike would manage to break the wall of silence imposed on the case by the Cuban government, I showed up in the office of Mari Paz and

Valle the morning of Monday, July 20, 1992, with chains and the two padlocks to chain me to the fence around the famous Retiro Park, just across from the Alcalá Gate and barely a few meters from the hotel where the visiting Presidents were staying as guests.

I knew that to attain credibility for the strike, I had to carry it out in the public's eye, where there would be no room for any doubts as to whether I might be eating on the sly, distracting attention from the real purpose of my fasting. For that reason, on the previous Friday night I'd taken ten laxative tablets to be sure that between Saturday and Sunday my intestines would have time to become totally emptied, and thus allow me to remain chained to the fence the entire week. Madrid was then experiencing temperatures of about 100°F, and I'd examined the spot on my daily trip to Mari Paz's office, convinced that I could avoid dehydration by remaining in the shade of the leafy elms that were so abundant there.

"You're out of your mind," Mari Paz told me when she saw the locks and chains in my hands. Convinced, however, that it would be futile to insist on my giving up the idea, she went off with Valle and her sister Alicia to break the story to the media.

Around noon they closed the locks on the chains wrapped around my wrists and attached to the lovely wrought-iron fence as the first photographers and reporters began to arrive. The only things accompanying me were the enlarged photo of Vicky and our sons, which I'd managed to hang on the fence with a sign that said CASTRO, STOP HOLDING MY FAMILY HOSTAGE! and a copy of Armando's *Against All Hope,* which served as inspiration for me to endure the worst moments of the hunger strike. The volunteers for the campaign in Madrid were soon mobilized and in a short time I found my little corner surrounded by chairs, a cooler for cold water, blankets, a radio for listening to the news, an enormous banner reading ON A HUNGER STRIKE TO PROTEST MY WIFE AND CHILDREN'S BEING HELD HOSTAGE IN CUBA, as well as hundreds of the first letters sent by listeners of Encarna's program to the offices of Mari Paz.

Troubled by the impunity with which any of the more than three hundred Cuban agents reportedly sent to guard Fidel Castro might attack me, a pilot friend from IBERIA, Oscar Pérez, insisted that his sons remain with me to look after me while I slept at night. Eventually a sort of constant guard was set up with the cooperation of a group of former Cuban political prisoners who now lived in Madrid. Encarna also sent over a mobile unit from her station, so that all her listeners who for months had been following the drama of our family would learn what I was doing in one more act of desperation. In a matter of hours the place was crowded with people who'd come to offer their sympathy and their help; and that first day of the hunger strike, but my third without ingesting any food, was to be the first of my battles with dozens of elderly well-meaning *Madrileña* women who were to come with tears in their eyes and food in hand to beg me to eat just a bit, on the sly.

In the afternoon a crew from the Spanish television station in Miami showed up, and I took the opportunity to make public what I'd already told the reporter from the newspaper *ABC:* I offered to the Cuban government my immediate return to the island to be tried for what they called "treason against the fatherland," if they would promise publicly the immediate release and departure from Cuba of my wife and my children, as soon as I turned myself in.

"Now you're really out of your mind!" Mari Paz exclaimed with horror at the possibility that the Cuban authorities might accept my proposal and immediately execute me without complying with their promise.

"If they did that," I started telling her, "we'd have won the battle. The Cuban government cannot admit publicly that they take innocent women and children hostage. My only intention is to deprive them of an argument in the face of international public opinion and force them that way to release my family. They would much rather do that than accept my proposal. They want me back, but not that way. They want me to come back quietly, to allow them to weave some other tale and conceal from the people and from the younger officers of the armed forces the real reasons I had for defecting."

Mari Paz looked me straight in the eye, then after a few more seconds she once again exploded: "Great, then we'll really have won the battle! We'll have one executed father, a widow, and two orphans. And we'll have lost the entire war!"

I had told Valle to take the keys to the locks with her, and as evening approached I realized that the length of the chains was insufficient to allow me to sleep on the ground. In any case, overcome by the heat and exhaustion, I let myself sink to the pavement, leaving my arms hanging by the chains while I heard the voices of my improvised bodyguards fade as I drifted off to sleep. In the night an unbearable pain in my wrists wakened me. They had become swollen from the tautness of the chains, but I decided it would be better to sleep sitting up than to remove them. Then toward morning what I was most afraid of happening occurred. Two policemen came up to me, demanding that I remove the chains. Thinking to put an end to the matter easily, I told them that I'd tossed the keys down the sewer before closing the locks. Still polite, they nevertheless were firm about their demand, warning me that if I didn't remove them they would call in a crew to cut the chains and then expel me from the area. That possibility filled me with dread, since it would mean that those who held my family as hostages would have scored another victory, at least indirectly. I was trying futilely to convince them otherwise when Mari Paz and Valle arrived, just in time.

"He doesn't have permission to carry on this hunger strike here," the police started to explain to Mari Paz, "and the use of chains, you have to understand, is something we cannot accept. But we sympathize with his cause. If he removes the chains, we'll let him carry on his hunger strike as long as he wishes."

Valle was jubilant at the policemen's offer and, taking the keys out of her pocket, she began unlocking the chains. In the days that followed there would always be a pair of Spanish policemen in the area who amiably lent their support.

The Cuban Leader was scheduled to arrive the next day, and his photo had already appeared in the daily paper *ABC* opposite one of me chained to the fence. The contrast was striking, and I felt jubilant at having managed something so difficult to ignore in the face of Spanish public opinion: now he didn't look like the charismatic, humanistic leader he portrayed himself to be, but like a tyrant who took innocent women and children as hostages.

Perhaps the embarrassment of it all will make him relent now, I thought to myself, encouraged. I was now ready to continue the strike as long as he remained in Madrid, or at least until he gave some sort of reply about the case to the press, which would be pursuing him.

It was now 104°F, but I wasn't feeling particularly weak. Mari Paz informed me that there was a popular demonstration condemning the dictator in the Plaza de Colón, and that the demonstrators were planning to march to where I was, with candles lit to participate in a vigil announced by Valle over the radio for Vicky and the children. Dusk was falling when I heard the police sirens and saw the crowd approaching along the Calle de Serrano with placards, Cuban flags, and chanting. They gathered around me to demonstrate their solidarity.

"You're not alone, brother!" shouted Luis Zúñiga, my roommate from Geneva, and others joined in. Then quite spontaneously we were also joined by various Spanish and Russian deputies who had come to Madrid to observe the summit meeting. Practically all the organizations fighting for a democratic Cuba were likewise present and I sensed in all this support the enormity of the tragedy lived out by Cuban families in the last three decades.

Hundreds of candles glowed as we all prayed for Vicky and our sons, covering the walled part of the fencing, permeating with the smell of wax for a long time thereafter all the cards, notes, and toys that people were leaving as tokens of their feelings. Kristina had airexpressed to us a gigantic photo of Vicky and the boys, and now it hung among the first thousand letters we'd received from the Spanish people. A mural made up of drawings and letters that free children were sending to my sons held hostage also covered part of the fence catching the attention of tourists and passersby, who stooped to read some of them and to sign their names in the book Alicia, Mari Paz's sister, had prepared with a petition to be sent to the Cuban leader.

A man and woman who stood out by their clothing as recently arrived Cubans stopped to observe the vigil and began hurling insults at us. Someone reacted indignantly, but I called him to order, asking everyone to ignore them, since what they wished was to create a public scandal to force the police to interrupt my hunger strike. So we ignored them until, tired of screaming insults that received no reply, they finally left.

It was my third day of the strike and I felt voraciously hungry, which made me constantly recall Armando's assuring me that I'd no longer feel any appetite after the second day. Just a few yards off was a kiosk selling all kinds of snacks, and how I suffered from the presence of people who innocently stopped to chat with me while they savored an ice cream or some other morsel. From the post office they called Mari Paz to say they'd received over 1,000 letters that day, which it was impossible for them to deliver, so Mari Paz sent for them in order to hang them from a string attached to the fence. Each passing day widened the space occupied by things people had brought, and more and more tourists and *Madrileños* came each day to sign their names and have their pictures taken with me. The Cuban Chief of State had arrived, but surrounded by a cordon of security impossible to penetrate. He was the only leader who hid from the press, and I had a horrible premonition he might succeed in avoiding any confrontation with a reporter about Vicky and the children.

Every day messages also arrived from Elena, Kristina, and Armando, lifting my spirits with their faxes or tapes of phone conversations with them that Mari Paz managed to record in her office. They had organized a protest in front of the Cuban Office of Interests in Washington, and Armando's children were parading among the protesters with placards of Vicky and the children as big as themselves.

On the fourth day I received a taped message from Armando and contentedly listened to the children reporting on their activities at the demonstration "to be able to get to see our cousins," as they explained.

"Now the worst is over; I'm sure you no longer feel the slightest bit hungry," Armando announced with conviction.

And I looked at the little tape recorder in my hands, saying, "Just be happy you're not standing here in front of me or I'd grab you by the neck! I could eat a live elephant to quell the hunger I feel!"

Then I laughed at myself and remarked to Mari Paz that I was going to write some suggestions for a *Manual for Hunger Strikes,* like not going on one in a public place where you end up watching people go by eating all sorts of tasty delicacies.

Elena also sent me messages filled with humor and faith, through our mutual friend from Miami, Rino Puig, who would visit me each day at my abode in the Parque del Retiro, always disposed to lift my spirits or to stuff a few hundred more dollars in my pocket for the campaign. I learned from Kristina that Elena was barely eating herself, so upset was she at the thought of my hunger strike.

The fourth day of my ordeal, but the sixth without eating, I was having a worse and worse time of it with the old women and even some physicians who kept coming by with food in hand and an infinite compassion to ask me to eat something even on the sly—which didn't help me.

"Please, try to understand that if I gave in, I'd lose the strength I need to carry on the struggle," I kept telling them, but they failed to comprehend and continued to insist with a naiveté that amused me and mortified me at the same time.

Each night a group of friends and journalists from Miami would gather, along with Mari Paz, Valle, and Alicia, to keep me company until I fell asleep. Those three in particular had barely slept or eaten either since my arrival, devoting their time to me to the point of exhaustion, and they might as well have been on a hunger strike themselves.

Thursday afternoon I was surprised to see Valle running down the street toward me with a look of jubilation on his face. He'd participated in the press conference given by the President of Spain, and he was bringing me the cassette recording of the President's reply to him when he'd asked if he would be willing to intercede with the Cuban government on behalf of my family.

"We are, of course, ready to intercede in the case," the head of the Spanish government began, "but we think that these matters are best resolved out of the public eye."

I listened and, pained at Valle's enthusiasm, was convinced that quiet diplomacy, such as had been undertaken up to now, would never bring results.

Early the next day the heads of state were already leaving Madrid and we were dismantling all the material we'd put up for the hunger strike, including the more than eight thousand letters we'd received from all over Spain, when we saw what looked like some sort of committee approaching us. It turned out to be the President of Chile with his retinue who were passing, and Valle immediately confronted him with his journalist's tape recorder in hand to ask him the same question he'd posed to the President of Spain.

"I think the worst step is the one not taken," the Chilean President replied, "and I'm ready to intercede with the Cuban President for this family." Then turning to me, he suggested, "Contact our ambassador in Washington and give him all the information about the case and he'll forward it to me."

The week of battle was over. I'd lost twenty-five pounds, and I wished to finish as quickly as possible cleaning up the area that had been my dwelling place under the stars. I wanted nothing so much as to have a bath, and eat, eat, eat.

As I bid good-bye to Mari Paz and Valle, I told them, "I'm tired of asking others for help. I'm going to get Vicky and the kids out myself."

They stared at me for a few seconds without saying a word. What good would it have done?

"May God be with you," Mari Paz whispered, kissing me farewell.

I returned from Madrid frustrated yet again by the fact that the Cuban Leader had managed to escape without anyone's having personally demanded from him that he release my loved ones. For the next four months Kristina, Brandon, and I attempted vainly to have an appointment with the Chilean embassy in Washington, in order to receive the red-carpet treatment we'd been promised.

"We'll let you know when you can come by with the material," they assured us by telephone whenever we insisted on meeting with the ambassador or one of his assistants. Then finally they stopped returning our calls. I realized once again that there was only one way to obtain freedom for Vicky and the children: rescue them myself.

Chapter 19

—

Someone

to

Confide In

With the arrival of August, I decided to make use of the information Mari Paz had given me concerning other Cuban families in the same situation as ours. I contacted those families living in the States, proposing that we join forces to fight publicly for our families' rights, instead of awaiting the nonexistent compassion of the Cuban authorities. Some families who had preferred the path of silent waiting had already spent more than eight years without seeing their loved ones. After many telephone calls and radio and television appeals to contact us, a group of people whose families had all been held hostage by the Cuban government met in Miami. Dissident intellectuals, doctors, engineers, and economists all got together to found an organization called Parents for Freedom, which had neither staff nor funds. Our only agenda was to maintain regular contact in order to share experiences and coordinate efforts to lend greater strength to each of our denunciations. In the following months Parents for Freedom became a leading voice in the struggle to call the world's attention to Cuba's practice of punishing the relatives of those who refused to submit to the government's tyranny. By the end of September our organization was able to present a document describing all the cases we'd compiled to the special United Nations representative investigating human rights abuses in Cuba.

—

Meanwhile, in Washington Frank Calzón was preparing a campaign with balloons upon which was printed the photo of Vicky and the children, and new postcards to send to the Cuban Leader demanding their release. Frank wanted to fill the streets of the capital with them, so one Sunday we set out for Georgetown with his group of volunteers from Of Human Rights to hand out the cards to passersby while offering their children the blown-up balloons.

After so many failed efforts, however, I felt uncomfortable, like somebody begging for his rights, imploring people in the streets to mail in those postcards. Some pedestrians walking toward us would veer off as if they were afraid we were going to ask them for something, and others tossed the postcards into the nearest trash can. Luckily most of them accepted the cards with an expression of doubt on their faces, unable to fathom how my family could be held hostage by a government. I would have quickly given up hounding innocent passersby were it not for the enthusiasm of Frank and his group of volunteers. Timidly and with evident embarrassment I continued to approach people. Then a young bearded man stopped to read the postcard, and staring at me with disdain, he commented, "I'm not going to mail anything. If you hadn't left, then they wouldn't be in the situation they're in now."

And feeling ashamed, I took back the postcard from him, saying simply, "Sorry, I didn't mean to bother you."

What could I tell him? How was he going to understand, living the way he lived, always free to say what he thought? It was his ignorance, more than cruelty, that made him act as he did.

Another man, also rather young, peered at me as if I were a repugnant insect, saying, "Why don't you go back and get them yourself?"

I ended the day in a terrible state. I'd need years to explain to people of the free world the situation in which my beloved found themselves, and why. And still they'd have a hard time comprehending. To attempt to rescue Vicky and the children on my own involved risking their lives. The Cuban government had ordered its coastal forces to fire at will upon anybody caught fleeing the country. Many innocent children had already been killed by machine guns manned by raw recruits indoctrinated to see a gang of CIA terrorists on each boat leaving the country; and by the time they discovered they were only innocent children, it was too late. The soldiers would then be released from duty and given psychological treatment, as if it were all a lamentable mistake for which no one was to blame. Other unfortunates were sent to replace them, ready to fire upon new "enemy" launches.

Such was the case in the notorious Canímar massacre of 1980. At the time the official press had reported that terrorists had taken a boat filled with tourists hostage and had opened fire on the children aboard when they saw themselves about to be captured by the coast guard. Witnesses of the event who later escaped to the United States told a very different story. Two soldiers completing their military service in a unit stationed near the Canímar River decided to flee with the help of their AKM rifles. They boarded a launch providing river passage for families visiting the area and aimed their weapons at the crew, demanding that they be taken to the United States. The crew radioed the coast guard and the latter, unable to intercept them on the high seas, sank the boat before it could escape. The children, some no more than a few months old, who'd simply gone on an outing with their relatives that day vanished forever in the waters of the Bay of Matanzas because of the cruelty of a system that preferred having them dead to having others escape the island.

Such was the risk we'd be facing if we happened to be surprised during the rescue attempt, and the possibility that one of my children could be struck down by a bullet horrified me. Yet what guarantees did I have that their lives, ruled by the will of the same people who ordered the death of so many other children, would be spared tomorrow? Each day the situation in Cuba was becoming more explosive, and I didn't harbor the slightest doubt that the moment the regime feared a rebellion of the people, it would impose open terror. Then the lives of Vicky and the children, like the lives of those victims from the Canímar River, wouldn't be worth anything.

Finally, I couldn't hope to see their lives respected by those who were already holding them hostage. We couldn't wait forever for the right to live together in freedom—we had to fight for it. Everything that it was possible to do we had done, and would continue to do; but from that point on, my number one priority was to find a way to rescue them by air.

I was a pilot, and it would be easy for me to evade any coast guard crew operating on the ground or in the water. I knew intimately the Cuban antiair defense system practically by heart: its deployment, the limitations of its radar and land-to-air missile installations, the inner workings of its command structure for ordering a military response. I could put together a plan with a real possibility of success, as long as I prepared everything in absolute secrecy. All I needed were my brains, a plane or helicopter, and somebody completely trustworthy who could get the details of the plan into Vicky's hands.

In addition, I didn't want to violate the laws of the United States, or to put its government in an embarrassing position. I was grateful to it, and wished above all to respect its laws, which now were my own, the same ones that protected my rights and liberties. Thus first of all I had to obtain a pilot's license, and then I had to act on my own in a legal, reasonable manner.

September 1992 arrived, and after various inquiries I found an aviation school in Virginia, which for two hundred dollars offered a course in the theoretical background for a private pilot's license. That was what I needed; I knew that actual flight experience wouldn't present a problem. I began the course, and before long I'd established close relations with the director of the school, Dr. Donald O. Robb, who was delighted to have me as a student and was only too happy to help me obtain my license as soon as possible.

"I need it to find a job," I'd told him during our conversations, just as I did with friends in order to allay any suspicion of what I was really planning.

One day I found out that someone I trusted totally was going to Cuba, and I sent Vicky a short verbal message.

"Tell her I'm coming for them myself," I confided. "Before Christmas, God willing."

In a store in Washington I was able to find maps of Cuba with the relief details I needed to make the first sketch of my plan. On it I began to fill in the locations of radar and missile installations on the western part of the island, calculating their limitations on the basis of their technical specifications and the elevation of the terrain where they were emplaced. With lines of different colors I began marking off the limits of their potential to locate and destroy targets at various altitudes, as well as the zones they were prevented from targeting due to interference from local peculiarities of terrain, which impeded the effectiveness of antiair detection at certain altitudes and approaches. This gave me a clear picture of the areas where I'd encounter the greatest concentration of antiair firepower; other areas that normally were protected minimally; and those areas where I could act with relative impunity, out of the reach of radar, artillery, or ground-to-air missiles.

There remained now the problem of selecting the most suitable place for a landing, depending upon the terrain and the possibilities for Vicky and the boys to get there without raising suspicions. Many factors influenced the decision I would finally make, and I went over them all each night in the privacy of my room, calculating and calculating, adding more and more data to my maps and the notes I hid along with them.

I knew, moreover, that the Cuban antiair defense system was incapable of responding swiftly to an air incursion because, due to the economic crisis and the lack of fuel, the majority of the radar installations remained disconnected most of the time, and many of the antiair missiles I'd depicted on my map would prove to be out of commission for the same reasons. In addition, the men who were normally on duty

---

at such installations now found themselves occupied with the agricultural tasks of growing their own food, and the lack of proper training would result in extremely slow and, at times, erroneous reactions. But I decided not to rely on these final factors and to base my plan on the supposition that the entire Cuban defense system was functioning perfectly. Only then could I select the surest alternative for my plan.

Over and over I revised the data, and each time I came up against the same disturbing fact: the safest places for the rescue were too distant for Vicky and the children, who wouldn't be able to get there without raising serious suspicions. I was going to have to choose, therefore, a site within the perimeter of their habitual activities: in Havana, near her parents; or in Matanzas, near mine, whom they regularly visited. But both cities were surrounded by radar and antiair missile complexes.

Only one thing might give us a certain edge, and that was the nearly inoperable system of the Cuban chain of command. Convinced that the country would never really be attacked and fearful that their own men in antiair defense might conspire to shoot them down when they traveled by air from one end of the island to the other, the Cuban Leaders had concocted a chain of command in which only they themselves could authorize the firing of weapons against airborne targets. The absence of adequate lines of communication and automated data transmission within the Cuban defense system, plus the actual difficulty of locating the Highest Leaders, who always clouded their movements in secrecy, were in our favor, and would afford us precious time in which to act.

So I added the time the radar operator would need to confirm the approach of an enemy target flying at very low altitude; the time it would take him to transmit his findings by the primitive means of communication available to the brigade command post; the time the officers on duty there would need to process the information and pass it on to divisional headquarters, and from there to Antiair Defense in Havana, and on to Armed Forces Central Command Post; then the time they would lose there trying to find the Highest Leaders to obtain a decision. I added to that the time consumed by the same process in reverse order, plus the time needed at the missile complexes to connect their own radar and launching pads, to initiate the search for the target, and to be ready to fire at it. On the supposition that the entire Cuban system managed to perform with precision, they'd need at least fifteen minutes after sighting me in order to be able to fire.

I had to know precisely, then, how much time it would take me from the moment of being detected by Cuban radar on my approach to the island until the instant I crossed the line of maximum reach by ground-to-air missiles during the return with my precious cargo aboard. This last part I couldn't determine precisely until I knew what kind of plane I'd use for the operation, the maximum airspeed it was capable of flying at very low altitude, and the exact distance at which it could be detected based upon the "effective surface" with which it reflected the electromagnetic waves of the Cuban radar systems. If this time turned out to be less than what was needed by the Cuban chain of command to transmit their information, make a decision, and deliver a response, then we could outwit the country's anti-air defenses!

It had been a long time since I'd talked to Vicky, when suddenly one morning I managed to get through to her. She was terribly upset at the setbacks we'd suffered in the face of the various efforts we'd made and at the pressure she was under. In a recent letter she'd sent with someone traveling out of Cuba, she had informed me that a neighborhood youth had scribbled some graffiti on the wall of a nearby building, demanding an end to tyranny. Somebody had reported it, and he was arrested. From jail he sent Vicky an important message: *Be careful, they're putting a lot of pressure on me to implicate you in the graffiti incident.*

Vicky then understood they'd use any pretext, even if it were some false accusation, to put her in jail. With that letter I became even more desperate, knowing that sooner or later they'd find a reason to put Vicky in prison among criminals, and take our sons away to be cared for by the State. That would spell the end of our family, and I didn't have much confidence in the reactions of a world that already seemed preoccupied with too many other things to be bothered stopping the Cuban authorities from committing such a crime. I had to act as swiftly as possible.

"I'll never give you up, never . . . whatever it takes . . ." I repeated over and over to her on the telephone, to make her realize that I'd already begun preparations for their rescue.

"Don't worry, Oré. Even if they burn me alive they'll never make me renounce you," she told me in tears.

I heard the voice of Alejandro, who insisted on speaking to me immediately, and the conversation I had with him shocked me completely.

"Daddy, listen," he began abruptly, but in a very low, confidential tone. "Look, you can come and get us. Late at night, when all the police are sleeping . . . then you come in a helicopter, but make sure there's no police around. . . ."

Vicky tried to interrupt the boy, fearful that his imagination might draw the attention of the authorities listening in on what we were actually planning.

"No, no, let him talk," I told her, hearing Alejandro's tearful protests in the background.

"Daddy," he began again his shrill, innocent voice. "Look, when there are no police in the street, you land the helicopter on top of the house. . . . Then you lower a sack on a rope. . . . We'll all get into the sack and you'll pull us up. . . . Then we'll all get away. . . ."

As my child continued, I felt my heart breaking. These last months I'd barely been able to sleep, always hearing voices at night, always calling me for help, always vanishing along with my nightmares; and now I was listening to him the same way, my six-year-old. How desperate he sounded! What a crime they were committing on such an innocent creature! *God, give me the strength to bear it!*

"Alé," I tried telling him as calmly as possible, while I felt my whole body resisting the struggle to control my emotions, ". . . Daddy would never do that. . . ."

I was lying to him purposefully, and it pained me to do so.

"You'll see, soon you'll be able to leave from the airport on a passenger plane, almost for sure before the Christmas holidays, which you've never seen before, but you'll love once you get here."

"With Santa Claus and the Three Wise Men?"

"You know about them?" I asked, happy to have drawn him out of the anguished silence into which he'd withdrawn.

"Yes, Mommy told me, and at church. . . . But I want to see you soon!" His last words exploded like thunder.

"You're going to see me soon." My voice was failing me again. And he protested in tears when Vicky took the phone from him.

"I want to see my daddy right away, I want to see him!"

"Criminals, cowards," the words burst hoarsely from my throat, filled with rage against the Cuban Leaders.

"My love . . ." It was Vicky again. "Forgive him, he spends the night dreaming up things before going to sleep, thinking about how to get away from here."

"I don't understand how they can torture children this way."

"Dad, it's Reyniel."

Everybody wanted, as always, to tell me something quickly before they cut off the call.

"Don't worry," he told me, "because I'm a man."

Reyniel was speaking firmly and proudly. The eighteen months since we'd last seen each other had toughened him.

"I'm taking care of Mom and my brother here. You keep fighting, Dad, 'cause we'll beat them."

—

After that conversation I thought I'd go mad. If only they'd accept my surrender in exchange for my family's freedom! But they wanted everything: me, Vicky, the boys. Only by feeding pitilessly on the blood of all Cubans could they keep themselves in power. From then on, I couldn't remain calm for an instant. I was consumed by sleeplessness and desperation to finish the course for a private pilot's license, to find an airplane and somebody I could trust to deliver the rescue plan to Vicky.

I wandered about like a madman from one place to another, in a flurry of activity, and often I felt the compassionate glances of people who saw me as a demented being, obsessed with an impossible struggle. One friend even came by to see me in order to convince me to begin a new life.

"You're eating yourself up little by little, slowly destroying yourself," he told me without looking up. "You need to give up this battle, which you'll never win. Vicky can't hold out much longer. . . . Find a woman and start a new relationship."

I looked at him with pity, then told him, "I know you believe in what you're saying, but our lives are different. You'll fall in love and feel loved one day, like us. . . . And then it won't matter to you whether other people think you're crazy."

One night Frank Calzón called to tell me that Tom Carter, the *Washington Times* reporter, would be traveling to Cuba in a few days.

"Maybe if he interviews your family, we'll be able to draw more attention to your case here," he suggested.

The following morning Kristina accompanied me to the offices of the *Washington Times*. Mr. Carter received us cordially and took an interest in everything I told him about Cuba. When I asked if he might interview Vicky and the children, a worried expression came over his face, and I realized that he feared the possible risks of such an undertaking.

A few days later, Tom landed in Havana and his European colleagues informed him of their own experiences.

"A number of journalists have interviewed political dissidents here without running into problems with the authorities, although it's difficult to predict how the Cubans will react to any given attempt," they confided. "But we don't advise you to visit that pilot's family— you can be sure the Cuban government won't like it."

The next morning Tom went to see my family with camera and tape recorder in hand. As he interviewed Vicky, he could barely hide the tension he felt as to the possible consequences of such behavior. That same afternoon, however, Tom returned to the house once again—this time without camera or tape recorder. Instead he carried a package, with food and other necessities for Vicky and the boys, despite the fact that his second visit also doubled the risks he was running. Later, as he walked off quickly, nervously, Vicky stood in the doorway watching him go, moved by the generosity of that man who'd so courageously overcome his own fear.

—

One afternoon toward the end of September Armando called me. "Come to the office. I'm here with some Mexican women who are going to Cuba soon."

They had come to him seeking support in their struggle for the rights of the mentally ill in Mexico. Filled with courage, love, and faith as their only weapons, they were standing up to the reigning corruption among bureaucrats who stole public funds destined for the mentally ill, forcing the latter to subsist under subhuman conditions.

"I'm Azul Landeros. How do you do?" said a woman with blond hair and lovely features as she stood to greet me. "And this is la Chaparra," she added, indicating a young woman with lively eyes who'd accompanied her.

Armando had explained the plight of Vicky and the children upon learning that they'd be attending a psychiatric congress the following week in Cuba, and they had immediately offered their help.

"Tell me what you want us to tell them or to give them. . . . Whatever you want, we'll do it," Azul told me. Her eyes filled with sweetness as I asked her to take Vicky and the boys some letters, photos, and tape recordings of the newscasts about their case, which had been broadcast on TV. I wanted them not to feel alone after so many setbacks, to know that the overwhelming majority of people, though not powerful, were with us.

The next morning I went to see them at the hotel where they were staying. Under my arm I carried a cardboard box that Kristina had prepared while I composed a long letter to Vicky. Medicines, vitamins, a little truck for the boys, and whatever else she imagined they might need, she packed into the carton along with videos and photos with that quiet efficiency characteristic of her.

At the hotel I met the third member of their team, whom I hadn't seen the day before. She greeted me with a smile.

"I'm Virginia, and I'm very moved by your family's beautiful love story."

We sat down, and I answered their questions over a cup of coffee. They wanted to know all about our lives, and I told them in a low voice, about our fight and our suffering, about how much I loved Vicky and my sons. After I'd finished, my eyes fixed upon my cup of coffee, I felt a compassionate hand take my own and squeeze it tenderly. I raised my eyes and met Virginia's overflowing with tears. She didn't have to speak; she had the gift of doing so with her eyes. I felt engulfed by the tenderness of an exceptional human being, capable of touching the most fragile corner of our soul, the part we conceal most fearfully, that of our pain. When we said good-bye, without my knowing anything about their lives, I felt that I could trust them to the point of putting our lives in their hands.

—

Soon thereafter they arrived in Cuba and awaited an opportunity to visit Vicky. Several times they passed by Vicky's street in their rental car, but the constant presence of a policeman on the corner made them nervous. Then Virginia decided to get out of the car ahead of time and stroll along the sidewalk unobtrusively while Azul rode around the block. At the policeman's first distraction Virginia would slip into the tenement.

Vicky was seated in front of the television with Alejandro on her knees, her eyes fixed on the screen but her mind as far away as ever, when that woman with black hair appeared suddenly in the doorway.

"Vicky?"

She understood by the woman's intonation and dress that she wasn't Cuban, and she jumped up in anticipation.

"He sent you, right?"

"Yes."

Virginia quickly entered the small room while setting down the carton and removing from her bag a photographic camera as well as a video camera.

"He sent you this, but first some photos, and a video. I want to bring him back some pictures and a video of all of you."

She spoke hurriedly, nervously, as if she feared that the arrival of the police would prevent her from taking pictures.

Reyniel had come out of the bedroom and, after greeting Virginia, began to rummage through the carton.

"Mom, photos! Dad sent lots of photos!" he said over and over, holding the photos of Geneva and Madrid, without paying any attention to the toys inside the box.

"He loves you very much. . . . Let me kiss you. You're an amazing family!" Virginia continued, talking hurriedly as she took more photos. "I'm not by myself, I've other friends here with me . . . and we're going to help you to be reunited, to escape from here!"

Vicky watched Virginia in silence, captivated as I was when I first met this woman. And she just kept crying. Virginia embraced her and cried along with her, only to interrupt her, smiling and saying, "Come on, woman. You'll see, it's all going to work out and in a very short time you'll be together. You'll see how we'll do it!"

And Vicky began crying again, moved by the presence of that guardian angel.

Azul appeared in the doorway and didn't have to introduce herself.

"Oh, my poor girl. How I love you and your children!"

And she took Vicky in her arms, in a long embrace, which Virginia captured on film forever.

Then they sat down, and Azul took Vicky's hands in hers and told her, "I saw him . . . and he asked me to tell you that he loves you, that he can't live without the three of you, that he's going to get you out of here somehow. How he loves you!"

After a few minutes the house was permeated with the enchantment of those strange women, whom my sons were now covering with kisses.

"You know?" Azul continued, now speaking to Virginia, "You scared the life out of me! You didn't wait outside for me while I was checking out the area, and when I didn't see you, I thought the police had arrested you!"

Virginia smiled without saying a word. She didn't need to speak, however—her whole being expressed faith and affection.

The next day they came back to see Vicky.

"We want to buy some little things for the boys," they explained before going off to one of those shops, veiled by curtains from prying eyes, which sell only to foreign tourists for dollars. And Vicky was overwhelmed with embarrassment by their generosity. They filled their trunk, the backseat, and even the trunk of another car with products that Vicky never imagined existed. It all seemed very little to those Mexican friends—clothes, shoes, food—for they seemed to want to put their very souls into those packages. But Vicky, who'd never seen so much food at once or so much spontaneous generosity, became faint after such a magnanimous gesture.

Then the moment of departure arrived on the heels of so much affection. In just a few days they had come to know each other, and now their good-byes left tears in everyone's eyes.

"I want you to have something very dear to me," Virginia told Vicky, taking the wooden cross from around her neck. "You'll give it back to me the day you're all reunited."

And with simple tears they spoke their silent farewell.

"We'll send someone by each month to buy you food," Azul promised, turning back as they departed. And not a month went by from then on when someone didn't come in their name with a load of food and a message of endearment for the family.

—

One afternoon I received word from Brandon: "Some representatives of the Union of Young Communists in Cuba are here on a tour of various cities around the country, and tonight they're holding a conference at my university."

Brandon, Kristina, and I decided immediately to attend, with photos of Vicky and the children in hand. We knew that the message they'd be bringing to North American students was of a democratic Cuba where they respected the rights of the individual as in no other country. Such was the model of communism they sold to the world, and we proposed, in the most courteous way possible, to defend the rights of those attending the conference, to receive information based on the truth.

We entered the room and noticed with shock that the staff of the Cuban Office of Interests in Washington had been allowed to determine exactly where people should be seated in the audience. A group of persons in their company denied our access to the empty seats in the first rows, stepping in front of us and ignoring our requests to be allowed to sit there.

At the back, a wide table was set up, filled with books containing the works of the most celebrated authors of communism, along with the speeches and interviews of Fidel Castro. At one end was a cardboard box labeled DONATIONS. I pitied those innocent enough to give money to a cause that intended to rob them of the freedom to read works other than those.

We took seats at the back of the room, and began to listen to the Cuban visitors, who'd arrived in the company of Professor Yvonne Captain-Hidalgo. They didn't seem to have used up their old arguments about the well-known free education and health care enjoyed under communism. And they knew what they were doing. Since Americans were becoming increasingly alarmed at the costs of health and education, it would be possible to gain sympathizers among the more romantic students.

When the time for questions and answers arrived, I raised my hand as insistently as I could, demanding the attention of Professor Captain-Hidalgo, who was serving as moderator. But she always called upon those who sat in the first rows, which had been reserved, and these guests didn't pose any questions but, rather, detailed the marvels they'd encountered in Cuba during their brief visits to the island.

I wanted to speak, I wanted to express myself, to tell the students who were listening to that string of lies that the free education and health available in Cuba was paid for with a price greater than money—with life itself, with the loss of the right to think or express opinions, to keep informed, to travel. I wanted to tell them of the plight of my wife and children, and to ask the panelists about that. But it seemed that I wasn't going to succeed, no matter how often I raised my hand—Professor Captain-Hidalgo had every intention of ignoring me. And this was in the United States!

Brandon tried to speak, and they wanted to prevent him as well— a young North American silenced in his own country by the hand of Cuba!

"This is a free country and nobody can prevent me from speaking!" Brandon protested while taking out the photo of Vicky and the children. "I want you to explain to me why this family isn't allowed to leave Cuba."

The visitors evidently were startled, and after a few seconds of confusion, one of them replied, "We don't know. We've only come here on a cultural exchange program with North American students."

Some cultural exchange that was!

The conference ended, and I left satisfied that at least the students present there had seen in the visitors' conduct a real example of the liberalities offered by communism. They hadn't managed to fool their audience this time, but I had experienced, for the first time since my escape, the asphyxiating impotence of not being able to say what one thinks.

How many will they manage to fool on their tour of so many American cities? I asked myself bitterly, seeing how they made use of this country's freedoms in order to destroy it.

That night I wrote a letter to Professor Captain-Hidalgo:

> *. . . I don't believe that the truth can be arrived at if others cannot express their opinions. . . . I'd be very thankful if you could set aside a few minutes whenever it's convenient for us to meet and have a friendly discussion on the subject of Cuba. . . .*

I took a copy of the video with the interview made by Canadian television with Vicky and our sons, and I added it to my letter, which Brandon deposited the following day in the personal mail slot belonging to Professor Captain-Hidalgo. I never received a reply. And, unfortunately, unlike the youths I had encountered on the streets of Georgetown on the day of the balloons, Professor Captain-Hidalgo wasn't acting this way out of ignorance.

One night in October, Frank Calzón called me with some exciting news. President Bush proposed to visit Miami and would take advantage of the occasion to direct part of his speech to the Cuban government asking for the release of Vicky and the children. That message would be picked up by all the international media, and thus would be very difficult for the Cuban Leader to ignore.

I was invited to take a seat with the President's family during the speech, and I listened, touched by his clear message calling Vicky and the boys by name, and then telling the Cuban government: "Castro, do it right, do it decent: Let the Lorenzo family go!"

I thanked President Bush for those words, the first to be spoken by an important world leader, courageously and without conditions, on behalf of my family. And when I was returning from the event with Frank, celebrating the deed, I couldn't help but remark to my friend, "If the President's message is ignored by the Cuban government, I'm going to get them myself."

"Don't tell me that. . . . I'd rather not know about it," Frank answered me, convinced that such secrets should not be shared with anybody.

I hope you're wrong, I kept thinking to myself in silence. *If there's no one I can confide in, then life's not worth living.*

Chapter 20

—

Messengers

of

Love

Days went by without any of the expected reaction in the media, without the Cuban government's responding to the plea from the President of the United States. Disgusted by so many failures, I decided to talk to Armando about something I'd only hinted at before.

"I'm going to Cuba to get Vicky and the boys," I told him as we took a short stroll in his backyard.

Armando stopped in his tracks, looking at me in alarm.

"Are you crazy? You're really thinking of doing that?"

"I can't take it anymore. I think I'm going to die if I don't try it."

"You have to be strong, to put up a fight."

"This campaign will never succeed; they'll never let them leave."

"They haven't let them go because the campaign hasn't produced enough pressure yet. I should know, I got out of a prison thanks to the campaign Martha waged."

Armando was obviously worried. He'd noticed my state of mind during the last few months, and he had a feeling I might do something drastic. We had a true friendship, and his greatest worry was that I might act blinded by feelings that would weaken my judgment. And now, with the example of his own experience, he felt sure that the campaign would lead to the release of my family. But times had changed. Then the Cuban government had felt strong; now it was intimidated by its own crimes as well as by the fall of the Eastern bloc countries. Above all it feared the youngest officers in the armed forces, and did not hesitate to send a clear message of intolerance to them.

No, my family would never be released, and now I tried to explain as much to Armando.

"I think you're mistaken," he insisted. "They might capture you, kill you, kill all of you. Vicky and the boys need you alive, not dead."

He looked really upset now. My capture and death would be a harsh blow not only for my own family, but for his as well, and for countless friends. He respected me and didn't want to hurt me, but the idea that they might kill me was tormenting him.

"You're my friend, Armando, and I've come to tell you of a decision I've already made. For months I've barely slept, thinking about it constantly. There's no other way out. I'm not acting on a whim, I've spent hours and hours making the most detailed calculations. I have a probability of success, and I'm going to risk it."

"Have you thought about the outcome if they capture you and kill you?"

"I tell you I'm already dying, eaten away by torment. I haven't got the strength to wait any longer, and I fear for the safety of Vicky and the boys. Each day the net tightens around them, and I have a terrible feeling something's going to happen, and it won't let me sleep. Imagine if you convince me, and then something happens to them tomorrow? It'd be the fault of my own cowardice, and then I couldn't go on living."

Armando's expression was now filled with dread. He stood in silence for a few seconds, and I could tell he was seeing himself in my position, desperate over what might happen to his children.

"Count on me for whatever you need. But I want to know how you'll get your plan into Vicky's hands. My experience in communicating by code in prison may be of some help there."

I hugged Armando, relieved that he understood. He was the first of my friends to know fully what I was planning.

"How will you inform them when you're going to come for them?"

"I'll send a detailed message with someone trustworthy. Then I'll give a password by telephone that means I'm coming the next day for them."

"What kind of password?"

"I plan to land on a highway, near a beach the two of us know quite well. I'll simply mention the place in the course of a normal conversation, as if I were recalling the time of our courtship there.''

"That's no good. You mustn't mention any place at all. . . . You have to use another code."

Together we worked out what seemed to us to be the most ordinary phrases in a phone conversation to utilize as codes. That night I went back to my apartment much calmer. I had a friend with whom to share the greatest secret of my life. I wasn't alone anymore.

The following day I spoke to Kristina. We'd worked together for many months; she'd shared with me every one of the torments afflicting me, looking after me like an older sister despite her young age. She almost went crazy when I began to tell her my plans. But finally she understood. "You mustn't give up the campaign until the last moment. There's still the chance that they might be able to get out without taking such a risk," she pleaded, adding: "I've even contacted David Asman. We have an appointment with him the day after tomorrow in New York."

She was referring to the well-known journalist from *The Wall Street Journal*, who we were hoping would write a piece on Vicky and the boys. Appearing in such a prestigious paper, it just might provide the last straw to embarrass the Cuban government enough to release them.

Skeptical about the probable results of the interview we were to have, I went with Kristina to meet Asman, who received us very cordially, suggesting in the end what seemed to him the best way of helping us in line with the style of the paper.

"Write your own article and we'll see if we can print it."

I wrote the article, which appeared in the edition of the twenty-first of November: "Message to Fidel: Execute Me, But Let My Family Go." But there was never any reaction by the Cuban government; the hangman didn't want to publicly accept my life in exchange for the freedom of my loved ones, except to send an intimidating message to Vicky.

—

Vicky was scrubbing some clothes on the washboard when her mother nervously informed her that a stranger was asking for her at the door.

"Asking for me?" Vicky commented in surprise, drying her hands on a small white rag cut from a flour sack as she headed for the living room.

"I've brought you a summons to appear at Villa Marista."

Vicky felt a chill at the mere mention of the place where the feared State security had their headquarters.

"You should be there promptly at eight tomorrow morning," the stranger concluded over his shoulder as he walked off, leaving Vicky standing there reading the piece of paper.

The following morning she presented herself with the children before the officer she was told would see her.

"Why have you brought the children?" he asked, annoyed.

"They go with me everywhere," Vicky replied, looking him in the eye.

He was wearing civilian clothes and held a lighted *puro* in his hand, of the kind that is normally exported. He'd taken a seat across from Vicky and leaned back in his chair, crossing his legs behind the desk, while throwing his head back and exhaling a large cloud of smoke. Then he stared at the *puro* between his fingers and, tilting his head to eye Vicky in what seemed a ridiculous posture, he addressed her in the gravest, honeyed voice he could muster.

"Do you know why we've sent for you?"

Now he was flexing his biceps in an unconscious gesture of one who spent a great deal of time in front of the mirror, examining the progress of his muscles after meticulous workouts in the gym.

"No, I don't know why. Have you finally decided to let us leave?"

The officer looked at her in perplexity and, getting to his feet, he took a few nervous steps around the room.

"No, absolutely not. We have nothing to do with that. That's a matter for Immigration."

"So?"

"Wait here, I'll be back in a while," he finally said, leaving the office.

Vicky then scanned the room, observing the desk, which was clean of any papers, the bench along the wall where the boys sat watching in silence, the television camera suspended from the ceiling at an angle from the wall. It was eight fifteen A.M. She took the toys out of her purse that Kristina had sent and handed them to the boys, watching as they began to play timidly. And then she settled down to wait.

Two hours went by and still no sign of the interrogator. Three hours—the boys were growing impatient, and she took out some chocolate, which Virginia and Azul had given her, handing it to the boys, who took it without much enthusiasm. Noon came and went, and she was asking herself if the waiting was going to be eternal, when the officer appeared at last.

"We've found out that certain persons have gone to your house offering you ways to leave the country illegally."

"Really?" *How could you not know when you're the ones who sent them,* she thought to herself as she stared at him coldly.

"We know that you haven't accepted such offers."

"I'll only leave my country in the normal way, when you've agreed to permit me to. We've committed no crime!" She felt she could no longer sit there quietly. "What have the children done wrong, for you to punish them this way? What crime have they committed?"

"Please, ma'am. I, I don't have anything to do with . . ." The man was stuttering without looking up from the papers he'd brought with him. "I only wish you to sign this declaration swearing that you'll never try to leave the country illegally."

Vicky took the declaration, which was already filled out in her name, and signed it while thinking, *You're the ones who break the law by keeping us in the country by force. The law says we can leave, so leave we will, by any means possible.*

—

I'd already passed the theoretical examinations, and after my first few flights at the Leesburg Aerodrome I felt ready for the flight test, so I went to see Dr. Robb.

"I think I can take the exam now."

"So quickly? You've flown very little."

"I've got sufficient hours on my record as a pilot. Legally I can already take the exam."

"But we don't normally—"

"Please, I have to. The fate of my family hangs on that license."

Dr. Robb seemed to understand.

"Let me first go up with you before the inspector."

After our flight together he gave me a phone number.

"That's Mr. Pears's number. He's the inspector for the Federal Aviation Administration. Call him, he can give you your test." And shaking my hand tightly as we said good-bye, he added, "Good luck, son!"

Inspector Pears attended to me politely.

"I can't take you for the exam until the thirteenth of December. Would you rather wait till January?"

"Absolutely not. Please, no later than December thirteenth."

"Then: ten in the morning at the Leesburg Aerodrome on the thirteenth."

"I'll be there."

After the thirteenth I'd be able to carry out the operation if I managed to find a plane. *If God is with us, the boys will soon have their first Christmas,* I told myself over and over, filled with joy.

—

Armando and I were invited with Kristina to Columbus once more by Elena, to initiate at her church the chain of prayers she'd organized around the world for Vicky and our sons; as well as to finalize the details of a meeting that the Moscow representative of the foundation had arranged between Armando and Gorbachev, who was to visit Mexico the following week. I was to serve as interpreter at the meeting, to be attended by the four of us, and we would take the opportunity to ask that prestigious statesman if he would intercede with the Cuban Leader on behalf of my family. We still continued to work at both alternatives, and my friends still felt hopeful that a miracle would occur to obtain the release of Vicky and the children at the last minute, making unnecessary the risks involved in my plan to rescue them.

Various gigantic billboards reproducing the photo of Vicky and the boys loomed up before us along the highway as we approached the city. We realized, deeply touched, that Elena was responsible for this. We attended the service, grateful to the Reverend Creede Hinshaw for his personal interest in helping us. As I addressed the parishioners, I couldn't hold back my tears at the sight of so many people crying. Clearly, wherever we found ourselves tomorrow, their prayers and faith would accompany us. In a world with so many who loved, hate could never destroy us.

That night the four of us met to work out the details of the trip to Mexico and to talk of my plans for the rescue attempt. For many months Elena had watched over me daily, filling me—if only at a distance when calling me on the phone—with her lively spirit and humor, with her faith. And now I watched her grow sadder and sadder as she listened to me, visibly tormented by what might happen.

"You have to understand that if I don't do it, I'll die."

She fixed her eyes on me, and I saw the tears there. She took my hand and said, "If my husband Johnny were alive, I know he'd approve. He was daring like you. Count on me. How will you find the plane?"

"I don't know, I still have to look for one."

"I have a friend who'd be delighted to help you. Just let me know when you come across that plane."

I knew that Elena was referring to herself. She'd always taken great pains not to wound my pride because of her wealth.

I took advantage of my visit to Columbus to lunch with the pilots who worked for Elena, whom I'd met on our first visit to the city.

"I'm looking for a plane. You can guess what I need it for."

Gary looked up from his plate in bewilderment. It was too much for him to imagine I could be planning what I suggested.

"Are you crazy? You'll be sticking your head in a noose."

"Please, let's drop it. I want you to help me find a cheap plane which can take off and land in a very confined space."

"I have a plane I want to sell," Ron interrupted. "It's a 1961 Cessna 310F."

I couldn't believe what I was hearing, and I jumped to my feet in jubilation.

"Where is it? Can we see it?"

Then Gary spoke up, this time to Ron.

"You know what he wants it for? You're going to get yourself in hot water."

I felt the blood rushing to my head. "I only want to buy your friend's plane!" Then I got hold of myself and spoke more calmly. "We're not talking about using his plane, but our plane, once we've bought it."

"But they'll investigate."

Gary's behavior seemed rather strange. I wasn't looking for an accomplice to a crime, but for someone who'd sell me a plane in a completely legal fashion. In any case, it was none of his business.

I began to worry about him, what he might do or say. More than once weak-minded men had endangered other people's efforts simply by being unable to accept the risks involved, even if these weren't their own. And in this case, what was at risk, should he be indiscreet, was the life of my family!

"Is there any law against selling what's yours to whomever you wish?" I asked, staring at him without concealing my irritation at his meddling.

Gary remained pensive.

"I want to sell my plane," Ron repeated then.

"How much?"

"Thirty thousand."

"I don't have the money now, but I'll have it soon. Promise me you won't sell it to anybody else. My family's life depends on it."

"It's a promise."

We returned to Virginia, and I had one more day to finalize my plan before leaving for Mexico. Virginia and Azul were the two people in the world best suited to get a message to Vicky. *If I could see them in Mexico,* I thought, and scribbled a brief note, which I immediately faxed to Azul.

We'll be in Monterrey. . . . It's important we see each other there. I think we can spend this Christmas together. . . .

Azul called me back immediately.

"Of course we'll go to Monterrey to meet you."

I unfolded the map on the table and began to calculate based on the data for a Cessna 310F and the four-lane highway along the coast of Matanzas in front of El Mamey Beach—the place I'd chosen for the rescue. It was near my parents' home, and Vicky could go there with the children without raising suspicions. I'd already calculated the time needed for the antiquated chain of command system to launch its missiles. What I needed to ascertain now was whether the time between the moment I was spotted and the instant I was out of missile range would be less than the time they needed to be able to fire upon us.

Flying nearly at sea level, I wouldn't be spotted until I was thirty nautical miles from my landing spot, and the ground-to-air missiles could reach no more than twelve nautical miles from the coast on our way back. We could fly at maximum airspeed of 212 knots. If we landed for no longer than one minute, we'd manage to cross the perimeter of the missiles' maximum range fourteen minutes and fifty seconds after being spotted. Ten seconds less than what the chain of command system required to launch its missiles.

Only their fighters could intercept us in international waters, and we'd attempt to elude them protected by darkness, but I'd need a little light to navigate and land on that highway. Dusk was therefore the best moment for the rescue. As a combat pilot I knew that it would be nearly impossible for my ex-comrades, in poor training now because of the fuel crisis and directed moreover by navigators giving radio instructions from radar screens with poor resolution, to locate a target moving above the sea at low speed and very low altitude in complete darkness.

I sat in front of the computer and wrote a detailed message, which I printed out in the smallest type possible:

Cuchita: it began. It was a name only I called Vicky in our more intimate moments, so she would know the note was genuine.

> *. . . On the highway in front of El Mamey beach . . . wait there starting a half hour before sunset. . . . Approach the plane from behind. Watch out for the propellers. Hold the boys by the hand. . . . The codes by telephone: Mine to ask if you approve of the plan is, "How's my father?" Your affirmative reply, "He's thinner, but he's fine." To tell you that I'm coming for you the next day at dusk, during the same or a subsequent phone conversation, "I'm sending you money for you to buy a VCR." Confirm the hour of sunset and let me know it by speaking of it as the size of a pair of shoes you're asking me to get you, to be sure that our times are synchronized . . .*

I finished writing at daybreak. The early light of day always surprised me at my most emotional moments. I looked at my airline ticket and discovered that I'd have no time to rest; in a few hours I had to be at the airport. In Mexico a rather interesting meeting awaited us with Gorbachev, and a more important one with Azul and Virginia.

We spent the flight laughing, thanks to Elena's gift for entertaining everyone in her path, and we readied ourselves for the brief meeting with Gorbachev at a small office in the convention center where he and Armando were to have their talk. I attended the meeting with a small tape recorder in hand. I no longer had any faith in efforts made out of the public eye.

Still, I felt a really great admiration for Gorbachev. I believed him responsible for the enormous changes that had occurred in the world, and I was grateful to him. If it hadn't been for Perestroika, perhaps I'd still have been submerged in the surrealistic world of the cult of hatred in which I had grown up. I had spoken to his wife, Raisa, during the dinner of the previous evening, and I felt hopeful when she took my hand tenderly in hers, promising she would speak to him that night.

"Trust in us," she'd told me before saying good night.

Now I was in the small office where we were to meet, and after a brief exchange between Gorbachev and Armando, I asked the latter if I could address Gorbachev directly.

"Mikhail Sergeievich, my wife and small children have been held hostage for two years in Cuba . . ."

Gorbachev ceased smiling at that point and, taking the hand in which I'd been holding the tape recorder, which hadn't bothered him until then, he pushed it to one side, saying, "The solution to isolated family problems ought to be in the context of the solution to the Cuban problem. For that reason . . ."

I'd already stopped listening. I'd shut off the tape recorder, which was worrying him, and took a few steps back, saying, "Don't trouble yourself, it's not necessary."

Minutes later I attended the press conference given by the celebrated statesman. Somebody in the audience asked him whether he believed in the existence of a divine will, and he lost himself in a web of words whose sense no one could make out.

Someone else repeated the question with even greater clarity: "Do you believe in God, or not?"

Again he didn't say yes or no, and I watched him fall from the altar of my heroes.

No, a man like that didn't initiate Perestroika willingly, I thought as I left in frustration at my meeting with one of the political figures I most admired. *He initiated it in order not to be destroyed!*

That afternoon Virginia and Azul arrived, enveloped as always in an enchanted aura of goodwill. We six met in the bar of the hotel, and speaking as quietly as possible I explained to them all the details of my secret undertaking, and the terrible presentiment I'd had that something would happen to Vicky and the boys if I didn't carry out the plan as soon as possible. Someone again brought up the risks I was posing to the lives of everyone involved, when Virginia intervened, her eyes moist with tears, "If he and Vicky both fear something terrible will happen if they don't do it, they should do it. Only they can decide."

Once again Virginia intuited the force of the human spirit. Then she added, smiling, "Well now, tell us what you want us to do to help."

"I need someone to take this message to Vicky," I said, taking the little folded piece of paper out of my wallet.

Virginia took it and put it away in her purse, saying, "Don't you worry, Vicky will get this as soon as possible."

On my way back to the States I had to ask myself, *What would happen to the person carrying the message if State security got ahold of it?* The probability that this might happen was extremely remote, yet I couldn't help feeling that I was acting selfishly in letting others run such a risk for my family, and it made me feel ashamed at how desperate I'd become.

It was the twelfth of December. There still remained my flight exam, scheduled for the following day, and the purchase of the plane. Elena, in her inimitable style, had already said that "a friend of hers" would donate the thirty thousand dollars to the foundation to purchase it.

God willing, we'll be together for Christmas, I thought excitedly as we landed at National Airport in Washington.

—

I'd taken the flight examination without a problem, and with the longed-for license in my pocket, I was pacing back and forth in my room trying to disentangle the manner in which events would proceed now. It was Tuesday evening, the fifteenth of December. The telephone rang and I grabbed it off the hook.

"Orestes?"

I'd been waiting to hear that voice!

"Yes?"

"It's Virginia, I'm leaving tomorrow with two friends for Cuba. We'll be back on Friday afternoon."

I was trembling from head to foot. I'd waited so long, suffered so much! Yet what had seemed nearly impossible only months ago was progressing now with extraordinary ease. That the hand of God should have placed in our path such miraculous friends! I threw myself down at my desk, and with my hands still shaking I began writing seven letters: to Armando, Kristina, Elena, Mari Paz, Valle, Azul, and Virginia.

> . . . *Know that I've never regretted leaving Cuba, nor anything I've done since then. . . . To have known you all is sufficient reason to be satisfied that I did it. . . . I've known freedom for twenty-one months, and not even death itself can take away from me the freedom I carry within me. As a result, I can say farewell joyfully. . . .*

I looked over the letters I was leaving for my dearest friends—six women and one exceptional man—and I felt certain of our triumph. What a lucky correlation! Oh, women! There's no failed undertaking wherever they place their love, their talent, and their devotion.

I took the map with my calculations, a walkie-talkie to communicate with the plane which I'd decided not to send to Vicky, and the check from the foundation for the thirty thousand dollars donated by Elena. Armando had left for Miami to do some work, and I called Kristina to say good-bye and to leave off the letters before leaving for Columbus, where I was to buy my plane.

"They're to be opened only if the worst happens," I told her as we waited for my flight in the airport lounge.

She kept silent, turning to wipe away the tears she'd held back the last several days. How much I loved her! We'd fought all those long months together, each time with new illusions, then new failures. She was always present in every undertaking, continually striving to touch the sensibilities of whoever might help, always thinking of some little thing to send Vicky and the children.

"You won't come back to Virginia first?"

"No."

She sat pensively a few seconds.

"I want to be there when you go."

It was time to board the plane. I gave her a hug, and without looking back, I ran to catch my flight.

—

Vicky had received a phone call from Virginia.

"I'm going to send you a Christmas present."

Now Vicky was playing with the boys in their room, when she heard her sister call with a cry of joy: "Vicky!"

She ran into the living room just in time to see that beloved person coming in, accompanied by her two friends Maribel and Mónica.

"Here I am! I'm the Christmas present!" Virginia exclaimed, running over to Vicky to hug her.

One by one she greeted everybody in the house. When Vicky was about to take a seat beside her, Virginia signaled that they should go to Vicky's room. They entered quietly, and Vicky turned on the radio to its highest volume. Putting a hand on Vicky's shoulder, Virginia placed her finger over her lips as a signal for silence. Then she opened her purse and searched among her cards and documents for a tiny piece of paper that had been meticulously folded.

Silently Vicky read the note she now held in her hands, overcome but not surprised. She'd been expecting it for a long time. She raised her eyes, which were radiant with happiness, and her gaze met Virginia's inquisitive look. She nodded her head then, biting her lips as if she feared letting words escape, and saw Virginia's fist punch the air in a fit of rejoicing. She took Virginia's hands in her own and squeezed them hard, letting her read in her eyes everything that she desired.

Vicky burned the message in the bathroom, and then they returned to the living room, where they talked loudly and happily of going the next day to the beach.

Now they were traveling crowded into the small car, singing together and exchanging looks of complicity, which went unnoticed by the children. On the way, they scrutinized the section of the highway where the rescue was to take place. Virginia insisted on stopping at a tourist shop, where she purchased three shirts and three caps of bright orange, which she handed over to Vicky whispering, "So he can spot you more easily from the air."

Only the children wanted to go in the water, and amid squeals of pleasure they anticipated the approaching waves. When Vicky and Virginia called them out of the water they all held hands, forming a circle in the sand. In the center was a bottle, filled half with sand and half with water. Then Virginia explained, "Now each one takes a little shell, puts it in the bottle, and silently makes a wish."

Silently they dropped in their shells and their wishes. Then they sat for a while in silence with their heads lowered, their eyes fixed on the sand. Reyniel was the first to break the silence, telling Alejandro, "I asked to be with Dad soon. And you?"

"I asked to be with Daddy soon, too."

On the way back to Havana, they watched the sun slip below the horizon. Vicky looked at her watch: it was five-thirty P.M., Thursday, the seventeenth of December.

—

I'd waited impatiently until Friday for Ron, and now we were trying out the Cessna No. N5819X before I bought it from him.

"Can you show me its stall speed with landing gear and flaps extended?" I asked, knowing that I'd have to maneuver within the plane's aerodynamic limitations.

"Seventy-four knots," he said, cutting his airspeed and pointing with a finger to the old-fashioned indicator, which was delineated in nautical miles.

"Could we cut it down a little more until we actually stall?"

Ron looked at me questioningly, then replied, "Okay, but do you mind if we get a little more altitude first?"

I suspected that the plane had a lower stall speed. Factories generally indicated a somewhat higher airspeed than the actual minimum sustainable by the aircraft in order to give the pilot a margin of safety, but I needed to know the actual limit. I was going to have to maneuver above a highway with traffic and land on the first attempt with very little light.

I was pleased with the characteristics of the Cessna 310F—an extremely short run for takeoff and landing, excellent maneuverability—exactly what I needed! Like my faithful, noble friends, it had been placed in my path and I thanked God for it.

After purchasing it, I asked Ron if he'd accompany me to Marathon Key, the place from which I planned to depart. I didn't want to talk over the radio; I wanted to exclude even the very remote possibility that Cuban radio interceptors might recognize my voice during radio contacts while flying to the Keys and have sufficient time to report it and increase surveillance of Vicky and the boys. He agreed, and we left it that we'd see each other for dinner at Elena's house.

Kristina had also arrived at Columbus a few hours earlier, and she confessed to me when I gave her a hug, "I just couldn't wait in Washington."

Virginia was about to arrive back from Cuba to Mexico at any moment, and now the three of us sat nervously by the phone. Elena, impatient, kept making brief trips to the kitchen, reappearing with more and more of her delicious snacks, as if eating might quicken the hands on our watches. The phone had rung various times, making us jump up from our seats, but they were all routine calls.

Eight o'clock. Elena seemed to be pacing infinitely, from the kitchen, to the bedroom, to the living room where we sat. She was smiling every time she reappeared, but I saw in her eyes the anguish she tried to hide with her laughter. If I failed this time, I'd pay with my life. Kristina wanted to take some pictures with her flash camera. I doubted the photos would turn out well, her hands were shaking so. I looked at mine, and found they were trembling as well.

Eight-thirty. The phone rang.

"Hello?"

It was the sweetest sound in the world.

"Virginia?"

"How are you? Well, I'm back."

"Virginia."

"It's all arranged. Our patient will be at the doctor's office at five forty-five on the day she has the appointment."

We stood frozen as we listened to her.

"Can you connect me to her in Havana? From here it's impossible—"

"I can get her for you on the other phone I have here. Hold on."

We waited in silence, listening to the sound Virginia's dialing produced.

"Hello?"

"I've gotten through!"

"Hello, Vicky? I'm back home. I have your husband on the other line. He's been trying for days to reach you but couldn't get through. Hold on."

I felt my pulse going through the roof.

"What shall I tell her?" She spoke now in a whisper.

"Ask her how my father's doing."

Again we heard her distantly, on the other telephone.

"He asked how his father's doing."

Silence.

"No, not yours. He wants to know how *his* father's doing.

Once again back on our line: "She says he's thinner but that he's fine."

I nearly leaped for joy. Elena and Kristina were listening, petrified.

"Tell her I'm sending money for a VCR and a TV set."

I couldn't contain myself for happiness. I jumped up and down and ran back and forth like a child, and with each turn I gave a hug to Elena and Kristina, who didn't know whether to laugh or cry.

"I'm not staying here tomorrow," Elena warned me with her usual directness, "I want to be at Marathon when you take off." And picking up the phone again, she called Gary to tell him she'd be flying to Miami the following morning. "I'll tell him tomorrow where we're really going," she remarked as she hung up the phone.

Ron showed up, ready to leave for Marathon, but I asked him to wait a bit. Elena had asked us to go to church, but discovering it was already closed she now called the hospital so that we could go say a prayer in their chapel. Sister Patrice led us to the chapel and opened it up for us. We went in quietly, each of us kneeling in a separate pew. I heard Kristina and Elena's quiet crying behind me, and as we withdrew from the chapel without a word, the sister intercepted us. She held a rosary in her hands and offered it to Kristina saying, "The Lord be with you."

"Take it," said Kristina, turning to me. "You'll need it on your trip."

I took the rosary and saw Sister Patrice nod her head as she squeezed my hand.

Back at Elena's house I asked for a video camera, which she brought out immediately. Then I requested that Kristina film me as I began explaining the details of my plan while unfolding the map:

"I know that if I'm captured the event will be used by the Cuban government to launch a campaign accusing the CIA and the U.S. government of terrorism against Cuba. . . . I also know that they can put the worst possible words in my mouth. I want to make clear to the world that I acted entirely on my own responsibility and with the help of only a few friends. I do not, nor will I ever, regret what I've done until now for my freedom and the freedom of my loved ones . . . I take no weapons on my flight. Only my love for my family . . ."

Elena still wanted to prepare a cooler with soda and chocolate for the children.

"It'll relieve the tension of the flight," she said as she filled it with ice.

Just before leaving, Kristina came back from her room with a package in hand.

"It's a jogging suit Brandon got for you. Our Christmas present to you. I want you to wear it," she said as she held it up for me to see.

I came back in a moment with the new outfit on, feeling extremely pressed to get going.

"One more thing . . ." It was Elena, extending her arms toward me. "It's a medal of Our Lady of Charity, which belonged to my mother. Take it with you, please!" she concluded, pinning it on my new outfit.

—

It was midnight when we took off from Columbus.

We flew the three and a half hours to Marathon in silence, interrupted only by the radio communications that Ron made.

Once there, we found a motel near the airport to spend the night, and I registered under a name that came to my mind by chance: Joao Garcia. We said good night to each other and went off to our rooms—Ron, to rest; and I, to go over my calculations one last time. I hadn't closed my eyes since Tuesday.

It was four-thirty A.M.

Chapter 21

The Final Day

Vicky had bid farewell to Virginia at noon, and from the moment she received her telephone call she knew she wouldn't be able to sleep.

She had thought it would take me more time to find the plane, and upon hearing the password so soon, she had to make an effort not to faint in front of everybody. Then she tried to control the excitement overwhelming her by visiting her neighbors in the tenement on some pretext or other. She'd been born and raised there, amid the clamor of those crowded dwellings, watching neighbors coming to the door of her home to ask for something with the same ease that her mother would send her to them for salt or sugar when she herself ran out. The last months had been very hard, but even though her neighbors were all from revolutionary families who attended meetings and stood watch for the Block Defense Committee, everyone had stood by her from the start, showing her special warmth, calling her to the phone with a cry whenever I'd telephone one of them to talk to her, and warning her of the presence of any stranger spying on her. Yes, they were part of her life. She loved them and was saying good-bye to them without their knowing, in these brief visits she made to their homes that night.

It was already late and her mother was going to bed, when she told her that the next day she planned to visit my family in Matanzas.

"That's crazy, with transportation so hard to come by," her mother replied, thinking of the trouble Vicky would have to go through to get there.

"I'll leave early in the morning for the bus terminal. If we don't manage to leave in a couple of hours, we'll come back home," she said then to reassure her mother, knowing that the 600 pesos Virginia had left her before departing would be sufficient to pay for the trip in one of those illegal taxis waiting near the terminal.

She had closed the door to her room so that they wouldn't notice the light shining. She began quietly to set her hair in front of the mirror. She realized that she hadn't bothered with it for a long time as she rolled it up with trembling hands.

I can't let him see me like this, she told herself later as she tried out the nail polish Kristina had sent her. Then she put on some makeup. Even on the edge of life and death she wanted to look beautiful for me.

Turning around, she contemplated our sons and her little niece lying there fast asleep. How far they were from imagining what she was about to do! How cruel their parents were in their love for each other, deciding their fate without asking them! And how cruel the innocence of those children was, preventing us from informing them of our plans! She knew that they would react by running toward the plane at the crucial moment. A thousand times over they'd voiced their hopes that they'd be rescued by their father. But what tormented her was that she couldn't let them know now for fear of their innocence, which might lead them to talk about it unwittingly without seeing the danger. Tomorrow, the outcome awaited them—their family reunited, freedom, perhaps death!—and she felt panic at her own thoughts.

What would they say when they grew up, if we hadn't tried? she asked herself once more, realizing that the risk we were taking was dictated above all by them, by their right to grow up free. *We won't let them be slaves!* she murmured, kissing them both on their checks.

Then she contemplated her only niece. She'd slept with her since they'd come back to live at her parents' home. Small, alert, and full of life, she trailed around behind Vicky all day clutching her skirt, exclaiming, "Aunty, Aunty . . ." And at night she'd curl up into a little ball against Vicky, in search of the warmth of her body. The child always insisted on her aunt's dressing her, on her aunt's being the first to see her in the new dress or pair of shoes that her uncle had sent her from that faraway place. And after tomorrow she wouldn't see her anymore, perhaps not ever. One of Vicky's tears fell on the little creature's face as she leaned over her to kiss her; then she hugged the child tight. How much she loved her!

She took down the Bible she kept in the old wardrobe and sat down next to the children to read. A slight scratching at the door drew her attention, and opening it, she saw darting past her that sweet, faithful creature whom the boys had named Motica.

She had arrived at their door a month before, on a rainy afternoon when Vicky was at a neighbor's. Reyniel and Alejandro had spotted her soaking wet at the doorstep, and there she remained, like someone seeking an invitation to come in. The boys were watching her with curiosity when their aunt suddenly yelled out: "Go on, dog, get away from here!" The dog ran off a safe distance from the doorway while Aurora exclaimed, "Just what we need in this house, where we can barely all fit!" Then she went back into the kitchen, and Motica came back to the door. Aurora rushed into the living room again, and once more Motica ran off. The scene was repeated several more times, and on each occasion Aurora looked sadder about chasing away the poor thing. The final time Reyniel and Alejandro had followed the dog out to the alley, where Vicky found them with her.

"Look, Mommy," they both said at once, as Motica wagged her tail with happiness at their feet.

Vicky looked at the dog closely and stepped back, enchanted, saying, "This little creature has so much compassion in her eyes. Let's take her home."

The four of them entered the house, and Motica acted as if it were her own place, running into the kitchen to curl up under the table. She'd become the last boarder in a house already filled with people, and she'd waited every day thereafter, stretched out in the doorway, until the children returned from school, to leap against their chests in a euphoria of playfulness.

Motica came into the room, and Vicky noticed that she wasn't wagging her tail happily as she normally would. She simply climbed onto the mattress where they all were sleeping and sat there in silence, crossing her forepaws and staring sadly at Vicky.

"You know the truth," Vicky told her.

And for the first time that night, Motica wagged her tail gently.

It was December nineteenth. The light of dawn was shining through her window when she finally picked up the knapsack in which Reyniel normally took his books to school, to pack things for the trip: the orange shirts and caps, the money from Virginia, the Bible, some caramels, and a snack, which she went to the kitchen to prepare. There she found her father already quietly having his first cup of coffee.

"It's very odd, this trip you're taking to Matanzas with the boys," he remarked, staring up at her thoughtfully.

"Dad," she pleaded at the same time she took him by the arm, squeezing it affectionately, "please . . ."

Gerardo lowered his gaze without saying another word, and Vicky kissed him on the forehead.

As she stepped into the alley of the tenement with the children, she turned around to look at her parents still standing in the doorway. She waved her hand in farewell and they waved back to her. She walked a little farther and turned around again. There they were still, with Motica between their legs and a sadness in their looks as they watched them going off.

They know, she thought as she walked along, regretting not having told them anything. *But what for? They would've died of worry.*

It was eight o'clock in the morning; if they were lucky they'd get an early start to Matanzas. They walked the six blocks to the bus stop, and they mingled with the people waiting there for what seemed an eternity. A man standing at the corner farther on kept staring at the bus stop, and Vicky felt a chill run through her.

Are they following us?

She tried to pretend she wasn't paying him any attention. Nearly an hour had passed by the time the bus appeared, coming around the corner, then passing by without stopping, its swarm of desperate passengers hanging out the doors.

"We're going to walk over to Calle Paseo," she told the boys, taking them by the hand.

"Are we going to ask one of those cars that go by to take us?" Reyniel asked her, ashamed at having to flag down one of them.

For some time, in order to alleviate people's anger somewhat at the horrible state of public transportation, the government had ordered civil servants with state vehicles at their disposal for work to pick up passengers along their normal routes.

At the corner Vicky turned to check behind her, and there was the man, a block behind, on the same corner as before, still staring at them.

They're obviously following us around, she told herself in horror as she thought about how to lose him.

A car finally stopped for them.

"I'm going to Revolution Square, no farther," the driver said leaning out, while the woman sitting beside him looked the other way.

"Thank you, that'll be fine," Vicky answered, opening the back door.

Revolution Square wasn't too far from the bus terminal. They could walk the rest of the way.

They got out of the car there, as did the woman in the front seat. And Vicky started walking quickly, pulling along the children, who were obviously in no mood to hurry. She looked back, and she saw the woman who'd sat in the front seat crossing the street in the direction of the Ministry of the Interior building, but turning around several times as she walked to observe them. Then Vicky looked up ahead on both sides of the street. The man from the corner by the bus stop was nowhere to be seen.

Maybe it was my imagination, but I'd better cut through those buildings just in case, she thought, and taking the boys by the hand, she changed direction to walk between the buildings and arrive at the bus terminal by a less common route.

She didn't go in. On an adjacent street were parked various

automobiles belonging to doctors, engineers, and other professionals who'd received them some time ago when the Revolution had awarded them to such people. Now they were waiting there for travelers willing to pay fees amounting to several months' wages.

"We're going to Matanzas," she said to the man leaning against the fender of the Moskovich at the head of the line of cars.

"It's a hundred pesos per person."

"That's fine."

Signaling two other passengers who were waiting for him to fill his car, he opened the doors for everyone.

Vicky gave one more glance behind her and didn't notice anyone following them. She got in beside the boys and checked her watch. It was ten A.M. *We'll get there in plenty of time,* she told herself, rejoicing.

———

Elena's plane landed at Marathon, piloted by Gary.

"Did you sleep at all?" Kristina asked me as I met her at the bottom of the ramp.

"Impossible. The time's dragging so."

"We couldn't sleep either."

"Let's go for a walk, then. I'm dying to have a look around Marathon," Elena added with her customary gaiety, trying to relieve the tension.

So the three of us went walking down the street, feeling the sun beating down on us and staring every minute at the hands on our watches, which seemed to have been soldered to the dials. We decided to eat pizza at a place we passed, and ran into Ron and Gary there. I'd noticed that, since his arrival at Marathon, Gary seemed particularly nervous, fidgeting about with an expression of fear and uncertainty on his face. His evident apprehension added another worry to the ones I already had, putting my nerves even more on edge.

"I'm afraid of what Gary might still do," I commented worriedly to Elena and Kristina while watching him sit with Ron at the other table. "If he calls anyone and I'm held off from departing for even a few minutes, then the whole plan is lost," I added, frightened by his lack of composure.

"He's a good boy. . . . Don't worry about him, I'll have a talk with him," Elena reassured me calmly.

I had another look at Gary, sitting with Ron, a disturbed expression on his face. No, I wasn't going to let him out of my sight for a second. It was noon.

———

They'd entered the city of Matanzas and, still sitting in the Moskovich, drove past a bus that was discharging passengers. Vicky turned her head as they went by and read the sign above the windshield: ROUTE 16—CANIMAR.

"We want to get out at the next bus stop," Vicky told the driver.

On the curb now, she and the boys watched the crowded bus pull over for them. There were no other cars on the road. No one seemed to be following them.

They got on, pushing their way in through the back door, the boys silent, accustomed since they were born to such shoving. They were already passing the street on which my brother lived at the edge of the city, when Reyniel exclaimed, "We passed our stop, Mom."

"No . . . they're at work now. Let's go to the beach for a while."

Reyniel regarded her curiously. December was not a time of year they were accustomed to going to the beach.

My mom's a little crazy today, he thought, but preferred not to contradict her. Something in Vicky's look told him he'd better keep quiet.

When they got to Canímar they still had to walk a good half mile to reach El Mamey Beach, and they crossed the bridge, walking along the edge of the highway until they saw the sea waiting below.

"Mommy, I'm tired of walking!" Alejandro exploded at last, after miraculously making the long trip in silence.

Vicky picked him up to humor him the rest of the way—the sweet tyranny of children, not knowing that their parents can also feel tired!

They spotted the beach, deserted, in a sort of cove carved out by centuries of salt water. And they descended to it by steps cut into the rocks. At the opposite end from the kiosk were four men who seemed to be sharing a bottle of rum. They sat on a rock close to the waves, while Vicky wondered what to do to distract the children. There were still five hours left till the appointed moment.

"Mom, what are we supposed to do here? I'm bored," Reyniel complained.

"For the moment, eat," Vicky answered, opening the knapsack. "There's no place we can go until your uncle gets back from work. The trip took less time than I thought it would."

Afterwards they walked along the sand, gathering shells of various sizes, chasing tiny crabs, which would vanish back into their holes.

Vicky looked up to check the kiosk, worried by the presence of those men who'd eyed them insistently as they came down the steps, and her heart froze: Two policemen were talking animatedly with them.

They've sent them to keep an eye on us because they suspect something! And I've no way of warning him not to land! she thought with her whole body shaking. She watched the boys running around in the sand, and took the Bible out of the knapsack to find some solace.

———

"Ma'am . . ."

The voice behind her startled her.

"Could you keep an eye on my clothes while I fish?"

The man was wearing a bathing suit. In one hand he held the harpoon and a pair of flippers; in the other, his clothes rolled up in a pile.

"One time they stole my clothes, you know? And I have to fish for something . . . life's gotten very tough."

"You can leave them here."

"Mom?" It was Reyniel, who'd come running up, followed by Alejandro. Both of them considered themselves their mother's protectors, and they'd noticed when the stranger approached her, little guardians that they were.

"Anything wrong, Mom?"

"Nothing. He just wants us to watch his clothes while he's fishing."

They both watched the man with curiosity, remembering the times they had come to the beach with me while I was fishing.

"There's two policemen over there," Reyniel told the man, nodding in the direction of the kiosk.

"I already saw them."

"They only allow foreigners to go underwater fishing," Reyniel added, recalling the prohibition for Cubans.

"Yes, but I still go fishing whenever I want. They've already taken away my equipment twice, and given me a fine. But I'm stubborn and I come back with another harpoon. I have to eat." And he hurriedly dove into the water.

Vicky looked over at the kiosk. The policemen were still there, talking.

"Go into the water, swim!" she told the boys quietly, barely moving her lips.

"But Mom, it's December. . . . It's a nice day, but the water's still cold."

"Reyniel, please."

The boy quietly observed his mother's look fixed directly on him. There was a great force in that look, something urgent. He didn't say anything. He turned around and ran into the water, followed by Alejandro, for whom any temperature was fine.

Vicky went back to her reading.

"Ma'am."

The man had returned from his fishing. His hair was still dripping and in his hand he held an enormous lobster.

"It's the only one I caught. Keep it."

"Thanks very much, but I can't."

"What do you mean, you can't? I've never seen anybody turn down a lobster in these hard times."

Where did such a character come from? All I need now is for them to stop me for having a lobster in my hands! she told herself. "I appreciate it, but I can't use it."

"Then I'll give it to the children," the man insisted.

"Don't trouble yourself. We're allergic to shellfish—we can't eat them."

The man looked at her, surprised and with a certain pity.

"Well, then . . . I guess I'll eat this one myself, or sell it." And thanking her for watching his clothes, he headed back up the rocks.

Vicky watched the kindly fellow go off on his way, and as he reached the top of the rocks she noticed that there was no longer anybody by the kiosk. She breathed a sigh of relief, checking her watch: five ..

"Reyniel, Alé. Come, change into your clothes! We're going!"

—

We'd noticed Elena talking briefly to Gary a few minutes after our lunch, and now I felt relieved to see him looking calmer, without that expression of fear on his face.

We were in the terminal now, sitting in comfortable armchairs set around a table filled with magazines. We remained silent a while, leafing through the magazines, staring at the undaunted clock on the wall. I'd checked the weather reports for navigation, and the day couldn't have been better. There were scarcely any clouds in the sky, and the visibility seemed limitless. It would take me thirty-eight minutes to reach El Mamey Beach, according to my calculations with the wind correction. I ought to take off at 5:07 exactly.

"I'm going out to the plane an hour before takeoff," I told them when I saw it was three-thirty.

"We have to take some photos," Kristina interrupted, taking out her camera. "Let's go, I want to get some pictures by the plane."

"Absolutely not. I don't want to draw anybody's attention."

"Don't be silly. Just one picture."

I stood up reluctantly to accompany her to the Cessna.

"Stand here, by the wing, like this. . . . Now, put your hand on the propeller . . ."

"Kristina, please . . . enough!"

"But what's wrong?"

She had no idea in her ingenuousness that I was terrified of drawing attention to us.

"We're at the southernmost tip of the country. . . . I arrived here last night in a private plane. Then all of you come, also in a private plane. We spend the morning walking around the town, and speaking Spanish in low voices. And we're strangers here!"

"What has that got to do with anything?"

"It's not normal, our behavior. Anybody could think we were involved in narcotics trafficking from the south!"

"Don't be idiotic!"

"It'd be idiotic if someone shows up now to search my plane when I'm supposed to be taking off! Not one more photo!"

"All right, don't get upset."

"I'm sorry. . . . I'm terrified of the tiny things that can destroy a larger undertaking."

"I didn't mean—"

"Come on, I've something to give you," I told her, taking her by the arm to go back to the terminal. There I handed her the small bag I'd prepared. "Here are all of my personal documents. Driver's license, Social Security number, everything. I don't want this to fall into their hands if I'm captured. Who knows how they might use them. The little I have is yours. . . ."

There were tears in her eyes.

We tested once again the frequency we'd set for the walkie-talkie to communicate during my return flight.

"Connect it at six o'clock in the evening. I'll call you by the name Bicycle One, I'll be Bicycle Two."

They both smiled. We'd always referred to the plane as the "bicycle" whenever we talked about it by phone during our preparations for the rescue.

I went over to say good-bye to Ron and Gary, then after hugging Elena and Kristina with all my strength, I headed out to the plane. In my hand was a small bag containing audiophones, the map, a Freedom AF-35 camera and a small ASA CX-1 flight computer.

In the cockpit I mentally went over each step of my flight from takeoff until my final return:

Coordinates for Mamey in the LORAN navigation system . . . Correct. I open the door this way . . . and close like this . . . no, no, I have to use both hands. This way . . .

I repeated the operation several more times, fearful of losing a second at the crucial moment.

Time to start the engines . . . batteries . . . engine start!

My hands and legs were shaking, and my heart wanted to leap out of my chest. In less than an hour I'd see those I loved dearest in the world!

The airport looked deserted, no traffic. I began to taxi, and then saw Elena and Kristina waving good-bye. I still had time to test the motors at the end of the taxiway.

When my watch read 5:06 I crossed onto the runway. Taking out the rosary from around my neck, and squeezing tightly the medal of Our Lady of Charity, I said aloud:

"Thy will be done, O Lord." Then lifting my right hand to the controls, I exclaimed, "Takeoff!"

"Is uncle back from work?" Alejandro asked.

They were already dressed in their orange shirts and caps, and now were climbing up the steps in the rocks, heading for the highway.

"No, not yet. First we're going to hunt for crabs."

"Crabs?!" exclaimed Reyniel with visible astonishment.

"Yes, crabs. There's nothing else to do right now."

They reached the highway, and Vicky began to drag the boys by the arm in the opposite direction from the city.

"Are you crazy, Mom? Where are we going?"

"To hunt for crabs."

Reyniel thought his mother had really gone out of her mind.

"Mom, no . . . Why are we going farther away, with all the distance we still have to walk?"

"Reyniel!" Vicky stopped to stare at the boy angrily. Alejandro looked on quietly waiting to see what would happen next, not caring very much about which way they walked.

"Listen to me! Do what I say without arguing! It's a matter of life and death! It has to do with your Dad."

Reyniel gazed at her in shock, lowered his head a second, then looking up again he said, "Okay, Mom, let's get going!"

Hand in hand they walked along the edge of the highway. Now and then Vicky would turn around to look back. No, no one was following them. She checked her watch: five-twenty P.M.

"Let's go down there and look for some crabs," she said to the boys, pointing to the field off the highway.

They descended along the culvert into the grass, which nearly covered them, and they spent a while hunting about until Reyniel exclaimed in frustration, "We'll find an elephant here before we find any crab!"

"Let's go," said Vicky, looking at her watch.

And they started walking once more in the same direction along the edge of the highway. She searched the sky up ahead and behind, toward the northern horizon. It was five-forty P.M.

———

Elena and Kristina watched the plane turn into a dot as it vanished over the water toward the horizon. They sat behind a concrete table outside the terminal, which had already closed, and settled down to wait quietly, checking their watches every moment. Time seemed to be standing still.

"It's five thirty-eight," Kristina remarked.

They knew that was my expected landing time in Cuba.

Elena was rummaging in her purse, without knowing what she was looking for. She said, "Whenever I'm nervous I get a terrible urge to clean my closets."

"Your closets?"

"Yes. Time goes by faster when you clean out a closet."

They both laughed nervously.

"It's a shame. I don't see any houses around here. . . . We could've cleaned their closets for them!"

———

In Mexico City it was one hour earlier: four-forty P.M. Virginia had invited family and various friends over to her house, along with Azul, la Chaparra, and the two young girls who'd accompanied her to Cuba. They all went into the biggest room of the house and sat on the floor, joining hands in a circle. In the center was a bottle; inside it, seawater, sand, some shells, and the dreams captured there two days before in Varadero. They closed their eyes and lowered their heads.

Virginia spoke, her voice resounding, "Oh God, they love each other. . . . Help them make it!"

———

I'd climbed to 1,000 feet after takeoff and flown at that altitude to ten nautical miles from the Twenty-fourth Parallel. Then I shut off the navigational lights and the automatic transponder. My own radio waves wouldn't give away my position now. I was flying above the waves as low as my eyes would permit me, ignoring the altimeter, which no longer mattered to me. Only three instruments had any importance for me: the airspeed indicator, LORAN indications, and compass.

Have they gotten to El Mamey without a mishap? What will I find on the highway? Too much traffic? I have to land on the first try. . . .

Some opaque crests loomed above the line of horizon, drawing my attention. *Is it the slopes of Pan de Matanzas? They must have already spotted me, the radar operator must be picking up the phone by now to inform command post. . . .*

Years ago I'd flown heading north and then south from those slopes, at very low altitude in a MiG-21, to synchronize their geography with the radar indications of the missile complexes at Matanzas. I couldn't have imagined then that someday I'd be trying to elude those missiles.

They're unmistakable. . . . It's the Pan de Matanzas! The bay is just to the left. . . . I'll come in across the middle. . . . Now I don't need the LORAN or compass!

They already know at divisional headquarters, they're calling Havana. . . .

Little by little the crests of the mountains loomed larger above the horizon, slightly to the right of my route. Then I saw the towers of the thermoelectrical plant supplying the city, the contours of the coast.

———

The bridge! There's the Canímar Bridge!

I checked my airspeed: 240 miles per hour.

Two miles more to the bridge . . . one . . . I have to cut my airspeed!

I cut back the throttles and pulled violently at the controls in order to reduce airspeed as quickly as possible. The motors rumbled with a vibration that shook the whole airplane while I climbed to the level of the bridge.

The engines, the engines! . . . Let them blow!

I was already over the bridge, and turned to the left banking steeply. It seemed like the wing was about to graze the outer edges.

Even if they're ready they won't be able to launch any missiles at me now; the new hotel on the far side blocks them from targeting me!

The highway, the highway . . .

I descended above it, searching for El Mamey Beach. Ahead it curved to the right. . . . *They should be waiting about a half-mile beyond the turn.* Two cars were going in my direction, and I overflew them. The low altitude and the trees to my right prevented me from seeing the highway beyond the curve. I followed the turn as though I were one more auto, in the air. In front of me appeared an oncoming trailer truck, as well as a bus attempting to pass him. They already had their headlights on.

Three bright orange dots were a little to the left and before the truck and bus.

"There they are! It's them!" I yelled in the cockpit.

Damn, another car!

A small, white auto was speeding in my direction, just between them and me. *I can't land in front of it! There's even less space than between the truck, the bus, and me!*

Overflying the car with my landing gear nearly touching its roof, I saw with horror that I still couldn't land. There was a rock in the center of the highway! I had no room to maneuver on my right—a traffic sign stood in the way! *If I hit it with my wing we're lost here for good.*

I nearly touched down in front of the rock. A gentle pull on the controls, a slight banking to the right . . .

Left rudder! Left rudder! You're going to miss!

There's the truck. . . . They're braking, they're getting out of my way! Stall out! You don't have the room! Stall it!

The Cessna fell abruptly on the pavement, and I hit the brakes with all my strength. Vicky and the boys were behind me. I was a mass of emotions. The plane halted in a matter of seconds. I was nose-to-nose with the truck, and could see every line on the driver's face. The bus was concealed behind him. The driver leaned forward, frozen at the wheel, stupefied with amazement. His eyes seemed to be popping out of his head.

Vicky had just checked behind her, peering up at the empty sky, when she saw drop before her eyes, "vertically, like a helicopter," the green and white mass of aluminum and iron. They hadn't heard it approaching—the noise of the trailer truck had been too loud.

"It's Daddy, it's Daddy! Run!" she screamed, holding the children's hands as tightly as she could.

"It's Da-a-d!" Reyniel yelled.

"The knapsack, Reyniel, drop the knapsack!"

He let it slide off his shoulders, and ran in front now, pulling his mother by the arm.

"My shoe, Mommy, I lost my shoe!" It was Alejandro shouting now as he ran along just behind her.

"Kick off the other one!"

—

Can the wing make it past without hitting it?, I wondered, watching the truck as I increased the right engine throttle and sat on the left brake pedal. *I've got to make the turn!* The plane swiftly turned, and righted itself on the highway with a final jolt.

They're coming, they're coming! Vicky! My sons!

One minute! We can't wait more than one minute!

They were running toward me, hand in hand, bent forward as they came. *They're getting here . . . the propellers, watch out for the propellers!* I turned to the left as I braked, till I was nearly perpendicular to the center of the highway. *The door! Pull the seat up!*

—

When I turned the plane, Reyniel recognized his father's face.

"Dad!" he screamed, tearing his hand free from his mother. He saw the door opening and crawled onto the wing.

"Da-ad-dy!"

"Reyniel!"

I saw a thousand emotions at once in my son's face, as there must have been in mine. He was crying, shaking, frightened, crazed. . . .

He jumped into the backseat, and I felt his hand on my shoulder, in my hair.

"Daddy!"

Now Alejandro was by the door. Pale, shocked, happy—petrified. Vicky pushed him in, and I felt his little hands hugging me around the neck.

"My love!" Vicky screamed hoarsely. Her eyes were very red, wide open. In her face were those two years of suffering, which now escaped from her in a flood. She was shaking, shaking from head to toe, as we all were. She got in and reached out with her hands to touch my own, still exclaiming, "Better to risk it all than to be slaves!"

"Don't touch me, don't talk to me."

I grabbed the door with one hand to close it. It wouldn't close. I tried again, but it wouldn't close. It felt like time itself was congealing, like everything was happening in slow motion.

"Calm yourself, calm yourself!" I told myself, screaming.

"Calmly, my love, calmly," Vicky repeated.

I took hold of the door with both hands. With all the calmness I could muster. It shut!

"We're on our way!" I cried, gunning the motors and trying to maneuver to the center of the highway. The plane swung around, tilting one way and then veering unstably from side to side, while I struggled with the pedals to bring it in line.

It seems like a century, but it's all happened in seconds—it still hasn't been a full minute since I touched down. The trailer truck and bus had been left behind. The automobile I overflew was closer now, in the lane to my left. *We have to pass each other.* My wing nearly grazed the car.

"Let's pray, let's pray!" Vicky told the boys.

Here comes the curve now. . . .

There's no highway left!

Sixty . . . Sixty-five . . .

It has to take off!

I eased the controls softly, but all the way. The plane lifted painfully over the hillside looming just at the edge of the curve, and I felt its wings stagger helplessly, as though we were poised on a needle with its point resting on a billiard ball.

We're airborne, airborne! Just don't stall out! Softly on the pedals, softly . . .

The motors roared with power, and our airspeed picked up rapidly. I felt we were safe, and I banked to the right, heading north, brushing treetops with my wing among the pines along El Mamey Beach.

Without thinking, a cry burst out of my lips: "We did it, you bastards! We did it!"

I could barely make out the surface of the water; it was almost dark. I heard Vicky and the boys praying behind me, and realized I was crying, crying my lungs out; but there were no tears in my eyes, I hadn't any tears. . . . *They've already made the decision to knock us out of the air. Now they're transmitting the order to the missile installations. . . .*

I took a quick look behind me, wanting to see my passengers, the sovereigns of my life. Alejandro was curled up with his eyes wide open, bewildered, his knees locked together and his white socks on.

Reyniel was still shaking from head to toe, staring at me in astonishment, unable to believe it.

"Dad . . . Dad . . ." he kept repeating.

"Cry, Reyniel, cry! Don't hold it back," Vicky told him, and the boy began crying.

The crews are already running to their posts in the missile silos. The launching ramps and targeting antenna have already begun rotating. . . .

The plane was vibrating as if it were about to disintegrate under the effects of our airspeed. I checked my watch and the LORAN indications.

Eleven nautical miles from the missiles. Eleven and a half . . .

They've already located us in the launching rooms. They've got our coordinates. . . .

Twelve nautical miles! The missiles are already pointed at us. . . .

Twelve and a half nautical miles! They can't reach us!

We made it!

It was getting impossible to fly at such a low altitude; the vault of the sky had joined the sea in a black sphere. I climbed to 200 feet, adjusting the cabin lights as dimly as possible.

If they've scrambled any fighter to intercept us, it's already too late. . . .

We were arriving at the Twenty-fourth Parallel. I remembered the camera then, which I'd brought along thinking I could take a shot of Cuba as I came and went, which of course had been impossible. I hadn't had the wherewithal to do that in the midst of so much tension. I took it out of the bag and, holding it in my right hand above my head, I pressed the shutter four times. The drama of that instant, illuminated in the faces of Vicky and the children, was captured forever. Then I asked Vicky to do the same, and I closed my right eye so that the flash wouldn't blind me. Part of the instrument panel was likewise perpetuated on film. The clock in the cockpit read 6:02.

We've passed the Twenty-fourth Parallel . . . out of danger! We continued to climb to 2,000 feet. I reached back with my right arm to feel many hands seizing my own.

"We did it. We're together . . . together forever!" I exclaimed.

"Forever!" Vicky repeated.

I switched on the navigation lights and automatic transponder. It was time to inform Kristina and Elena.

"Bicycle One, Bicycle Two here."

Silence.

"Bicycle One, Bicycle Two," I repeated.

—

Kristina was holding the walkie-talkie when she heard my voice, broken by static, too faint to make out clearly. She answered over the walkie-talkie, but received no reply. The apparatus wasn't powerful enough at that distance. She ran to the phone and dialed Armando's number at home, since he was now back from Washington. Mari Paz, who'd come from Spain, was also anxiously waiting there.

"He's on his way back, we can hear his voice. But we don't know yet if he's got the family with him," she said, speaking uncontrollably.

"If he's coming back, he's got his family with him," Armando replied at the other end. And positive of what he was saying, he hung up to call in the news to the radio stations in Miami. Mari Paz, who was sitting beside him, jumped up to hug Martha, who thanked God, bursting into tears.

Kristina ran to Elena's plane. Ron and Gary had the radio on and were signaling her from the cabin door. She hurried aboard and heard my voice clearly as I radioed the Key West Approach Tower, reporting my position and altitude. She ran back to the cabin door to meet Elena, who was already on the ramp.

"He's coming, he's coming!" she was saying, when she heard another call on the walkie-talkie she was carrying with her.

"Go ahead Bicycle Two, Bicycle One here," she answered with emotion.

"Bicycle Two reporting," she heard me say in my broken voice, hoarse with excitement, "I'm bringing a plane filled with love, a plane filled with love!"

They both started jumping around and crying, hugging each other. Gary and Ron, seeing them, understood and also began jumping up and down, yelling and hugging. They looked like four crazy, solitary beings who were lost in jubilation in the middle of a ramp at an empty airport.

—

Nelson was alone at home, stretched out on the sofa watching "CNN News" when the telephone rang. It was Armando.

"Nelson! Nelson!" Armando was talking too fast, yelling. "He's coming with the family, with the family!"

Nelson didn't understand. "What family?"

"He's flying back with them, right now! They're going to land at Marathon Key."

Suddenly, like a light going on, he saw everything in a flash. Who else could it be? He ran all around the house, jumping up and down, repeating aloud Armando's words. No, he couldn't wait for his wife to come home—he ran out into the street. His neighbors looked at him suspiciously as he rang all their doorbells, yelling the news. Then he ran to his car and drove off like a shot, straight to Armando's house.

—

Uncle Raúl was getting ready to take a bath. He'd gotten out of his clothes and turned on the portable radio, which he'd hung from the mirror. It was the same newscast he always heard on the Spanish station at that hour.

Aunt Fela was straightening out the living room. She heard a cry, and then she saw a completely naked Raúl come out of the bathroom, dripping water everywhere.

"Fela, Fela!" he exclaimed, waving his arms.

"My God, you scalded yourself with the hot water!" she screamed in fright, running over to him, and he reached out to grab her by the shoulders.

"Fela, Fela!" he kept yelling while shaking her.

"What's wrong?" she replied, horrified.

"Our nephew, our nephew!"

"What's wrong with our nephew!"

"He rescued Vicky and the kids!" Raúl took a breath, then stammered on, "It's, it's on the radio. They say they still haven't landed."

—

The lights of the Keys appeared on the horizon, and Vicky was jumping for joy in her seat.

"The United States!" she exclaimed.

We touched down on the runway at the aerodrome, which appeared deserted; Elena, Kristina, Ron, and Gary were waiting at the ramp. Vicky was the first to jump out and was swept up into their arms. Reyniel and Alejandro were hugging me around the neck in the cockpit. I felt the downy skin of their faces caressing mine, which was soaked in sweat. They climbed out of the plane, and I followed behind.

—

On the ground, Vicky comes running for me and swings herself round my neck, shouting, trembling, crying.

"Together at last! How we suffered! How we suffered!" she repeats over and over, as I kiss her euphorically on the forehead, on her eyes, her cheeks, her lips.

I feel Reyniel and Alejandro hugging me around the waist and I bend over to take them too in my arms. How long since I've held them like this! I lift them up, hugging them to my chest. The whole universe is contained in my happiness.

Reyniel raises his fist and shakes it in the air, shouting, "I'm free! I'm free!"

And Alejandro imitates his brother: "I'm free! I'm free!"

A f t e r w o r d

It was through my grandparents that I learned to appreciate the value of one's word—not simply as a means of expression, but as a principle of behavior. My father told me how once a stranger came by the house and offered my grandfather a miserable sum for his next tobacco harvest. My grandfather nevertheless accepted his offer, because at least he would be sure of earning something to counter the desperate poverty in which he lived with his huge family. Months went by, and a pestilence destroyed the plantings throughout the country, but not my grandfather's, which by the grace of God were more beautiful than ever that year. Prices soared and plenty of buyers were willing to pay my grandfather even five times the sum he had promised the stranger he would accept. But my grandfather still refused to sell his harvest, awaiting the stranger who took his time arriving to collect his spoils. "My word is worth more than all the tobacco in the world," my grandfather would say.

Today one's word seems to have lost its value. Only a signature, sanctioned by our lawyers, seems worthy of respect. And each day written agreements invade more and more of our lives in our relations with colleagues, friends, and even our own families, replacing our feelings and God's teachings. Thus we protect ourselves from possible trickery or betrayal, forgetting that human laws will never be able to substitute for the sacred values we have lost.

I believe that my life would have been very different if the principles my grandfather defended had not been devalued so, since the communism under which I grew up would not have found space to forage upon society's soul. Each time we experience a crisis of values there hangs over us the danger of communism or some other doctrine ready to destroy us as thinking creatures, who are created by and for love.

When I decided to write my memoirs I drew upon such feelings, which flooded my heart. Then, as I began to spend sleepless nights before my word processor, I slowly discovered the tremendous difference between feeling and telling: the harsh awakening of any writer. Little by little, the memories—like torn strips of grief—took shape as a book, thanks to the understanding of my wife, my children, and my friends, who found ways to encourage me in my most difficult moments. Nor would I have attained the necessary harmony between what I wrote and what I felt without the useful advice of my literary agent, Thomas Colchier, my translator, E. K. Max, and my editor, Michael Denneny, who captured the essence of what I wished to express; as well as those who shared with me details of certain episodes herein narrated in which I was not present. To all of them I express my appreciation for their collaboration.

More important still was the help of those who made the freedom of my loved ones possible. Most of them are not even mentioned in this book, since the list would have been interminable. Such is the case for so many of those who offered me their homes and shared their tables with me during my continual wanderings in search of help; the tens of thousands of people who from five continents wrote letters demanding the release of my wife and sons; and the many more who prayed for us around the world. They proved to me that human solidarity is still a potent force, restoring my faith in a world ruled by love for one's fellow being. To all of them, my eternal gratitude.